U0330204

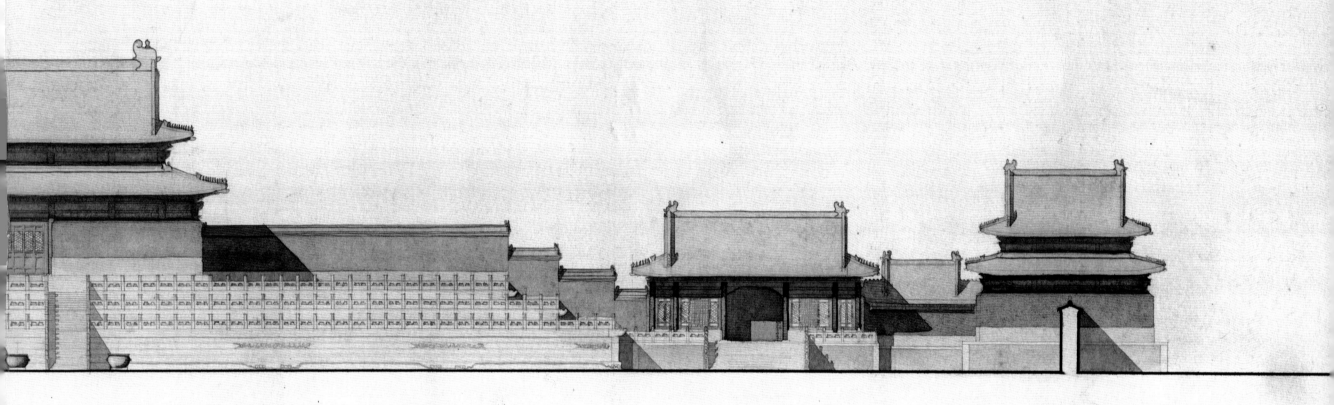

殿　　　　　　　　　　　　　　　後右門　　　　　　崇樓

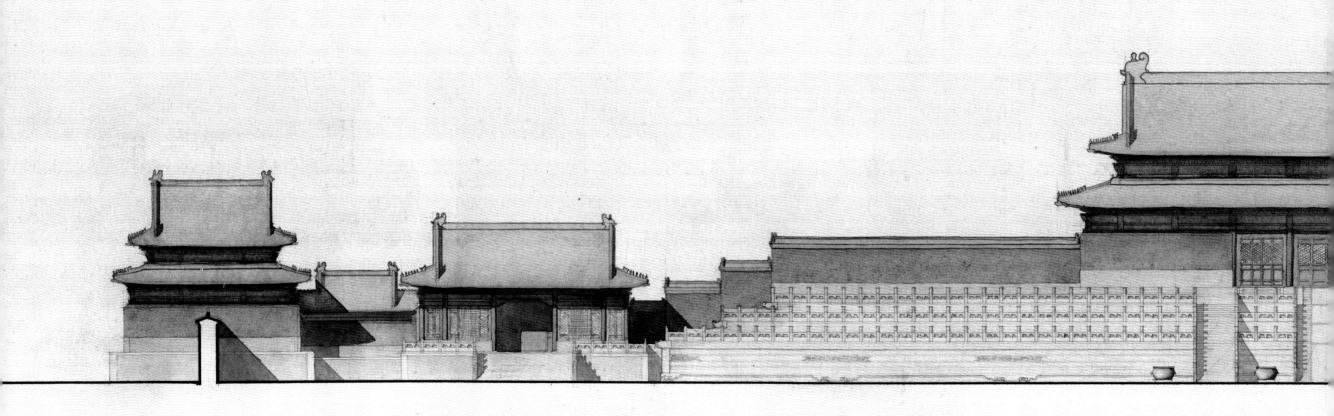

崇　樓　　　　　　後　左　門　　　　　　保

三大殿总背立面图
Back Elevation of the Three Main Halls

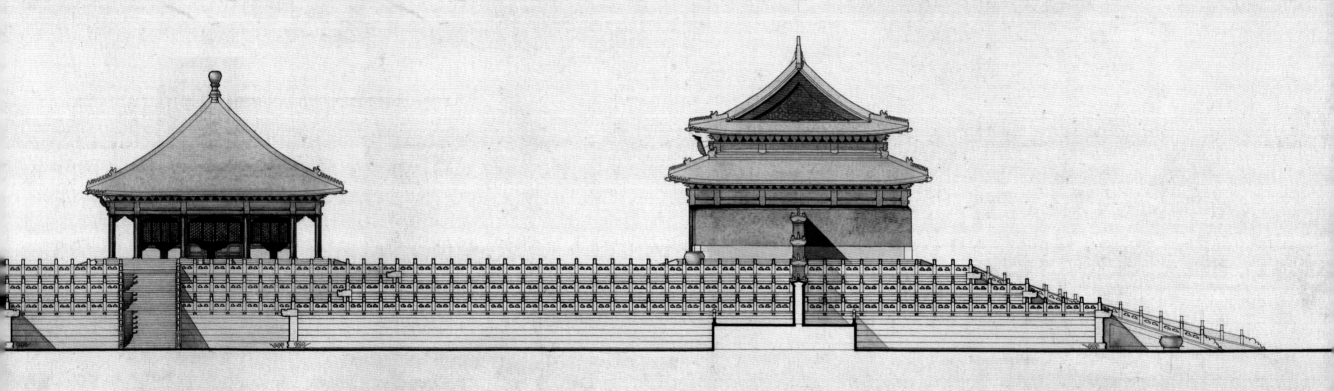

中　和　殿　　　　　　　　　　　　　保　和　殿

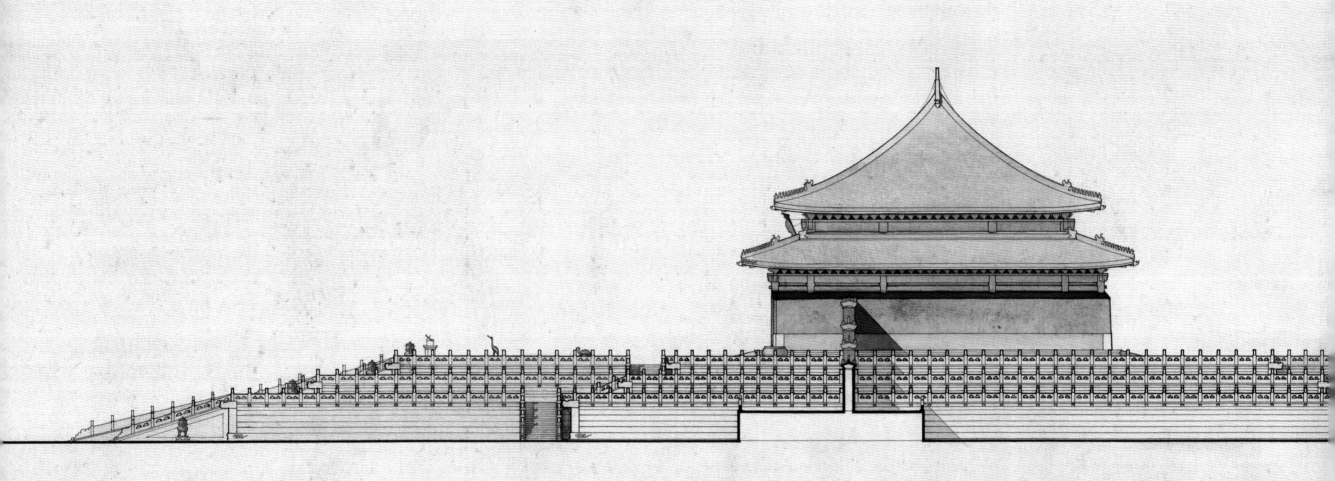

太 和 殿

三大殿总侧立面图
Side Elevation of the Three Main Halls

太和门正立面图

Front Elevation of the Gate of Supreme Harmony

太和殿背立面图
Back Elevation of the Hall of Supreme Harmony

太和门细部图
Detailed Drawing of the Gate of Supreme Harmony

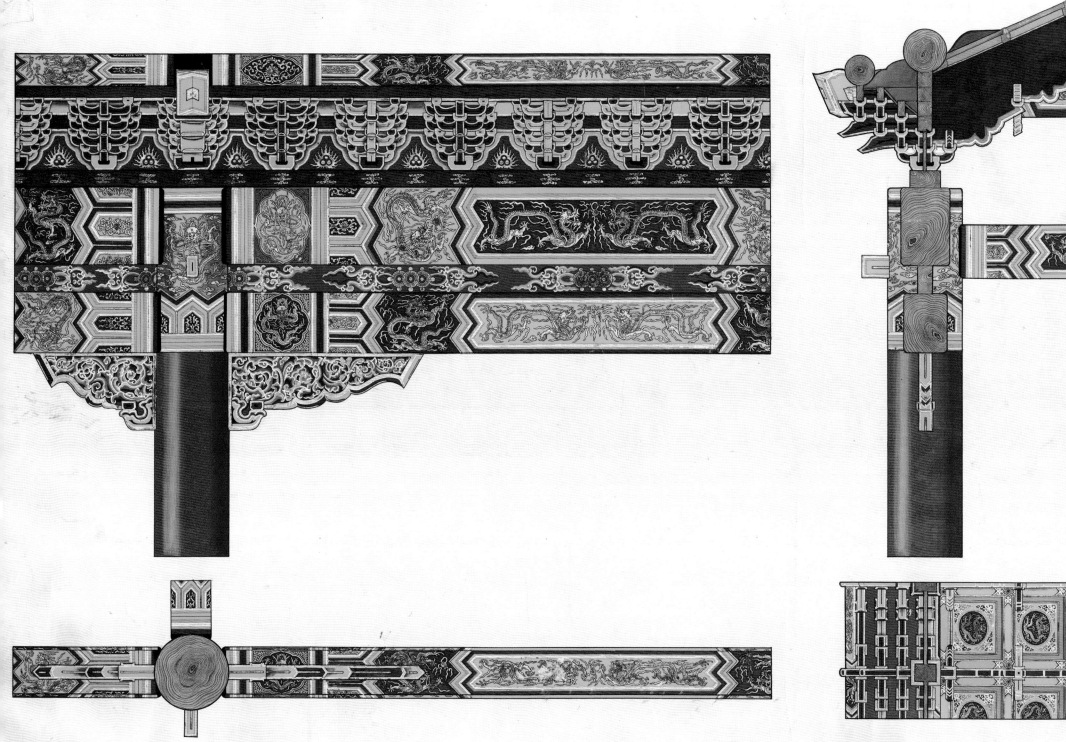
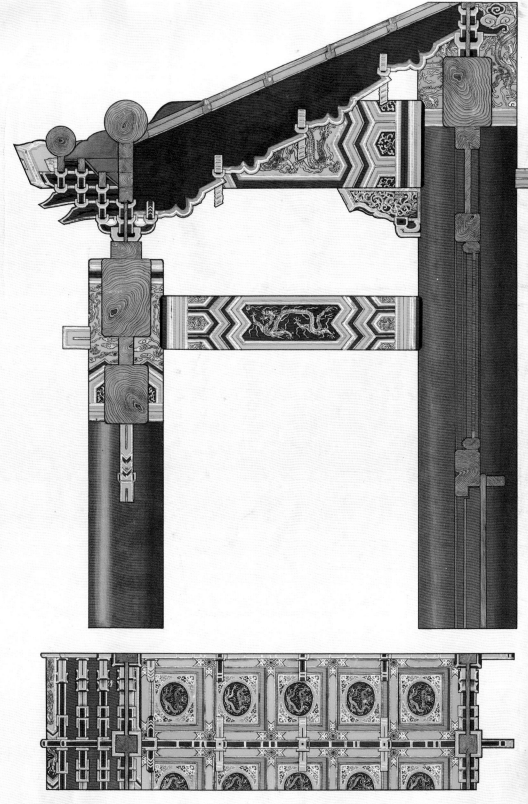

太和殿外檐细部图

Detailed Drawing of the Exterior of the Hall of Supreme Harmony

中和殿正立面图

Front Elevation of the Hall of Central Harmony

保和殿背立面图
Back Elevation of the Hall of Preserving Harmony

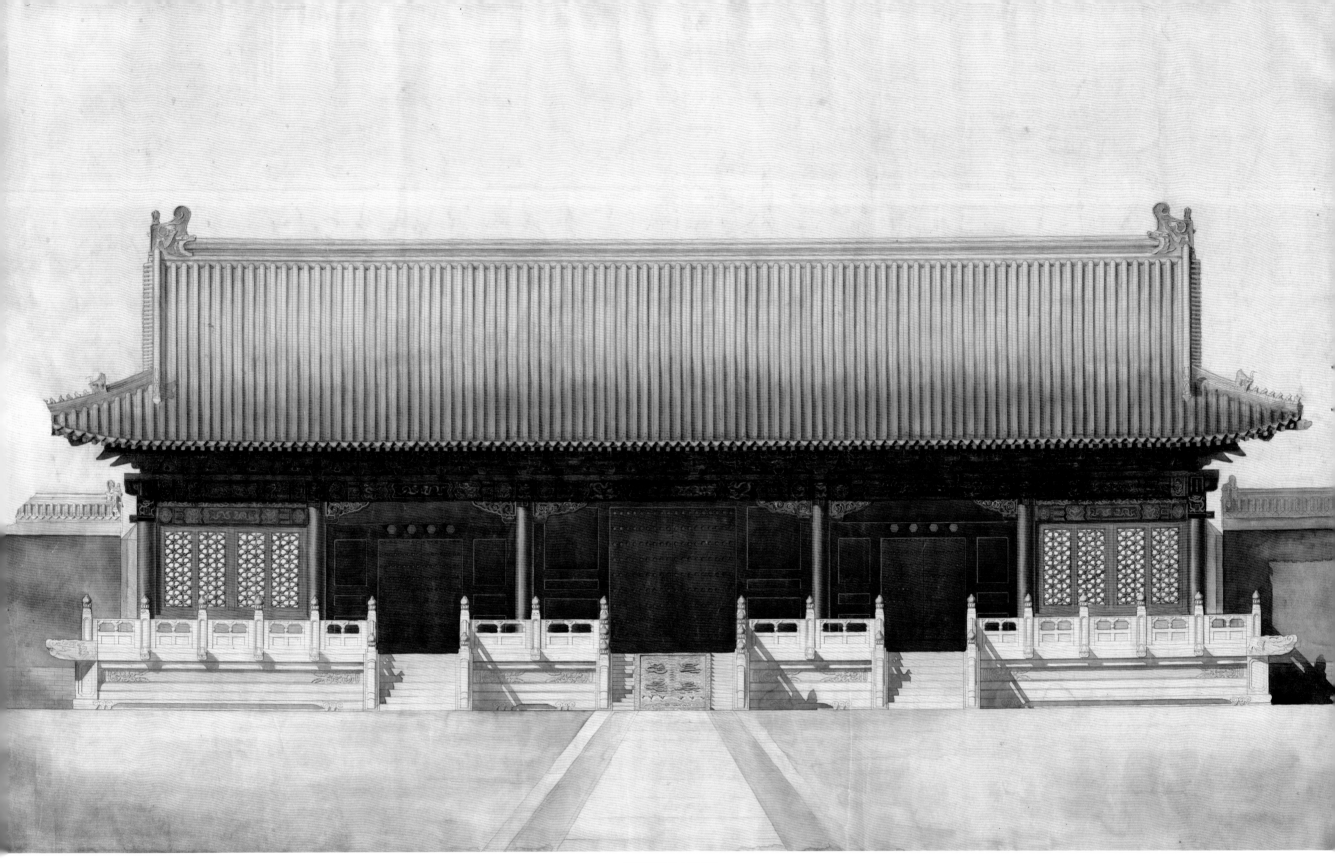

武英门正立面图
Front Elevation of the Gate of Martial Valor

神武门透视图
Perspective View of the Gate of Divine Prowess

乾清门透视图

Perspective View of the Gate of Heavenly Purity

乾清宫透视图

Perspective View of the Palace of Heavenly Purity

交泰殿透视图

Perspective View of the Hall of Union

坤宁宫透视图
Perspective View of the Palace of Earthly Tranquility

文华殿透视图

Perspective View of the Hall of Literary Brilliance

文华殿配殿立面及彩画大样图

Front Elevation and the Colored Paintings of the Side, Hall of Literary Brilliance

西华门透视图

Perspective View of the West Prosperity Gate

协和门正立面图

Front Elevation of the Gate of Blending Harmony

顺贞门透视图

Perspective View of the Gate of Loyal Obedience

延晖阁透视图

Perspective View of the Pavilion of Prolonging Splendor

绛雪轩透视图
Perspective View of the Belvedere of Crimson Snow

角楼立面图
Elevation of the Corner Tower

御景亭透视图
Perspective View of the Pavilion of Imperial Prospect

琉璃吻兽大样图
Detailed Drawing of the Glazed Roof-ridge-figurine Wenshou

石阶细部图

Detailed Drawing of the Stone Steps

国家出版基金项目

中国古建筑测绘大系 · 宫殿建筑

故 宫

故宫博物院古建部　编著

赵鹏　王莫　主编

『十二五』国家重点图书出版规划项目

中国建筑工业出版社

Traditional Chinese Architecture Surveying and
Mapping Series:
Palace Architecture

THE FORBIDDEN CITY

Compiled by Department of Architectural Heritage, The Palace Museum
Edited by ZHAO Peng, WANG Mo

China Architecture & Building Press

Editorial Board of the Traditional Chinese Architecture Surveying and Mapping Series

Editorial Advisory Board: FU Xinian, HOU Youbin

Editorial Director: SHEN Yuanqin

Deputy Editorial Director: WANG Lihui

Editors in Chief: WANG Qiheng, WANG Guixiang, CHEN Wei, CHANG Qing

Editorial Team Members (Characters arranged according to stroke counts):

DING Yao, WANG Nan, WANG Wei, WANG Mo, BAI Ying, BAI Chengjun, FENG Di, ZHU Lei, ZHU Yuhui, LIU Chang, LIU Yang, LIU Daping, LIU Tongtong, LI Luke, YANG Jing, XIAO Dong, WU Cong, WU Xiaomin, HE Jie, HE Beijie, WANG Zhiyang, ZHANG Long, ZHANG Shiqing, ZHANG Fengwu, ZHANG Xingguo, ZHANG Chunyan, LIN Yuan, YUE Yanmin, SHI Fei, YAO Hongfeng, HE Congrong, JIA Jun, GUO Xuan, GUO Huazhan, ZHUGE Jing, CAO Peng, YU Mengzhe, CHENG Fei, LIAO Huinong

『中国古建筑测绘大系』编委会

顾问　傅熹年　侯幼彬

主任　沈元勤

副主任　王莉慧

主编（以姓氏笔画为序）　王其亨　王贵祥　陈薇　常青

编委（以姓氏笔画为序）

丁垚　王南　王蔚　王莫　白颖　白成军　冯棣

朱蕾　朱宇晖　刘畅　刘洋　刘大平　刘彤彤　李路珂

杨菁　肖东　吴葱　吴晓敏　何捷　何蓓洁　汪智洋

张龙　张十庆　张凤梧　张兴国　张春彦　林源　岳岩敏

是霏　姚洪峰　贺从容　贾珺　郭璇　郭华瞻　诸葛净

曹鹏　喻梦哲　程霏　廖慧农

Contents

目　录

Introduction

The Forbidden City, which is now the Palace Museum, is the imperial palace of the consecutive Ming (1368—1644) and Qing (1644—1911) dynasties. In nearly five hundred years, fourteen emperors of the Ming dynasty and ten emperors of the Qing dynasty successively issued orders and ruled the country here.

Completed in the eighteenth year of the reign of Yongle Emperor (1420),the Forbidden City has a history of more than six hundred years. Situated in the heart of Beijing, the Forbidden City covers an area of seventy-two hectares and has more than 8,700 bays of rooms. As the largest and best-preserved ancient palace in China, the Forbidden City embodies the wisdom and quality of ancient Chinese architecture; while as one of the palace complexes surviving throughout China's two thousand year history as a unified country, it has witnessed the evolution of China's feudal social system, politics, economy and history. In 1961, the State Council designated the former imperial residence as one of China's foremost-protected cultural heritage sites. It was listed as a UNESCO World Heritage site in 1987.

Rectangular in shape, the Forbidden City measures 961 meters from north to south and 753 meters from east to west. Surrounded by ten-meter-high walls in all four sides and a fifty-two-meter-wide moat, the complex looks virtually impregnable. The Forbidden City has one gate along the city wall on each side. These four gates are the Meridian Gate (*Wu men*) on the south, the Gate of Divine Prowess (*Shenwu men*) on the north, and the East and West Prosperity Gates (*Donghua men* and *Xihua men*) on the east and west, respectively. On top of the lofty walls, there are four structural complicated Corner Tower, each of which has nine girders, eighteen posts and seventy-two ridges according to local folklore. For different functions, the Forbidden City is divided into the Outer Court in the south and the Inner Court in the north. Known as the Outer Court, the southern portion of the Forbidden City features three main halls—the Hall of Supreme Harmony (*Taihe dian*), the Hall of Central Harmony (*Zhonghe dian*), and the Hall of Preserving Harmony (*Baohe dian*), the venue for the emperor's court and grand audiences in the Ming and

导　言

紫禁城，又称故宫，是明清两代的皇宫，明代的14位皇帝和清代的10位皇帝，先后共491年在这里发号施令、统治中国。

紫禁城建成于明代永乐十八年（1420年），至今已有逾600年的历史。它位于北京城的中心，占地72万平方米，有房屋8700多间，是中国现存最大最完整的古代宫殿建筑群，集中体现了中国古代建筑智慧与水平。故宫是中国自形成统一的国家后，2000多年的历史过程中遗留下来的一座完整宫城，是封建社会制度和政治、经济、历史沿革的实物见证。1961年，国务院颁布故宫为第一批全国重点文物保护单位；1987年，联合国教科文组织将故宫列入世界文化遗产保护项目。

紫禁城南北长961米，东西宽753米，四面围有高10米的城墙，城外有宽52米的护城河，真可谓『有金城汤池之固』。紫禁城有四座城门，南面为午门，北面为神武门，东面为东华门，西面为西华门。城墙的四角，各有一座风姿绰约的

Qing dynasties (Figs.1~4). Lying to the far east and west of the three main halls are the complex of the Hall of Literary Brilliance (*Wenhua dian*) and the complex of the Hall of Martial Valor (*Wuying dian*) respectively. Located on the north of the Outer Court, the Inner Court centers on the Palace of Heavenly Purity (*Qianqing gong*), the Hall of Union (*Jiaotai dian*), and the Palace of Earthly Tranquility (*Kunning gong*), which were built for accommodating the emperor and his chief consort in Ming dynasty. The far north end of the Inner Court is the Imperial Garden. On respective sides of the main axis of the Inner Court lie the Six Eastern Palaces and the Six Western Palaces, the residences of the emperor's consorts. Apart from serving the emperor and his consorts, the Inner Court also comprises venues for religious rituals activities, such as the Numinous Firmament Treasure Hall (*Tianqiong baodian*) to the east of the Six Eastern Palaces, where Taoist ceremonies were held, and the Hall of Rectitude (*Zhongzheng dian*) and the Belvedere of Raining Flowers (*Yuhua ge*) to the west of the Six Eastern Palaces, which were the centers of Buddhism activities in Qing dynasty. Further from the axis of the Inner Court, there are two groups of complexes—the Far East Road and the Far West Road. The major complexes in the Far East Road include the Hall of Plucking Fragrance (*Xiefang dian*) in the south, commonly known as the three southern halls, and the Palace of Tranquil Longevity (*Ningshou gong*) in the north, which was reconstructed by Qianlong Emperor (1736—1796) in Qing dynasty as his palace for retirement; while the major complexes in the Far West Road include residences of the Empress Dowagers—the Palace of Compassion and Tranquility (*Cining gong*) and the Palace of Longevity and Health (*Shoukang gong*) in the south, the Palace of Peaceful Longevity (*Shouan gong*) in the north, and Buddhism buildings such as the Hall of Exuberance (*Yinghua dian*).

1. The Planning of the Forbidden City

In the history of traditional Chinese architecture, the imperial palace has always been one of the most brilliant and magnificent kind. China has been ruled by emperors for a long time. As the highest monarch of the imperial realm, emperors of that time had supreme power over the whole country. Imperial palaces, accordingly, were regarded as the symbol of the emperors' authority, and were assigned the most important kind of buildings in ancient society. Monarchs of all dynasties spent millions of money, tons of precious materials and countless craftsmen to built the imperial palace, with no expense spared. Marvelous imperial palaces were therefore presented one after another. Unfortunately, due to the Chinese tradition to destroy the old dynasty's palaces to suppress the former rulers of the country, most of China's imperial palaces were demolished or burnt down during

一、紫禁城的营建

宫殿建筑是中国古代建筑史中最辉煌的篇章。在古代中国，皇帝制度曾长期延续。皇帝是国家的最高统治者，拥有至高无上的权力。宫殿作为皇帝权威的象征，一直是古代社会中最重要的建筑。历朝历代的统治者都不惜动用全国的财力，采用最好的材料，使用最高超的技术来建造宫殿，因此出现了一个又一个建筑奇迹。然而不幸的是，每逢改朝换代，新旧王朝交替之际，新政的统治者总要毁坏旧王朝的宫殿，而另建新的皇宫。据说这样做可以镇压旧王朝的王气，以防止其死灰复燃，东山再起。这也从反面印证了宫殿建筑在显示和象征皇权方面的重要作用。这种大规模的破坏，使众多的建筑杰作毁于一旦。

角楼，民间有『九梁十八柱七十二条脊』之说，形容其结构的复杂。紫禁城内的建筑分为外朝和内廷两部分。外朝的中心为太和殿、中和殿、保和殿，统称『三大殿』，是国家举行重大典礼的地方（图一~图四）。三大殿左右两翼辅以文华殿、武英殿两组建筑。内廷的中心是乾清宫、交泰殿、坤宁宫，统称『后三宫』，在明代是皇帝和皇后居住的正宫。其后为御花园。后三宫两侧排列着东、西六宫，是妃们居住休息的地方。东六宫东侧是天穹宝殿等道教建筑，西六宫西侧是中正殿、雨花阁等清代佛堂建筑。此外还有外东路、外西路两部分建筑。外东路南部是皇太后、太妃等居住的慈宁宫、寿康宫、北部除皇太后、帝营建的太上皇宫殿——宁寿宫。外西路南部是皇子居住的撷芳殿，俗称『南三所』；北部是乾隆皇太妃等居住的寿安宫外，还有英华殿等佛堂建筑。

图一　三大殿全景

Fig.1 Panorama of the Three Main Halls

图2 三大殿总平面图

图3 三大殿总横剖面图

图4 三大殿总纵剖面图

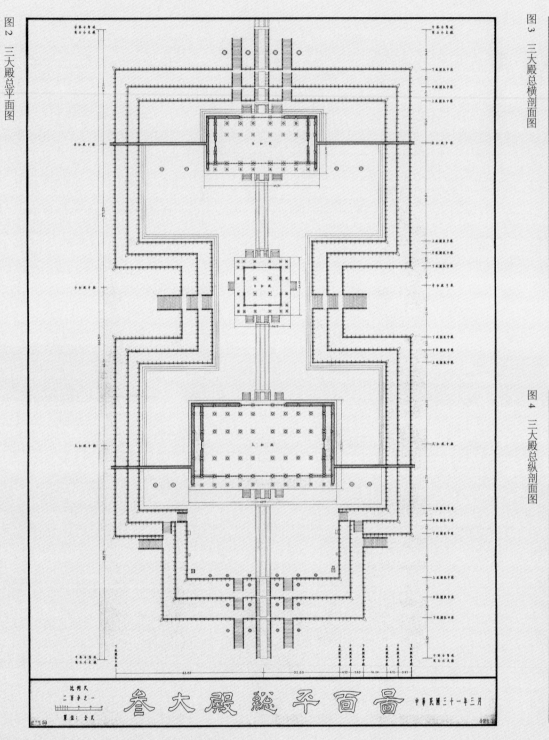

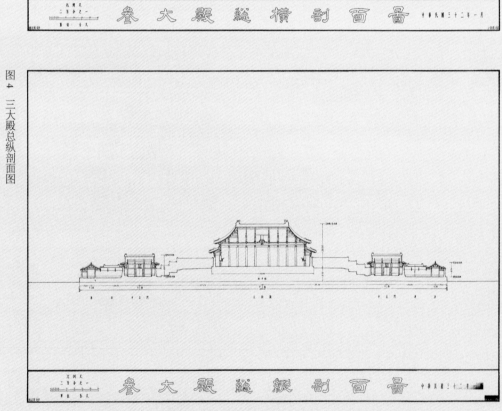

Fig.2 Overall Layout of the Three Main Halls
Fig.3 Overall Cross Section of the Three Main Halls
Fig.4 Overall Longitudinal Section of the Three Main Halls

the transfer of power. This is a big loss in the history of Chinese architecture on one hand, but proves the importance of imperial palaces and encourages the development of this kind of architecture on the other hand. It is only in this way that the art and technology of imperial palaces could develop and achieve today's success.

The construction of the Forbidden City started during the reign of Yongle Emperor, *Zhu Di* in Ming dynasty (1403—1424), but the story had begun long before. In 1368, *Zhu Yuanzhang*, the founder of the Ming dynasty, ascended the throne and appointed Nanjing as the capital of Ming later. In the third year of his reign (1370), *Zhu Yuanzhang* enfeoffed his sons with estates and titles of nobility. At this time, *Zhu Di*, the fourth son of *Zhu Yuanzhang*, was granted the Prince of Yan, with the capital of his princedom at *Beiping* (modern Beijing). Twenty-eight years later (1398), *Zhu Yuanzhang* passed away. Before his death, he appointed his grandson *Zhu Yunwen*, the child of his eldest son[①] as the future emperor. This reign did not last long. As *Zhu Yunwen* attempted to restrain his powerful uncles, *Zhu Di* rose in rebellion against his nephew. In 1402, *Zhu Di* overthrew *Zhu Yunwen* and was proclaimed emperor. He adopted the era name Yongle, which means 'perpetual happiness'. In the fourth year of his reign (1406), considering the endless struggles against the Mongols of the former Yuan dynasty, *Zhu Di* issued the edict to re-establish *Beiping* as the new imperial capital to consolidate his regime of the northern Ming dynasty. The next year, the construction of the imperial palace in *Beiping* started. Massive ministers were sent out to find proper logs, to make bricks and tiles, and to supervise the renovation planning of *Beiping* and the Forbidden City. The planning at that time had three considerations in special. (1) Considerations of the Sites of Former Yuan Dynasty: The site of the Forbidden City was situated on the capital city of the Mongol Yuan dynasty (called Khanbaliq or *Dadu* in Chinese). To make full use of the relics, the planners spent a lot of time investigating the former imperial city, learning the surviving buildings, river systems and drainage systems, which as a result saved a lot of resources. Notably, during the planning of the river systems, due to a lack of water, the Pond of Heavenly Dew (*Taiye chi*)[②] of Yuan dynasty was reused to introduce water sources inside the Forbidden City. The water was drawn through the northwest corner of the Forbidden City. Winding south, it converged to form the Golden River (*Jinshui he*) to the north of the

① The eldest son of *Zhu Yuanzhang* is *Zhu Biao*. He was appointed as the crown prince once his father ascended the throne, and passed away six years before his father died.
② Pond of Heavenly Dew (*Taiye chi*) was later turned into *Beihai* and *Zhonghai*, the imperial garden to the northwest of the Forbidden City.

但从另一个角度看，每一次大规模的毁建，都是一次宫殿建筑在走向成熟过程中的脱胎换骨。宫殿建筑的艺术与技术就是在这种不断扬弃的过程中逐渐发展、进步的。

紫禁城宫殿是明成祖朱棣在位时营建的。1368年，明太祖朱元璋建立明朝，之后定都南京。洪武三年（1370年），分封诸子为藩王，皇四子朱棣被封为燕王，驻守北平。朱元璋去世后，因皇太子早逝，由其皇太孙朱允炆继位，是为建文帝。朱棣不服，于建文四年（1402年）以武力攻下南京，并夺取了皇位，改年号为永乐，他于永乐四年（1406年）下诏迁都北京，并明令次年五月开始营建北京宫殿。他首先选派大臣分赴全国各地采伐木材、烧造砖瓦，且委派专员督制北京城与紫禁城的改建规划。当时的规划有三大特点。第一，明代的北京宫殿是在元大都的基址上营建的。当拟制规划时，规划师们不仅掌握元大都的基本情况，而且十分熟悉地上建筑的情况、水系的来龙去脉，以及暗沟的排水高程和坡度，因此在营建新城时得以充分利用原有的遗物，节省了很多工程量。由于紫禁城中缺乏水面，所以把太液池中的水从城墙的西北角引入，向南迁绕，在紫禁城内的一段就是美丽的内金水河，然后从东南方向流出，经菖蒲河、御河，与通惠河接通。第二，明代的都城规划吸取了历代都城规划的优点，对元大都宫殿布局作了许多改动（图5）。元朝的大内正门崇天门至大都正门丽正门的距离较近，没有北宋汴京宫殿布置那种雄伟深邃的气魄，于是明代的北京城规划吸取了北宋汴京宫前『周桥南北是天街』的布局，使明代的北京城规划吸取了北宋汴京宫前天街的那种雄伟深邃的气魄，

Meridian Gate (*Wu men*), flowed out of the Forbidden City from the southeast and finally flowed into Tonghui River through Changpu River and Yu River. (2) Considerations of the Former Capitals: The urban planning of *Beiping* had drawn advantages of capitals of previous dynasties (Fig.5). As a consequence, many changes were made to Khanbaliq, the capital city of Yuan dynasty. To start with, the south boundary of Khanbaliq was pushed southwards and a new gate, namely the Gate of South (*Zhengyang men*), was established along the boundary, replacing the south gate of Yuan (*Lizheng men*), a gate that is too close to the south gate of the imperial city of Yuan (*Chongtian men*), to continue the tradition of having a spacious plaza and a series of gates in front of the imperial city set in Song dynasty (960—1279). Between the Gate of South and the front gate of the Forbidden City, a series of gates and constructions were built, including the Gate of Great Ming (*Daming men*)[①], the Outer Golden River Bridges (*Wai jinshui qiao*), the Gate of Celestial Favor (*Chengtian men*)[②] and the Gate of Correct Deportment (*Duan men*), forming an axis of divinity and a space of sequence. These gates were the prelude of the Forbidden City that would add to the pomp and solemnity of the Forbidden City. Corridor halls were built to accommodate ministers of Ming in front of the Gate of Celestial Favor. Moreover, the Temple of Imperial Ancestral (*Tai miao*) and the Altar of Land and Grain (*Sheji tan*) were moved to the east and west of the gate, following the tradition laid down in the Confucian classic *The Rites of Zhou*. (3) Considerations of Defense: The planning of the Forbidden City in Ming times paid much attention to defense. In the Yuan dynasty, the imperial palace of Khanbaliq mainly consisted of three groups of palaces built around the Jade Island (*Qiong dao*) in the Pond of Heavenly Dew, namely the Main Imperial Palace (*Da nei*), the Palace of Thriving Divinity (*Xingsheng gong*) and the Palace of Flourishing Blessings (*Longfu gong*). Among the palaces, the Palace of Thriving Divinity and the Palace of Flourishing Blessings primarily served the empress dowagers, concubines and princes, whereas the Main Imperial Palace was used by the emperors and empresses. Though enclosed by walls, there was no moat or high hill around the palace. To remedy the defect, the imperial palace in the Ming dynasty was built intensively. A moat of fifty-two meters wide was built beyond the enclosing city walls, forming another layer of fortification for the Forbidden City. The soil excavated from the moats was up to a million cubic meters. It was moved to the north of the Forbidden City and thus formed the forty-

① Gate of Great Ming (*Daming men*) was later renamed as Gate of Great Qing (*Daqing men*) in Qing dynasty, and was torn down in 1954.
② Gate of Celestial Favor (*Chengtian men*)was the main entrance to the imperial city. It was later renamed as Gate of Heavenly Peace (*Tianan men*) in Qing dynasty.

把京城的南面城墙向南推出数百米，到正阳门的位置，从而使正阳门到紫禁城之间形成了一条笔直而漫长的中轴线。从正阳门向北，经过大明门（清代称大清门，现已无存）、外金水桥、承天门（清代称天安门）及端门，才能看到巍峨雄峙的紫禁城大门——午门。这些门阙构成引人入胜的空间，有如宫前的序幕，增加了紫禁城庄严肃穆的气氛。明代在承天门外中轴线的两侧布置有千步廊和衙署，在承天门内东西朝房两旁布置了『左祖右社』的太庙和社稷坛。这样的布置改变了元朝『左祖右社』远离皇城的情况，使太庙和社稷坛紧连皇宫。第三，明代的宫殿规划更重防守。元朝的宫殿布局是以琼岛为中心的三处宫殿群，即兴圣宫、隆福宫和大内。其中兴圣宫和隆福宫是太后、嫔妃及太子的宫室，大内则为帝后的正衙和寝宫。大内周围虽环以城墙，但无护城河，宫后的御苑中也无高山。明代的宫殿规划则是把所有宫室都布置在了紫禁城内，并沿紫禁城四周挖了一条 52 米宽的护城河，使紫禁城增加了一道防御工事。从护城河中挖出的土方多达百万立方米，运至宫后的御苑堆成高约 46 米的万岁山（清代称景山）。这个设计既符合南京明宫殿后面以万岁山为屏障的雄伟构想，又节省了土方的运输。在筹工备料、大兴土木历时十余年之久后，至永乐十八年（1420 年），紫禁城落成，帝京建设终于实现。永乐十九年（1421 年），朱棣正式迁都北京。

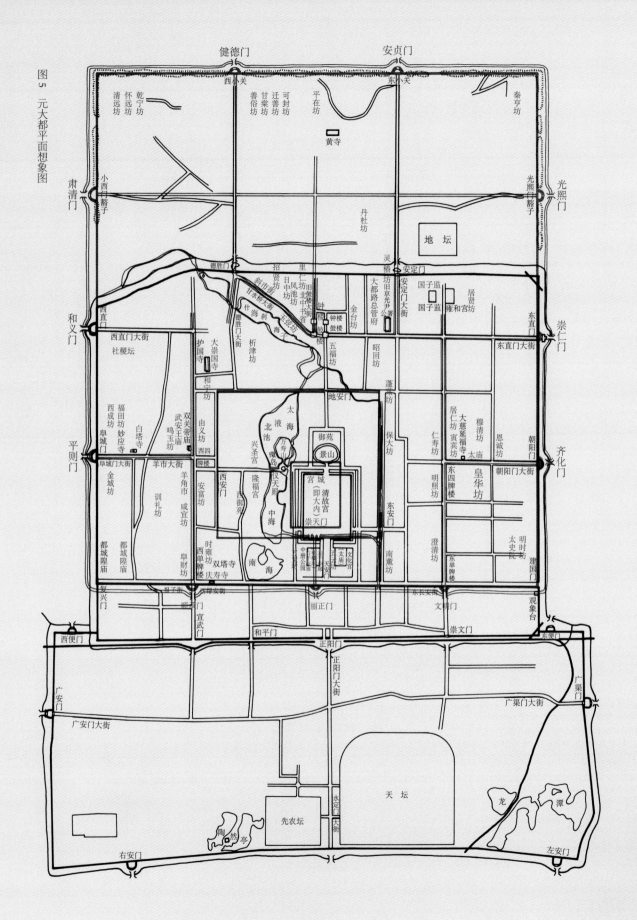

图5 元大都平面想象图

Fig.5 Restored Map of the Capital of Yuan Dynasty

—— 元大都城坊宫苑平面配置想象图

—— 北京市内外城平面略图

six-meter high artificial hill, the Hill of Long Life (*Wansui shan*)① . The construction of the Hill of Long Life served the purpose of siting residences south of a nearby hill for better *Fengshui*② conditions, and saved the cost of transportation. After years of preparation and construction, in the eighteenth year of Yongle reign (1420) finally, the capital city and the Forbidden City were both completed. The next year (1421), *Zhu Di* moved to *Beiping* officially and made here the primary capital of the empire.

Palaces are built under certain guiding ideology and theory, among which the most important concept is the norms of etiquette. Norms of etiquette, or *Li* in Chinese, is the core ideology that runs throughout the Chinese history and traditional culture. As the epitome of traditional Chinese architecture, the Forbidden City embodies the norms of etiquette in its siting and layout, as well as in the scales, forms, colors and decorations of single buildings. In fact, it was out of the consideration of etiquette③ that the Forbidden City was sited in the center of Beijing City. Apart from the norms of etiquette derived from Confucianism, the theory of *Yin*, *Yang*④ and Five Elements (*Wu Xing*)⑤ was widely practiced during construction in Ming dynasty as well and was generally reflected in three aspects. (1) Overall Layout: During the planning of the Forbidden City, the layout of the Outer Court was designed to be grand and the buildings masculine and magnificent, whereas layout of the Inner Court was planned to be compact and the buildings feminine and delicate. That is because in the Chinese theory of *Yin* and *Yang*, it is generally believed that the Outer Court of the Forbidden City is of the power of *Yang*, the sun principle, and the Inner Court is of the power of *Yin*, the dark principle. (2) Special Numbers: In the Chinese theory of *Yin* and *Yang*, odd numbers are numbers of *Yang*; while even numbers

① The Hill of Long Life (*Wansui shan*) was later renamed the Hill of Prospect (*Jing shan*) in Qing dynasty.
② *Fengshui* is literally translated as Wind Water. It is a method of investigating geographical features used in site selection and construction of dwellings, cities, and tombs, etc. by means of examining soil and tasting water. Its core concept is the harmonious coexistence between human beings and nature.
③ It is recorded in *Xunzi* that it is required by the norms of etiquette that emperors should live in the center of the world.
④ The concept of *Yin* and *Yang* originated from people's attitude toward nature in ancient China. The observation of mutually related and apposite aspects inspired the theory philosophically. Theory of *Yin* and *Yang* had come to pervade every aspect of Chinese traditional culture, including religion, philosophy, calligraphy and architecture.
⑤ Five Elements, namely fire, water, metal, earth and wood, are regarded as the foundation of everything in the universe and natural phenomena in China. They have their own characters and they can generate or destroy one other. They also correspond to massive things in daily life.

宫殿建筑的规划必然有其指导思想与理论依据。『礼』是贯穿中国传统文化的核心思想。紫禁城宫殿作为古代建筑文化集大成的载体，无论其位置、布局，还是建筑单体的规模、形制、色彩，乃至装饰等方面，都鲜明地体现着『礼』文化的渗透和影响。例如，紫禁城位于北京城中心，正是符合了『王者必居天下之中，礼也』的思想。此外，明代营建紫禁城时除了遵循儒家礼制，也充分运用了『阴阳五行』学说。『阴阳』说在紫禁城建筑中主要表现在以下三个方面：（1）宫殿布局——外朝为阳，内廷为阴。外朝建筑布局疏朗，气势雄伟，体现阳刚之美；内廷建筑布局严谨，内檐装修纤巧精美，体现阴柔之美。

（2）数目奇偶——奇数为阳，偶数为阴。外朝反复运用三、五、九等奇数，如中轴线上的三大殿坐落于三台之上；奉天殿（清代称太和殿）以南安排有五门，大殿面阔9间，进深5间暗示天子『九五之尊』；且外朝建筑的踏跺级数、台基和槛墙的砖皮层数也多用奇数。与之相对应，内廷则多用偶数，如中轴线上的主要建筑是乾清、坤宁两宫（交泰殿是后来增建的）；其两侧分布有十二宫、十所，以象征星辰拱

are numbers of *Yin*. Therefore, odd numbers such as three, five and nine are repeatedly used in Outer Court. For instance, the three main halls on the central axis are located on a terrace of three tiers; the Hall of Venerating Heaven (later renamed as the Hall of Supreme Harmony in Qing dynasty) is located to the north of a series of five gates, and has nine bays in width and five bays in depth[1]; and the numbers of steps, terraces, and brick layers used on Outer Court's buildings are also in most cases odd numbers. Conversely, even numbers are used extensively in the Inner Court. In comparison to the three main halls in the Outer Court, there were two halls only standing on the central axis when first constructed, that is, the Palace of Heavenly Purity (*Qianqing gong*) and the Palace of Earthly Tranquility (*Kunning gong*)[2] and twelve consort-accommodating palaces (Six Eastern and Western Palaces) in similar forms and ten abodes (Western and Eastern Five Abodes) in total in the Inner Court, surrounding the Palace of Heavenly Purity and the Palace of Earthly Tranquility like stars. The numbers of steps, terraces, and brick layers used on Inner Court's buildings are in most cases even numbers. (3) Names of Parallelism: To emphasize the complementarily and harmony of *Yin* and *Yang*, the names of the buildings in the Forbidden City are mostly names of parallelism. For instance, the main buildings of the Inner Court are the Palace of Heavenly Purity and the Palace of Earthly Tranquility. The gates on respective sides of the Gate of Heavenly Purity are the Gate of Solar Essence (*Rijing men*) and the Gate of Lunar Essence (*Yuehua men*). In addition to the philosophy of *Yin* and *Yang*, the Five Elements theory was also widely applied in the planning of the Forbidden City. For instance, the Hall of Literary Brilliance (*Wenhua dian*), where the crown prince worked in the Ming dynasty, and the Hall of Plucking Fragrance (*Xiefang dian*), where the princes lived in the Qing dynasty, are both set near the East Prosperity Gate (*Donghua men*) and are designated to use green glazed roofing tiles, because wood corresponds to the east in terms of orientation, to azure in terms of color and to growth in terms of character. For the same reason, the Meridian Gate is dominated by red colored paintings, because fire corresponds to red in terms of color; the palaces for empress dowagers are set in the west part of the Forbidden City, because metal corresponds to decay in terms of character and corresponds to west in terms of orientation; the central balustrade on the north side of the Hall of Imperial Peace (*Qin'an dian*), which is on the north end of the central axis of the Forbidden City, is decorated with water motif,

[1] To use number nine and five at the same time is deemed authoritative and sacred in ancient China. Sometimes they are used to indicate emperors.

[2] The Hall of Union (*Jiaotai dian*) was built later and thus formed the three rear halls together with the Palace of Heavenly Purity and the Palace of Earthly Tranquility.

卫；内廷建筑的踏跺级数、台基和槛墙的砖皮层数亦多为偶数。（3）建筑命名——大多使用对偶之词，以强调阴阳互补与调和，如乾清宫与坤宁宫、日精门与月华门，等等。紫禁城中有许多『礼象五行』之处，则是『五行』说在宫殿中的鲜明体现。东方属木，为青色，主生长，故明代『太子视事之所』文华殿和清代皇子居住的南三所均安排在东华门内，建筑屋面采用绿色琉璃瓦。南方属火，为赤色，所以午门采用独特的红色彩画。西方属金，生化过程为『收』，太后居住的宫室因此被安排在内廷西侧。北方属水，所以中轴线尽端的钦安殿北面正中的石栏板采用水纹雕饰，与其他栏板的穿花龙雕饰不同。中央属土，为黄色，设计者巧妙地将三台平面做成『土』字形，并在紫禁城中大面积使用黄色琉璃瓦，以象征王者居中统摄天下。『五行』说中还有『相生相克』的说法，因此三大殿多用红色墙壁和油饰体现『火生土』的规律，并尽量少用绿色，也不种植树木，就是为了防止『木克土』。凡此种种，以灵活多样的手法，充分展示了五行方位、色彩、生化过程间的相互关系。紫禁城的总体空间布局处理亦受到传统风水『形势』说的深刻影响与制约，具体表现为以下两个方面：（1）在单体构成上——构成紫禁城建筑组群的各个单体建筑，其空间尺度莫不遵循『百尺为形』的原则，即以23～35米为律来控制单体建筑的平面及竖向尺度。例如，午门是宫中最高的单体建筑，总高37.95米，其镇压威慑作用高于其他建筑，奉天殿

because water corresponds to north in terms of orientation; the three-tier terrace that the three main halls stand on is in the shape of Chinese character ' 土 ' (earth) and yellow glazed roofing tiles are widely applied in the Forbidden City, because earth corresponds to center in terms of orientation and to yellow in terms of color. The Five Elements can generate or destroy one other. According to the interaction, fire creates earth/ash while wood break up earth, so the dominant hue of the three main halls are red rather than green, and no trees are planted around the halls and the terrace. The above facets not only indicate the intrinsic relations among the orientation, color and biochemical process of the Five Elements, but also show the impact of the Five Elements theory on the Forbidden City. *Fengshui* is another important factor that deeply influenced and restricted the planning of the Forbidden City. It has manifests itself as follows: (1) For Single Buildings: The buildings of the Forbidden City shall not exceed a hundred *chi*[①] in scale, following the theory of *Fengshui*. That is to say, the buildings shall be no more than twenty-three to thirty-five meters in length, depth and height. In fact, the buildings in the Forbidden City are all lower than thirty-five meters, except the overwhelming Meridian Gate, the highest building of the Forbidden City (37.95m in height), and the grand Hall of Venerating Heaven (later renamed as the Hall of Supreme Harmony in Qing dynasty, 35.05m in height). the most important building of the Forbidden City. (2) For Overall Layout: On one hand, constructions within the range of visibility, such as platforms, courtyards and plazas, shall not exceed a hundred *chi* in scale; while constructions over the range of visibility shall not exceed a thousand *chi* in scale, following the theory of *Fengshui*. For example, the length and depth of the three main halls and the distance among them are all within thirty-five meters, same as the length and depth of most courtyards in the Inner Court. Yet the distances among different single buildings, plazas and alleys are no more than three hundred and fifty meters, except for the distance between the East Prosperity Gate (*Donghua men*) and the Northeast Corner Building, and the distance between the West Prosperity Gate (*Xihua men*) and the Northwest Corner Building.

2. The Construction of the Forbidden City

In the past six hundred years, the Forbidden City has been maintained, restored and even reconstructed for multiple times. Although the layout of the palace remains much the same as it was first constructed, new buildings were added by different rulers. To sum up,

① The length unit *chi* was widely used in ancient China. In Qing dynasty, one *chi* is about zero point three two meters in length.

二、紫禁城修建历程概述

在漫长的岁月中，紫禁城宫殿虽然经历多次保养性修缮，甚至改建、重建，但至今仍保持了始建时的基本格局，并遗存了许多具有时代特征的历史建筑。其修建历程大致可分为以下几个阶段：

（清代称太和殿）位尊九五，全高 35.05 米；其他建筑的高度均在 35 米限下。（2）在视距构成上——月台、庭院、广场的围合空间，其平面尺度限定了观赏视距，近观皆以『百尺为形』控制，如三大殿丹陛的面阔、进深以及间距都在 35 米之内，内廷大多数庭院的通面阔和进深也都不逾此数；而远观则不超过『千尺为势』的限制，除东北、西北城外角到东华、西华门距离过大，属于特例外，其余所有广场、街巷或相邻单体建筑的间距最大只在 350 米左右。

the buildings of the Forbidden City were primarily built in the following periods:

(1) Yongle Reign in Ming Dynasty: In the fourth year of Yongle reign (1406), upon *Zhu Di*'s edict to construct *Beiping* as the new capital, stock preparation was started. Later on, the first phase of the construction started. Considering the limited resources and time, the first phase of the construction aimed to complete important buildings only. Started with the water supply and sewerage system underground, the buildings on the central axis, of the Six Eastern and Western Palaces and of the Western and Eastern Five Abodes were completed, while a great number of buildings on the east and west sides of the palace remained un-built. From Hongxi reign to Zhengde reign (1425—1521), these spare areas were gradually filled with buildings of different forms and functions.

(2) After Zhengde Reign in Ming Dynasty: Multiple expansion, restoration, reconstruction and relocation projects were carried out after Zhengde reign in Ming dynasty. This was especially true during Jiajing reign (1522—1566) when the quantity and quality of the buildings both increased and buildings of rare forms appeared frequently. According to archives, the buildings constructed during Jiajing reign included the Beamless Hall (*Wuliang dian*) for alchemy, the building on stilts behind the Hall of Literary Brilliance (*Wenhua dian*) built for catastrophe, which were both destroyed; the wood frame-structures of the Six Western Palaces, the Pavilion of Myriad Spring times (*Wanchun ting*), the Gate of Heavenly Unity (*Tianyi men*), the Gate of Earthly Tranquility (*Kunning men*), and the yellow glazed roofing tiles on the Hall of Literary Brilliance, which were remained and still could be seen now. From Wanli reign to the end of the Ming dynasty (1573—1644), renovation projects took over the dominant position instead of constructions with the exception of the construction inside the Imperial Garden (*Yuhua yuan*). During Wanli reign (1573—1620), the Mountain of Accumulated Elegance (*Duixiu shan*), the Imperial Prospect Pavilion (*Yujing ting*), and the two square pavilions of the Pavilion of Floating Jade (*Fubi ting*) and the Pavilion of Auspicious Water-cleansed (*Chengrui ting*), were added to the Imperial Garden, as an unique example of architecture of Wanli. In the fifteenth year of Chongzhen reign (1642) when the Ming dynasty was in its dusk, corridor halls were added symmetrically to the south of the Pavilion of Spreading Righteousness (*Hongyi ge*) and the Pavilion of Embodying Benevolence (*Tiren ge*) that were located on both sides of the plaza in front of the Hall of Supreme Harmony (*Taihe dian*).

(3) During the Transfer of Power: By 1644, the Manchus had achieved supremacy in northern China and proclaimed the Qing dynasty as the successor to the Ming. According

（一）《日下旧闻考》卷九。

（1）明代永乐四年（1406年）筹建北京宫殿时，由于采用全面规划、重点实施的方针，因此第一期工程为给水排水的地下工程先行，随即进行大规模的备料；建筑方面是以中轴线为主，包括东、西六宫的单元式宫室及乾清宫东、西五所的营建工程，而紫禁城两侧则留有大量余地。自洪熙到正德的90余年间，房屋多在留有余地的空地上营建，所以故宫的基本格局是始建时的原状。

（2）自明代正德以后，尤其在嘉靖年间大肆进行增建、重建、改建、移建工程。不仅建筑数量增多，而且宫中出现了罕见的品种，如为炼丹增建的无梁殿、为防天灾在文华殿后增建了孤立的干阑式建筑等，但多已无存。现存的西六宫太极等殿的木构架，御花园万春亭、天一门和坤宁门的修建与改建，以及文华殿屋顶改为黄瓦等，都是明代嘉靖年间的遗物。万历年以后多是重修工程，但御花园的叠山以及山上的御景亭、鱼池中的浮碧、澄瑞两亭的四角攒尖方亭均是明代万历年间的遗物。明代崇祯十五年（1642年）在弘义、体仁两阁以南的隙地增建左右对称的值房。

（3）清军攻克北京后，对明代宫殿十分满意，便全盘接收了。为了利用这座极其典范的宫殿，『世祖章皇帝（顺治）定鼎燕京，顺治元年（1644年）肇定大清门名额，有若殿庙宫阙制度，皆不振鸿谟，因胜国（明代）之旧而斟酌损益之』。因而清代顺治、康熙年间对外朝、内廷建筑普遍进行维修，除

to *the Compendium of Beiping* (*Rixia jiuwen kao*), after the young Shunzhi Emperor (1644—1661) proclaimed himself as ruler of all China, he decided to largely maintained the Forbidden City's Ming dynasty scheme, except for the names of some of the principal buildings. Thanks to his decision, the Forbidden City was able to retain its original appearance and style regardless of the change of regime. Buildings burnt down in wars were reconstructed following their original designs, whereas others were maintained to be in good conditions. The Meridian Gate (*Wu men*) and the Hall of Supreme Harmony, however, were reconstructed smaller than they were in Ming dynasty. That is because these two buildings were so huge that no logs of appropriate sizes could be found. To solve the problem, the Hall of Supreme Harmony was changed into a hall of shorter length and more bays so that shorter beams could be used; while the Meridian Gate remained much the same from outside, but were differentiated from the inner structure—to reduce the use of long logs and to maintain the large, open, partition-less interior space at the same time, the column grid of the Meridian Gate was remained, but two groups of trusses were added on top of the original columns and beams to break the long axis into pieces. The Palace of Earthly Tranquility (*Kunning gong*) was also greatly renovated upon the succession of Qing. Different from the above two buildings which were reconstructed smaller because of the limitation of materials, the Palace of Earthly Tranquility was converted for religious beliefs. Following the Palace of Purity and Tranquility (*Qingning gong*) in the Shenyang Palace, the Palace of Earthly Tranquility was turned into a place of Shamanist worship and was filled with a linked heated brick *kang*[1] platform along the north, the west, and the south walls, and a large kitchen where sacrificial meat was prepared. Moreover, the doors of the palace were relocated and the window papers were changed to be pasted from outside.

(4) Qianlong Reign in Qing Dynasty: The Forbidden City was greatly renovated in Qianlong reign (1736—1796). For instance, the symmetric layout of the Western and Eastern Five Abodes was changed to build the Garden of Established Happiness (*Jianfugong huayuan*) for Qianlong Emperor. Yet the Hall of Benevolent Longevity (*Renshou dian*), the Hall of Whistling Blue-phoenix (*Huiluan gong*) and the Hall of Flying Red-phoenix (*Jiefeng gong*) of Ming dynasty were pulled down to make room for constructing the Palace of Tranquil Longevity (*Ningshou gong*), the palace for Qianlong Emperor's retirement. Occupied an area of forty-eight thousand square meters,

① *Kang* is the special kind of beds made of wood platforms with heated stoves beneath, mainly used in the northern China.

个别的特殊原因外，大都保持原状，如今故宫建筑中能够遗存很多明代建筑与这个时期的修缮原则是分不开的。只是午门、太和殿两座建筑由于开间过大，无此栋梁之材，最后把太和殿改为面阔二间，以减小桁条的跨度；午门的修缮方案则更为巧妙，下部木架不动，以维持明代的大开间，但上架里围金柱间的内额上增加两缝梁架，以缩短桁条的跨度，外观上仍未改变明代原有形制。但在坤宁宫装修工程中，为了符合满族的风俗习惯与宗教信仰，仿照盛京皇宫（今沈阳故宫）清宁宫的格调，做了通连的大炕，增设了煮肉的大锅，改变了门的位置，并将窗户纸糊在外。

（4）清代乾隆年间在紫禁城中做了大量改建。为了营建建福宫花园，拆除了乾清宫西五所西端的两所建筑，改变了东、西五所对称的布局。在紫禁城东部，为乾隆皇帝营建太上皇宫殿时，把内廷原明代仁寿殿一号殿、哕鸾宫、喈凤宫予以拆除，在 4.8 万平方米的基地上营建了宁寿宫一区，是紫禁城宫殿建筑改动最大之处。

the renovation of Palace of Tranquil Longevity was the largest project carried out in the history of the Forbidden City.

(5) Late Qing Dynasty: Due to a lack of money, the number of constructions inside the imperial palace began to decline in the late Qing Dynasty. At that time, only a few renovation projects of small scales were accomplished. The Palace of Eternal Spring (*Changchun gong*), for instance, were connected with the former Palace of Auspicious Beginning (*Qixiang gong*) and united with it as a large compound to possess more space. To achieve this, the former Gate of Eternal Spring as well as the rear wall of the Palace of Auspicious Beginning were dismantled; walls of the main hall and two side halls were moved from peripheral columns to hypostyle columns to form a connecting winding porch; and sparrow braces, a kind of components that only appear in high-class architecture, were added among peripheral columns. Having a porch and sparrow braces at the same time is regarded as a symbol of high-class architecture at that time. That is to say, the renovation project has made the Palace of Eternal Spring the only high-class example in the Six Western Palaces area. Learning from this, the Palace of Gathered Elegance (*Chuxiu gong*) and the Palace of Earthly Honor (*Yikun gong*) were both turned into a series of four courtyards with porches. The six western palaces have therefore merged into four palaces and the symmetric layout of the Six Eastern and Western Palaces was changed.

In the fourteenth year of Guangxu reign (1888) in Qing dynasty, the Gate of Supreme Harmony (*Taihe men*) caught on fire. The next year, the structure was rebuilt according to the original scheme. Aiming to build exactly the same as the former structure, the gate actually applied techniques of the time and shaped its components such as brackets and sparrow braces in the forms that were popular in Guangxu reign. In the sense of conservation, the intervention approach did decrease the authenticity of the buildings. But it chronicles the history of constructions and benefits the later researcher a lot. Like the Gate of Supreme Harmony, buildings of characteristics of different times are routinely seen in the Forbidden City. This could probably explain why the Forbidden City is often referred as the museum of Chinese architecture.

(6) After the Fall of Qing Dynasty: In 1912, with the abdication of Puyi, the last Emperor of China, the Outer Court of the Forbidden City was turned over to the new Republic of China government, while the Inner Court retained to serve the imperial family. In 1914, a museum was established in the Outer Court, and the Hall of Martial Valor (*Wuying dian*) and the Hall of Respectful Thoughts (*Jingsi dian*) in the complex of the Hall of Martial

（5）清代晚期，因财政匮乏，所以无力进行古建筑养护，但宫室的修饰还是不少的。为了扩展后妃宫室的庭院规模，把两进院的长春宫与启祥宫联系组成四进院的宫室，不仅拆掉了长春门及其两侧院墙，而且拆除了启祥宫后檐墙，并接建了后廊与抱厦，为了体现庭院中四面游廊的气氛，把原来六宫中不设外廊的形制改为前出廊，于是把原来的装修从檐柱推至金柱，并在檐柱上添装雀替，使西六宫中出现了既出廊又有雀替的高等级建筑形制。继而储秀宫、翊坤宫也仿照该做法，改为四进院带游廊的形式，于是西六宫变为四宫，改变了原来东、西六宫的格局。

清代光绪十四年（1888年）太和门发生火灾，次年虽在原基础上按原形重建，但各部件的手法，尤其斗栱、雀替等构件明显采用当时光绪年间形制手法建造。说明当时的重建工程只是大体相似的重新营建，并不是恢复原状的重建，因而工艺手法均用当时流行的规程，使人一看便知是清代晚期的建筑。不仅在太和门，这种做法在历代重建工程中也是如此，因而形成了古建筑的时代特征，方便了考古工作的可识别性。

（6）民国3年（1914年），内务部下令将武英殿、敬思殿改造为陈列室，于是门窗均改成近代门窗的边抹样式，室内铺水泥花砖地面，增建文物库房——宝蕴楼，采用欧洲19世纪的建筑形式，如砖墙、木楼楞、木屋架。民国5年（1916年），由于认为武英殿的改造很好，也仿照武英殿的做法给文华殿室内铺墁水泥花砖地面，更换门窗。

Valor were reformed into exhibition rooms: the paper on the partition windows and doors were replaced by modern glass; cement tiles were applied on the floor. A storehouse for collections was established, that is the Hall of Embodied Treasures (*Baoyun lou*), in the nineteenth-century European style, with brick walls, wood furring channels and wood trusses. In 1916, with massive positive responses, the Hall of Literary Brilliance was renovated following the example of the Hall of Martial Valor.

Apparently, constructions of above periods could not meet the requirements of modern conservation. That is probably because the Forbidden City was no more than a group of buildings for living in the eyes of people of that time. It is understandable that the rulers favored the most popular or functional forms and techniques rather than the ancient, authentic ones, and that renovations were carried out frequently for needs of reality.. It was not until the rise of heritage preservation when ancient buildings were finally considered cultural relics that this understanding gradually changed.

In 1961, the State Council promulgated *the Provisional Regulations on the Protection and Control of Cultural Relics* and designated the Forbidden City as one of China's foremost-protected cultural heritage sites. *The Provisional Regulations on the Protection and Control of Cultural Relics* were issued based on China's eleven-year practice on cultural relic preservations and had positive effects on promoting the scientific management of cultural relics above- and under-ground throughout China. It pointed out the importance of understanding the historical values, artistic values and scientific values of cultural relics, thus leading to the transition from perceptual to rational knowledge in terms of cultural relics cognition and promoting the development of architectural heritage preservation and research. In 1982, on inheritance and development of the Provisional Regulations, the *Law of the People's Republic of China on Protection of Cultural Relics* was adopted. Principles of preserving and restoring historic buildings were clearly stipulated in the law as the guiding ideology and theoretical basis for practice. After the law was promulgated, the awareness of treating buildings of history as cultural relics was greatly strengthened. Nowadays, keeping the authenticity of the historic buildings to the greatest extent has been a fundamental principle of heritage preservation and conservation inside the Forbidden City.

3. Magnificent Halls in the Outer Court

The Meridian Gate (*Wu men*) is the main entrance to the imperial palace (Fig.6). Following the institution of setting up 'Three Courts and Five Gates' to show respects to the emperor,

三、雄伟壮丽的外朝殿宇

午门是紫禁城的正门，位于北京的中轴线上（图6）。其前有端门、天安门（皇城的正门，明代称承天门）、大清门（明代称大明门，现已无存），其后有太和门（明代称奉天门，后改称皇极门，清代

上述几个阶段的修建方法，都是把古建筑看作一般建筑，丝毫没有文物意识，因而把当时流行的，或者是认为最好的形式与做法应用到古建筑修建当中，甚至提出改造的指示。这种修建思想由来已久，直到把古建筑纳入文物范畴后才逐渐得以转变。

1961年国务院通过《文物保护管理暂行条例》，同时通过第一批全国重点文物保护单位名单，故宫即在第一批名单中。该条例是在中华人民共和国成立以来文物工作总结的基础上形成的，对全国的地上、地下文物纳入科学管理起到了积极的推动作用。它指出了文物的历史、艺术、科学价值的重要性，是文物意识从感性阶段到理性认识的飞跃，促进了古建筑保护与研究工作的发展与提高。1982年，在《文物保护管理暂行条例》的继承与发展中，我国颁布了《中华人民共和国文物保护法》，该法明确规定了古建筑的保护及修缮原则，使这项工作有了更为准确的指导思想和依据，视古建筑为文物的意识也更加增强了。如今，故宫的古建筑修缮工作都以『不改变文物原状』为根本原则。

图 6 午门

Fig.6 Meridian Gate

the Forbidden City was designed to have Gate of Great Ming (*Daming men*)[1], Gate of Celestial Favor (*Chengtian men*)[2], Gate of Correct Deportment (*Duan men*), the Meridian Gate and Gate of Venerating Heaven (*Fengtian men*)[3] from south to north on the central axis of Beijing when first constructed in Ming dynasty. There are corridor rooms on both sides of each gate, forming a series of open squares together with the gate buildings. The alignment of gates and squares strengthens the rhythm of the central axis and highlights the solemn and profound atmosphere of the Forbidden City at the same time. The Meridian Gate was first built in the eighteenth year of Yongle reign (1420) and was reconstructed in the fourth year of Shunzhi reign (1647) and the sixth year of Jiaqing reign (1801). Following the Hall of Origins (*Hanyuan dian*) in Palace of Highest Virtue (*Daming gong*) of Tang dynasty (618—907) and the Gate of Red Phoenix (*Danfeng men*) of Song dynasty (960—1279), the layout of the Meridian Gate is concave. This form originates from *Que* - a kind of watchtowers in Han dynasty (202BC—220AD). The Meridian Gate can be roughly divided into two parts – the upper towers and the twelve-meter-high abutment. These two parts are connected by bridle paths on both sides of the abutment. On the abutment, there are in total three doorways on the frontispiece and two smaller doors at the corners of the flanking buildings. The five doors served different groups of people in ancient times. The center passage-way was reserved solely for the emperor. However, the emperor's main consort – the empress - was granted the privilege of using this opening once, and once only, on her wedding day. As a special honor, the top three scholars, who achieved the highest awards in the national examinations presided over by the emperor, would be permitted to march through this door, following their interview with the emperor. The door to the east was used by officials whereas that to the west was used by members of the imperial family. The remaining two small doors at the corners were only used when there were grand ceremonies. The upper towers of the Meridian Gate consist of five tower buildings. With a double-eaved hip roof, nine bays in width and five bays in depth, the central tower is undoubtfully the largest. To the east and west of the central tower, two corridor-like buildings with thirteen bays extend southward, connecting two towers with double spires on their ends separately. The appearances of these constructions look much like the wings of a bird. Consequently the two wings are often referred as 'the Hall of Wild Geese's Wings'

① Gate of Great Ming (*Daming men*) was later renamed as Gate of Great Qing (*Daqing men*) in Qing dynasty, and was torn down in 1954.
② Gate of Celestial Favor (*Chengtian men*) was the main entrance to the imperial city. It was later renamed as Gate of Heavenly Peace (*Tianan men*) in Qing dynasty.
③ Gate of Celestial Worship (*Fengtian men*) was later renamed as Gate of Imperial Supremacy (*Huangji men*), Gate of Supreme Harmony (*Taihe men*) in Ming and Qing dynasties successively.

改今名）。各门之内，两侧均有排列整齐的廊庑。在中国古代『五门三朝』制度的影响下，这种以门庑围成广场、层层递进的空间布局形式不但强化了中轴线的感染力，更突出了紫禁城肃穆深邃的庄严气氛。

午门建成于明代永乐十八年（1420 年），清代顺治四年（1647 年）重修，嘉庆六年（1801 年）又修。

午门的平面呈『凹』字形，沿袭了唐朝大明宫含元殿以及宋朝宫殿丹凤门的形制，是从汉代的门阙演变而成的。午门分上、下两部分。下为墩台，高 12 米，正中开三门，俗称『明三暗五』，墩台两侧设上下城台的马道。五个门洞各有用途。中门为皇帝专用；此外，只有皇帝大婚时，皇后乘坐的喜轿可以从中门进宫；在宣布殿试结果后，通过殿试选拔的状元、榜眼、探花可以从中门出宫。东侧门供文武官员出入，西侧门供宗室王公出入。两掖门只在举行大型活动时开启。墩台上正中有门楼一座，面阔 9 间，进深 5 间，重檐庑殿顶。墩台两翼各有廊庑 13 间，俗称『雁翅楼』，廊庑两端建有重檐攒尖顶的方亭。正楼两侧有钟、鼓亭各 3 间，每遇皇帝亲临天坛、地坛祭祀或举行大型活动则钟鼓齐鸣，去太庙祭祀则击鼓。午门整座建筑高低错落，左右呼应，形若朱雀展翅，故又有『五凤楼』之称。午门

(*Yanchi lou*). On two ends of the central tower, there are three bell-and-drum pavilions separately. The bells would ring and the drums would be struck to announce the emperor's departure for the Temple of Heaven (*Tian tan*) and the Temple of Earth (*Di tan*), or to show the imperial dignity when emperor went to the Hall of Supreme Harmony (*Taihe dian*) to hold grand ceremonies. In cases of departure for the Imperial Ancestral Temple (*Tai miao*), the drums would be played solely. With heights varying and towers symmetric, the Meridian Gate appears in the shape of a flying phoenix, which gives it the name 'the Five-Phoenix Tower' (*Wufeng lou*). The Meridian Gate was the usual place for the promulgation of the emperors' rescripts. Every year the official lunar calendar was issued from here in a special ceremony. Moreover, when the troops returned from an important battle in triumph, there would be a grand Captives Sacrifice Ceremony that allowed the emperor to sit on the Meridian Gate and inspect his troops.

The Gate of Supreme Harmony (*Taihe men*) is the grand formal entrance to the Forbidden City and the Outer Court. Built during the Yongle reign of the Ming dynasty, it was first named as the Gate of Venerating Heaven (*Fengtian men*). Later, the Jiajing Emperor (1522—1566) of Ming dynasty renamed it as the Gate of Imperial Supremacy (*Huangji men*). Its current name was assigned in the second year of Shunzhi reign (1645) after the Qing regime moved its capital to Beijing and began its rule over China. In the third year of Shunzhi reign (1646) and the seventh year of Jiaqing reign (1802), renovation has been carried on the Gate of Supreme Harmony. The gate now seen was rebuilt in the fifteenth year of Guangxu reign (1889) after it was destroyed by fire the year before. The Gate of Supreme Harmony has nine bays in width and four bays in depth, covering an area of about 1,300 square meters. Situated on top of a marble abutment, it has a double-eaved gable-and-hip roof and beams decorated with dragons pattern paintings (*Hexi caihua*). In front of the Gate of Supreme Harmony are symbols of legitimacy to rule: a pair of bronze lions and four bronze *ding* tripods cast in Ming dynasty. In respective sides are the Gate of Manifest Virtue (*Zhaode men*) to the east[①] and the Gate of Correct Conduct (*Zhendu men*)[②] to the west. The square in front of the gate covers an area of about 2.6 hectares, in the center of which the Inner Golden Water River (*Nei jinshui he*) bends like

① Gate of Manifest Virtue (*Zhaode men*) was initially called East Corner Gate (*Dong jiaomen*) in the Ming dynasty, was dubbed the Gate of Spreading Administration (*Hongzheng men*), and was given the present name by the Qing rulers.
② Gate of Correct Conduct (*Zhendu men*) was originally named the West Corner Gate (*Xi jiaomen*), in 1562 was changed to Gate of Proclaiming Governance (*Xuanzhi men*) by the Jiajing Emperor, and was given the present name by the Qing rulers.

是颁发皇帝诏书的地方。每年腊月初一，都要在午门举行颁布次年历书的『颁朔』典礼。遇有重大战争，大军凯旋归来，要在午门举行向皇帝敬献战俘的『献俘』礼。

太和门是紫禁城内最大的宫门，也是外朝宫殿的正门。明代建成时称奉天门，明代嘉靖四十一年（1562年）改称皇极门，清代顺治二年（1645年）改今名。顺治三年（1646年）、嘉庆七年（1802年）重修，于光绪十四年（1888年）被焚毁，次年重建。太和门面阔 9 间，进深 4 间，建筑面积约 1300 平方米，上覆重檐歇山顶，下为汉白玉基座，梁、枋等构件饰以和玺彩画。门前列铜狮 1 对，铜鼎 4 只，为明代铸造的陈设铜器。太和门左右各设一门，东为昭德门（明代称东角门、弘政门），西为贞度门（明代称西角门、宣治门）。门前有面积约 2.6 万平方米的广场，内金水河形如弯弓自西向东蜿蜒流过，好似一

a bow leading from west to east. Five marble bridges span the river, namely the Inner Golden Water Bridge (*Nei jinshui qiao*). This set of assemblage, featuring a fallen silk ribbon, brings a picturesque scenery to the solemn Forbidden City (Fig.7). The Gate of Supreme Harmony was used by emperors to hold morning audience to accept memoranda from officials, issue orders and deal with political affairs during the Ming and early Qing dynasties. Later, the morning audience was moved to the Gate of Heavenly Purity (*Qianqing gong*). In the ninth month of the year following the Manchu conquest (1644), Shunzhi Emperor ascended the throne and issued the proclamation of Qing dynasty rule over the country at the Gate of Supreme Harmony.

The Hall of Supreme Harmony (*Taihe dian*), the most dignified building in the Forbidden City and the most significant hall of the three main halls of the Outer Court, is commonly referred to as the Hall of Golden Chimes (*Jinluan dian*) (Fig.8). When first built in the eighteenth year of Yongle reign (1420) in the Ming dynasty, it was named the Hall of Venerating Heaven (*Fengtian dian*). In the forty-first year of Jiajing reign (1562), Jiajing Emperor renamed it the Hall of Imperial Supremacy (*Huangji dian*). Upon making Beijing their capital, the Qing rulers quickly changed it to its present name. The Hall of Supreme Harmony has been burned to the ground and reconstructed for several times. The current building was reconstructed in the Qing dynasty. As the largest hall in the Forbidden City, the Hall of Supreme Harmony has eleven bays in width and five bays in depth, covering 2,377 square meters. The building itself is 26.92 meters high, while the building and the abutment together is about 35.05 meters high. The double-eaved hip roof, the 3.4-meter-high 4,300-kilogram-weight mythical animals at the ends of the main ridge and the ten figurines at each of its roof corners, imply that the hall is architecturally the highest-ranking building in China superior to other ancient ones (Fig.9). The decorations of the hall are also superior and splendid. Beneath the eave, there are bunch of concentrated brackets (*Dou gong*) and beams decorated with dragons paintings (*Hexi caihua*). The lattice windows and lattice doors of the hall are adorned with water chestnut blossom pattern on the upper parts and in relief with cloud and dragon motif on the lower parts, while the joints are covered by gilded bronze wares decorated with dragons (Fig.10). Inside the Hall of Supreme Harmony, the floor is paved with special bricks called Gold Bricks (*Jin zhuan*). As a symbol of imperial power, the sandalwood throne, standing under the signboard inscribed with '建极绥猷' (*Jianjisuiyou*)[①] by Qianlong Emperor,

① '建极绥猷' means that the emperor shall obey the heaven and comfort the people at the same time.

条玉带飘落，为庄严肃穆的紫禁城增添了几分画意。河上横架五座石桥，习称内金水桥（图7）。太和门在明代是『御门听政』之处，皇帝在此接受臣下的朝拜和上奏，颁发诏令，处理政事。清代初年的皇帝也曾在太和门听政、赐宴，后来『御门听政』改在乾清门。清代顺治元年（1644年）九月，满族统治者定鼎北京即在太和门颁布大赦令。

太和殿俗称『金銮殿』，是外朝三大殿的正殿，位于紫禁城中轴线的显要位置（图8）。明代永乐十八年（1420年）建成时称奉天殿，明代嘉靖四十一年（1562年）改称皇极殿，清代顺治二年（1645年）改今名。自建成后屡遭焚毁，又多次重建，今天所见为清代重建后的形制。太和殿面阔11间，进深5间，建筑面积约2377平方米，高26.92米，连同台基通高35.05米，为紫禁城内规模最大的殿宇。其上为重檐庑殿顶，正脊两端安有高3.4米、重约4300公斤的大吻，檐角安有10个走兽，数量之多为现存古建筑中的孤例（图9）。太和殿的装饰十分豪华。其檐下施以密集的斗栱，室内外梁枋上饰以和玺彩画。门窗上部嵌成菱花格纹，下部浮雕云龙图案，接榫处安有镌刻龙纹的镏金铜叶（图10）。殿内金砖铺地，明间设宝座，上悬清代乾隆皇帝御笔『建极绥猷』匾额，宝座两侧排列有6根直径一米的沥粉贴金云龙

图7 太和门广场（内金水河、内金水桥）

Fig.7 Plaza in front of the Gate of Supreme Harmony (with the Inner Golden Water River and Bridge in sight)

图 8　太和殿

图 9　太和殿檐角走兽

图 10　太和殿槅扇门

Fig.8 Hall of Supreme Harmony
Fig.9 Figurines on the Eaves of the Hall of Supreme Harmony
Fig.10 Lattice Doors of the Hall of Supreme Harmony

is located in the center and surrounded by six thick gold-lacquered pillars decorated with dragons and clouds (Fig.11, Fig.12). Two kinds of gold in different colors were used on the pillars to create a distinct pattern. The ceiling above the throne is an upward raised umbrella-shaped caisson ceiling (*Zaojing*), in the middle of which lies a dragon playing with pearls (Fig.13, Fig.14). In front of the Hall of Supreme Harmony, there are a sundial (*Rigui*), a measuring vessel (*Jialiang*), a pair of bronze crane and bronze tortoise, and eighteen bronze *ding*s. The *Rigui* and the *Jialiang* demonstrate that the emperor was both just and fair, whereas the crane and tortoise symbolize longevity. Under the Hall of Supreme Harmony, as well as the other two main halls of the Outer Court, there stands a three-tier marble terrace in the shape of the Chinese character ' 土 ', the land, symbolizing that all land under heaven belongs to the emperor. 8.13 in height, the terrace ascends the three main halls, enabling the emperor to inspect the empire as far as he could. Balustrades and stone-carved dragon heads used for drainage are set on the edges of all three tiers. On rainy days, chances are that the breathtaking sight of a thousand dragons disgorging water can be seen (Fig.15). In conclusion, the Hall of Supreme Harmony is the largest hall in the Forbidden City and architecturally the highest-ranking building of the surviving traditional architecture in China. The overwhelming architecture design and dragon-dominate décor distinguish it as superior to other ancient buildings in China. During the twenty-four emperors' reign in Ming and Qing dynasties, a great amount of grand ceremonies were held in the Hall of Supreme Harmony, including the enthronement ceremonies, wedding ceremonies and other important occasions such as the appointment of the emperor's main consort - the empress, and the dispatch of generals into fields of war. Celebrations also marked the three main festivals in Qing dynasty, that is the Winter Solstice, the Chinese New Year and the emperors' birthdays, when emperors received greetings from high officials and awarded them the court banquet. In the early Qing dynasty, the Hall of Supreme Harmony had been used to hold the Palace Examination where the scholars achieved the highest awards were inspected by the emperor. In the fifty-fourth year of Qianlong reign (1789), the examination was moved to the Hall of Preserving Harmony (*Baohe dian*).

Located between the Hall of Supreme Harmony (*Taihe dian*) and the Hall of Preserving Harmony (*Baohe dian*), the Hall of Central Harmony (*Zhonghe dian*) is the smallest hall among the three main halls of the Outer Court (Fig.16). Built in the eighteenth year of Yonle reign (1420) in the Ming dynasty as part of the original design of the Forbidden City, it was first named the Hall of Splendid Canopy (*Huagai dian*). After several conflagrations and reconstructions, it was renamed the Hall of Central Supremacy

图案巨柱，所贴金箔采用深、浅两种颜色，以使图案突出鲜明（图11、图12）。宝座上方天花正中安置形若伞盖、向上隆起的藻井，藻井正中雕有蟠卧的巨龙，龙头下探，口衔宝珠（图13、图14）。太和殿前的月台上陈设有日晷、嘉量各一个，铜龟、铜鹤各一对，铜鼎18座。日晷是古代的计时仪器，嘉量是古代的标准量器，二者都是皇权的象征。龟、鹤则为长寿的象征。太和殿下面是高8.13米的三层汉白玉石雕基座，周围环以栏杆。栏杆下安有排水用的石雕龙头，每逢雨季可呈现『千龙吐水』的奇观（图15）。三层的汉白玉须弥座石基俗称『三台』，其平面呈『土』字形，象征『普天之下，莫非王土』。它像一座巨大的玉盘，承托着三大殿。太和殿是紫禁城内体量最大、等级最高的建筑，其建筑规制之高、装饰手法之精堪列中国古代建筑之首。明清两代24位皇帝都在太和殿举行盛大典礼，如皇帝登基即位、皇帝大婚、册立皇后、命将出征；此外，每年万寿、元旦、冬至三大节日，皇帝均在此接受文武官员的朝贺，并向王公大臣赐宴。清初，还曾在太和殿举行新进士的殿试，乾隆五十四年（1789年）始，改在保和殿举行。

中和殿是外朝三大殿中体量最小的一座，位于太和殿与保和殿之间（图16）。明代永乐十八年（1420年）建成时称华盖殿；明代嘉靖时期遭遇火灾，重修后改称中极殿，现天花内构件上仍遗留有明代题写的『中极殿』墨迹；清代顺治二年（1645年）改今名，『中和』取自《礼记·中庸》的『中也者，天下之本也』；『和也者，天下之道也』之意。中和殿平面呈正方形，面阔、进深各3间，四面出廊，金砖铺

图12　太和殿内毗卢帽

Fig.11　Throne of the Hall of Supreme Harmony
Fig.12　Vairocana Hat of the Hall of Supreme Harmony

图13 太和殿室内彩画

图14 太和殿藻井天花

图15 三台须弥座上的石雕龙头

Fig.13 Colored Paintings inside the Hall of Supreme Harmony
Fig.14 The Caisson Ceiling of the Hall of Supreme Harmony
Fig.15 Stone-carved Dragon's Heads on the Three-tier Sumeru-seat Style Terrace

图 16　中和殿

Fig.16 Hall of Central Harmony

(*Zhongji dian*) by Jiajing Emperor in the Ming dynasty, scripts of which can be found on the ceiling panels of the hall. The current name, the Hall of Central Harmony, was designated by Shunzhi Emperor of the Qing dynasty in the second year of his reign (1645), conveying the philosophy of using the Golden Mean (*Zhongyong*) to achieve universal peace and harmony recorded in *Book of Rites* (*Li Ji*). Square in shape, the Hall of Central Harmony has three bays and porches on four sides, covering a total area of 580 square meters. It has a single-eaved roof paved with yellow glazed tiles and a gilded pinnacle in the middle. The beams beneath the eave are decorated with gilded dragons pattern paintings (*Hexi caihua*), while the ceiling panels are decorated with dragon-motif gilded embossed paintings (*Li fen*). As for the doors and windows, there are twelve lattice doors in the front facade; and four lattice doors and eight lattice windows in other facades respectively. All doors are adorned with triple-crossed six-curved water chestnut blossom pattern. This kind of design with doors and windows on four sides is an imitation of the ancient Bright Hall (*Ming tang*) recorded in *Dadailiji*, and differentiated the Hall of Central Harmony from the other two main halls. Three sets of stairs extend on the south, east and west sides of the hall respectively, the central set of which has a dragon-and-cloud-relief marble plate in the middle, known as the Imperial Way (*Yu lu*); whereas the other two sets of which have steps (*Taduo*) and drooping belt stone (*Chuidai shi*) decorated with floral-scroll carvings. Inside the Hall of Central Harmony, Gold Bricks (*Jin zhuan*) can be seen on the floor. In the center of the bricks stand the emperor's throne and screen, and the signboard inscribed with '允执厥中' (*Yunzhijuezhong*)[1] by Qianlong Emperor hanging over. In the Ming and Qing dynasties, the emperor would have a rest and receive obeisance from his officials in the Hall of Central Harmony before presiding over grand ceremonies in the Hall of Supreme Harmony; examine sacrificial writings and farm implements before offering sacrifices to heaven, to earth and to agriculture god; examine memorials before conferring titles on the empress dowagers; read the compilation of the imperial family tree, and hold grand ceremonies for the compilation here in the hall.

The third hall of the three main halls, the Hall of Preserving Harmony (*Baohe dian*) is architecturally second only to the Hall of Supreme Harmony (Fig.17). Completed in the eighteenth year of Yongle reign (1420) in the Ming dynasty, it was first called the Hall of Scrupulous Behavior (*Jinshen dian*). During Jiajing Emperor's reign in the Ming dynasty,

---

① '允执厥中' means that one's words and deeds should be fair and impartial, following the philosophy of *Zhongzheng* (中正) recorded *in the Book of Documents*.

地，建筑面积约 580 平方米。屋顶为单檐四角攒尖式，上覆黄色琉璃瓦，正中为铜胎镏金宝顶。檐下饰以金龙和玺彩画，天花为沥粉贴金正面龙。殿四面开门，正面为三交六椀菱花槅扇门 12 扇；其余三面均为三交六椀菱花槅扇门 4 扇，两侧置槅扇槛窗各 4 扇。中和殿四面安设门窗的形制取自《大戴礼记》中所述的『明堂』，避免了三大殿的雷同。殿门前石阶为南、北各三出，东、西各一出；踏跺、垂带浅刻卷草纹。殿内设地平宝座，上悬清代乾隆皇帝御笔『允执厥中』匾额。明清两朝，在太和殿举行各种大典前，皇帝要先在中和殿小憩，并接受执事官员的朝拜。凡遇皇帝亲祭，如祭天坛、地坛，皇帝便于前一日在中和殿阅视祝文；祭先农坛举行亲耕仪式前，皇帝还要在此查验种子和农具。皇太后上徽号，皇帝在此阅视奏书。玉牒（即皇族族谱）告成，大臣恭进中和殿呈御览，同时要在此举行隆重的存放仪式。

保和殿是外朝三大殿的最后一座，规格等级仅次于太和殿（图 17）。明代永乐十八年（1420 年）建成时称谨身殿；明代嘉靖时期遭遇火灾，重修后改称建极殿；清代顺治二年（1645 年）改今名。保

the hall was burnt, reconstructed and renamed as the Hall of Establishing Supremacy (*Jianji dian*), and was finally named the Hall of Preserving Harmony in the second year of Shunzhi reign (1645). Nine bays in width and five bays in depth, the hall covers an area of 1,240 square meters. The overall height of the hall is 29.5 meters. Second to the Hall of Supreme Harmony, the Hall of Preserving Harmony has a double-eaved gable-and-hip roof paved with yellow glazed tiles, and nine figurines at each of its roof corners. The beams of the interior and exterior are all painted with gilded dragon patterns (*Hexi caihua*), while the ceiling panels are painted with gilded embossed dragon-motif (*Li fen*). The floor of the Hall of Preserving Harmony was paved with Golden Bricks (*Jin zhuan*). A golden carved-lacquer throne was placed in the central bay inside the hall, facing south, upon which hangs the signboard inscribed with '皇建有极' (*Huangjianyouji*)[①] by Qianlong Emperor. Two partition doors decorated with wood-based cloud-and-dragon-relief gilded Vairocana hats (*Pilu mao*), a kind of architectural components derived from Buddhism, separate the central bay from the south and east bays. The south and east bays are warm chambers, which means that they were designated to have heating stoves. To adapt to the function, subtraction was used on the hall's structure design. To be specific, six hypostyle columns have been taken off to broaden the space inside the Hall of Preserving Harmony. The hall was used differently in Ming and Qing dynasties. In Ming times, before attending a grand ritual or ceremony, the emperor was usually brought to the Hall of Preserving Harmony to change into ceremonial robes. While in Qing times, the hall served as the venue for imperial banquets on New Year's Eve and on the fifteenth day of the first lunar month (that is, the full moon). The hall was also used for the Shunzhi Emperor as a temporary residence for him and his successor, the Kangxi Emperor (1662—1722), when the three main halls in the Inner Court were under restoration. When the Shunzhi Emperor lived here, the hall was temporarily called the Palace of Inoculation (*Weiyu gong*), while when his son moved here, it was renamed the Palace of Purity and Tranquility (*Qingning gong*). The wedding ceremony of the Shunzhi Emperor was also held here. From the fifty-fourth year of Qianlong reign (1789), the Hall of Preserving Harmony began to hold the Palace Examination every three years.

The complex of the Hall of Martial Valor (*Wuying dian*) is an architectural compound that lies to the far west of the Gate of Glorious Harmony (*Xihe men*), the gate leading to the Hall of Supreme Harmony (*Taihe dian*) (Fig.18). First constructed in the early Ming, the total floor area of the complex is about 23,000 square meters, and the building area is

---

① '皇建有极' means that the emperor shall establish the supreme rules in the world.

和殿面阔 9 间，进深 5 间，建筑面积约 1240 平方米，通高 29.5 米。黄琉璃瓦重檐歇山顶，檐角安有走兽 9 个。建筑内、外檐均饰以金龙和玺彩画，天花为沥粉贴金正面龙。殿内金砖铺地，明间坐北朝南设雕镂金漆宝座，上悬清代乾隆皇帝御笔『皇建有极』匾额。东、西两梢间为暖阁，安板门两扇，上置木质浮雕如意云龙浑金毗卢帽。其在建筑结构上采用了减柱造做法，将殿内前檐金柱减去 6 根，以扩大室内空间。保和殿在明清两代用途不同。明代大典前，皇帝常在此更衣。清代每年除夕、正月十五，皇帝赐宴均于保和殿举行。清代顺治三年（1646 年）至十三年（1656 年），皇帝福临曾居住保和殿，时称『位育宫』，大婚亦在此举行。康熙皇帝自即位至八年（1669 年）也曾居住保和殿，时称『清宁宫』。清代殿试自乾隆五十四年（1789 年）始在此举行。

武英殿区始建于明初，位于外朝熙和门以西，是一组独立的建筑群，总占地面积约 2.3 万平方米，建筑面积约 6575 平方米（图 18）。位于外朝协和门以东的文华殿区，与其东西遥对。文华殿、武英殿

图 18 武英殿鸟瞰

图 17 保和殿

Fig.17 Hall of Preserving Harmony
Fig.18 Bird View of the Hall of Martial Valor

about 6,575 square meters. Symmetrically in the east, the complex of the Hall of Literary Glory (*Wenhua dian*) echoes the design of the complex of the Hall of Martial Valor, southeast to the Gate of Blending Harmony (*Xiehe men*). These two compounds together would add to the magnanimity of the Outer Court and the Forbidden City. The main building of the complex, the Hall of Martial Valor, is five bays in width and three bays in depth. Facing south, the hall has a hip-and-gable roof paved with yellow glazed tiles and a Sumeru-seat (*Xumi zuo*) style terrace. Surrounded by marble balustrades, the I-shaped terrace extends to the Gate of Martial Valor (*Wuying men*). To the back of the main hall stands the Hall of Respectful Thoughts (*Jingsi dian*) in similar architectural style, which is connected to the main hall by a lobby; to the east and west locate sixty-three-bay corridor rooms, in the centers of which are the Hall of Concentrated Doctrines (*Ningdao dian*) and the Hall of Luminous Appeals (*Huanzhang dian*); whereas to the northeast is the Studio of Eternal Longevity (*Hengshou zhai*) and to the northwest the Hall for Cultivating Virtues (*Yude tang*). In the early Ming dynasty, the Hall of Martial Valor was the place where emperors went on a fast and receive ministers. In the late Ming dynasty, the peasant rebellion troop broke into the imperial palace and burnt down many of the buildings. Remaining intact, the Hall of Martial Valor was the place where *Li Zicheng* (1606—1645), the peasant unrest leader, ascended the throne as the emperor and handled business before he hurriedly fled from Beijing. After the Manchu Qing regime moved its capital to Beijing to rule across China, the hall became the office for *Dorgon* (1612—1650), one of the four regents, for handling state business. In the early Qing dynasty, emperors also attended small-sized ceremonies here. From Kangxi reign (1662—1722) on, the Hall of Martial Valor became an imperial cultural center - a workshop for amending, compiling, and printing books with carved wooden blocks. Books printed here were marked with the authoritative "Hall edition". In 1869, the eighth year of Tongzhi reign, the complex was damaged by a fire-thirty-seven buildings was burnt down, including the main hall, the rear hall, the gate, the east hall and the Hall for Cultivating Virtues; and books were all destroyed. In the same year it was reconstructed.

The Gate of Divine Prowess (*Shenwu men*) is the northern gate of the imperial palace. Completed in the eighteenth year of Yongle reign (1420) in the Ming dynasty, it was first named after the God of the Northern sky, *Xuanwu* (Fig.19). During the reconstruction in Kangxi reign, to avoid using the personal name of Kangxi Emperor, the gate was renamed as the Gate of Divine Prowess. Similar to the Meridian Gate, the Gate of Divine Prowess can also be divided into two parts—the upper tower and the three-opening abutment, which are connected by bridle paths on both sides of the abutment (Fig.20). Standing

作为左辅右弼，使外朝气势恢宏，更加雄伟壮丽。正殿武英殿为南向，面阔 5 间，进深 3 间，黄琉璃瓦歇山顶，下部须弥座围以汉白玉石栏杆，前出月台，有甬路直通武英门。后殿敬思殿与武英殿形制略似，前后殿间以穿廊相连。东、西配殿分别是凝道殿、焕章殿，左右共有廊房 63 间。院落东北有恒寿斋，西北有浴德堂。武英殿在明初为皇帝斋戒和召见臣工的地方。明末农民起义军领袖李自成曾在此办理政务。清兵入关时，曾为摄政王多尔衮的治事之所。清初，武英殿用作皇帝便殿，举行小型朝贺，赏赐、祭祀等仪典。康熙以后则作为编印图书之地。清代同治八年（1869 年）武英殿被火焚，烧毁正殿、后殿、殿门、东配殿、浴德堂等建筑共 37 间，书籍版片焚烧殆尽。同年重建。

神武门是紫禁城的北门，明代永乐十八年（1420 年）建成，称玄武门（图 19）。清代康熙年间重修时，因避康熙皇帝玄烨的名讳而改称神武门。神武门分上、下两部分，下为墩台，正中开三门，墩台两侧设有上下城台的马道（图 20）。墩台上正中门楼一座，平面呈矩形，面阔 5 间，进深 1 间，四面出廊，东、西两山面设双扇板门，南、北面明间与左、右次间开门，均为菱花槅扇门；东、西两山面设双扇板门，楼前、后檐明间与左、右次间开门，均为菱花槅扇门；楼为黄琉璃瓦重檐庑殿顶，上层单翘重昂七踩斗栱，下层基部为汉白玉石须弥座。楼前、后檐明间与左、右次间开门，均为菱花槅扇门；通往城墙及左、右马道。四面门前各出踏跺。

图19 神武门

图20 神武门东侧

Fig.19 Gate of Divine Prowess
Fig.20 East side of the Gate of Divine Prowess

on top of a marble Sumeru-seat (*Xumi zuo*) style terrace, the upper tower is rectangle in shape, five bays in width and one bay in depth. The doors of the three bays in the middle on the front and back facades are lattice doors; while that of the east and west facades are double-leaf wooden panel doors that leads to the City Wall and the bridle paths. Four flights of marble stairs were fitted for access of the doors. Architecturally important, the upper tower is equipped with a double-eaved yellow-glazed-tile-paved hip roof , two layers of brackets (*Dou gong*) beneath the eave (namely single-petal two-lever seven-*cai*[1] brackets in the top layer, and single-petal two-lever five-*cai* brackets in the lower layer), black-edge gilded tangent circle pattern paintings (*Xuezi caihua*) on the beams, and a blue-based signboard inscribed with the gate's Manchu and Chinese names written with gilded bronze. Inside the upper tower of the Gate of Divine Prowess, there are gilded lotus-and-waterweeds pattern ceiling panels on the top and Golden Bricks on the floor. Formerly, the upper tower housed a drum and a bell, which were used to announce the time. Every day after evenfall, the bell would ring for a hundred and eight times, announcing the arrival of dusk. Afterwards, the drums would be struck every *geng*[2] during night, until the dawn came and the bell was back in charge. However, the bells were not used when the emperor was in the Forbidden City. As the back gate of the Forbidden City, the Gate of Divine Prowess was used when the empress and imperial concubines were leaving for worshipping the silkworms God. Selected girls (*Xiunv*) would also enter into the Forbidden City through this gate every three years. In 1924, the last emperor, Xuantong Emperor (1909—1911), was deported out of his palace from the Gate of Divine Prowess.

The Outer Court that consists of three main halls, the complex of Hall of Literary Brilliance (*Wenhua dian*) and the complex of Hall of Martial Valor (*Wuying dian*) is located on the Central Axis of Beijing. Starting from the Gate of Eternal Peace (*Yongding men*) on the south, running across the Gate of South (*Zhengyang men*), Gate of Great Qing (*Daqing men*), Gate of Heavenly Peace (*Tianan men*), Gate of Correct Deportment (*Duan men*), the Outer Court, the Inner Court, the Hill of Prospect (*Jing shan*) sequently, and ending with the Drum Tower and Bell Tower, the Central Axis of Beijing is often compared to a grand symphony. Lofty and majestic, the three main halls of the Outer Court are akin to the rousing climax of the symphony; while the Hall of Literary Brilliance and the Hall of Martial Valor in respective sides of the axis can be described

[1] *Cai* is the unit to count the extension of brackets used in Qing dynasty.
[2] *Geng* is the unit of nighttime used in ancient China. Traditionally, one night is divided into five *gengs*. One *geng* is about two hours.

单翘重昂五踩斗栱，梁枋间饰墨线大点金旋子彩画。上檐悬蓝底镏金铜字满汉文「神武门」匾额。楼内顶部为金莲水草天花，地面铺墁金砖。神武门旧设钟、鼓，由銮仪卫负责管理。每日黄昏后鸣钟108响，钟后敲鼓起更。其后每更打钟击鼓，启明时复鸣钟报晓。皇帝住宫内时则不鸣钟。神武门作为皇宫的后门，是宫内日常出入的重要门禁，明清两代皇后、妃、嫔行亲蚕礼即由此门出入。清代每三年选一次秀女，备选者经由此偏门入宫候选。1924年末代皇帝溥仪被逐出宫，即日出宫之时亦由此门离去。

三大殿及文华、武英殿一带为紫禁城外朝之所在，殿宇高大，气势巍峨。端坐太和殿，透过太和门，视线望远，过午门、端门、天安门、大清门，再过正阳门可直达永定门，承中轴一线，统领北京城，精彩的建筑华章如珍珠落盘般奏响。收纳外气，凝为序曲；反向回溯，城墙夹峙，殿阁高耸，三大殿气势雄浑，有如轰然奏响的高潮之章扑面而来，萦绕耳畔；乐章蔓散，延至两翼文华、武英，于威严端庄中又不失平和之气，自然不同凡响。

as the sedate movements. As a whole, the Outer Court is the core and the most imposing part of the Forbidden City and demonstrates the magnificent spatial pattern of ancient China.

4. Strictly Managed Palaces in the Inner Court

In opposite to the Hall of Preserving Harmony, the Gate of Heavenly Purity (*Qianqing men*) is the principal entrance to the Inner Court of the Forbidden City. Since its completion in early fifteenth century, it has been rebuilt many times because of damage or total destruction by fire. The current gate is datable to the twelfth year of Shunzhi reign (1655). Five bays wide, three bays deep and sixteen meters high, the Gate of Heavenly Purity is a structure with single-eaved yellow-glazed-tile hip-and-gable roof, resting on a 1.5-meter-high white marble terrace of Sumeru-seat (*Xumi zuo*) style surrounded by carved stone balustrades (Fig.21, Fig.22). Beneath the eave, there are brackets (*Dou gong*) of single petal and three *cai*, and beams painted with dragons pattern (*Hexi caihua*). Three partition doors are set among the rear hypostyle columns, while brick walls with lattice windows are set between the front cave columns of the westernmost bay and the easternmost bay. In the front, there lie three flights of stairs, in the center of which is the ascending dragon-and-cloud-relief marble plate, known as the Imperial Way (*Yu lu*), and a pair of glided bronze lions as guardians. Flanking the south face of the Gate of Heavenly Purity is a group of splayed glaze-tile screens of 8-meter height and 9.7-meter depth. Lifelike and gorgeous glazed flowers are embellished to the center and four corners of the screen. The gleaming flowers dignify the Gate of Heavenly Purity to an extraordinary extent. The glazed doors on the walls on respective sides of the gate, videlicet, the Left Gate of the Inner Court (*Neizuo men*) leading to the Primary East Corridor (*Dongyi changjie*) and the Right Gate of the Inner Court (*Neiyou men*) leading to the Primary West Corridor (*Xiyi changjie*), are major passages to the Six Eastern Palaces and the Six Western Palaces. Extending to the east and west, the plaza in front of the Gate of Heavenly Purity connects the Outer Court and the Inner Court. In Qing times, state business including Morning Audience (*Yumen tingzheng*), ceremonies for fast and ceremonies for treasures were processed here at times. Consequently, huts for Waiting Room for High Officials (*Jiuqing zhifang*) and Office of the Grand Council of State (*Junji chu*) were built here to accommodate ministers to be interviewed. The Office of the Grand Council of State was first established during Yongzheng Emperor's reign (1722—1735). As the head of the imperial privy council, the presence of the Office of the Grand Council of State made the plaza one of the most significant spaces in the Forbidden City.

四、门户森严的内廷殿宇

乾清门是紫禁城内廷的正门。建于明代永乐十八年（1420年），清代顺治十二年（1655年）重修。乾清门面阔5间，进深3间，高约16米，坐落在高1.5米的汉白玉须弥座上，周围环以雕石栏杆（图21、图22）。上覆黄琉璃瓦歇山顶，檐下施单昂三踩斗栱，梁枋绘金龙和玺彩画。其正中开三门，门扉安设在后檐，前檐两侧梢间为青砖槛墙，上置方格窗。门前石阶为三出，中间浮雕云龙纹御路，两侧列铜镏金狮子一对。乾清门两侧为『八』字形琉璃影壁，高8米，长9.7米，壁心及岔角以琉璃花装饰，花形自然逼真，色彩绚美艳丽，在阳光的照射下流光溢彩，将乾清门映衬得华贵富丽。东西两侧的随墙琉璃门——内左、内右门，分别通向东、西一长街，是去往东、西六宫的重要通道。乾清门与保和殿相对，门前为一东西向狭长的庭院。它是连接内廷与外朝往来的重要通道，在清代又兼为处理政务的场所，如清代的『御门听政』、斋戒、请宝接宝等典礼仪式都在乾清门举行，故庭院两侧分布有朝臣的值舍，特别是清代雍正年间设立的军机处，为皇帝统治国家的枢密机构，使得乾清门前庭院愈显重要。

乾清宫、交泰殿、坤宁宫即所谓『后三宫』，其建筑形制、体量、装饰等方面较之外朝三大殿有所缩减。

Inside the Gate of Heavenly Purity, the Palace of Heavenly Purity (*Qianqing gong*), the Hall of Union (*Jiaotai dian*) and the Palace of Earthly Tranquility (*Kunning gong*) constitute the three rear halls of the Inner Court. As it is deemed inferior to the Hall of Supreme Harmony, the Palace of Heavenly Purity is a similar but smaller version of the Hall of Supreme Harmony. That is to say, everything within the Palace of Heavenly Purity is smaller than similar components in the superior palace. However, it is still the largest palace in the Inner Court and is superior to any other structures here. The Palace of Heavenly Purity was first built in the eighteenth year of Yongle reign (1420) in the Ming dynasty. Having been rebuilt several times after conflagrations, the current building is datable to 1798, the third year of Jiaqing reign in Qing dynasty (Fig.23). Located on a single-tier marble terrace, the Palace of Heavenly Purity has nine bays in width, five bays in depth and twenty meters in height, covering an area of 1,240 square meters. Paved with yellow glazed tiles, the roof of the palace is in the style of double-eaved hip and has nine figurines at each of its roof corners. Beneath the eave, from top to bottom there are single-petal two-lever seven-*cai* brackets (*Dou gong*), single-petal single-lever five-*cai* brackets, beams decorated with gilded dragons pattern paintings (*Hexi caihua*) and lattice doors and windows adorned with triple-crossed six-curved water chestnut blossom pattern. Inside the Palace of Heavenly Purity, to enlarge the interior space, the central bay has been interlinked with the east and west bays, and hypostyle columns in the front have been taken off. A set of screen and throne is set between the two central hypostyle columns in the rear (Fig.24). Hanging high above the throne is a signboard inscribed with '正大光明' (*Zhengda guangming*)① by Shunzhi Emperor. On respective sides of the open space, the east bay and west bay of the Palace of Heavenly Purity are designed to be warm chambers with mezzanines (*Xianlou*, literally 'immortal's pavilion') in the north (Fig.25); while the easternmost and westernmost bays are hallways leading to the Hall of Union and the Palace of Earthly Tranquility. Golden Bricks were paved all over the palace. Same as the Hall of Supreme Harmony, a sundial (*Rigui*), a measuring vessel (*Jialiang*), and a pair of bronze crane and bronze tortoise are placed in front of the Palace of Heavenly Purity, as well as four gilded bronze incense burner. A huge marble relief extends in the centre of the stairway to the Gate of Heavenly Purity (*Qianqing men*). As the emperors' private palace, from Yongle Emperor, the first emperor of the Forbidden City, to Chongzhen Emperor (1628—1644), the last emperor of the Ming dynasty, there were fourteen emperors in total living in the Palace of Heavenly Purity. As the palace is too spacious, partitions are added

① '正大光明' means that man shall be upright and pure in mind.

乾清宫的建筑规模为内廷之首，始建于明代永乐十八年（1420 年），明清两代曾数次因被焚毁而重建，现有建筑为清代嘉庆三年（1798 年）所建（图 23）。乾清宫坐落在单层汉白玉石台基上，面阔 9 间，进深 5 间，建筑面积约 1240 平方米，自台面至正脊高 20 余米。黄琉璃瓦重檐庑殿顶，檐角安有走兽 9 个，上层单翘重昂七踩斗栱，下层单翘单昂五踩斗栱，梁枋间饰金龙和玺彩画。三交六椀菱花槅扇门窗。殿内明间与东西次间相通，明间前檐减去金柱，梁架结构为减柱造形式，以扩大室内空间；后檐两金柱间设屏，屏前设宝座（图 24），上悬清代顺治皇帝御笔『正大光明』匾额。东、西两梢间为暖阁（图 25），后檐设仙楼。两尽间为穿堂，可通交泰殿、坤宁宫。地面铺墁金砖。殿前宽敞的月台上，左右分别有铜龟、铜鹤及日晷、嘉量，前设镏金香炉 4 座，正中出丹陛，接高台甬路与乾清门相连。明代作为皇帝的寝宫，自永乐至崇祯，共有 14 位皇帝曾在乾清宫居住。因宫殿高大、空间过敞，皇帝在此居住时曾分隔成数室。据记载，明代乾清宫内有暖阁 9 间，分为上、下两层，共置床 27 张。由于室多床多，皇帝每晚就寝之处很少有人知道，以防不测。清代康熙以前仍沿袭明制，自雍正皇帝移居养心殿

图21 乾清门前庭院

Fig.21 Plaza in front of the Gate of Heavenly Purity
Fig.22 Gate of Heavenly Purity
Fig.23 Palace of Heavenly Purity

图22 乾清门

图23 乾清宫

图 24 乾清宫内宝座

图 25 乾清宫西暖阁

Fig.24 Throne of the Palace of Heavenly Purity
Fig.25 West Warm−Chamber of the Palace of Heavenly Purity

to divide it into smaller rooms. According to records, the Palace of Heavenly Purity in Ming times had nine warm chambers, two storeys and twenty-seven beds, allowing the emperor to sleep in different places every night to keep safe. Beginning in the Yongzheng reign in Qing dynasty, with the nearby Hall of Mental Cultivation (*Yangxin dian*, Figs.26~31) taking over the function, the Palace of Heavenly Purity was no longer a residence, but a venue in which emperors conducted routine government business, interviewed officials, met foreign envoys, responded ministers' reports, and celebrated major festivals and rituals.

North of the Hall of Union (*Jiaotai dian*), the Palace of Earthly Tranquility (*Kunning gong*) was built in the eighteenth year of Yongle reign (1420) in the Ming dynasty (Fig.32). Having been rebuilt several times after conflagrations, the current building is datable to the third year of Jiaqing reign (1798) in Qing dynasty, after it was burnt down in the same fire that destroyed the Palace of Heavenly Purity the year before. Facing south, the Palace of Earthly Tranquility is nine bays wide and five bays deep, and has a double-eaved hip roof with yellow glazed tiles. It was originally built for the chief consort of the emperor. In the twelfth year of Shunzhi reigh (1655) in Qing times, the palace was remodeled into a Manchu-style house, a Shamanism sacrificial hall, following the design of the Palace of Purity and Tranquility (*Qingning gong*) in the Shenyang Palace: the house had its main door off center to the east rather than in the middle; wooden panel doors were replaced lattice doors; lattice windows were changed into windows that open from the bottom (swinging out on hinges fastened at the top) and were propped up by sticks. Inside the palace, the east two bays were partitioned as warm chambers for living during the renovation; whereas the other bays were connected and had a linked heated brick *Kang* platforms for sacrificing along the north, the west, and the south walls (Fig.33). A separate room with lattice doors and gilded Vairocana hat (*Pilu mao*) was divided opposite to the wooden panel doors, inside which three caldrons were set to cook meat for the imperial family during sacrifices. After the renovation, the Palace of Earthly Tranquility was used mainly for Shamanism sacrifices, but also served as the imperial bridal chamber for Kangxi, Tongzhi (1862—1874), Guangxu (1875—1908), and the abdicated Xuantong emperors (Fig.34).

The Six Eastern Palaces and the Six Western Palaces on respective sides of the three rear halls were used as the residence of concubines in the Ming dynasty, and served the empresses and concubines at the same time in the Qing dynasty. As the name indicates, these two regions house six palaces of same styles located on the east side of the axis in the Inner Court, and six palaces located on the west side of the axis. In the regions, there are more than a hundred and forty buildings and over five hundred buildings in total.

（图 26～图 31）以后，乾清宫遂成为听政之地。皇帝在此召见臣工、接见外国使节、批阅奏章、处理日常政务，并举行重大赐宴活动。

坤宁宫是内廷后三宫之一，始建于明代永乐十八年（1420 年），明清两代曾数次重建（图 32）。清代嘉庆二年（1797 年）乾清宫失火，延烧此殿前檐，三年（1798 年）重修。坤宁宫坐北朝南，面阔连廊 9 间，进深 5 间，黄琉璃瓦重檐庑殿顶。明代是皇后的寝宫。清代顺治十二年（1655 年）仿照盛京皇宫（今沈阳故宫）的清宁宫改建后，为清宫萨满教祭神的主要场所。改原明间开门为东次间开门，原槅扇门改为双扇板门，其余各间的棂花槅扇窗均改为直棂吊搭式窗。室内东侧两间隔出为暖阁，作为居住的寝室；西侧四间设南、北、西三面炕，作为祭神的场所（图 33）；与门相对的后檐设锅灶，作为杀牲煮肉之用。坤宁宫改建后，虽主要为祭祀场所，由于是皇家所用，灶间设棂花扇门，浑金毗卢帽，装饰考究华丽。但其中宫的地位并未改变。清代康熙四年（1665 年）玄烨大婚时，太皇太后就指定其在坤宁宫行『合卺』礼。同治、光绪两位皇帝大婚，以及末代皇帝溥仪婚礼也都是在坤宁宫举行（图 34）。

东、西六宫分别位于后三宫的左右两侧，明代为妃嫔所居，清代为后妃所居。两个区域内共有建筑 140 多座，房屋 500 多间，其位置之醒目、布局之严谨为历代后宫所不及。东、西六宫的平面布局既遵从传统礼制，又富于变化。从内廷的总体布局来看，乾清、坤宁两宫作为主要建筑沿紫禁城中轴线纵向

Though the forms of the Six Eastern and Six Western Palaces have some similarities from palaces of same kinds in the past dynasties, the prominent locations and rigorous layouts make them incomparable. To be specific, the twelve palaces are located on respective sides of the main buildings of the Inner Court, namely the Palace of Heavenly Purity (*Qianqing gong*) and the Palace of Earthly Tranquility (*Kunning gong*), guarding them like stars surrounding moon. This layout clearly reflects the philosophy of "being in center" in traditional Chinese culture as mentioned before. Apart from the grand layout, the Six Eastern Palaces and the Six Western Palaces are also neatly arranged inside. Two groups of complexes are formed in the Six Eastern Palaces and the Six Western Palaces respectively, within which three palaces runs from north to south on either side of an alley. The alleys are called 'Long Alley' (*Changjie*). Together with the passages in front of the palaces, these lanes separate the palaces while connect them at the same time, forming a crisscross and rational configuration. Inside each single palace, the layout and the buildings are almost the same. Covering an area of about two thousand and five hundred square meters, there are two layers of courtyards and high enclosing walls on four sides in every palace. The courtyards have different functions - the first courtyards are generally used for living, whereas the second courtyards are used for rest. The main buildings of both courtyards are designated to face south, and the side halls are distributed symmetrically, following the traditional Chinese philosophy. Doors are open on the front main buildings' gable walls to connect two courtyards. With these considerations, the buildings of the Six Eastern and Western Palaces are reasonable and arrange in order, achieving a high degree of harmony and unity. All built in 1420, the twelve palaces had different destiny. The palaces in the Six Western Palaces have been greatly renovated during Qing dynasty, thus presenting a flexible style. Comparatively, the palaces in the Six Eastern Palaces has kept their original forms basically as they were first built, demonstrating the thoughtful layout of Ming Dynasty.

The Palace of Eternal Spring (*Changchun gong*) is one of the Six Western Palaces, where the emperor's consorts would reside (Fig.35). Completed in the eighteenth year of Yongle reign (1420) in the Ming dynasty, the palace was first named as the Palace of Eternal Spring. In the fourteenth year of Jiajing reign (1535), it was renamed the Palace of Eternal Tranquility (*Yongning gong*), while in the forty-third year of Wanli reign (1615), it was renamed once again the Palace of Eternal Spring. In the twenty-second year of Kangxi reign (1683) in Qing dynasty, the palace was renovated. Afterwards, several maintenance projects have been carried out. In the ninth year of Xianfeng reign (1859), the Gate of Eternal Spring was dismantled, and the palace was connected with the back hall of the

排列，有如天地；而『六寝六宫』分立于东西两侧横向展开，如众星拱卫，这清晰地反映出『王者必居

其中』的营建思想。东、西六宫在以乾清、坤宁两宫为中心横向排开的同时，还保持着自身布局的纵向

排列，呈『三横二纵』的格局，每列纵向串联三宫，列与列之间形成了以二长街构成的虚轴线。十二座

院落之间以东、西二长街及各宫前巷道纵横分隔，构成了条条街巷、座座门墙相通而又相隔，规整、严

谨的空间。这种布局方式使后宫众多房屋建筑得以合理地排列组合，达到了高度的和谐统一。从局部看，

十二宫的主体建筑均朝南向，采用了『取正』的布局方式。每座院落的平面布局和建筑形式基本相同，

均为两进的三合院，各占地 2500 平方米左右，四周环以高墙。宫中前殿后寝，有左右配殿，严格讲求对称。

前殿两山有卡墙，以便门与后殿相通。清代晚期曾对西六宫进行过两次较大的改建，因此，目前东六宫

仍基本保持着明代周密的布局风格，而西六宫则体现为灵活多变的清代风格。

长春宫为内廷西六宫之一（图 35）。明代永乐十八年（1420 年）建成，初名长春宫，嘉靖十四

年（1535 年）改称永宁宫，万历四十三年（1615 年）复称长春宫。清代康熙二十二年（1683 年）重修，

后又多次修整。清代咸丰九年（1859 年）不仅拆除了长春宫的宫门——长春门及前宫墙，而且拆除了

启祥宫（原名未央宫，清代晚期改称太极殿）后殿的后檐墙，接建了后廊与抱厦，并将启祥宫后殿改

为体元殿，使原来独立的两进院落联系成为四进院。这打破了明代六宫独立的格局，加强了建筑室外

为体元殿，使原来独立的两进院落联系成为四进院。这打破了明代六宫独立的格局，加强了建筑室外

图 26　养心殿鸟瞰

图 27　养心殿

图 28　养心殿明间

图 29　养心殿东暖阁

Fig.26　Bird View of the Hall of Mental Cultivation
Fig.27　Hall of Mental Cultivation
Fig.28　Central Bay of the Hall of Mental Cultivation
Fig.29　East Warm-Chamber of the Hall of Mental Cultivation

图30 养心殿「勤政亲贤」

图31 养心殿「三希堂」

Fig.30 Panel in the Hall of Mental Cultivation inscribed with 'Diligent and Affectionate'
Fig.31 Hall of Three Rarities of the Hall of Mental Cultivation

图 32　坤宁宫

图 33　坤宁宫西侧室内

图 34　坤宁宫婚房

Fig.32 Palace of Earthly Tranquility
Fig.33 West Side of the Interior of the Palace of Earthly Tranquility
Fig.34 Bridal Chamber inside the Palace of Earthly Tranquility

Hall of Supreme Principle (*Taiji dian*)[①] and united with it as a large compound. The union of the two palaces converts the layout of the Six Western Palaces drawn in Ming times greatly. In comparison with independent palaces, the new united compound reinforces the continuity of the exterior space, enlarges the open space, lightens the atmosphere and facilitates daily life. Measuring five bays wide, the main hall of the now Palace of Eternal Spring has a front of double-layer bamboo-relief lattice doors[②] in the central bay, step-by-step pattern (*Bubu jin*) removable windows in the other bays, a porch sheltering these doors and windows, and a gable-and-hip roof with yellow glazed tiles on top of all these assemblage (Fig.36). The interior of the main hall is decorated with a throne in the central bay, upon which hangs the signboard inscribed with '敬修内则' (*Jingxiuneize*)[③] by Qianlong Emperor; curtains in the east and west bays partitioning the space; and *Kangs* in the easternmost and westernmost bays for sleeping. In front of the main hall, there is a pair of copper turtles and a pair of copper cranes on the right and left. The east side hall of the Palace of Eternal Spring is the Hall of Secure Longevity (*Suishou dian*), yet the west side hall is the Hall of Collecting Happiness (*Chengxi dian*). Both halls have three bays in width and a porch in the front. The porches of the main hall and side halls are connected, enclosing the courtyard of the palace. On the walls of the porches are a series of eighteen paintings of scenes from *Dream of the Red Chamber* (*Honglou meng*) (Fig.37). This novel, written by *Cao Xueqin*, is one of the Four Great Classical Novels of Chinese literature and is universally considered one of the greatest novels of China. Extended from the rear of the Hall of Manifest Origin (*Tiyuan dian*), a hall in the south of the Palace of Eternal Spring, there is a veranda that was used as a theatrical stage, where the Empress Dowager Cixi would watch opera performances from here (Fig.38). In the tenth year of Guangxu reign (1884), to celebrate Cixi's fiftieth birthday, operas were played here for half a month. The back hall of the Palace of Eternal Spring was built the same time as the main hall, named Taking Pleasure in Classics and History (*Yiqing Shushi*). It was equipped with three side rooms on the east and west respectively, two side halls, namely the Lodge of Benefitting Longevity (*Yishou zhai*) and the Belvedere of Lofty Pleasures (*Lezhi xuan*), and a Well Pavilion in the front. In terms of function, the Palace of Eternal Spring was used as the residence of concubines in the Ming dynasty, and served the empresses and

① The hall was originally called the Palace of Endless (*Weiyang gong*). It was renamed the Palace of Auspicious Beginning (*Qixiang gong*) in the fourteenth year of Jiajing reign (1535), and later changed into the current name in late Qing.
② Double-layer doors consists of the doors for preventing wind (*Feng men*) in the front and lattice doors for access in the back.
③ '敬修内则' means that the concubines should regulate their words and deeds and abide by their duties.

空间的连续性，扩大了活动场所，增加了生活气氛，为日常使用提供了便利。长春宫面阔5间，前出廊（图36）。明间开门，为槅扇风门，竹纹裙板；次、梢间均为步步锦支摘窗。上覆黄琉璃瓦歇山顶。

殿内明间设地平宝座，上悬清代乾隆皇帝御笔『敬修内则』匾额，左右有帘帐与次间相隔，梢间靠北设落地罩炕，为寝室。殿前左右设铜龟、铜鹤各1对。长春宫的东配殿为绥寿殿，西配殿为承禧殿，各3间，前出廊，与转角廊相连，可通各殿。廊内壁上绘有18幅以《红楼梦》为题材的巨幅壁画（图37），属清代晚期作品。长春宫南面，即体元殿的后抱厦，为长春宫院内的戏台（图38）。清代光绪十年（1884年），为庆祝慈禧太后的五十寿辰，曾在此演戏达半月之久。长春宫的后殿为怡情书史，与长春宫同期建成，面阔5间，东、西各有耳房3间。其东配殿为益寿斋，西配殿为乐志轩，各3间。后院东南有井亭一座。此宫明代为妃嫔所居，清代为后妃所居。清代乾隆皇帝的孝贤皇后曾

图35 长春宫鸟瞰

图36 长春宫

Fig.35 Bird View of the Palace of Eternal Spring
Fig.36 Palace of Eternal Spring

图 37　长春宫壁画

图 38　长春宫院内戏台

Fig.37　Wall Paintings of the Palace of Eternal Spring
Fig.38　Stage in the Courtyard of the Palace of Eternal Spring

concubines in Qing times. Xiaoxian Empress, the empress of Qianlong Emperor in Qing dynasty, once resided here. When she passed on unfortunately in 1748, her coffin was placed in the Palace of Eternal Spring during her funeral. Years later, upon the regency of the Tongzhi Emperor, the Empress Dowager Cixi made the Palace of Eternal Spring her residence, until her fiftieth birthday when she moved to the Palace of Gathered Elegance (*Chuxiu gong*) in the tenth year of Guangxu reign (1884).

Located in the Far West Road of the Inner Court, the Palace of Longevity and Health (*Shoukang gong*) was constructed from the thirteenth year of Yongzheng reign (1735) to the first year of Qianlong reign (1736). After multiple renovations during the reigns of Jiaqing and Guangxu, it turned out as a series of three courtyards in alignment. The southernmost part of the palace is a small squares surrounded by houses with yellow glazed tiles on the west and south. On the east of the square is the Right Gate of Dulcet Music (*Huiyin you men*) which connects to the Palace of Compassion and Tranquility (*Cining gong*), whereas on the north is the Gate of Longevity and Health (*Shoukang men*) made of glaze. Passing through the Gate of Longevity and Health, the south-facing main hall could be seen. Five bays in width and three bays in depth, it has a gable-and-hip roof in yellow glazed tiles (Fig.39). Inside the main hall, the central bay is crowned by a plaque inscribed with '慈寿凝禧' (*Cishouningxi*)[1] written by Qianlong Emperor, while the easternmost and westernmost bays are warm chambers for worshipping Buddha. Outside the main hall, a platform extends to the north. The east and west side halls sandwich the main hall, each of which has three bays decorated with yellow glazed tiles and side rooms on the south. To the north of the two side halls, there are long corridor rooms that connect directly to the north end of the main hall. Behind the main hall, there is the sleeping hall of the empress dowagers with inscribed panel '长乐敷华' (*Changlefuhua*)[2] hanging in the middle. Five bays in width and three bays in depth, the sleeping hall is connected to the main hall by a paved pathway and is connected to the rear hall by a covered corridor. It has a gable-and-hip roof of yellow glazed tiles. The interior of the sleeping hall is divided into five rooms by partitions (Fig.40). In Qing dynasty, the Palace of Longevity and Health is exclusively reserved for empress dowagers. Every two or three days, the emperor would come and visit the empress dowagers here. The famous imperial dowager consorts lived here include the Empress Dowager Chongqing in Qianlong reign, the Dowager Consort Ying in Jiaqing reign and the Empress Dowager Kangci in Xianfeng reign. After the Empress Dowager Chongqing passed away, his son, the Qianlong Emperor would worship her in the Palace of

① '慈寿凝禧' is a blessing to the empress dowagers for compassion, longevity and happiness.
② '长乐敷华' means to live like flowers in blossom with eternal happiness.

居住长春宫，并于死后在此停放灵柩。同治年至光绪十年，慈禧太后一直在此宫居住。

寿康宫位于内廷外西路，清代雍正十三年（1735 年）始建，至乾隆元年（1736 年）建成，嘉庆二十五年（1820 年）、光绪十六年（1890 年）重修。寿康宫南北共三进院落。南端的寿康门为琉璃门，门前是一个封闭的小广场，广场东侧为徽音右门，可通慈宁宫。正殿寿康宫坐北朝南，面阔 5 间，进深 3 间，上覆黄琉璃瓦歇山顶（图 39）。殿内悬清代乾隆皇帝御笔『慈寿凝禧』匾额；东、西梢间被辟为暖阁，其中东暖阁为皇太后日常礼佛所用的佛堂。殿前出月台。东、西配殿均为面阔 3 间，前出廊，黄琉璃瓦硬山顶。两配殿南设耳房，北为连檐通脊庑房，与后罩房相接。后殿为寿康宫的寝殿，额曰『长乐敷华』，有甬道与寿康宫相连。后殿面阔 5 间，进深 3 间，上覆黄琉璃瓦歇山顶。殿内以槅扇分为 5 间，其后檐明间开槅扇门，接叠落式穿堂（图 40），直达后罩房。寿康宫是清代太皇太后、皇太后的居所，太妃、太嫔随居于此，皇帝每隔两三日即至此行问安礼。乾隆朝的崇庆皇太后、嘉庆朝的颖贵太妃、咸丰朝的康慈皇太后都曾在此颐养天年。崇庆皇太后去世后，乾隆皇帝仍于每年的圣诞令节及上元节前一

图39　寿康宫

图40　寿康宫后殿北侧叠落式穿堂

Fig.39 Palace of Longevity and Health
Fig.40 Hallway on the North Side of the Rear Hall, Palace of Longevity and Health

Longevity and Health for memorial every year.

5. Unique Imperial Gardens

There are in total four gardens in the Forbidden City, that is, the Imperial Garden (*Yu huayuan*), the Garden of Compassion and Tranquility (*Cininggong huayuan*), the Garden of Established Happiness (*Jianfugong huayuan*) and the Garden of Tranquil Longevity (*Ningshougong huayuan*). Compared with the large-scale imperial gardens such as the Summer Palace, the conditions inside the Forbidden city are unfavorable for gardening. There are high enclosing walls everywhere and there is a lack of water. In fact, the conditions are so limited that little creation can be carried out during planning. Consequently, the gardens inside the Forbidden City look more like those small single-complex gardens in grand royal gardens in terms of scale. However, the real single-complex gardens could rely on the royal gardens belonging to—they could draw water and raise rockery as their pleases. The gardens in the Forbidden City comparably could only take the buildings as background and have still water or squat rockery with secondary sources. There is one thing that the two kinds of gardens share in common, however, that is the use of massive buildings in gardens. From Kangxi to Qianlong reign in Qing Dynasty, the emperor spent more and more time in the royal gardens in suburban. Accordingly, the quantity and form of buildings in the gardens increased greatly to meet the needs of emperors. In Qianlong reign, buildings accounts for a great part in royal gardens and an even larger part in gardens in the Forbidden City. That is because the emperor would spend most of his time in suburbs and return to the Forbidden City in winter only when trees are leafless and flowers are withered. Gorgeous buildings are built hence to adorn gardens. The gross floor area of the Imperial Garden accounts for one third of the total area, and that of the Garden of Established Happiness and the Garden of Tranquil Longevity accounts for about a half. While in the Garden of Compassion and Tranquility, where the buildings are widely scattered, the gross floor area still accounts for one fifth of the total area. The buildings undoubtedly add to the magnificence of the gardens and differentiate the gardens inside the Forbidden City from the private gardens by clear axis and grand architecture despite the generous similarities between the two.

Situated to the southwest of the Palace of Compassion and Tranquility (*Cining gong*) at the west road of the inner court, the Garden of Compassion and Tranquility (*Cininggong huayuan*) was first constructed in Ming dynasty. In the thirty-fourth year of Qianlong reign (1769), the emperor had the garden renovated to provide his mother, a faithful Buddhist, a

五、独具特色的宫廷园林

紫禁城内共有宫廷园林四座，分别为：御花园、慈宁宫花园、建福宫花园和宁寿宫花园。与大型皇家园林相比，宫廷园林不具备一般皇家园林范围广阔和便于造园的条件。宫廷园林地处宫禁之内，占地狭小，无发挥余地；周围有高墙遮挡，又缺乏水源，不利于规划布局。因此在规模上，宫廷园林近似于皇家园林中的园中园。然而园中园可以皇家园林为依托，叠石引水各随其便；但宫廷园林却只能以高大宫殿为背景，且只有无土之山、无源之水，要构成园林气氛实在不易。宫廷园林和皇家园林仅有一点是共同的，那就是突出建筑的功用。从清代的康熙到乾隆，皇帝在郊外园居的时间越来越长，园居活动的内容也愈加广泛，相应地就要增加园内建筑的数量和类型，以满足其所需。再者，北方气候不同南方，每到冬季百树凋零，多一些建筑点缀就少一分萧杀景象，所以乾隆时期皇家园林中建筑所占的比重相当之大。宫廷园林在这方面表现就更为突出。一年之中，皇帝大部分时间在外园居住，只在冬季回宫居住，因而必须突出建筑的功用。御花园的建筑面积占全园面积的三分之一；建福宫花园、宁寿宫花园的约占三分之一；慈宁宫花园建筑布局最为疏朗，亦占全园面积的五分之一。所以宫廷园林更显富丽堂皇。虽然在造园手法上，宫廷园林与私家园林有颇多相似之处，但宫廷园林轴线分明，建筑富丽，与私家园林显然有别。

慈宁宫花园位于内廷外西路慈宁宫西南，始建于明代。花园中原有临溪观、咸若亭等建筑，明代万历十一年（1583年）改名为临溪亭、咸若馆。清代乾隆三十四年（1769年）曾进行过大规模的改建，

日至寿康宫拈香礼拜、瞻仰宝座，以申哀思之情。

place to worship the Buddha. Several renovations were carried afterwards, but the overall scale and layout of the garden remained much alike the ones in Qianlong reign. As seen in today, the Garden of Compassion and Tranquility runs 130 meters north-south and 50 meters east-west and contains eleven architectural features, including the Studio of Understanding and Bringing Peace (*Xianruo guan*), the Building of Benevolent Sanctuary (*Ciyin lou*), the Building of Auspicious Clouds (*Jiyun lou*), the Building of the Solemn Buddha (*Baoxiang lou,* Fig.41), the Hall of Prolonged Longevity (*Yanshou tang*), the Lodge of Enclosed Purity (*Hanqing zhai*), the Pavilion over the Stream (*Linxi ting,* Fig.42) and its two side halls. These building structures are concentrated in the northern part of the garden, leaving the south area flat and open, stuffed with natural elements such as pond, rockery, flora and fauna. Passing through the main gate, the Gate of Enjoying Sceneries (*Lansheng men*), located on the east wall of the garden, the main building of the Garden of Compassion and Tranquility, the Studio of Understanding and Bringing Peace, emerges. The hall was initially named the Pavilion of Understanding and Bringing Peace (*Xianruo ting*), and was given the current name in the eleventh year of Wanli reign (1583). Five bays in width, the studio has a hip-and-gable roof in yellow glazed tiles, a protruding facet (*Baosha*), and a parterre in the front. To the north of the studio, the Building of Benevolent Sanctuary is located, flanking by the Building of the Solemn Buddha and the Building of Auspicious Clouds to the east and the west. Similar in forms, the three buildings are all two-storey C-shaped constructions decorated with round-ridge gable-and-hip roof of green glazed tiles and yellow glazed tiles trimmings. The easternmost bay of the Building of Benevolent Sanctuary on the first floor is a pass way leading to the plaza of the Palace of Compassion and Tranquility. To the south of the Building of the Solemn Buddha and the Building of Auspicious Clouds, there are two courtyards in which Qianlong Emperor served his mother traditional herb infusions, videlicet, the Hall of Prolonged Longevity in the west and the Lodge of Enclosed Purity in the east. Simple but novel, the main building of each courtyard is designated with a grey-tile roof with three linking round-ridges. In the south of the Garden of Compassion and Tranquility, there situates a pond, over which is a white marble bridge. On the bridge there is the Pavilion over the Stream, facing the Studio of Understanding and Bringing Peace. The Pavilion over the Stream was initially named the Studio of over the Stream (*Linxi guan*) when constructed. The current name was given in the eleventh year of Wanli reign (1583). To the east and the west of the Pavilion over the Stream, there used to be a pavilion called Emerald Aroma, and a pavilion called Greenish Clouds. After years of renovations, they are now replaced by two side halls of five bays. Two parterres of Sumeru-seat (*Xumi zuo*) style stand symmetrically to the north and south of the Pavilion over the Stream, six and a half meters square and one meter high. Further south, after bypassing the

此后虽『颇有更动』，但花园总体规模和布局始终没有大的变化。花园南北长约130米，东西宽约50米。

园中仅有建筑11座，集中于花园北部，南部则地势平坦开阔，莳花种树、叠石垒池。花园入口揽胜门设在东墙，为一朴素的随墙门。进门北望，主殿为咸若馆，面阔5间，前出抱厦，黄琉璃瓦顶。馆前有花坛一座，东西两侧有宝相楼（图41）和吉云楼，馆后正北为慈荫楼。三座楼形制相近，皆为两层，覆绿琉璃瓦黄剪边卷棚歇山顶，成『口』形环抱咸若馆。慈荫楼底层东梢间开一小门，与慈宁宫前广场相通。宝相楼和吉云楼正南各有小院一座，名为含清斋、延寿堂，是乾隆皇帝侍奉皇太后汤药之处。小院中的主体建筑为灰瓦三卷勾连搭卷棚顶，素雅新颖。花园南部有一东西窄长的矩形水池，当中横跨汉白玉石桥，桥上建亭一座，名曰临溪亭（图42），北与咸若馆相对。亭的东西两侧原有翠芳亭、绿云亭，现为面阔5间的配殿各一座。临溪亭南侧的花坛呈正方形，边长6.5米，高1米，为须弥座式，与北花坛相对称。再向南绕过太湖石叠山，即为花园的南入口。慈宁宫花园是明清两代太皇太后、皇太后及太妃、太嫔们的游憩、礼佛之处。由于受礼制、宗法、风水等多种因素制约，园中建筑按照主次相辅、左右对称的格局安排，布局规整严谨却略显单调，因此主要依靠内部精巧的装修和院落里的水池、山石以

图四一 慈宁宫花园宝相楼

图四二 慈宁宫花园临溪亭

Fig.41 Building of the Solemn Buddha of the Garden of Compassion and Tranquility
Fig.42 Pavilion over the Stream of the Garden of Compassion and Tranquility

rockery made of decorative *Taihu* Stone, the south entrance of the Garden of Compassion and Tranquility can be seen. In Ming and Qing dynasties, the Garden of Compassion and Tranquility mainly served as the venue where empress dowagers and imperial dowager consorts worshiped the Buddha, entertained themselves and rested. Due to the constraint of various factors such as rites, patriarch and *Fengshui*[①], the buildings in the garden are in a hierarchical and symmetrical layout, which is orderly neat yet somehow monotonous. The garden atmosphere is enhanced by sophisticated interior embellishment as well as the ponds, rockery, and a wide variety of plants in the courtyards. The garden trees, mostly pine and cypress with occasionally Chinese parasol tree, ginkgo, magnolia, and clove, are densely planted in front of the Studio of Understanding and Bringing Peace and around the Pavilion over the Stream, while the parterres see profuse peony. With the changes of seasons and time, different sentiments and feelings are thus created in this garden ground. Having spent the whole life in the Forbidden City where hierarchies and etiquettes are ubiquitous, the Garden of Compassion and Tranquility is perhaps the only place where the former consorts could find spiritual comforts and reliefs.

Garden of Tranquil Longevity (*Ningshougong huayuan*) (Fig.43) locates at the northwest part of the Palace of Tranquil Longevity area (*Ningshou gong*) in the Far East Road. The current layout is datable to the reconstruction from the thirty-seventh year to the forty-first year of Qianlong reign (1772—1776) that was carried out to provide the emperor a place of seclusion for his life after retirement. Consequently, the garden is also referred to colloquially as the 'Qianlong Garden'. The area allotted for the garden is a narrow rectangle, 160 meters in length, north to south, and 40 meters in width, within which were incorporated 27 buildings and pavilions surrounding courtyards, rockeries, paths, caves and plants. The architectural features, the natural elements and the open spaces are divided into four courtyards. Each of the courtyards has its own individual plan and design, featuring different sceneries and views. Passing through the main gate, the Gate of Extending Auspiciousness (*Yanqi men*), the first courtyard welcomes visitors with its main hall, the Bower of Ancient Catalpa (*Guhua xuan*) which was named after the catalpa tree in front of it (Fig.44). The Bower of Ancient Catalpa is surrounded by rockeries to the east, the west and the south: the eastern rockery has the Terrace for Collecting Morning Dew (*Chenglu tai*) on the top; the western one has the Pavilion for Greeting the Rising Sun (*Xuhui ting*) standing on the summit, the name of which means standing high and eastward to greet sunrise; whereas the southern rockery has a winding path back to the

① *Fengshui* is the traditional Chinese theory for planning.

及品种繁多的花木来烘托浓厚的园林气氛。园中树木以松柏为主，间有梧桐、银杏、玉兰、丁香，集中分布在咸若馆前和临溪亭周围，花坛中则密植牡丹、芍药。其春华秋实，晨昏四季，各有不同的情趣。

在礼制森严的紫禁城中，慈宁宫花园是唯一能令前代后妃们寻得心灵慰藉的轻松所在。

宁寿宫花园（图 43）位于内廷外东路宁寿宫西北。清代乾隆三十七年（1772 年）至四十一年（1776 年）重建宁寿宫时，在后区西部南北长约 160 米、东西宽约 40 米的窄长地段内建成一座花园，以备乾隆皇帝归政后游赏，故又称乾隆花园。全园南北分隔成四进院落，每进院落的布局各具特色，景色各不相同。花园正门衍祺门内为第一进院落。主体建筑古华轩（图 44），因轩前有一株古楸树而得名。轩东山峦上有承露台；轩西为凿有流杯渠的禊赏亭（图 45）；亭北山上是旭辉庭，因其坐西朝东，且高居于堆山之上，可迎日出，遂得乾隆皇帝御笔『旭辉』；轩南堆假山，其间有曲径。轩东南角为曲廊、矩亭、抑斋围合成的小院，小院内东南侧假山上建有高出墙垣的撷芳亭，可登临远眺，也为园中一景。

古华轩北侧垂花门（图 46）内即为第二进院落。正殿遂初堂，有东西两座配殿，四周游廊将正殿、配殿、

图43　宁寿宫花园鸟瞰示意图

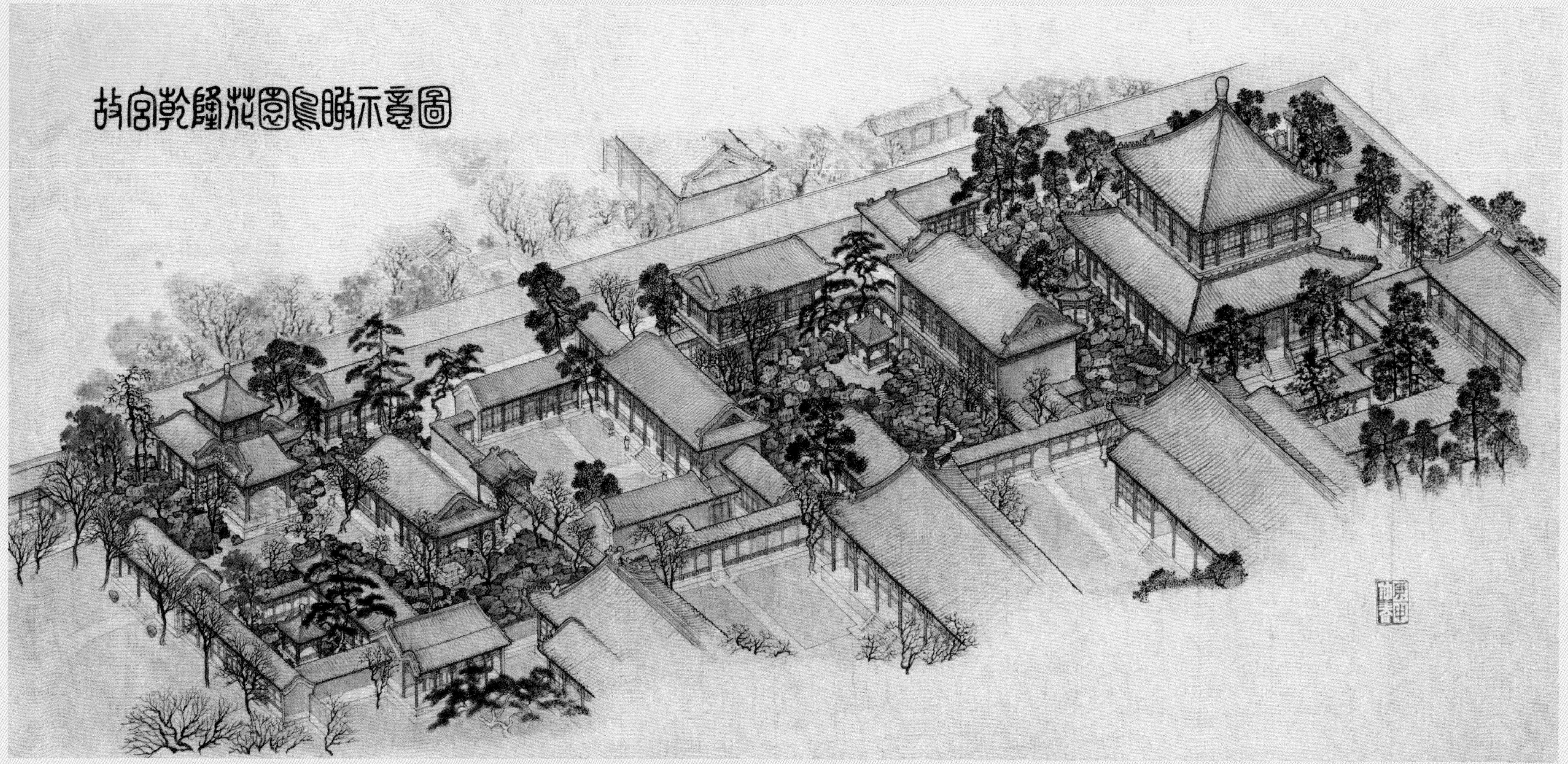

故宫乾隆花园鸟瞰示意图

Fig.43 Bird View of the Garden of Tranquil Longevity

图44 宁寿宫花园古华轩内景

Fig.44 Inner View of the Bower of Ancient Catalpa, Garden of Tranquil Longevity

图 45　宁寿宫花园禊赏亭

图 46　宁寿宫花园垂花门

Fig.45　Pavilion of the Purification Ceremony of the Garden of Tranquil Longevity
Fig.46　Floral-pendant Gate of the Garden of Tranquil Longevity

Gate of Extending Auspiciousness. To the southwest of the bower, there is the famous Pavilion of the Purification Ceremony (*Xishang ting*) with a twisting water channel in accordance with the verse of 'a twisting water channel for floating wine cup and enjoying the drinking festival' (Fig.45). Apart from the above buildings, the first courtyard also contains a small complex in the southeast, enclosed with winding corridors and the Pavilion of Properties (*Ju ting*) and the Studio of Self Restraint (*Yi zhai*) at corners. The Pavilion of Plucking Fragrance (*Xiefang ting*) stands tall and erect on the rockery in the southeast of the small complex. Further north from the Bower of Ancient Catalpa, there is a floral-pendant gate (*Chuihua men*, Fig.46) and then the second courtyard of the Garden of Tranquil Longevity. The buildings of the second courtyard include the main hall, the Hall of Fulfilling Original Wishes (*Suichu tang*), and two side halls on both sides. These three halls and the floral-pendant gate are connected by corridors, forming a typical Chinese courtyard of compounds on three sides (*San heyuan*). To the north of the second courtyard, the third courtyard appears with undulating rockeries and caves that lead to different directions. On top of the rockeries is the Pavilion of Lofty Elegance (*Songxiu ting*, Fig.47), whereas to the north, the west and the east are the Building for Enjoying Lush Scenery (*Cuishang lou*), the Building of Extending Delight (*Yanqu lou*), and the Bower of Three Friends (*Sanyou xuan*). Notably, a new roof form was invented for the Bower of Three Friends because the east end of its roof has ran into the west gable wall of the Hall of Joyful Longevity (*Leshou tang*). The new roof is designed to be flush-gable in the east and gable-and-hip in the west, both round ridge and paved with yellow glazed tiles. To the north of the Building for Enjoying Lush Scenery lies the fourth and the last courtyard of the Garden of Tranquil Longevity, in which the Belvedere of Viewing Achievements (*Fuwang ge*) is the largest and the most prominent feature. Square in shape, the Belvedere of Viewing Achievements, seemingly two-storied structure has, in fact, three interior stories. The pyramidal hip roof of the belvedere is crowned with a spherical finial and the unique interior design of it is intricately ornate and ingeniously partitioned into various spaces lavishly decorated with a dazzling array of gold, jade, and enamel inlays. Casually passing through a door or stepping over a threshold can lead to disorientation in what has been referred to colloquially as the 'maze building' (*Mi lou*). To the south of the Belvedere of Viewing Achievements, there is a mountainous rockery with the Pavilion of Jade-green Conch (*Biluo ting*) standing on the top (Fig.48). The Pavilion of Jade-green Conch is also known as the Pavilion of Plum Flowers for its wide use of five-petal plum flowers. A marble bridge is erected to the south of the pavilion for easy access of the second floor of the Building for Enjoying Lush Scenery in the third courtyard. Southwest to the rockery, there is the L-shaped two-storey Hall of Luminescent Clouds

垂花门联为一体，是个典型的三合院。遂初堂北侧则是第三进院落，以山景为主。院中峰峦起伏，山间有深谷峭壁，山下有隧洞通向四方。沿蹬道上山，可见耸秀亭（图47）屹立山顶。环山北面建有萃赏楼；西有延趣楼，东有三友轩，轩东面紧靠乐寿堂西廊，黄琉璃瓦卷棚顶，东为硬山式，西为歇山式——这是一种巧借地形的屋顶构造形式，为宫中仅有。萃赏楼以北是第四进，也是花园的最后一进院落。主体建筑符望阁为宁寿宫花园中最高大的建筑，其平面呈方形，外观两层，内部实际三层，四角攒尖顶。符望阁的室内装修颇具特色，它以各种不同类型的装修巧妙地分隔空间，穿门越槛之际往往迷失方向，故俗有「迷楼」之称。碧螺亭位于符望阁南侧的叠山主峰之上，其建筑造型独特，采用五瓣梅花形，构件也以各种梅花纹装饰，亭南有白石小桥通萃赏楼两层（图48）。符望阁西南建有云光楼，楼内匾额「养和精舍」为乾隆皇帝御笔，楼平面呈曲尺形，东侧外接上下两层游廊与萃赏楼相连。符望阁西为玉粹轩

图47　宁寿宫花园耸秀亭

图48　宁寿宫花园碧螺亭

Fig.47　Pavilion of Lofty Elegance of the Garden of Tranquil Longevity
Fig.48　Pavilion of Jade-green Conch of the Garden of Tranquil Longevity

054

(*Yunguang lou*), in which hangs the inscribed panel '养和精舍' (*Yanghe jingshe*)[①] by Qianlong Emperor. There are porches on both floors of the Hall of Luminescent Clouds, connecting to the Building for Enjoying Lush Scenery. South from the rockery, there are Bower of Purest Jade (*Yucui xuan,* Fig.49) in the west of the fourth courtyard, the Studio of Exhaustion from Diligent Service (*Juanqin zhai,* Fig.50, Fig.51) in the north, and the Lodge of Bamboo Fragrant (*Zhuxiang guan*) in the northwest (Fig.52). An arced wall with an octagonal entrance is placed in front of the Lodge of Bamboo Fragrance, facing east, and the Studio of Exhaustion from Diligent Service and the Bower of Purest Jade are connected to the Lodge of Bamboo Fragrant by ascending covered walkways. As a whole, features are concentrated and design are ingenious in the Garden of Tranquil Longevity. With various and colorful roofs, gilded Suzhou style embellishments (*Sushi caihua*) painted on beams, the Garden of Tranquil Longevity inherits the exquisite and delicate design from the private gardens and demonstrates the lavish and sumptuous taste of the imperial family.

Notes:

In 1937, the Lugouqiao Incident broke out. For fear that the architectural heritage in Beijing would suffer from the warfare, Mr. Zhu Qiqian, founder of the Society for the Study of Chinese Architecture (*Yingzao Xueshe*) initiated the Surveying and Mapping Project of the Ancient Buildings on Beijing Central Axis to accurately measure and retain the authentic works, and Zhang Bo, the architect of the Kwan, Chu and Yang Architects & Engineers (*Jitai Gongchengsi*) was entrusted by the Urban Planning Bureau of Japanese Puppet Regime as the project leader. Starting in June 1941 (the 30th year of the Republic of China) and ending at the end of 1944 (the 33rd year of the Republic of China), the Surveying and Mapping Project of the Ancient Buildings on Beijing Central Axis could be divided into three stages. The initial stage was mainly accomplished by graduates of year 1941 from the Department of architecture and the Department of civil engineering of Institut des Hautes Etudes et Commerciales (*Tianjin Gongshang Xueyuan*). The surveying and mapping project turned out as a great success — over 700 drawings were made during the project and all of them were preserved till now (654 of these drawings were stored in China's mainland and 50 were in Taiwan).

Among the surveying and mapping drawings selected in this publication, the drawings

[①] '养和精舍' means the Studio of Cultivated Harmony and Supreme Spirits.

图纸说明：

1937 年卢沟桥事变后，恐北京城内的古建筑文化遗产遭受兵火之灾，以『精确实测』留存真迹』为目的，在中国营造学社创始人朱启钤先生的策划下，日伪北平工务总署都市计划局委托基泰工程司的张镈主持实施了北京中轴线古建筑测绘项目。项目共分为三个阶段，始于 1941 年（民国 30 年）6 月，至 1944 年（民国 33 年）底结束。测绘工作初期的参与人员以天津工商学院 1941 年的建筑系和土木系毕业生为主。这次测绘取得的重要成果——700 多张古建筑测绘图纸被完整地保存了下来（其中大陆保存有 654 张，另有 50 张现收藏于台湾）。

秀巧的风貌，又与皇宫富丽华贵的氛围相协调。

（图 49）；北为倦勤斋（图 50、图 51）；西北有竹香馆，馆外围是一道南北向弓形矮墙（图 52）。玉粹轩北、倦勤斋南接有爬山廊，可直达竹香馆二层。宁寿宫花园建筑密集，布局紧凑，中轴线在后半部分略往东移；屋顶类型多样，且色彩丰富；梁枋上大量使用金线苏式彩画。整座花园既有私家园林玲珑

图50　宁寿宫花园倦勤斋室内

图49　宁寿宫花园玉粹轩

Fig.49 Bower of Purest Jade of the Garden of Tranquil Longevity
Fig.50 Interior of the Studio of Exhaustion from Diligent Service, Garden of Tranquil Longevity

图 51　宁寿宫花园倦勤斋室内戏台

图 52　宁寿宫花园竹香馆

Fig.51 Stage inside the Studio of Exhaustion from Diligent Service, Garden of Tranquil Longevity

Fig.52 Lodge of Bamboo Fragrant of the Garden of Tranquil Longevity

of the Meridian Gate (*Wu men*), the Gate of Supreme Harmony (*Taihe men*), the Hall of Supreme Harmony (*Taihe dian*), the Hall of Central Harmony (*Zhonghe dian*), the Hall of Preserving Harmony (*Baohe dian*), the Gate of Heavenly Purity (*Qianqing men*), the Palace of Heavenly Purity (*Qianqing gong*) (elevation excepted), the Palace of Earthly Tranquility (*Kunning gong*) and the Gate of Divine Prowess (*Shenwu men*) on the central axis of the Forbidden City all originate from this project in the Republic of China era. Other architectural drawings and all drawings for colored paintings are achieved with computer-aided software.

Reference:

[1] Yu, Z. The palaces of the Forbidden City [M]. Hong Kong: Commercial Press of Hong Kong, 1982.

[2] Yu, Z. Restorations in the Forbidden City - discussion on the preservation of architectural heritages [C]// Yu, Z. Research and Preservation of the buildings in the Forbidden City. Beijing: Forbidden City Press, 1995: 449-454.

Image Source:

All pictures are provided by The Palace Museum

Written by WANG Mo

Department of Architectural Heritage,

The Palace Museum

Translated by LIU Renhao

在本书选用的测绘图纸当中，位于中轴线上的午门、太和门、太和殿、中和殿、保和殿、乾清门、乾清宫（除立面图外）、坤宁宫和神武门的古建筑图纸均为民国时期的手绘图，其余古建筑及全部彩画图纸则为近年的计算机辅助制图。

主要参考文献：

【一】于倬云．紫禁城宫殿 [M]．香港：商务印书馆香港分馆，1982．

【二】于倬云．紫禁城宫殿修建历程——兼论保护古建筑原状 [C]// 于倬云主编．紫禁城建筑研究与保护．北京：紫禁城出版社，1995：449-454．

图片来源：

所有图片均由故宫博物院提供。

执笔人　王莫

故宫博物院古建部

养性斋透视图
Perspective View of the Lodge of Spiritual Cultivation

坤宁门透视图
Perspective View of the Gate of Earthly Tranquility

景和门透视图
Perspective View of the Gate of Auspicious Harmony

景运门透视图

Perspective View of the Gate of Auspicious Harmony

日精门透视图

Perspective View of the Gate of Solar Essence

澄瑞亭透视图
Perspective View of the Pavilion of Auspicious Water-cleansed

浮碧亭透视图
Perspective View of the Pavilion of Floating Jade

图版

Figures

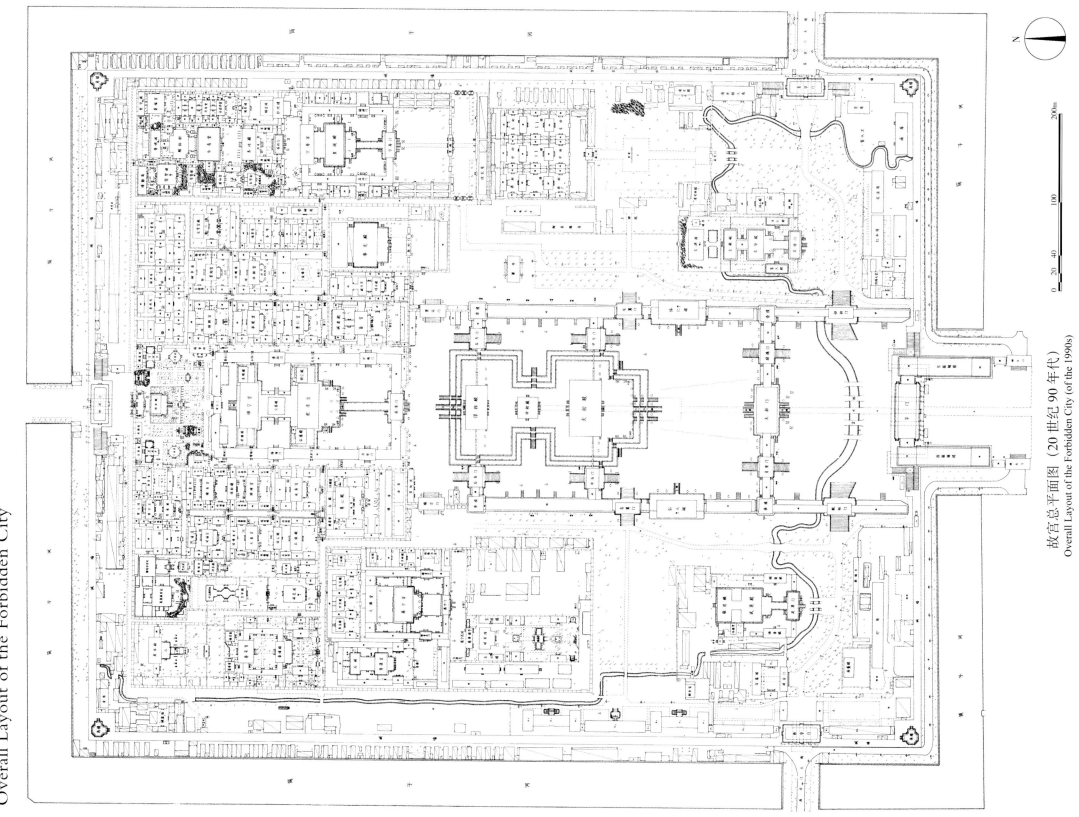

故宫总平面图
Overall Layout of the Forbidden City

故宫总平面图（20 世纪 90 年代）
Overall Layout of the Forbidden City (of the 1990s)

午门
Meridian Gate (*Wu men*)

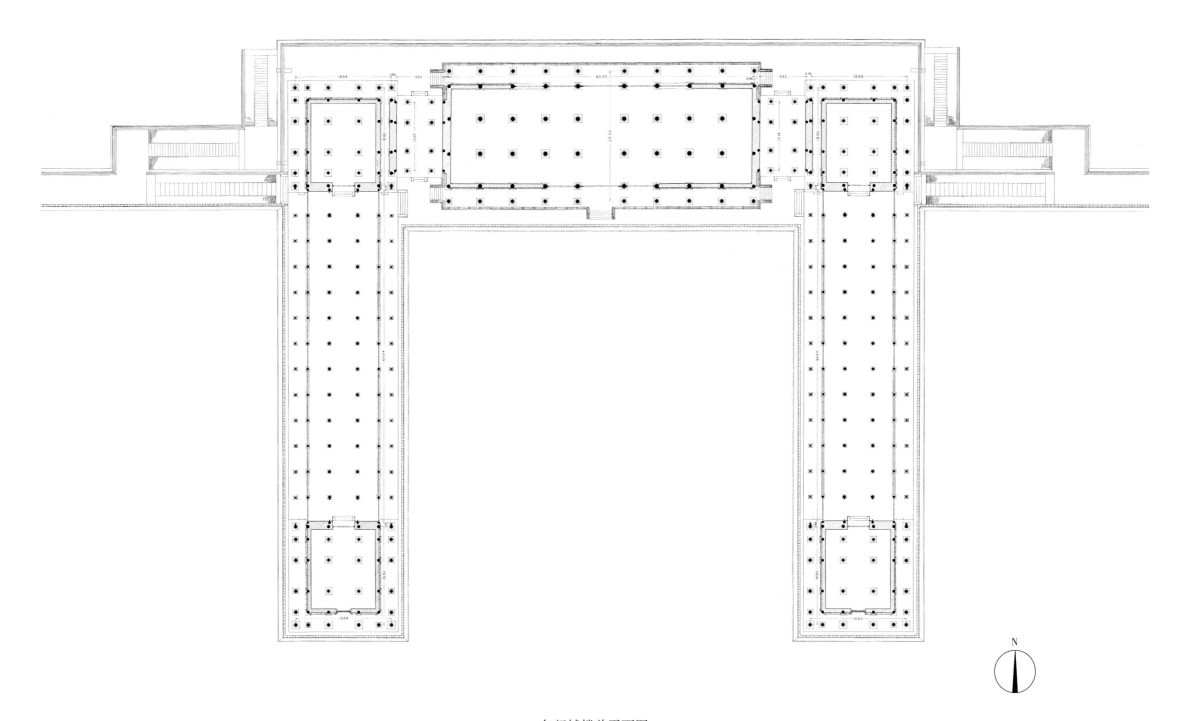

午门城楼总平面图
Overall Layout of the Upper Towers, Meridian Gate

0 5 10 15 20 25 30m

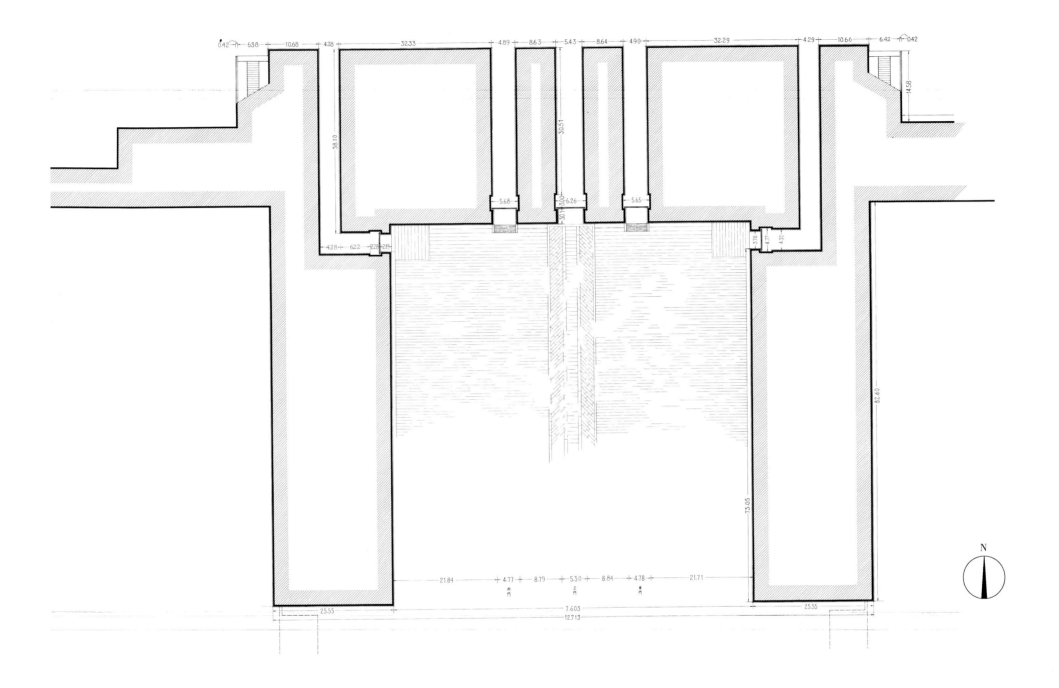

午门城台总平面图
Overall Layout of the Abutment, Meridian Gate

0　5　10　15　20m

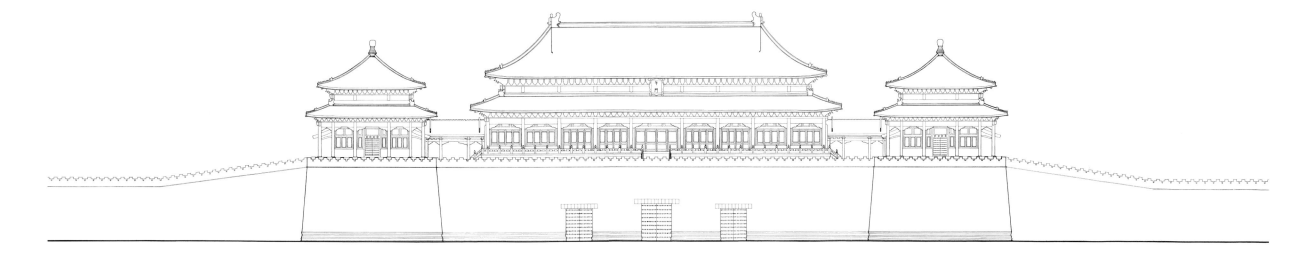

0　5　10　15　20m

午门总正立面图
Front Elevation of the Meridian Gate

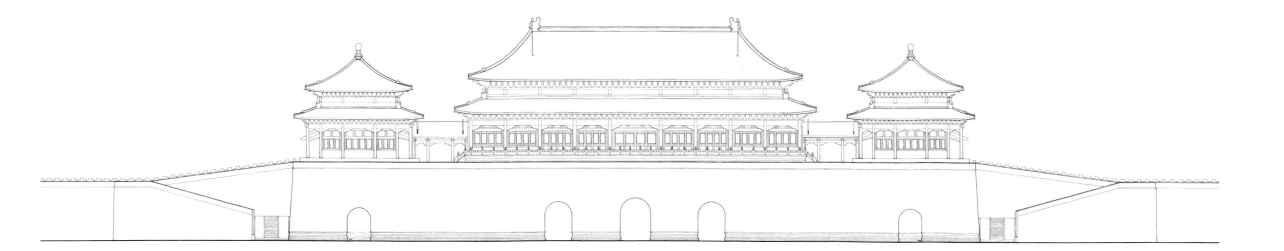

午门总背立面图
Back Elevation of the Meridian Gate

0　5　10　15　20m

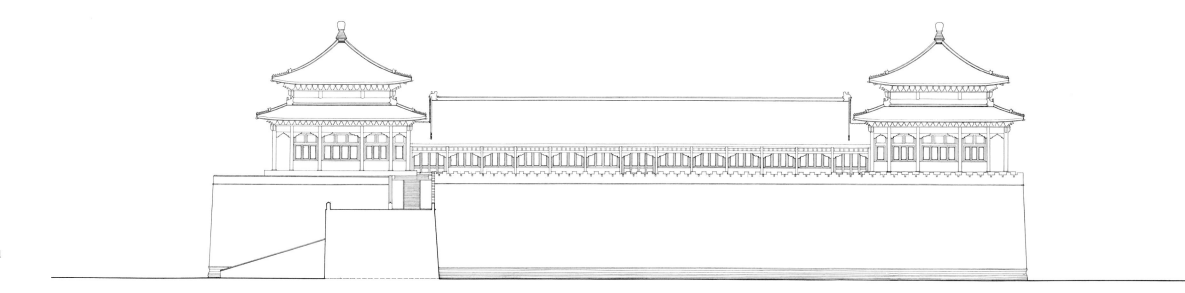

0　　5　　10　　15　　20m

午门总侧立面图（外视）
Side Elevation of the Meridian Gate (View from Sides)

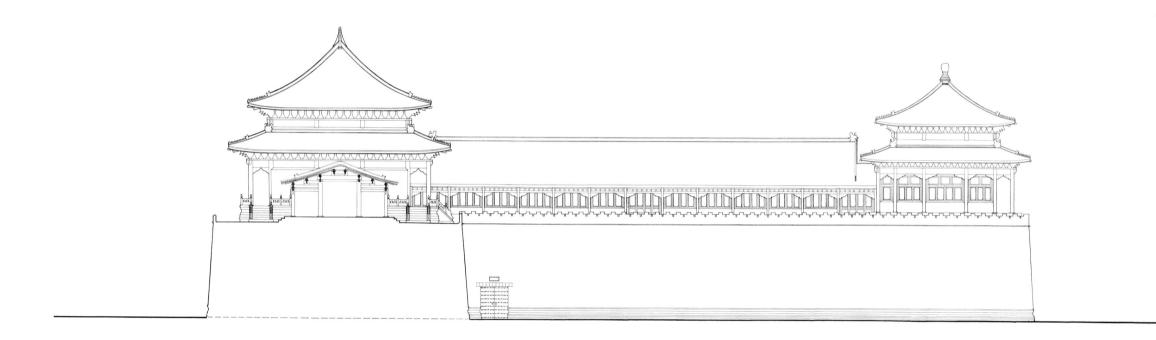

午门总侧立面图（内视）
Side Elevation of the Meridian Gate (View from the Center)

0　5　10　15　20m

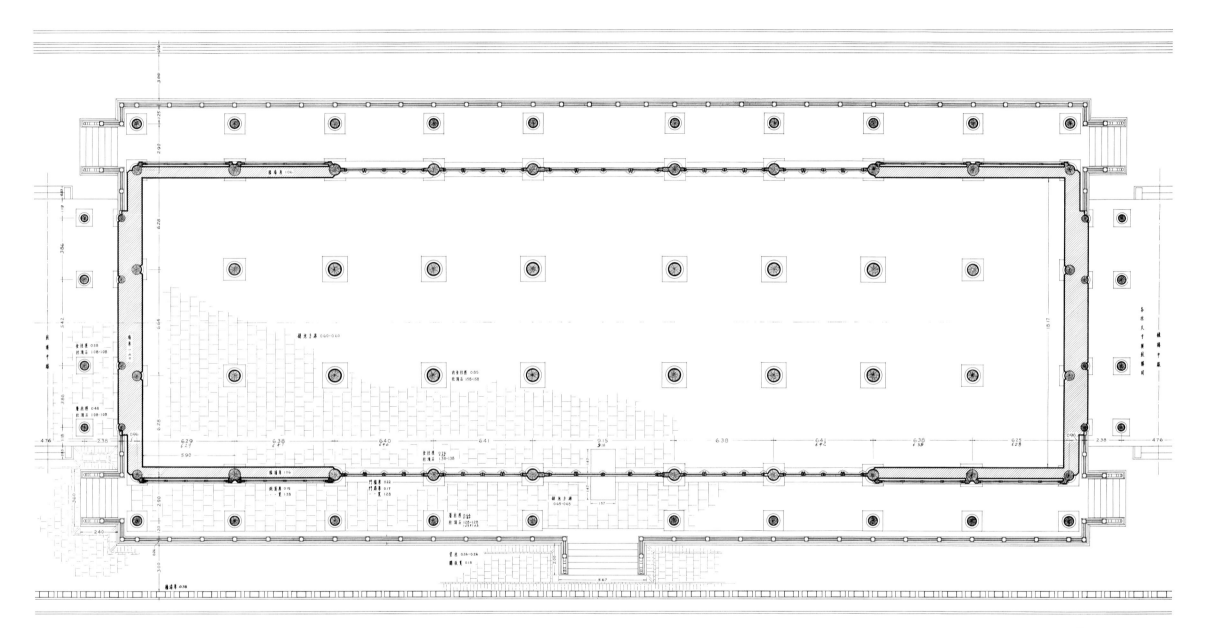

午门城楼平面图
Floor Plan of the Central Tower, Meridian Gate

N

0 1 2 3 4 5   10m

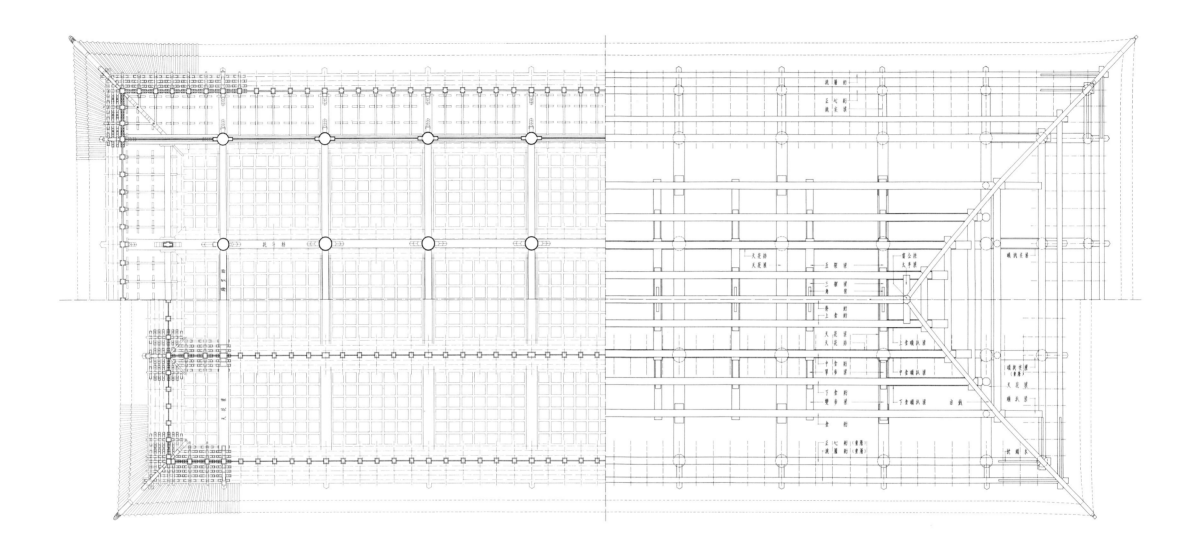

午门城楼天花屋架平面图
Bottom View of the Ceiling Panels and Top View of the Trusses of the Central Tower, Meridian Gate

0 1 2 3 4 5   10m

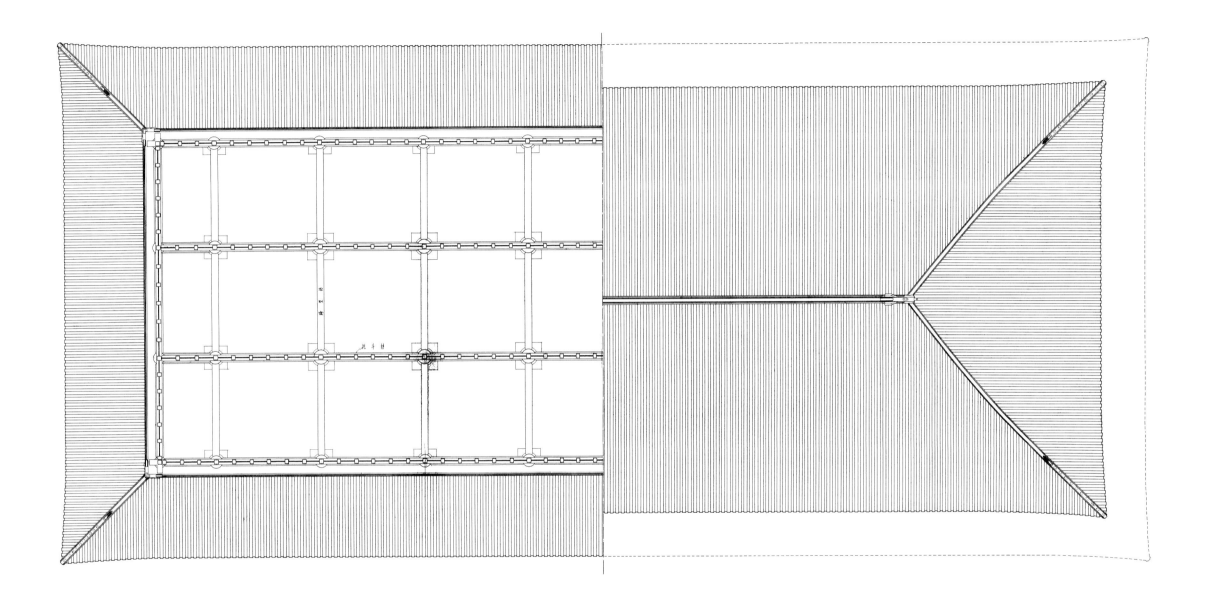

午门城楼屋顶平面图
Top View of the Roof of the Central Tower, Meridian Gate

0 1 2 3 4 5　　　　10m

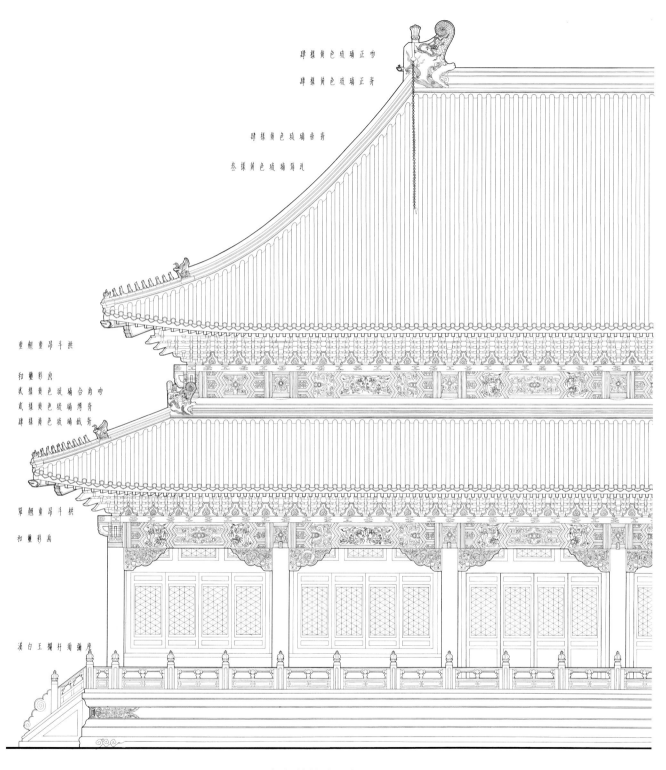

肆样黄色琉璃正吻

肆样黄色琉璃正脊

肆样黄色琉璃垂脊

叁样黄色琉璃筒瓦

重翘重昂斗栱

扣墨彩画
贰样黄色琉璃合角吻
贰样黄色琉璃博脊
肆样黄色琉璃戗脊

单翘重昂斗栱

扣墨彩画

汉白玉栏杆须弥座

午门城楼立面细部图
Detailed Drawing of the Elevation of the Central Tower, Meridian Gate

0 1 2 3 4 5m

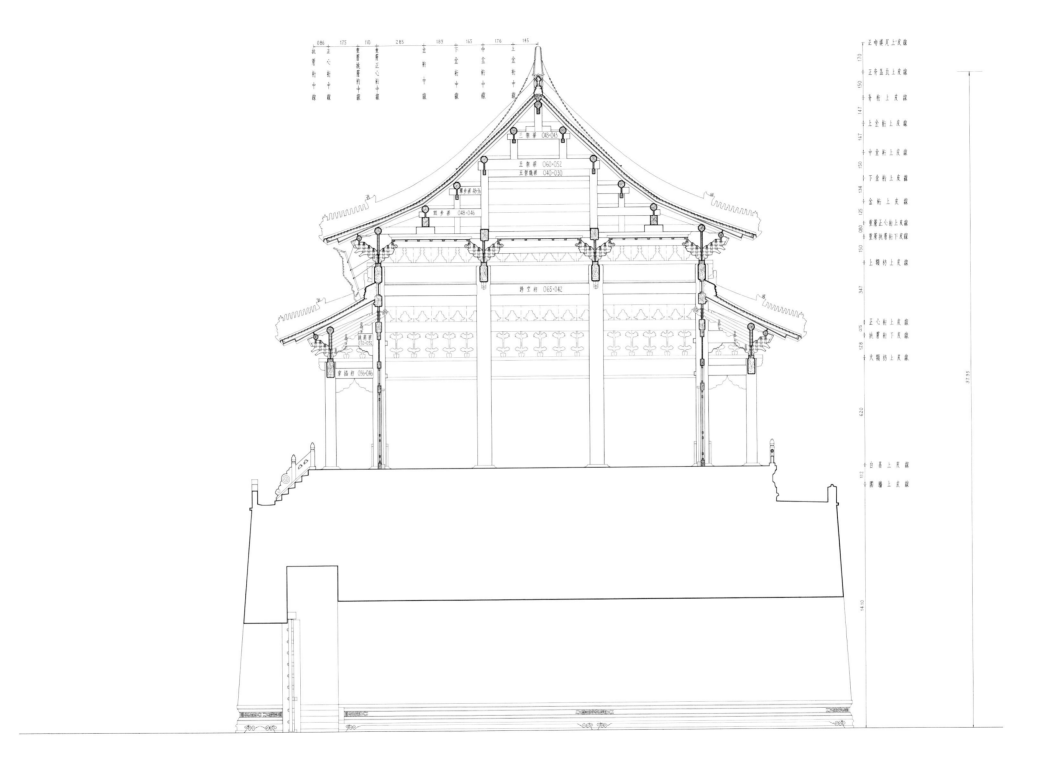

午门城楼横剖面图
Cross Section of the Central Tower, Meridian Gate

0 1 2 3 4 5 6 7 8m

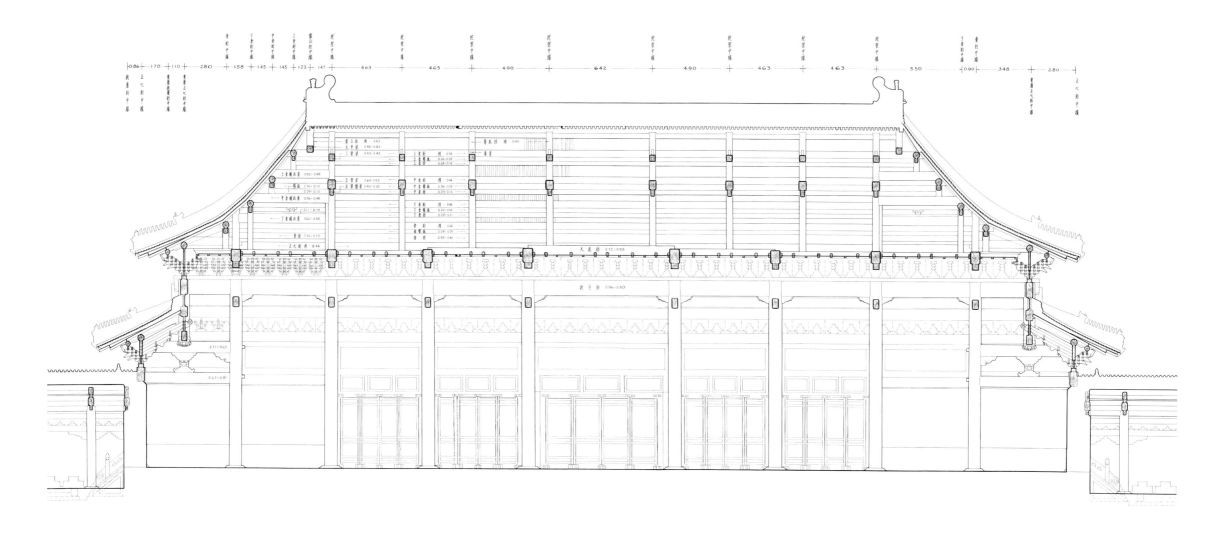

午门城楼纵剖面图
Longitudinal Section of the Central Tower, Meridian Gate

0 1 2 3 4 5   10m

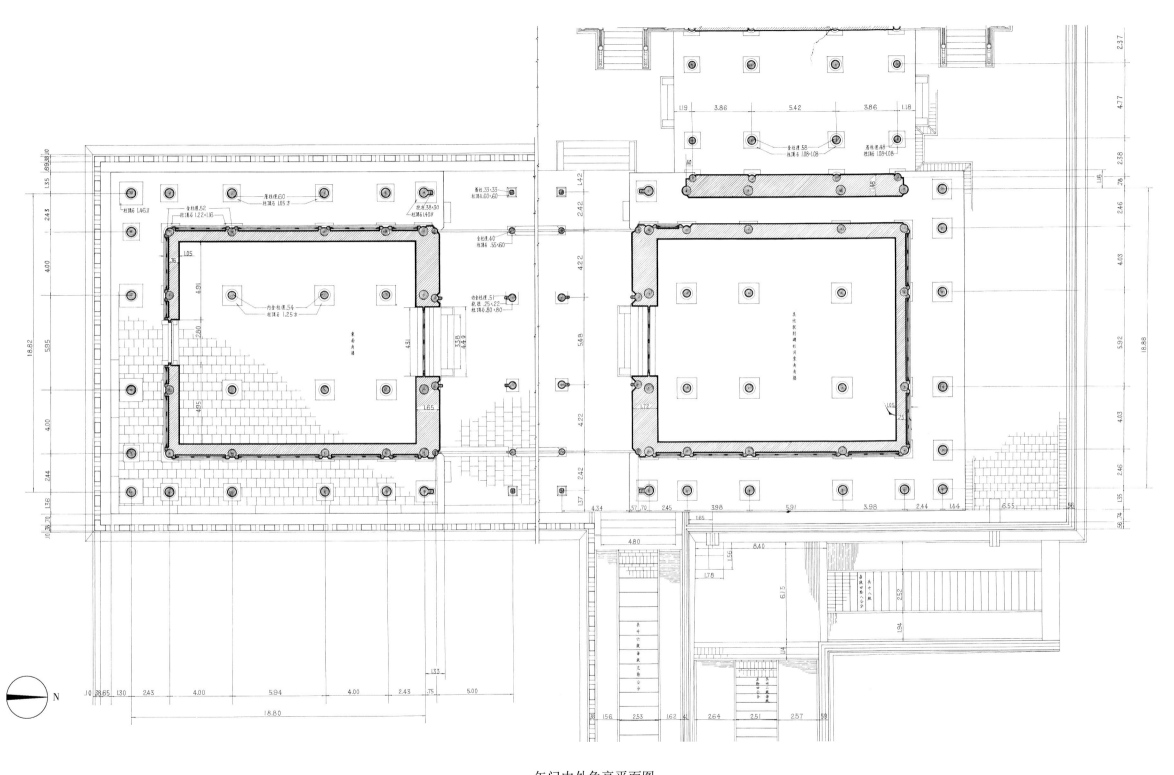

午门内外角亭平面图
Floor Plan of the Corner Towers, Meridian Gate

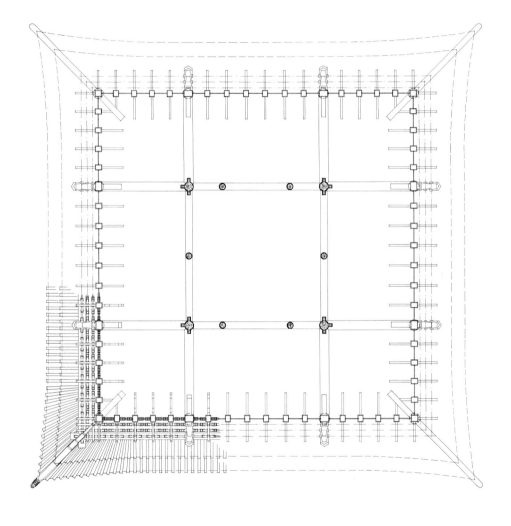

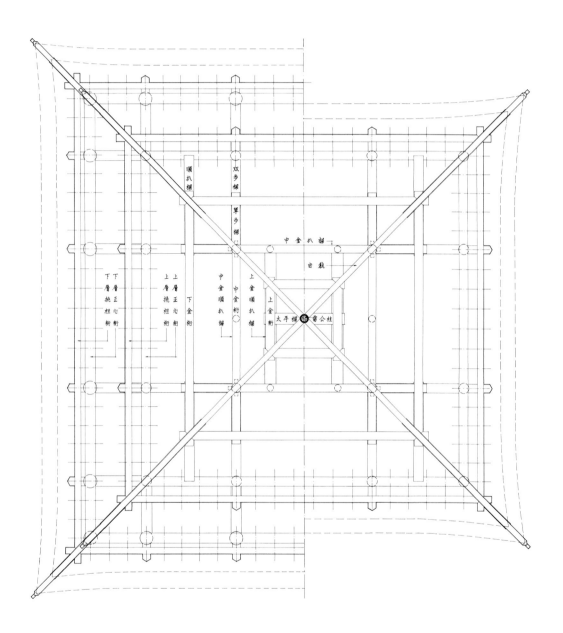

午门角亭斗栱屋架平面图
Bottom View of the Brackets and Top View of the Trusses of the Corner Tower, Meridian Gate

0 1 2 3 4 5 6 7 8m

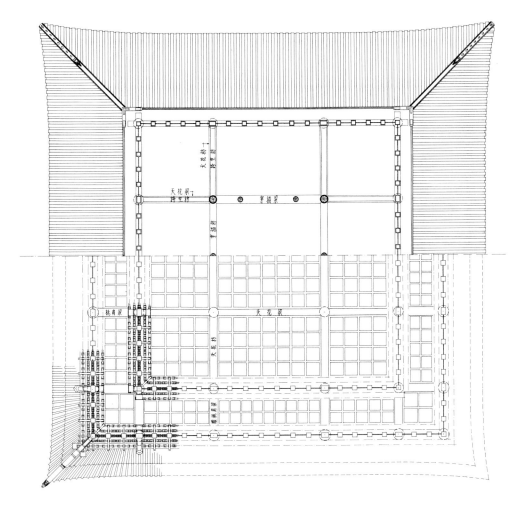
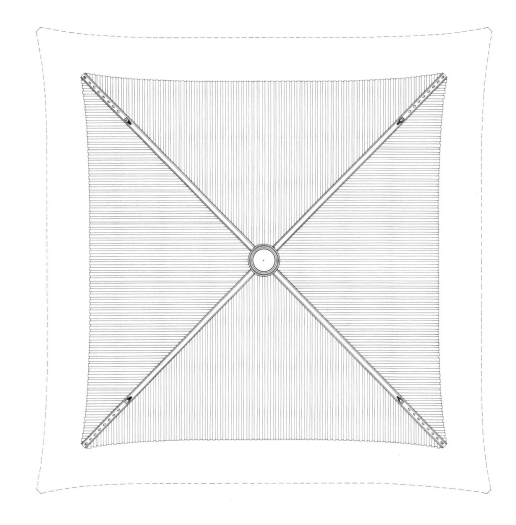

午门角亭天花屋顶平面图
Bottom View of the Ceiling Panels and Top View of the Roof of the Corner Tower, Meridian Gate

0 1 2 3 4 5 6 7 8m

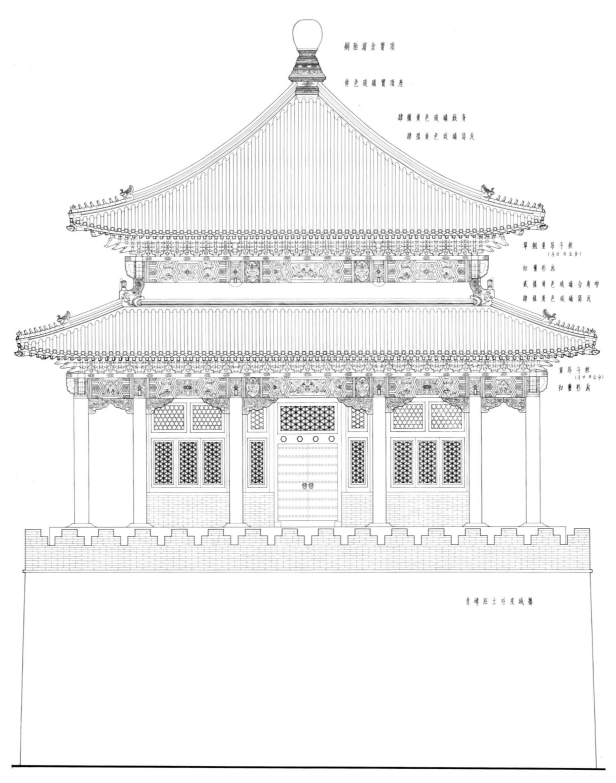

铜胎溜金宝顶

黄色玻璃宝顶座

肆样黄色玻璃脊背
肆样黄色玻璃筒瓦

翠鮑童昂斗栱
（斗口五公分）
扣垂彩画
贰样黄色玻璃合角吻
肆样黄色玻璃筒瓦

童昂斗栱
（斗口五公分）
扣垂彩画

月台挡土外皮城墙

午门角亭立面图
Elevation of the Corner Tower, Meridian Gate

0 1 2 3m

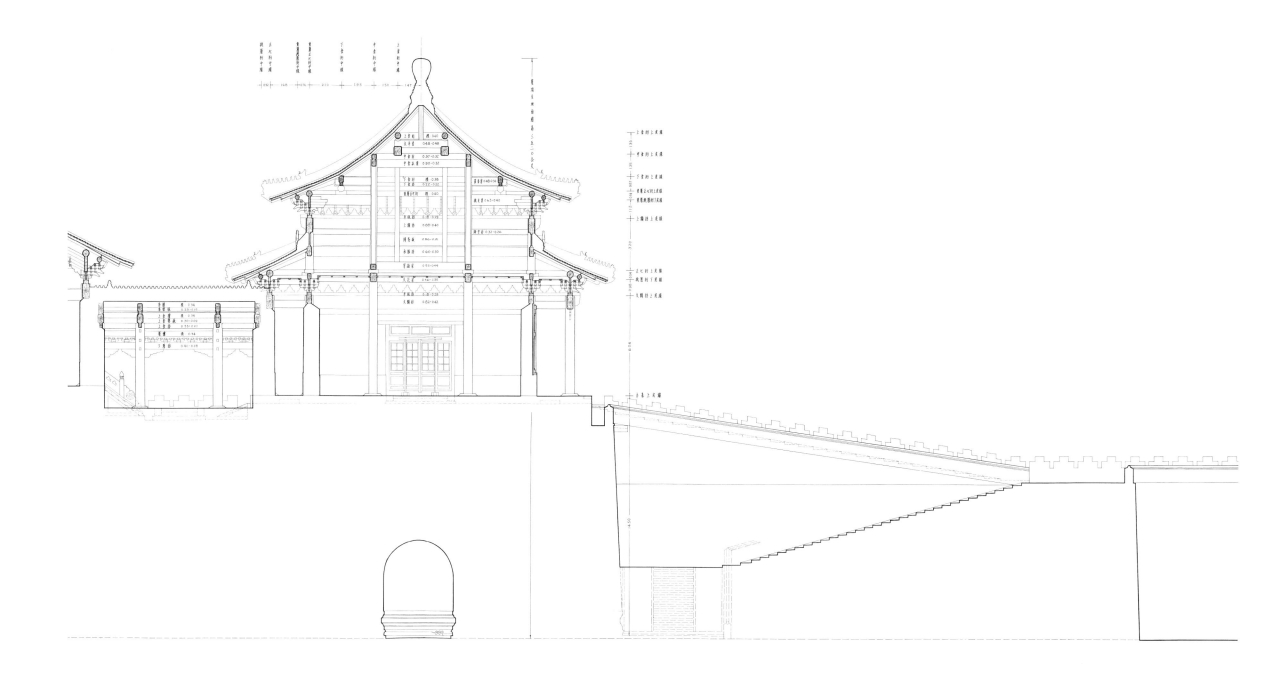

午门角亭横剖面图
Cross Section of the Corner Tower, Meridian Gate

0 1 2 3 4 5 6 7 8m

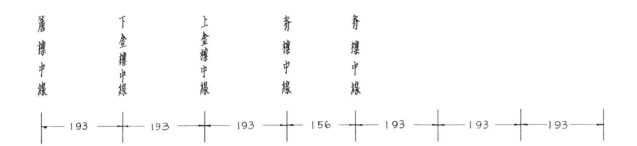

檐檩中線　　下金檩中線　　上金檩中線　　脊檩中線　　脊檩中線　　　　　　　　　　

├─ 193 ─┼─ 193 ─┼─ 193 ─┼─ 156 ─┼─ 193 ─┼─ 193 ─┼─ 193 ─┤

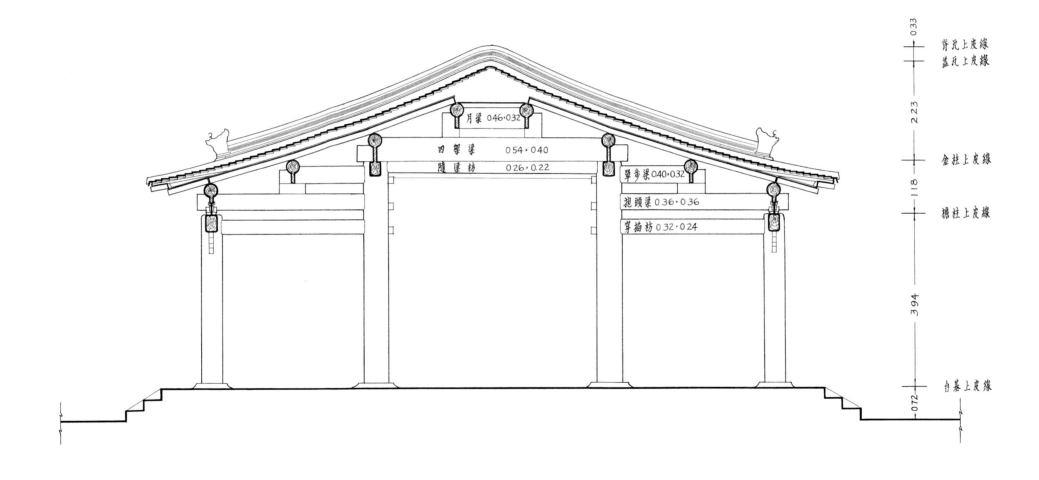

月梁 046·032

四架梁　　054·040
隨梁枋　　026·0.22

單步梁 040·032

抱頭梁 036·036

穿插枋 032·024

脊瓦上皮線　0 33
蓋瓦上皮線　2 23

金柱上皮線　118

檐柱上皮線　394

台基上皮線　072

午门鼓楼横剖面图
Cross Section of the Drum Tower, Meridian Gate

0　1　2　3　4　5　6　7　8m

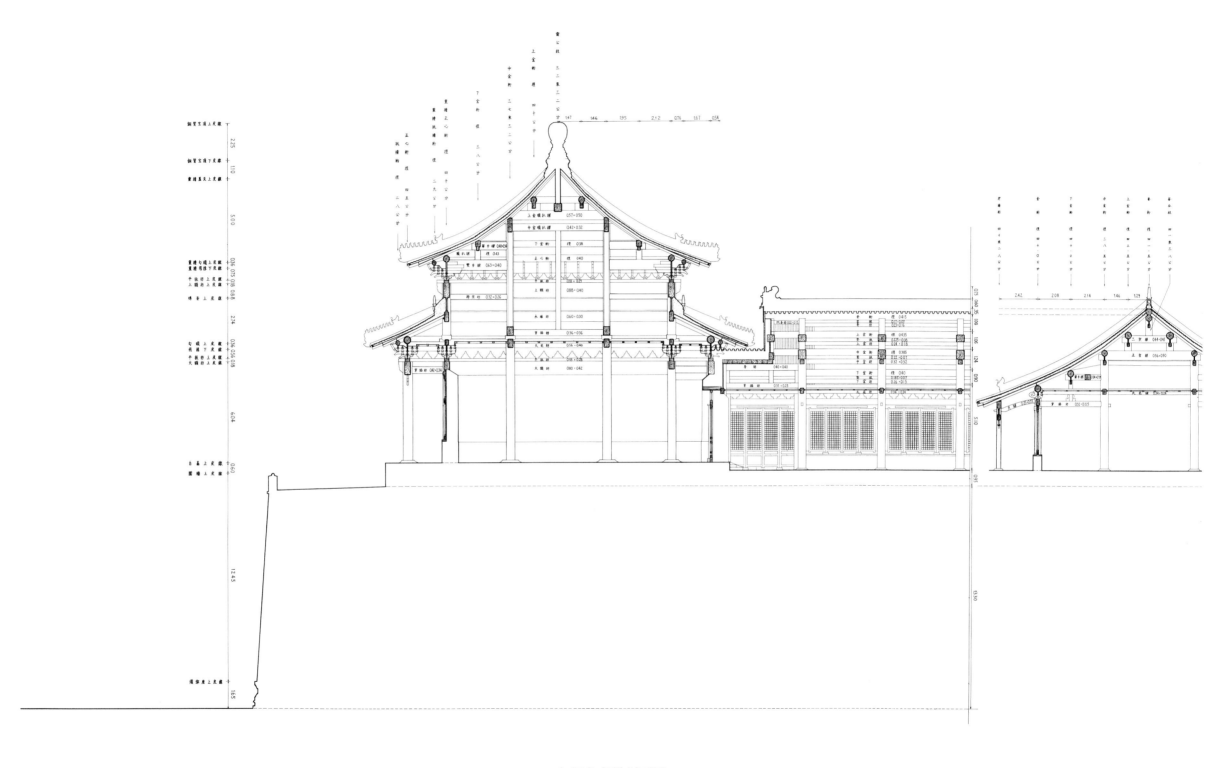

午门角亭纵剖面图
Longitudinal Section of the Corner Tower, Meridian Gate

0 1 2 3 4 5 6 7 8m

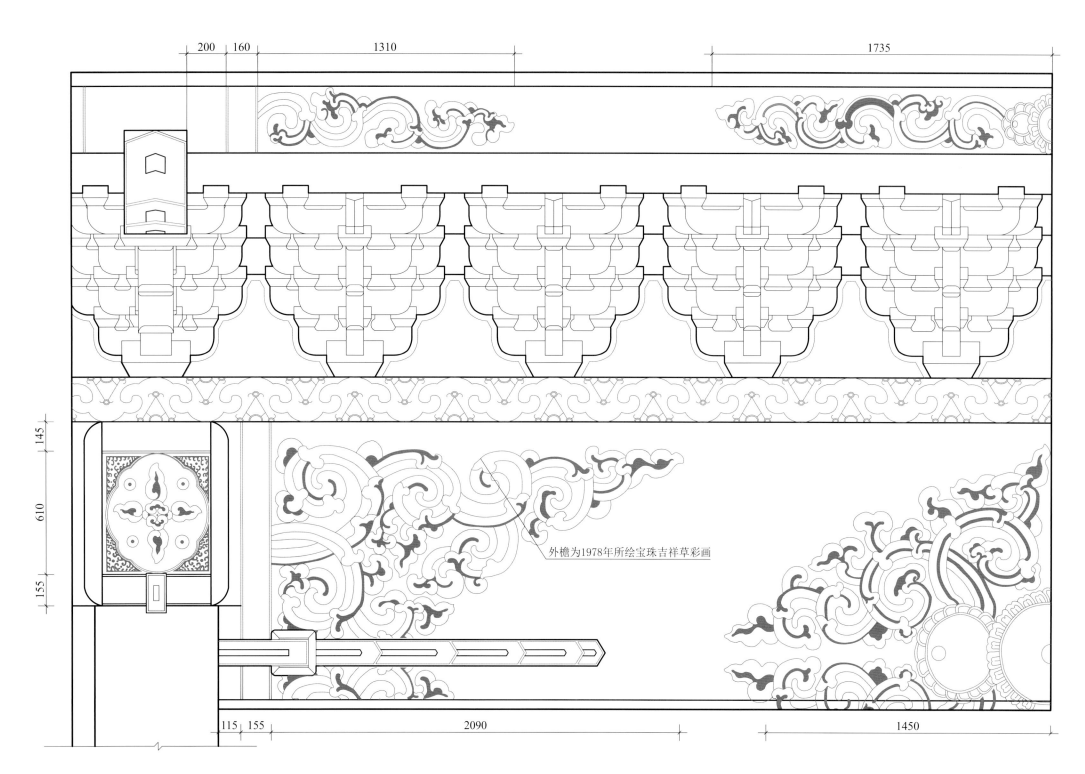

外檐为1978年所绘宝珠吉祥草彩画

午门城楼下檐明间前后外檐彩画现状图
Present Condition of the Colored Paintings of the Front and Back Elevations' Central Bays under the Lower Eave of the Central Tower, Meridian Gate

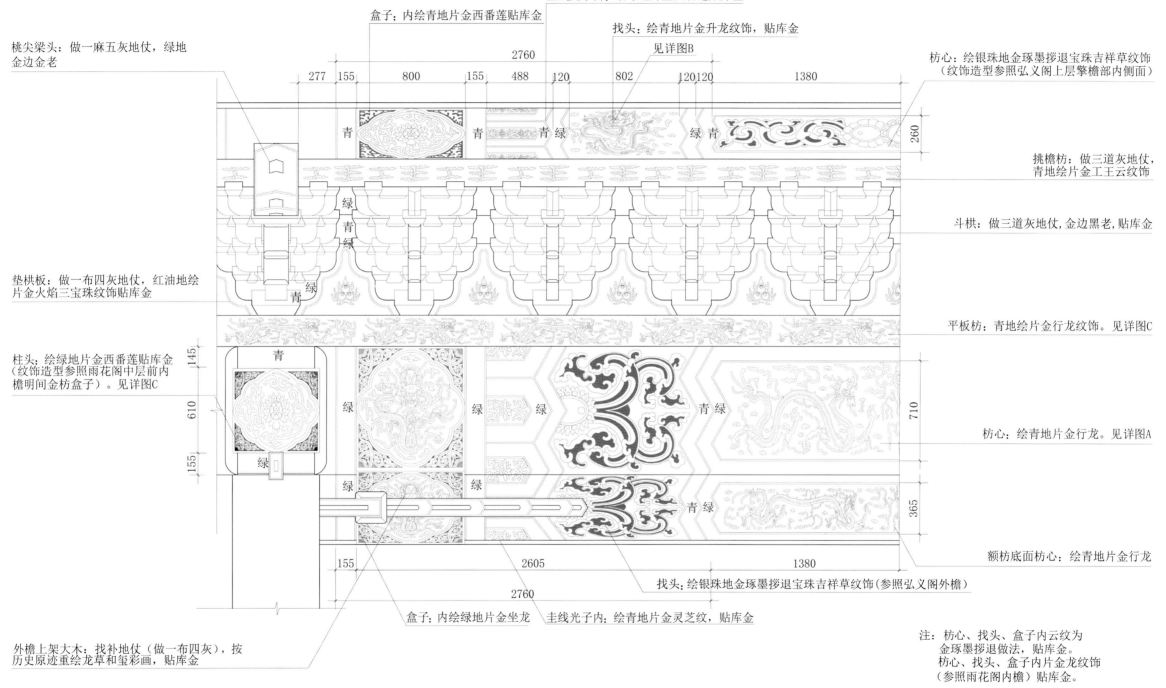

桃尖梁头：做一麻五灰地仗，绿地金边金老

圭线光子内：绘绿地片金西番莲贴库金

盒子：内绘青地片金西番莲贴库金

找头：绘青地片金升龙纹饰，贴库金

见详图B

枋心：绘银珠地金琢墨拶退宝珠吉祥草纹饰（纹饰造型参照弘义阁上层擎檐部内侧面）

挑檐枋：做三道灰地仗，青地绘片金工王云纹饰

斗栱：做三道灰地仗，金边黑老，贴库金

垫栱板：做一布四灰地仗，红油地绘片金火焰三宝珠纹饰贴库金

平板枋：青地绘片金行龙纹饰。见详图C

柱头：绘绿地片金西番莲贴库金（纹饰造型参照雨花阁中层前内檐明间金枋盒子）。见详图C

枋心：绘青地片金行龙。见详图A

额枋底面枋心：绘青地片金行龙

找头：绘银珠地金琢墨拶退宝珠吉祥草纹饰（参照弘义阁外檐）

盒子：内绘绿地片金坐龙

圭线光子内：绘青地片金灵芝纹，贴库金

外檐上架大木：找补地仗（做一布四灰），按历史原迹重绘龙草和玺彩画，贴库金

注：枋心、找头、盒子内云纹为金琢墨拶退做法，贴库金。枋心、找头、盒子内片金龙纹饰（参照雨花阁内檐）贴库金。

277 155 800 155 488 120 802 120 120 1380

2760

260

145 610 155 710 365

155 2605 1380

2760

青 青 青 绿 绿 青

绿 青 青 绿 绿

青 绿

绿 绿 绿 青绿

青绿

绿 绿

青绿

午门城楼下檐明间前后外檐彩画设计图

Design Drawing of the Colored Paintings of the Front and Back Elevations' Central Bays under the Lower Eave of the Central Tower, Meridian Gate

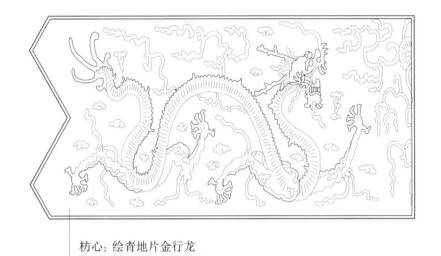

枋心：绘青地片金行龙

详图 A

详图 B

青

绿

详图 C

午门城楼下檐明间前后外檐彩画设计图详图
Design Drawing of the Colored Paintings of the Front and Back Elevations' Central Bays under the Lower Eave of the Central Tower, Meridian Gate

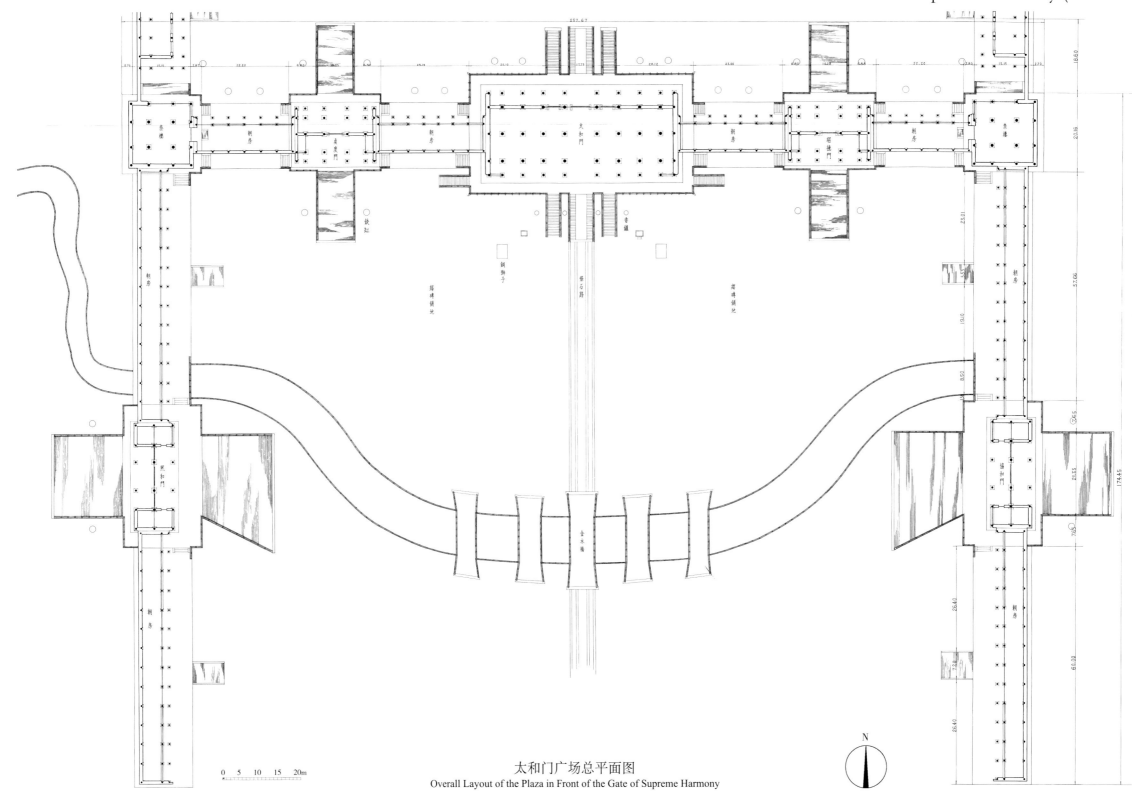

太和门广场总平面图
Overall Layout of the Plaza in Front of the Gate of Supreme Harmony

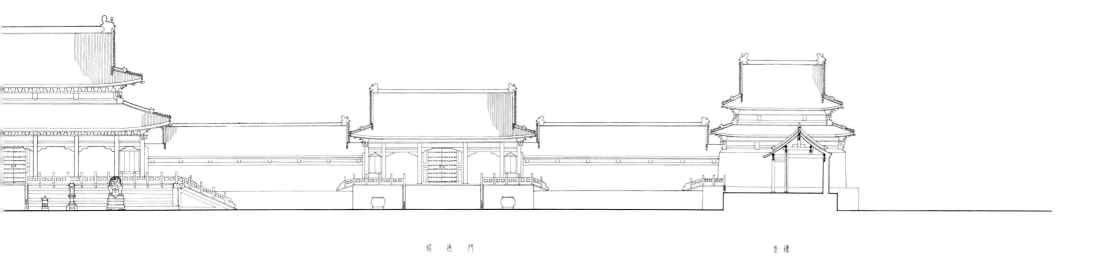

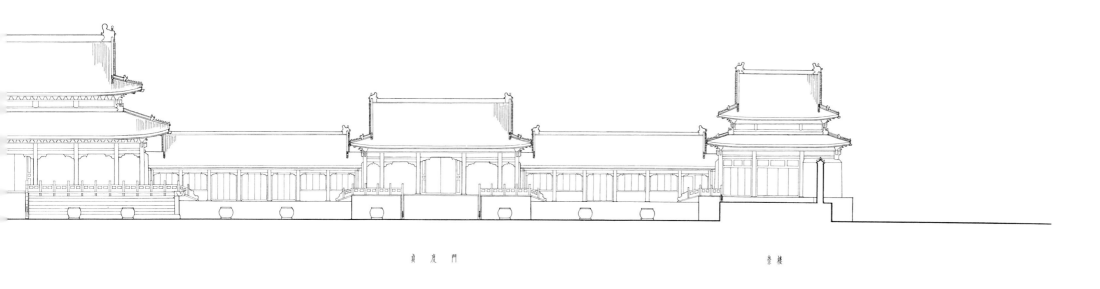

昭德门　　　　　　　　崇楼

太和门广场总正立面图
Front Elevation of the Plaza in Front of the Gate of Supreme Harmony

贞度门　　　　　　　　崇楼

太和门广场总背立面图
Back Elevation of the Plaza in Front of the Gate of Supreme Harmony

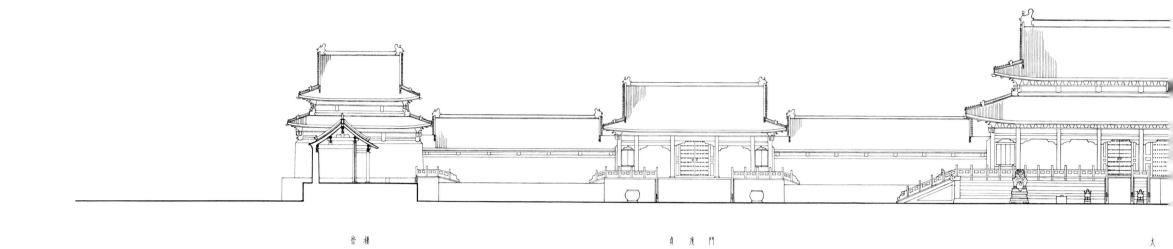

崇楼　　　　　　　　　　　　　　　　　貞度門　　　　　　　　　　　　　　　　　　　大

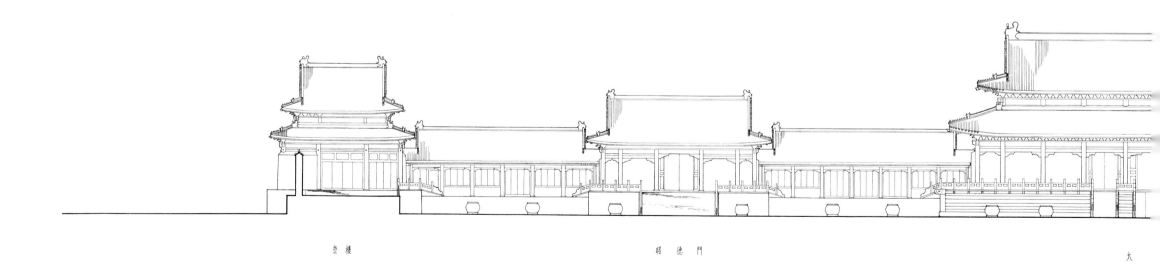

崇楼　　　　　　　　　　　　　　　　　昭德門　　　　　　　　　　　　　　　　　　　大

0　　5　　10　　15　　20　　25　　30m

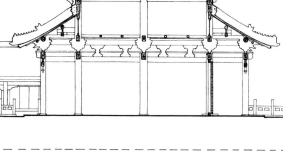

太和門

太和门广场总侧立面图
Side Elevation of the Plaza in Front of the Gate of Supreme Harmony

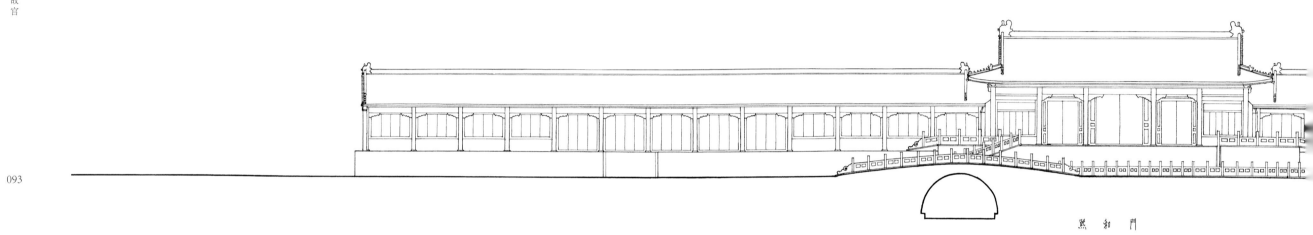

熙 和 門

0 1 2 3 4 5　　10　　15　　20　　25　　30m

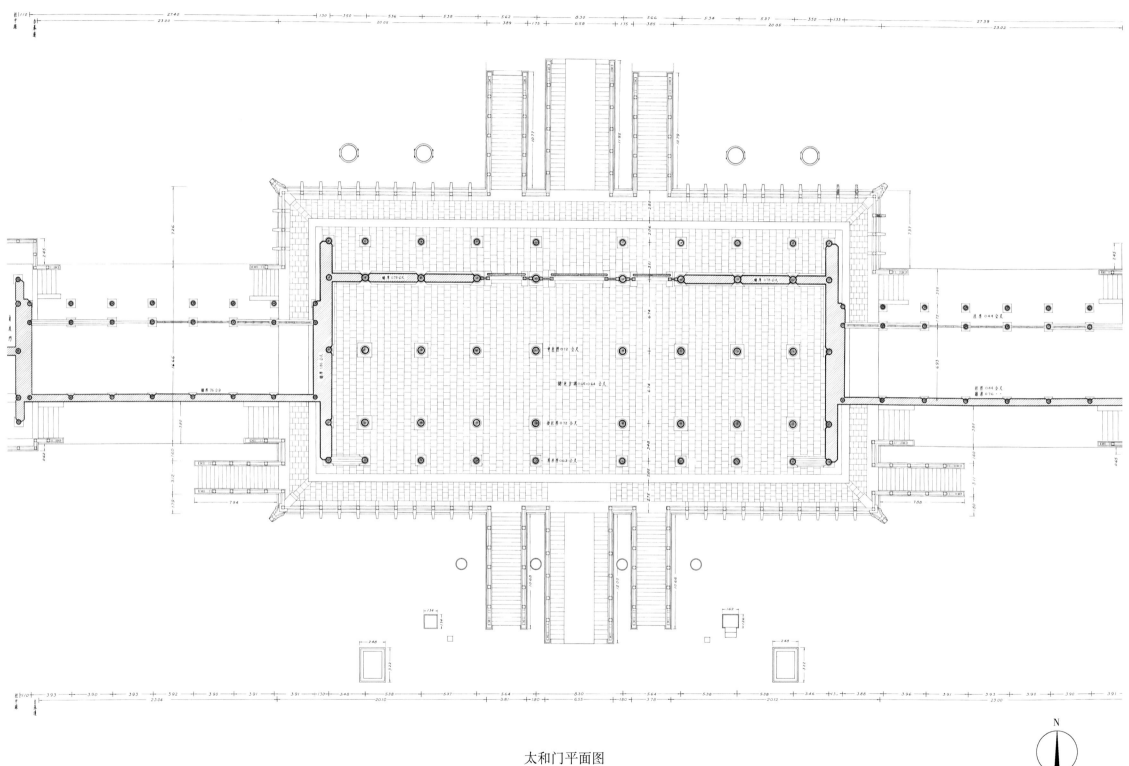

太和门平面图

Floor Plan of the Gate of Supreme Harmony

0　5　10　15m

N

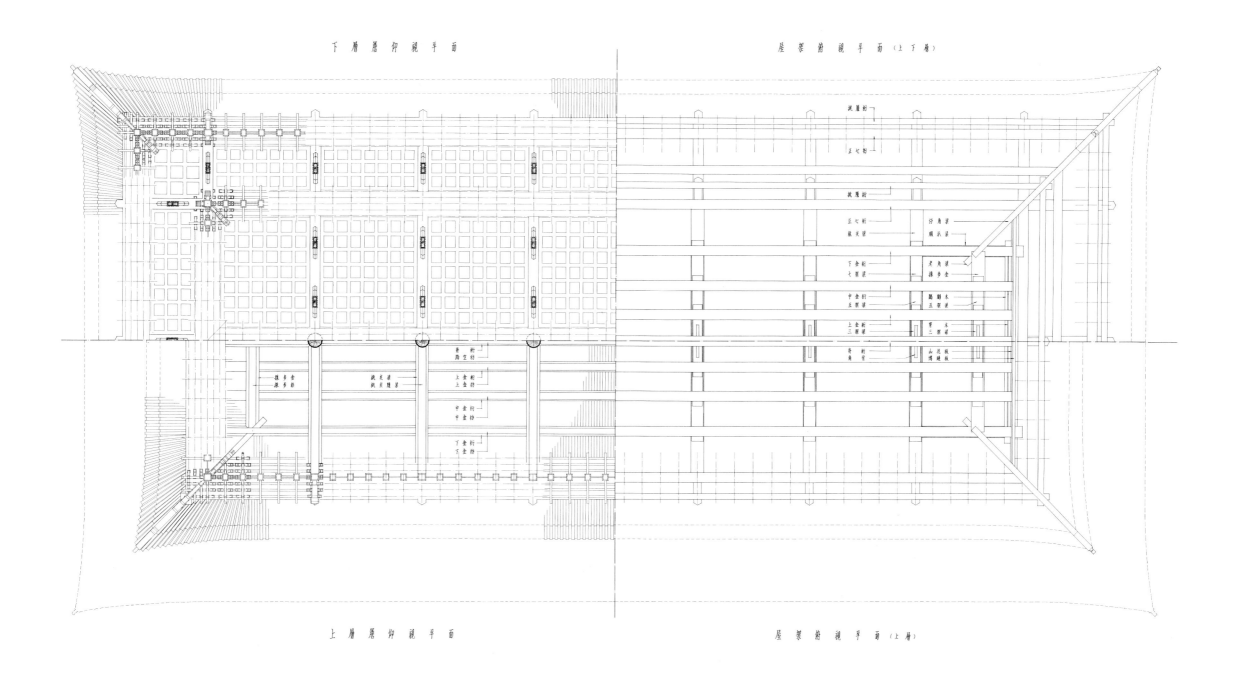

下 层 藻 卯 视 平 面

屋 架 俯 视 平 面 （上 下 层）

上 层 藻 卯 视 平 面

屋 架 俯 视 平 面 （上 层）

太和门天花屋架平面图
Bottom View of the Ceiling Panels and Top View of the Trusses, Gate of Supreme Harmony

0 1 2 3 4 5　　　　　10m

正吻　肆樣黄色琉璃
正脊　叁樣黄色琉璃

垂脊　叁樣黄色琉璃

筒瓦　肆樣黄色琉璃　上下層相同
斗栱　上層单翘重昂七踩　下層单翘单昂五踩
斗口　玖公分　　　　　上下層相同
彩画　扣豆影彩画　　　上下層相同

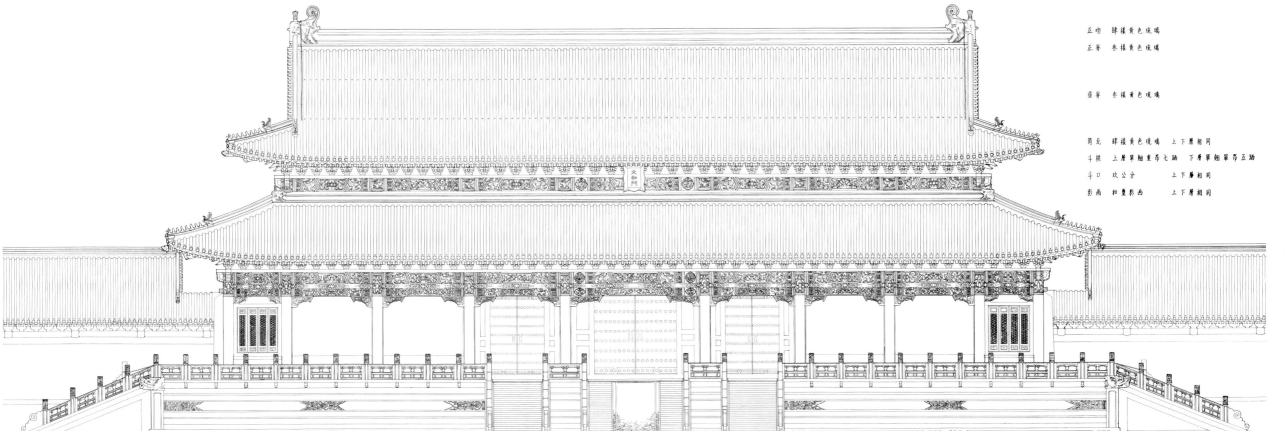

太和门正立面图
Front Elevation of the Gate of Supreme Harmony

0 1 2 3 4 5 6 7 8 9 10m

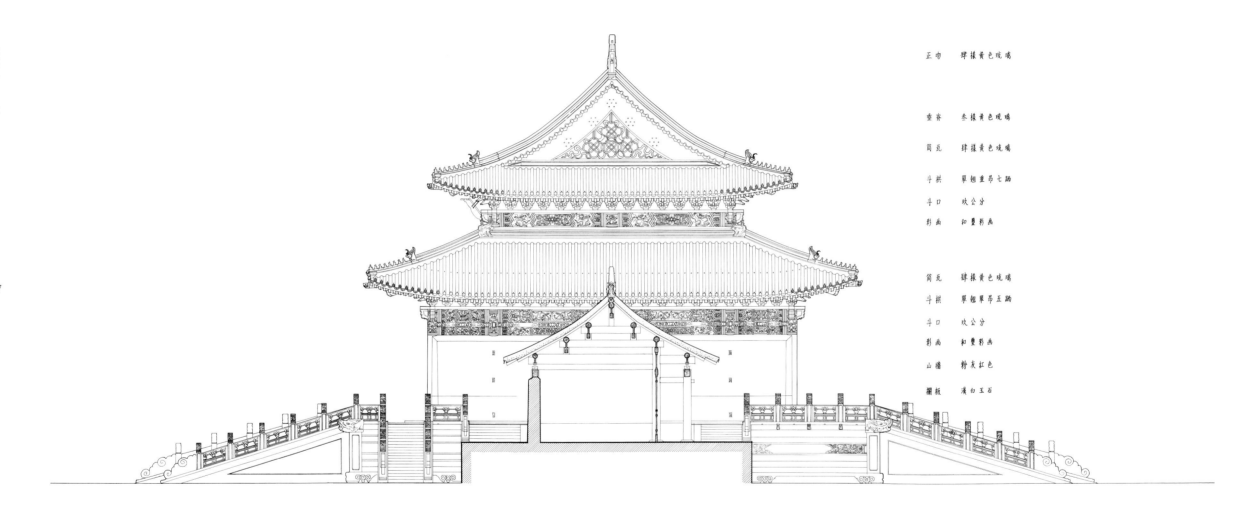

正吻　肆樣黄色琉璃

垂脊　叁樣黄色琉璃

筒瓦　肆樣黄色琉璃

斗拱　單翘重昂七踩

斗口　玖公分

彩画　和璽彩画

筒瓦　肆樣黄色琉璃

斗拱　單翘單昂五踩

斗口　玖公分

彩画　和璽彩画

山墙　粉炭红色

栏板　汉白玉石

0 1 2 3 4 5 6 7 8 9 10m

太和门侧立面图
Side Elevation of the Gate of Supreme Harmony

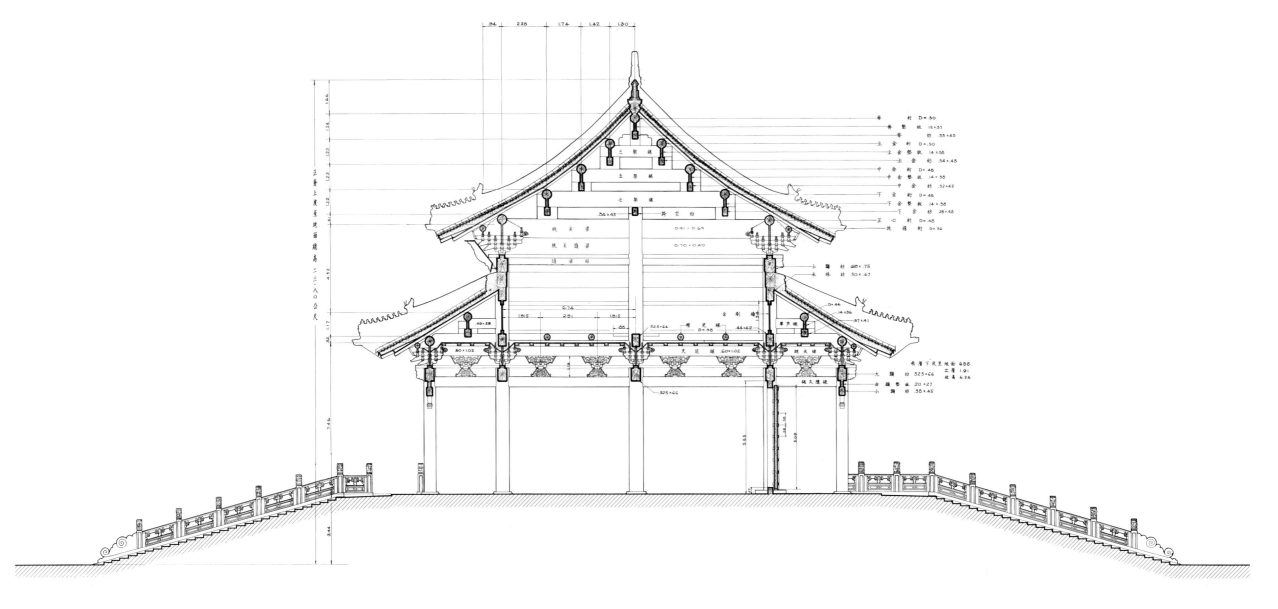

太和门横剖面图

Cross Section of the Gate of Supreme Harmony

0 1 2 3 4 5　　　　10m

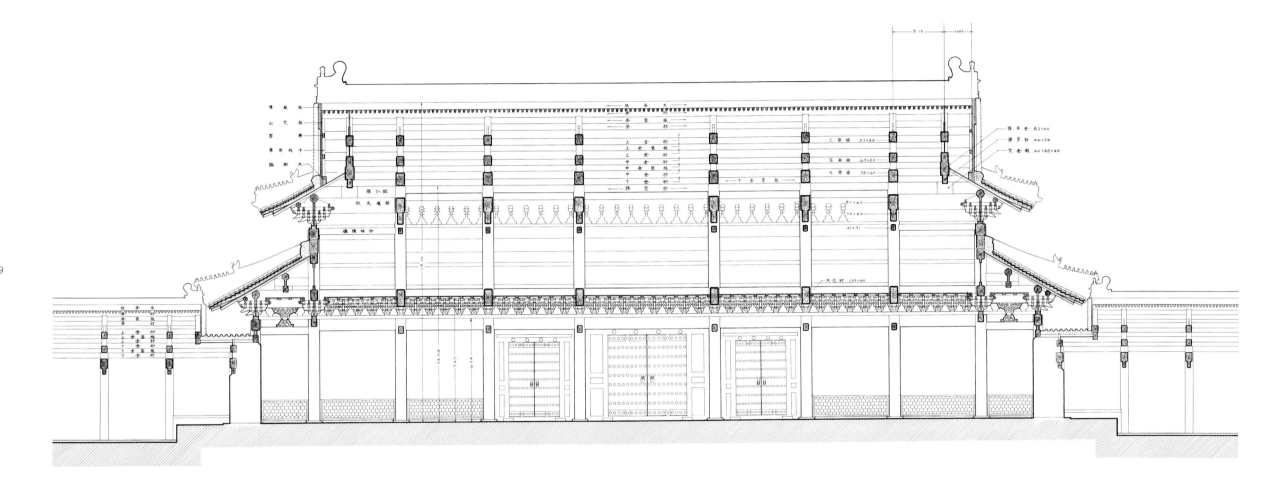

太和门纵剖面图
Longitudinal Section of the Gate of Supreme Harmony

0 1 2 3 4 5   10m

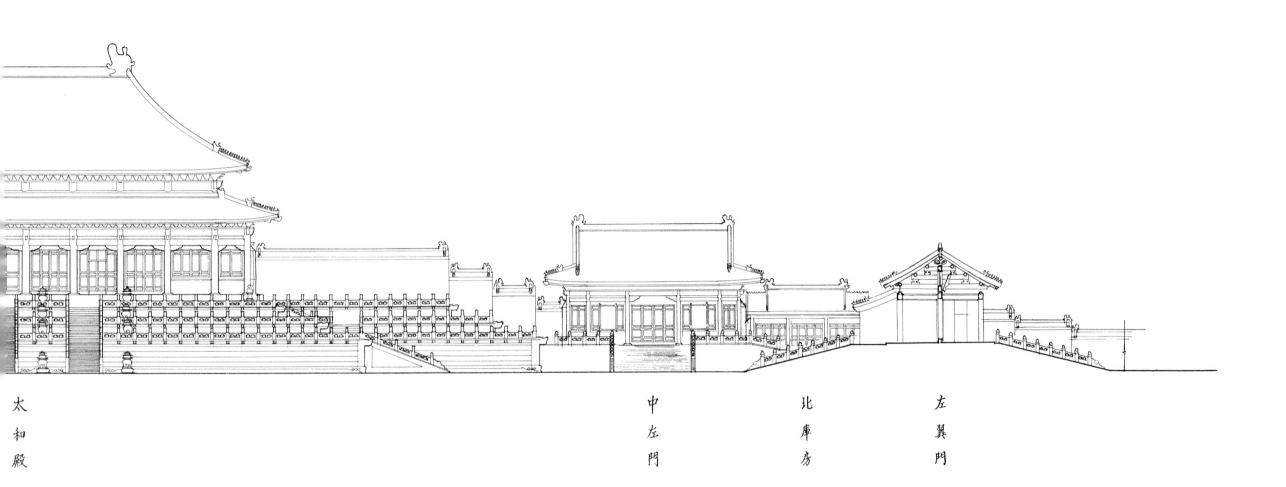

太和殿

中左门

北库房

左翼门

三大殿总正立面图
Overall Elevation of the Three Main Halls

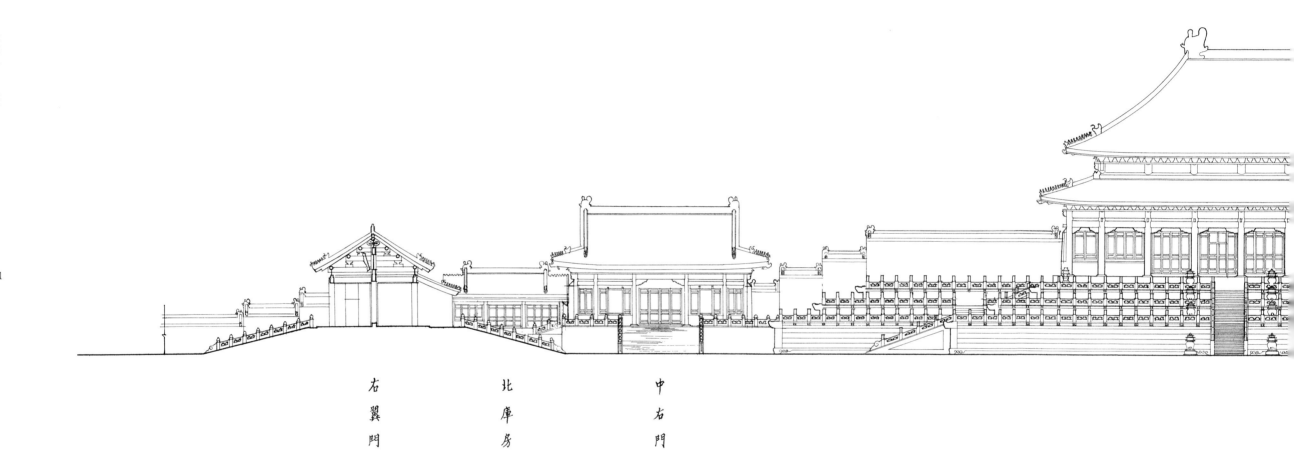

右
翼
門

北
庫
房

中
右
門

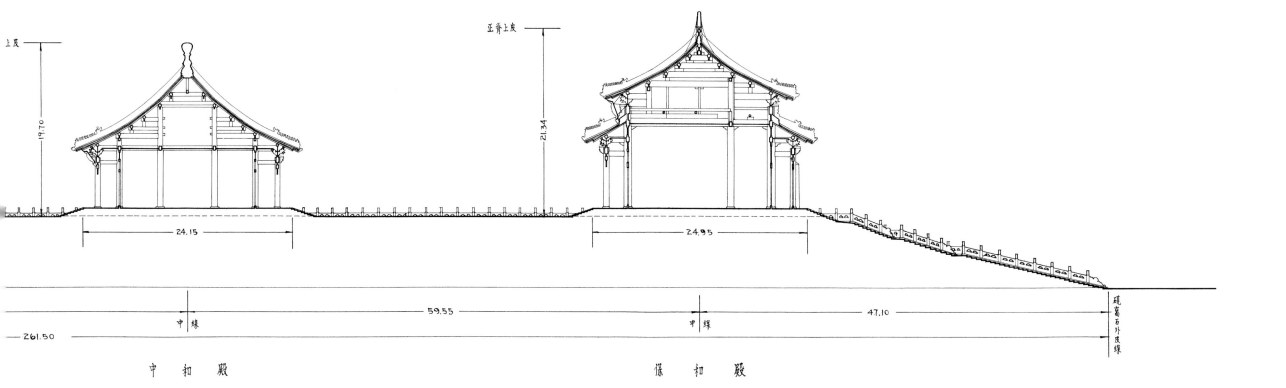

上皮

19.70

正脊上皮

21.34

24.15

24.95

中线

中线

59.55

47.10

碳墁石外皮线

261.50

中和殿

保和殿

三大殿总横剖面图
Overall Cross Section of the Three Main Halls

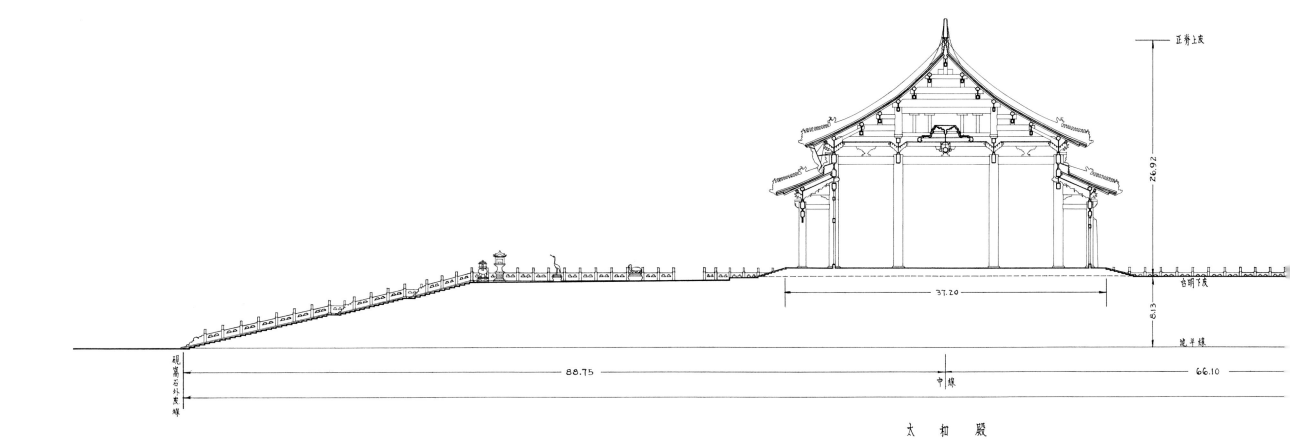

26.92

古明下皮

8.13

施平線

37.20

砚窝石外皮線

88.75

中線

66.10

太 和 殿

0 1 2 3 4 5　　10　　15　　20　　25　　30m

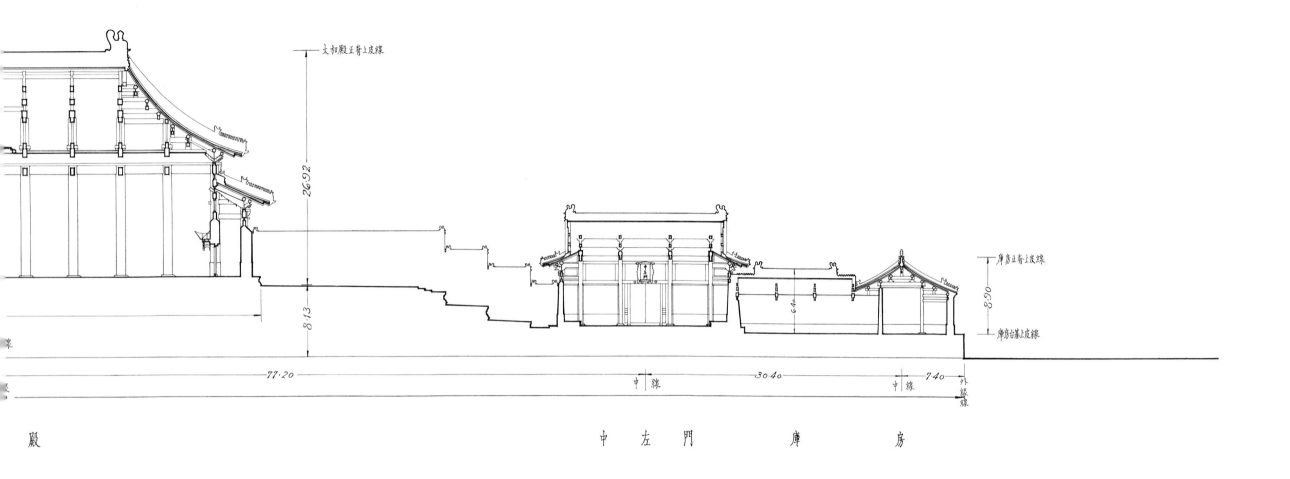

太和殿正脊上皮線

2692

8·13

廊房正脊上皮線

8·90

廊房台基上皮線

6·40

77·20

中線

30·40

中線

7·40

外線線

殿　　　　　　　　　　中　左　門　廊　房

三大殿总纵剖面图
Overall Longitudinal Section of the Three Main Halls

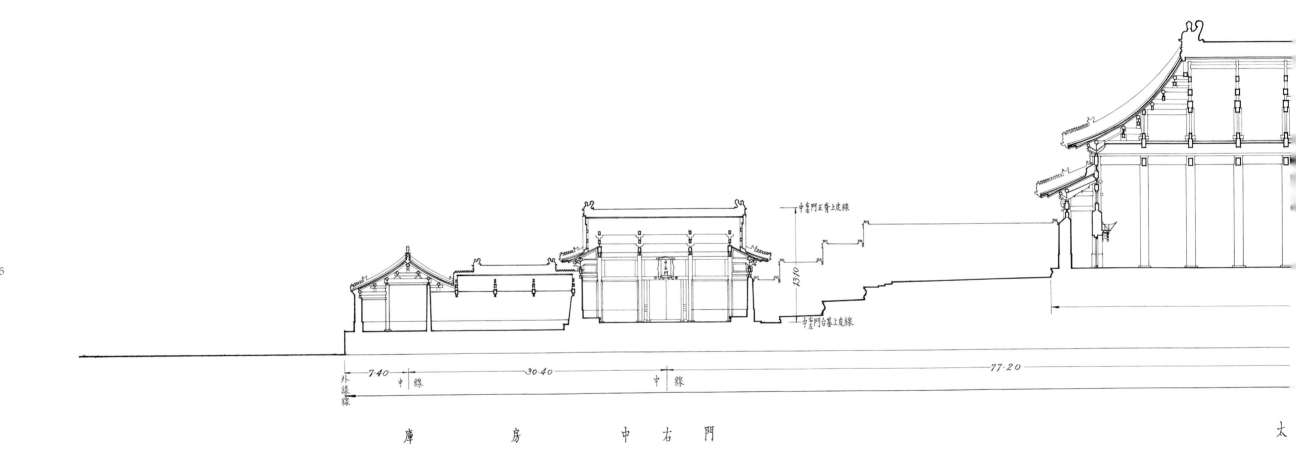

中室門正脊上皮綫

中室門台基上皮綫

1310

7·40 中綫

30·40 中綫

77·20

外緣綫

庫　　房　　中　右　門　　　　　　　　　　　　　　　　　　　　　　　　　太

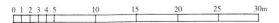

0 1 2 3 4 5　　10　　15　　20　　25　　30m

三大殿总平面图
Overall Layout of the Three Main Halls

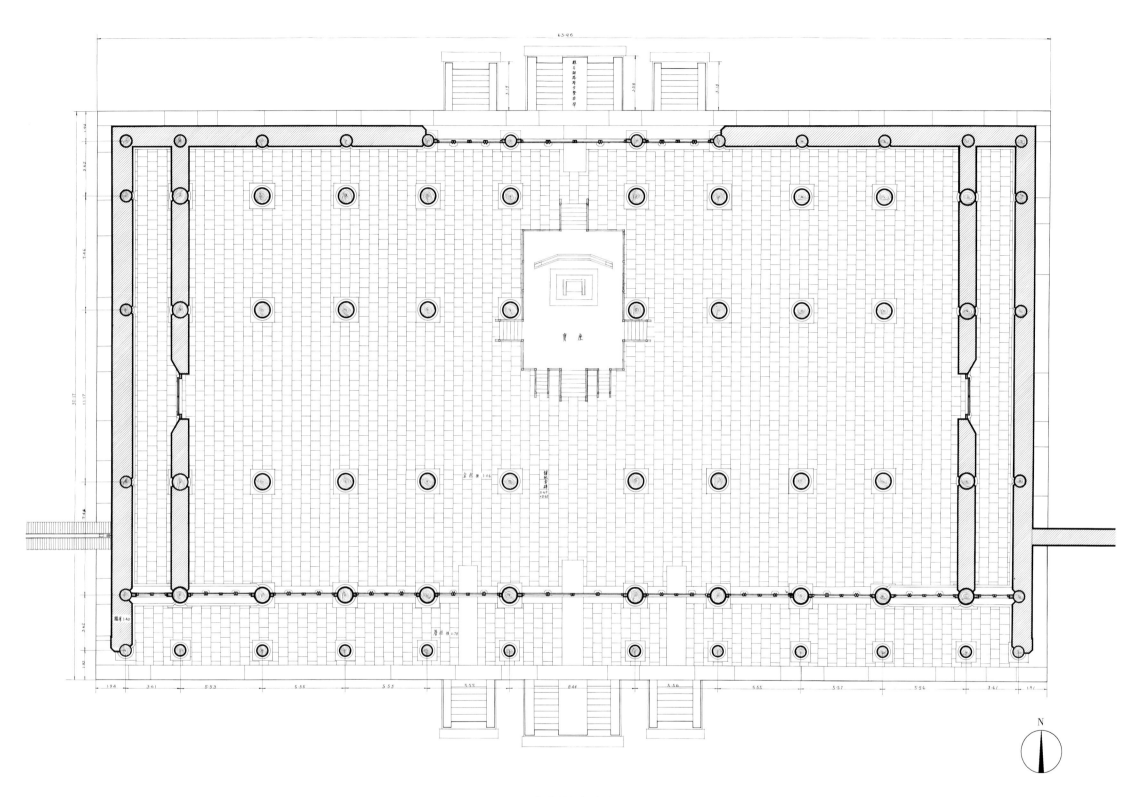

太和殿平面图
Floor Plan of the Hall of Supreme Harmony

N

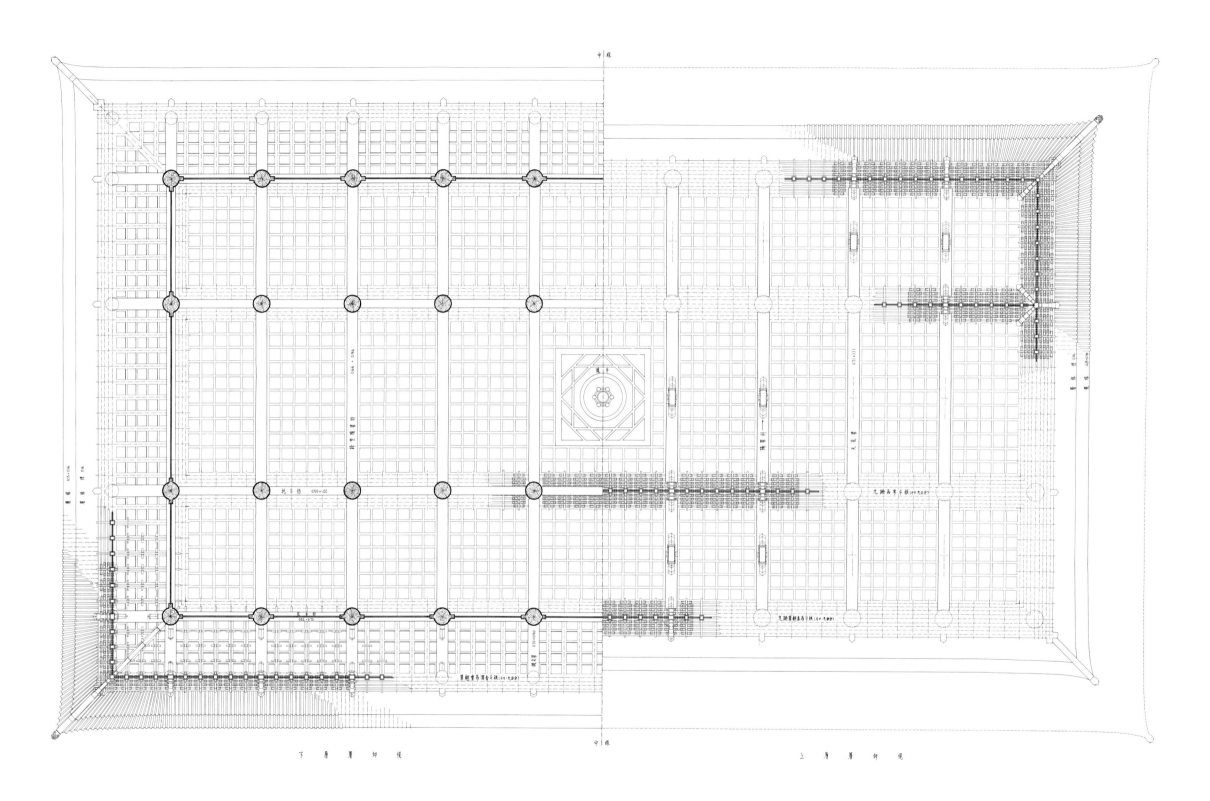

太和殿天花平面图
Bottom View of the Ceiling Panels, Hall of Supreme Harmony

0 1 2 3 4 5 6 7 8 9 10m

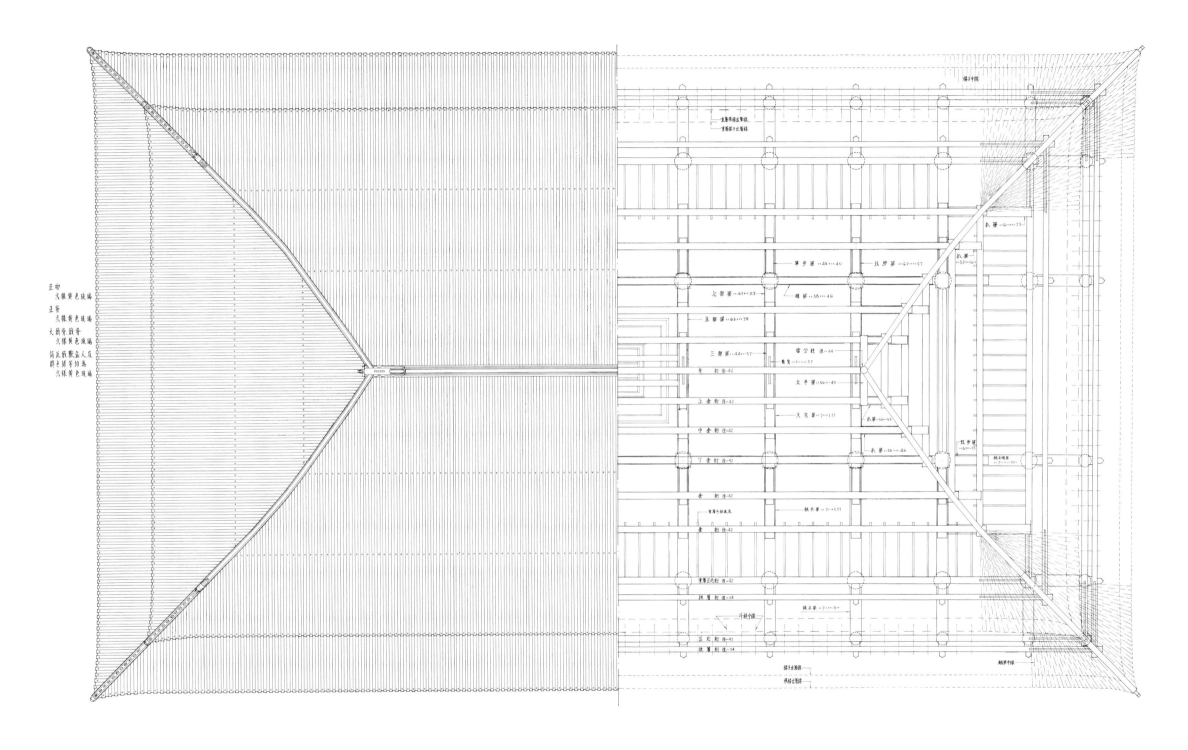

太和殿屋顶屋架平面图
Top Views of the Roof and Trusses, Hall of Supreme Harmony

0 1 2 3 4 5   10m

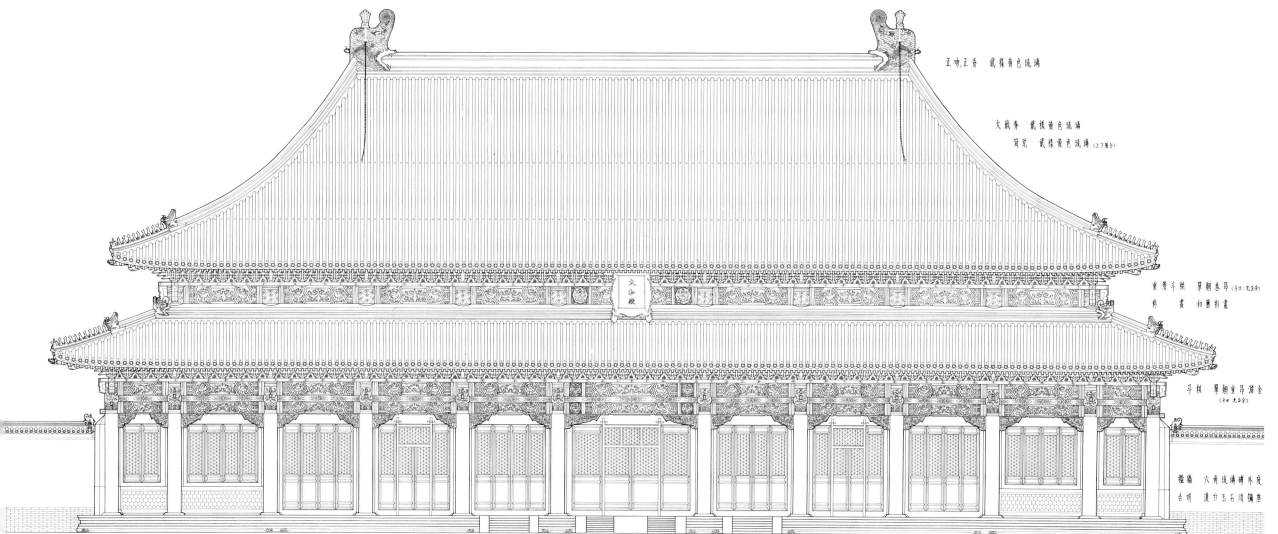

正吻,正脊 貳樣黄色琉璃

大瓦筒 貳樣黄色琉璃
筒瓦 貳樣黄色琉璃(上丁層合)

重昂斗栱 單翹重昂(斗口:九金分)
彩畫 和璽彩畫

斗栱 單翹重昂鎏金
(斗口:九金分)

檻牆 六角玻璃磚外皮
台明 漢白玉石須彌座

太和殿正立面图

Front Elevation of the Hall of Supreme Harmony

0 1 2 3 4 5   10m

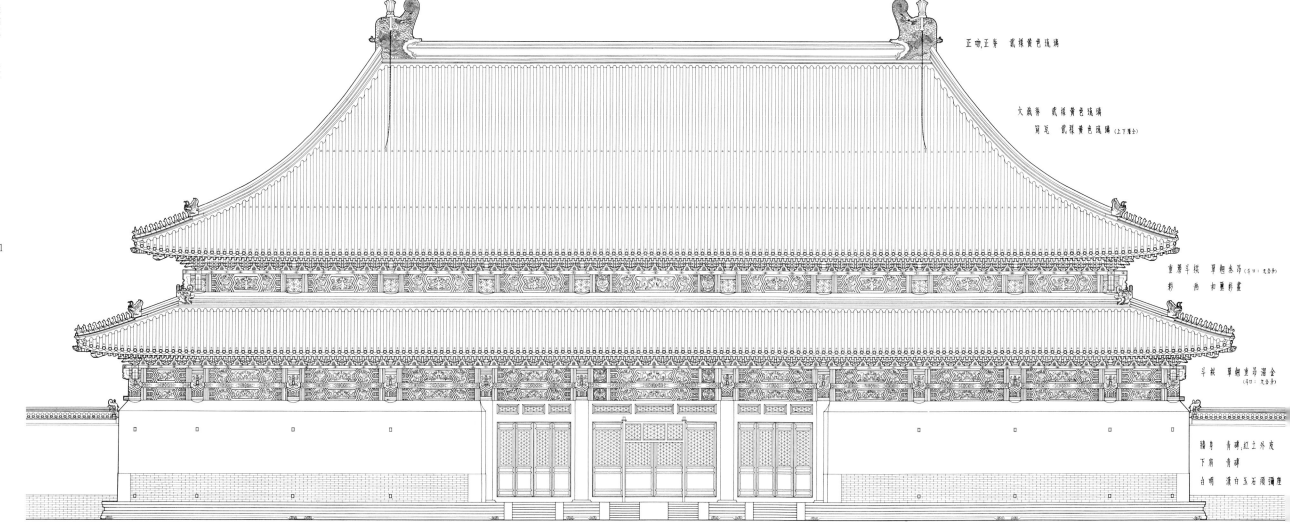

正吻正脊　贰样黄色琉璃

大戗脊　贰样黄色琉璃
筒瓦　贰样黄色琉璃（上下层全）

重檐斗栱　单翘叁昂（斗口：九公分）
彩　画　和玺彩画

斗栱　单翘重昂溜金
（斗口：九公分）

墙身　青砖,红土刷皮
下肩　青砖
白明　汉白玉须弥座

太和殿背立面图
Back Elevation of the Hall of Supreme Harmony

0 1 2 3 4 5　　　10m

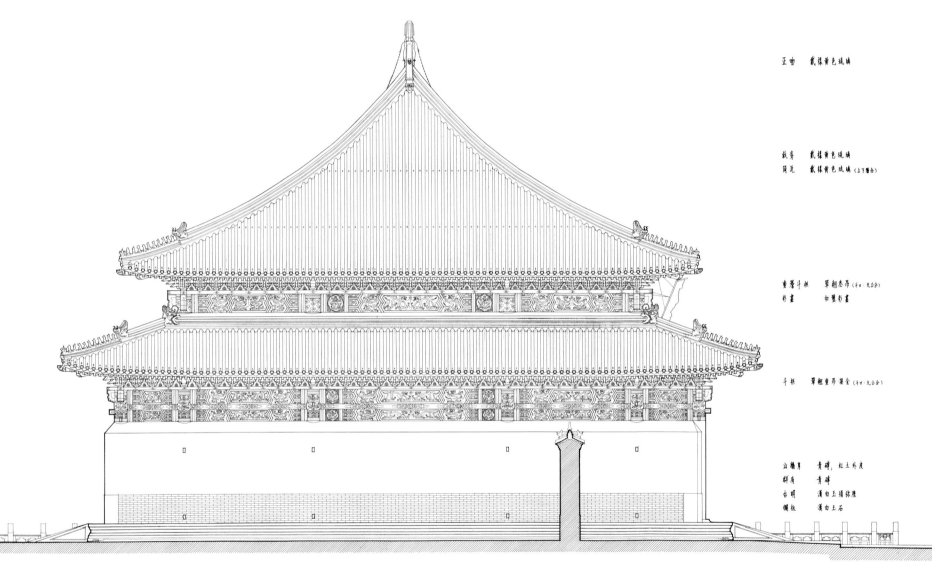

正吻　　载揲黄色琉璃

鸱兽　　载揲黄色琉璃
仙冠　　载揲黄色琉璃（工丁醬金）

重檐斗栱　　翠翘泰草（和口·九合金）
彩画　　如意彩画

平板　　翠翘重草潭金（和口·九合金）

山墙身　　青砖，红土外皮
群肩　　青砖
台明　　汉白玉猪张座
栏板　　汉白玉石

0　1　2　3　4　5　　　　　10m

太和殿侧立面图
Side Elevation of the Hall of Supreme Harmony

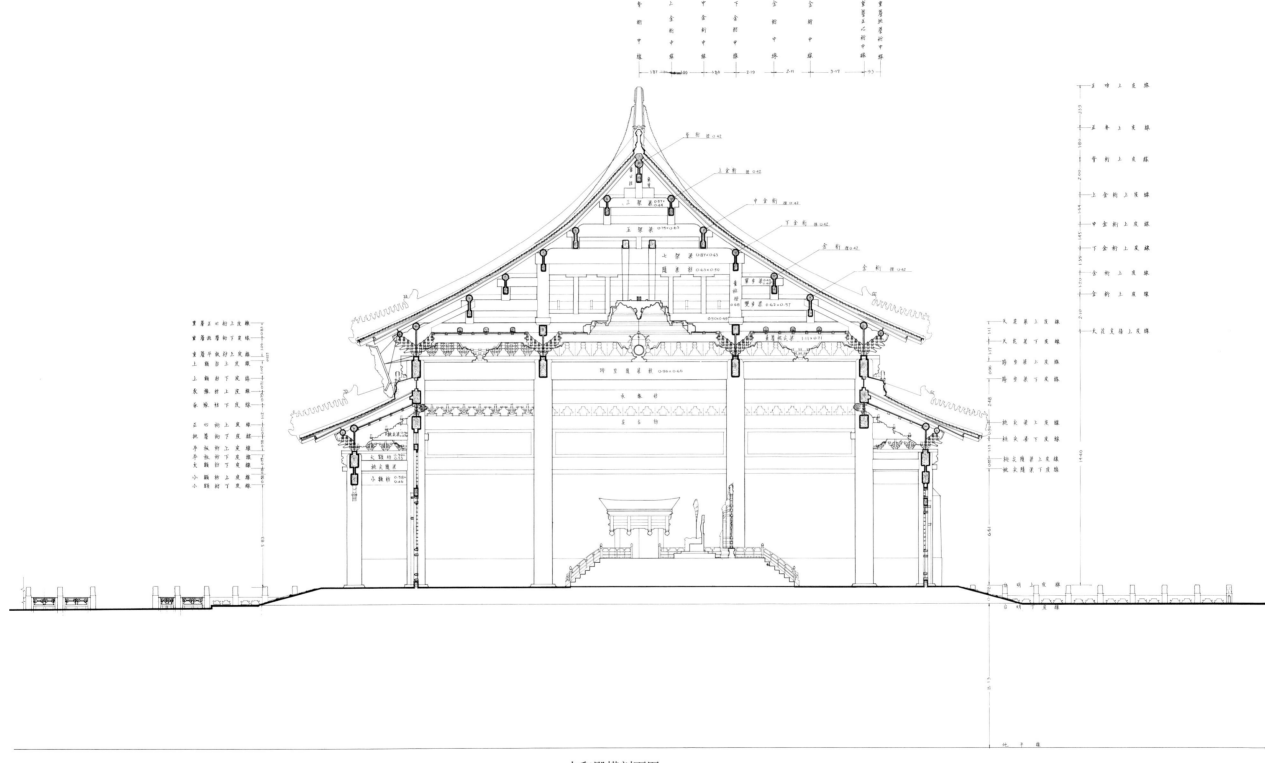

太和殿横剖面图
Cross Section of the Hall of Supreme Harmony

0 1 2 5 10m

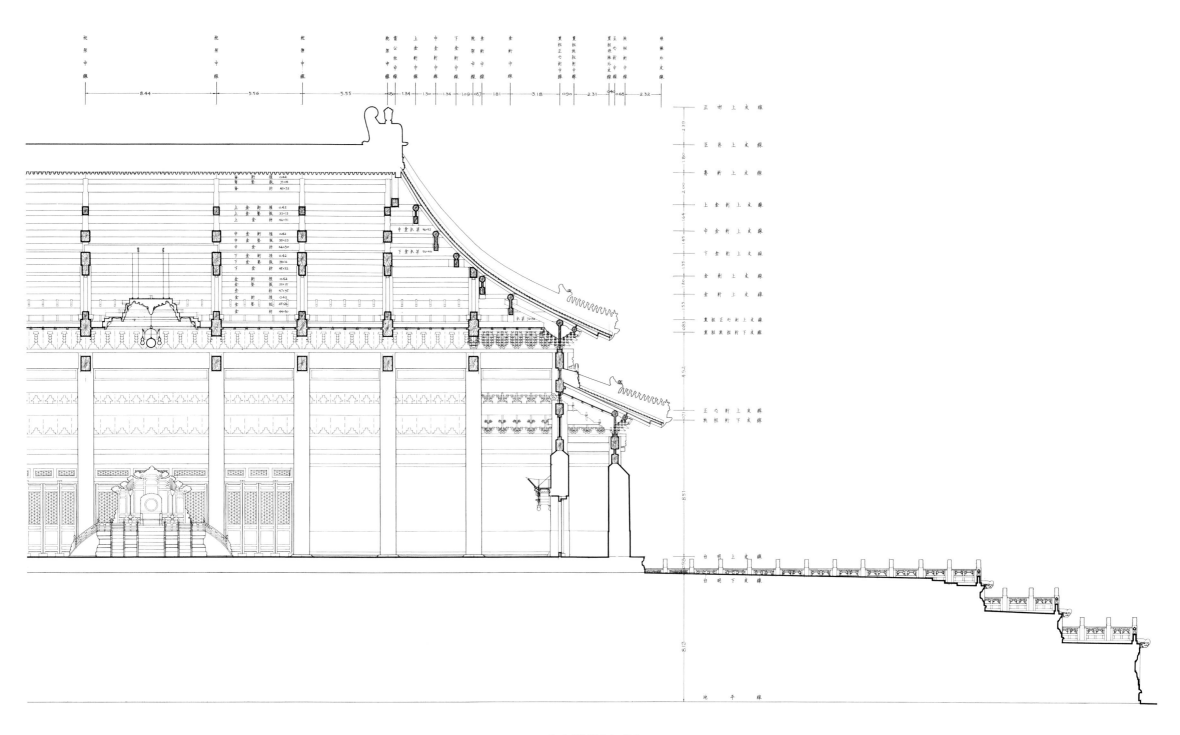

太和殿纵剖面图
Longitudinal Section of the Hall of Supreme Harmony

0 1 2 5 10m

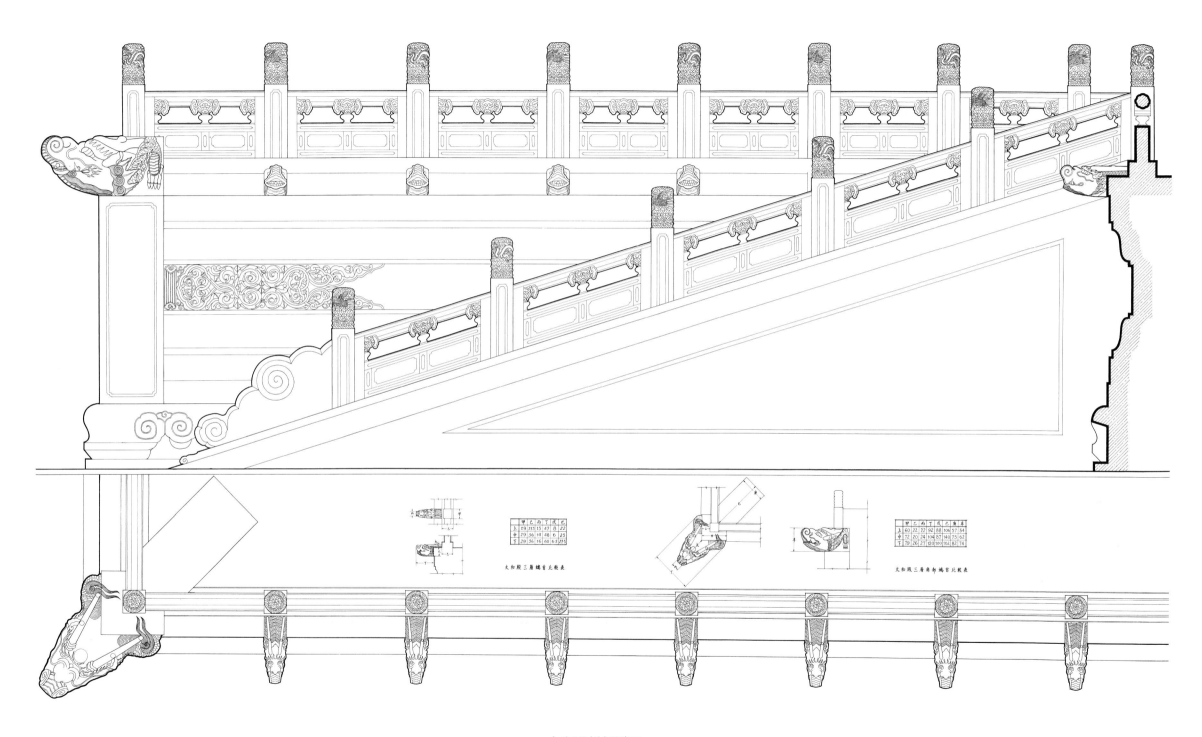

太和殿栏板详图
Detailed Drawing of Balustrades, Hall of Supreme Harmony

0   0.5   1   1.5m

盒子: 绘绿地片金坐龙

圭线光子内: 绘绿地片金灵芝纹

找头: 绘青地片金升龙

枋心: 绘绿地片金行龙

桃尖梁头: 绿地片金西蕃莲

2325

150 135　　770　　140　340　　940　　1290

245

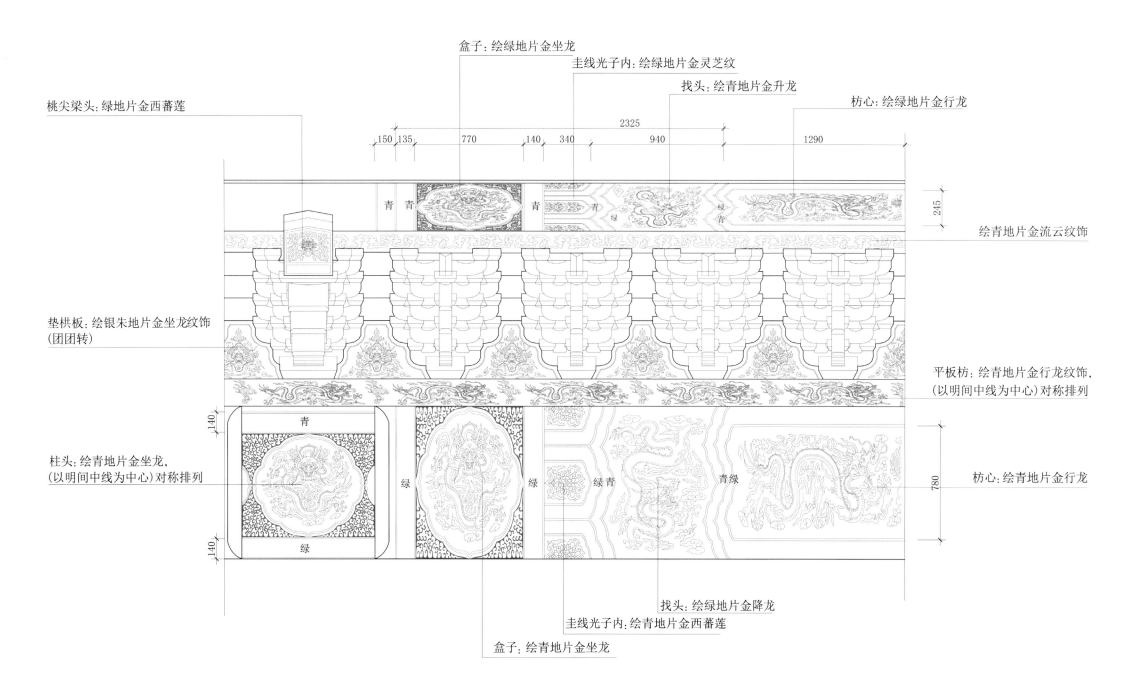

绘青地片金流云纹饰

垫栱板: 绘银朱地片金坐龙纹饰
(团团转)

平板枋: 绘青地片金行龙纹饰,
(以明间中线为中心)对称排列

140

柱头: 绘青地片金坐龙,
(以明间中线为中心)对称排列

780

枋心: 绘青地片金行龙

140

找头: 绘绿地片金降龙

圭线光子内: 绘青地片金西蕃莲

盒子: 绘青地片金坐龙

太和殿上檐明间前外檐彩画现状图
Present Condition of the Colored Painting of the Front Elevation's Central Bay under the Upper Eave, Hall of Supreme Harmony

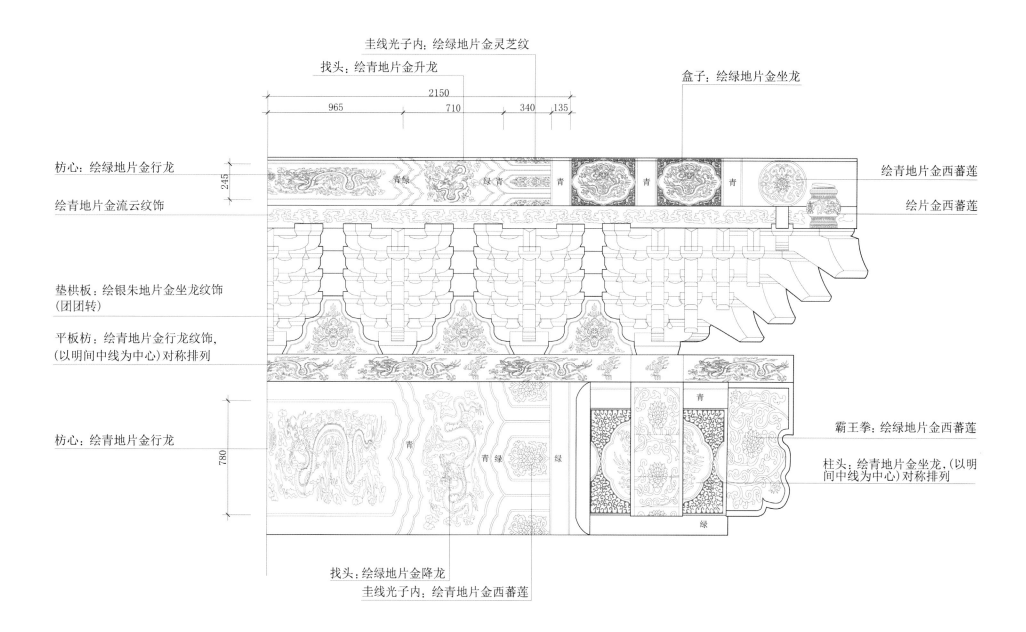

圭线光子内：绘绿地片金灵芝纹

找头：绘青地片金升龙

盒子：绘绿地片金坐龙

枋心：绘绿地片金行龙

绘青地片金流云纹饰

绘青地片金西蕃莲

绘片金西蕃莲

2150

965　　710　　340　135

245

青绿　　绿青　　青　　青　　青

垫栱板：绘银朱地片金坐龙纹饰
（团团转）

平板枋：绘青地片金行龙纹饰，
（以明间中线为中心）对称排列

枋心：绘青地片金行龙

780

青　　青绿　　绿

青

霸王拳：绘绿地片金西蕃莲

柱头：绘青地片金坐龙,（以明间中线为中心）对称排列

绿

找头：绘绿地片金降龙

圭线光子内：绘青地片金西蕃莲

太和殿上檐东梢间前外檐彩画现状图

Present Condition of the Colored Painting of the Front Elevation's Eastmost Bay under the Upper Eave, Hall of Supreme Harmony

桃尖梁头：绿地片金西蕃莲

盒子：绘绿地片金坐龙

圭线光子内：绘绿地片金灵芝纹

找头：绘青地片金升降龙

枋心：绘绿地片金行龙

3440

135　135　　770　　140　400　　　　1995　　　　　　1690

245

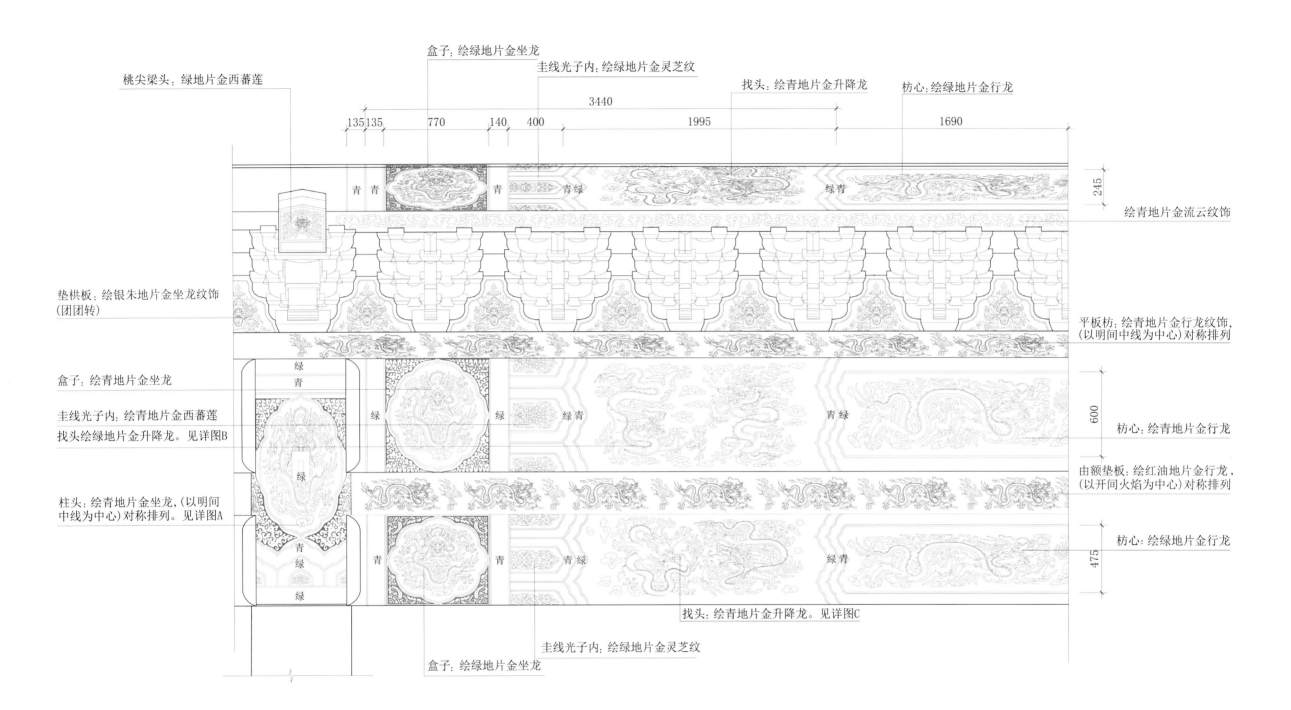

绘青地片金流云纹饰

垫栱板：绘银朱地片金坐龙纹饰
（团团转）

平板枋：绘青地片金行龙纹饰，
（以明间中线为中心）对称排列

盒子：绘青地片金坐龙

圭线光子内：绘青地片金西蕃莲
找头绘绿地片金升降龙。见详图B

600

枋心：绘青地片金行龙

由额垫板：绘红油地片金行龙，
（以开间火焰为中心）对称排列

柱头：绘青地片金坐龙，（以明间
中线为中心）对称排列。见详图A

475

枋心：绘绿地片金行龙

找头：绘青地片金升降龙。见详图C

圭线光子内：绘绿地片金灵芝纹

盒子：绘绿地片金坐龙

太和殿下檐东山面明间外檐彩画现状图
Present Condition of the Colored Painting, the East Elevation's Central Bay under the Lower Eave, Hall of Supreme Harmony

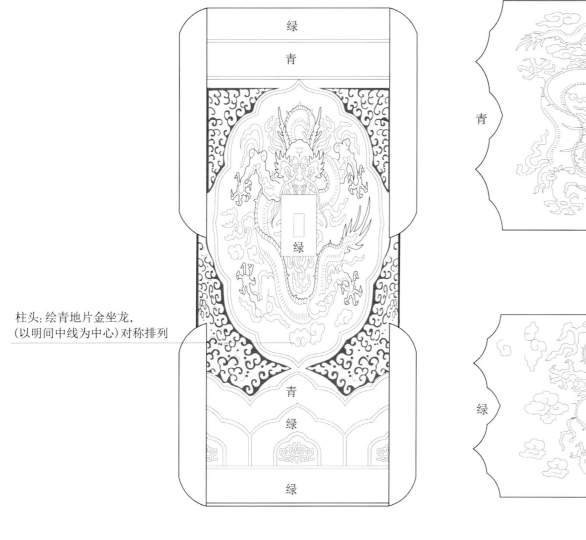

柱头: 绘青地片金坐龙,
(以明间中线为中心)对称排列

详图 A

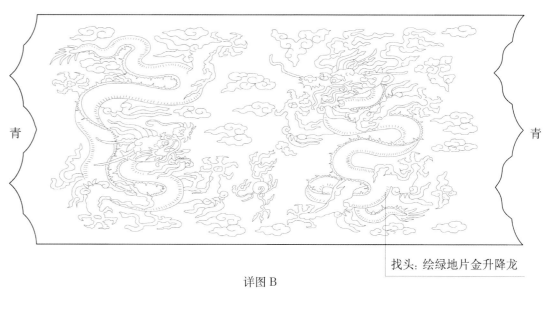

找头: 绘绿地片金升降龙

详图 B

找头: 绘青地片金升降龙

详图 C

太和殿下檐东山面明间外檐彩画现状图详图
Detailed Drawing of Present Condition of the Colored Painting, the East Elevation's Central Bay under the Lower Eave, Hall of Supreme Harmony

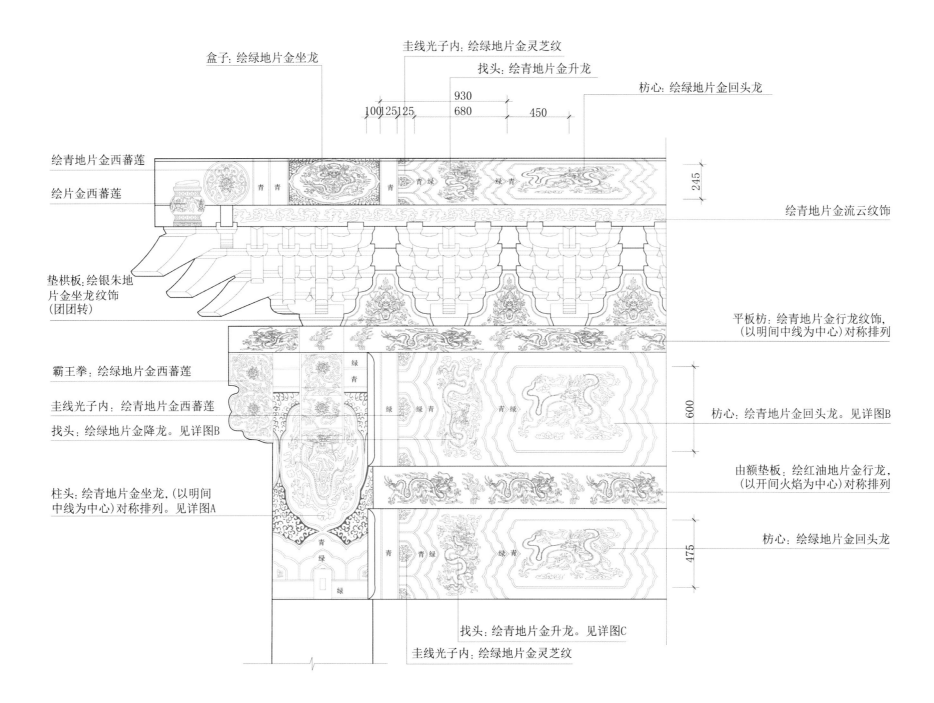

盒子：绘绿地片金坐龙

圭线光子内：绘绿地片金灵芝纹

找头：绘青地片金升龙

枋心：绘绿地片金回头龙

绘青地片金西蕃莲

绘片金西蕃莲

绘青地片金流云纹饰

垫栱板：绘银朱地片金坐龙纹饰（团团转）

平板枋：绘青地片金行龙纹饰，（以明间中线为中心）对称排列

霸王拳：绘绿地片金西蕃莲

圭线光子内：绘青地片金西蕃莲

找头：绘绿地片金降龙。见详图B

枋心：绘青地片金回头龙。见详图B

由额垫板：绘红油地片金行龙，（以开间火焰为中心）对称排列

柱头：绘青地片金坐龙，（以明间中线为中心）对称排列。见详图A

枋心：绘绿地片金回头龙

找头：绘青地片金升龙。见详图C

圭线光子内：绘绿地片金灵芝纹

245

930
680
450

1001 25125

600

475

青 青 青 青绿 绿青 绿青 青绿

绿青

绿青

绿 绿青 青绿

青 青绿 绿青

绿

太和殿下檐东山面南梢间外檐彩画现状图

Present Condition of the Colored Painting, the East Elevation's Southmost Bay under the Lower Eave, Hall of Supreme Harmony

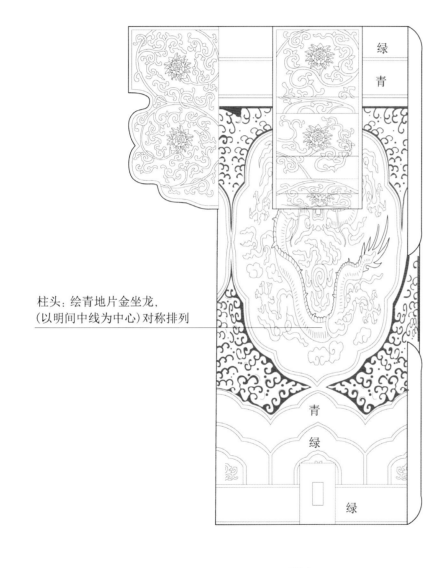

柱头: 绘青地片金坐龙,
(以明间中线为中心) 对称排列

详图 A

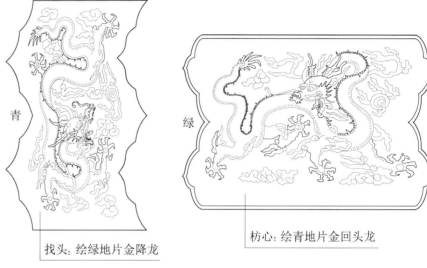

找头: 绘绿地片金降龙

枋心: 绘青地片金回头龙

详图 B

找头: 绘青地片金升龙

详图 C

太和殿下檐东山面南梢间外檐彩画现状图详图
Present Condition of the Colored Painting, the East Elevation's Southmost Bay under the Lower Eave, Hall of Supreme Harmony

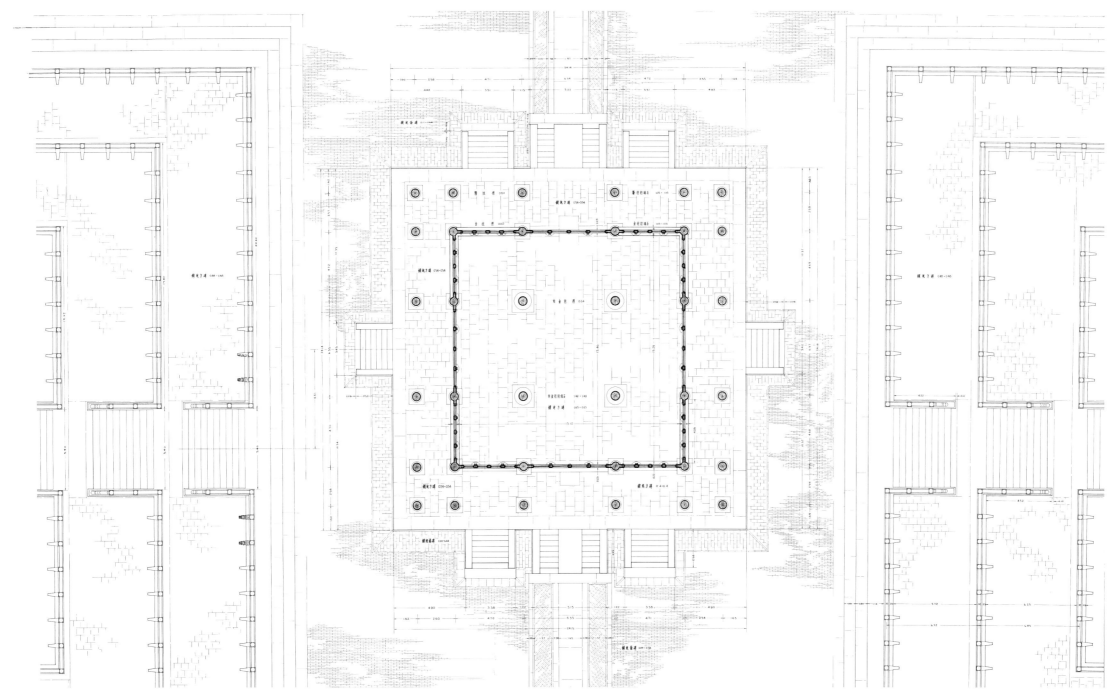

中和殿平面图
Floor Plan of the Hall of Central Harmony

0 1 2   5   10m

N

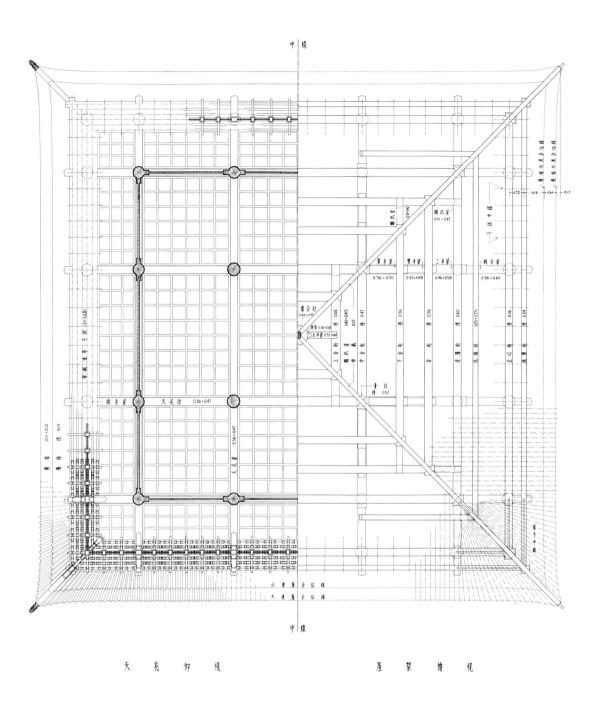

天 花 仰 视　　　　屋 架 俯 视

中和殿天花屋架平面图
Bottom View of the Ceiling Panels and Top View of the Trusses, Hall of Central Harmony

0　1　2　　　5　　　　　　10m

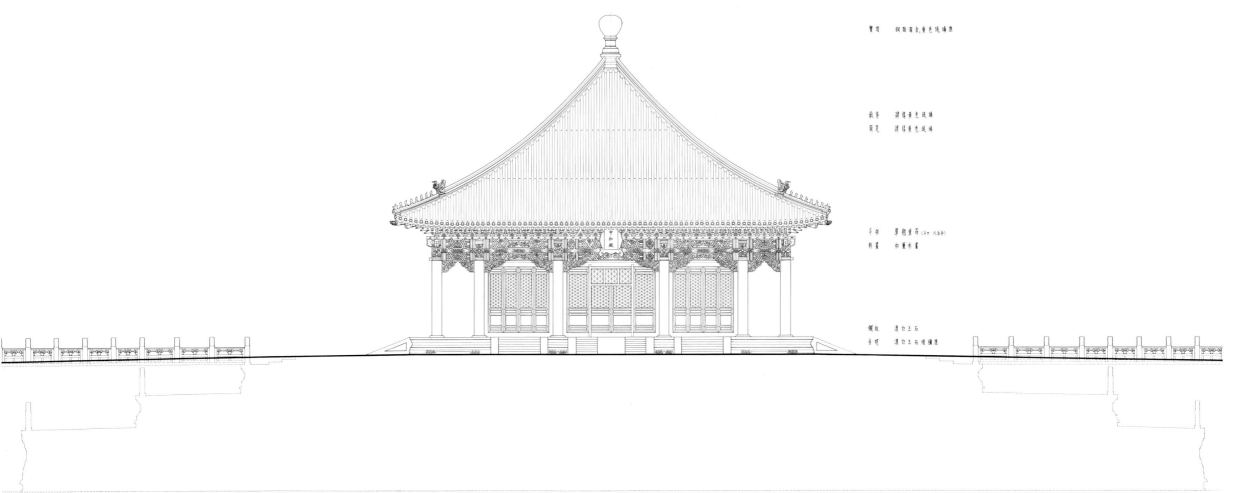

中和殿正立面图
Front Elevation of the Hall of Central Harmony

0 1 2 5 10m

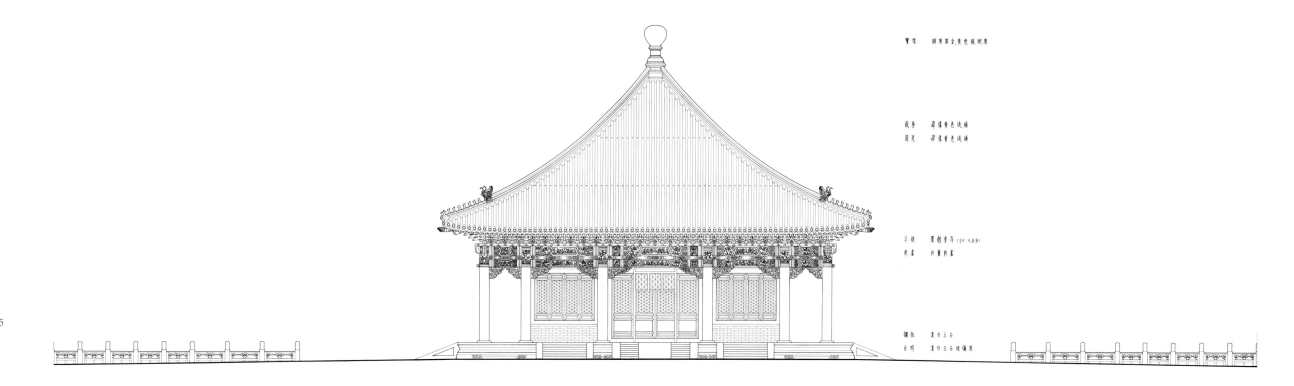

宝顶　铜胎鎏金黄色玻璃构建

戗兽　琉璃黄色玻璃
脊兽　琉璃黄色玻璃

斗栱　双翘重昂（斗口八分金）
彩画　和玺彩画

栏板　汉白玉石
台明　汉白玉石须弥座

0 1 2   5   10m

中和殿背立面图
Back Elevation of the Hall of Central Harmony

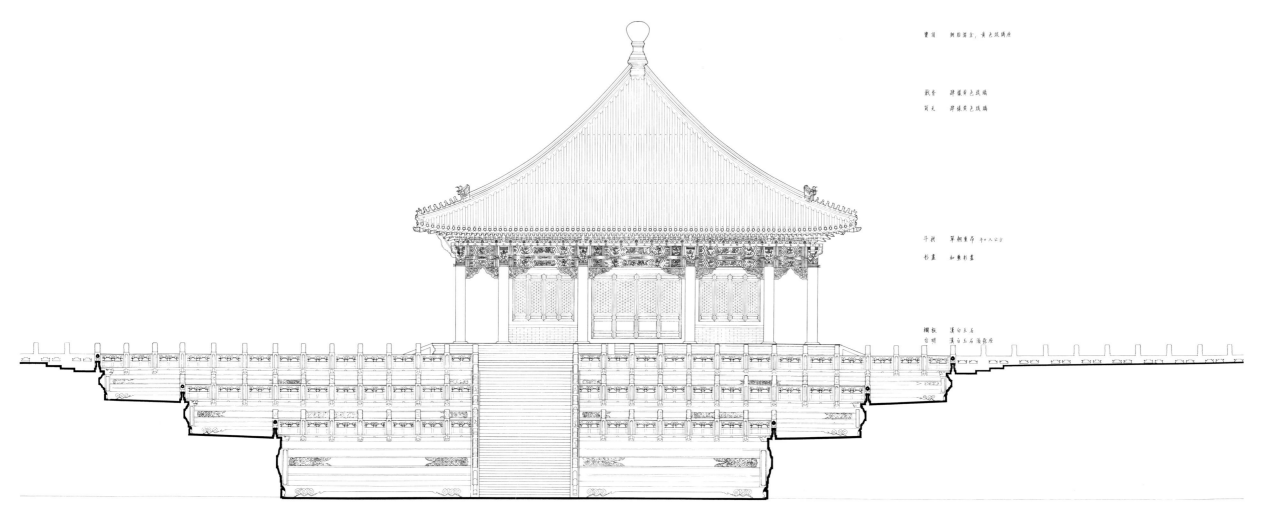

中和殿侧立面图

Side Elevation of the Hall of Central Harmony

0 1 2 5 10m

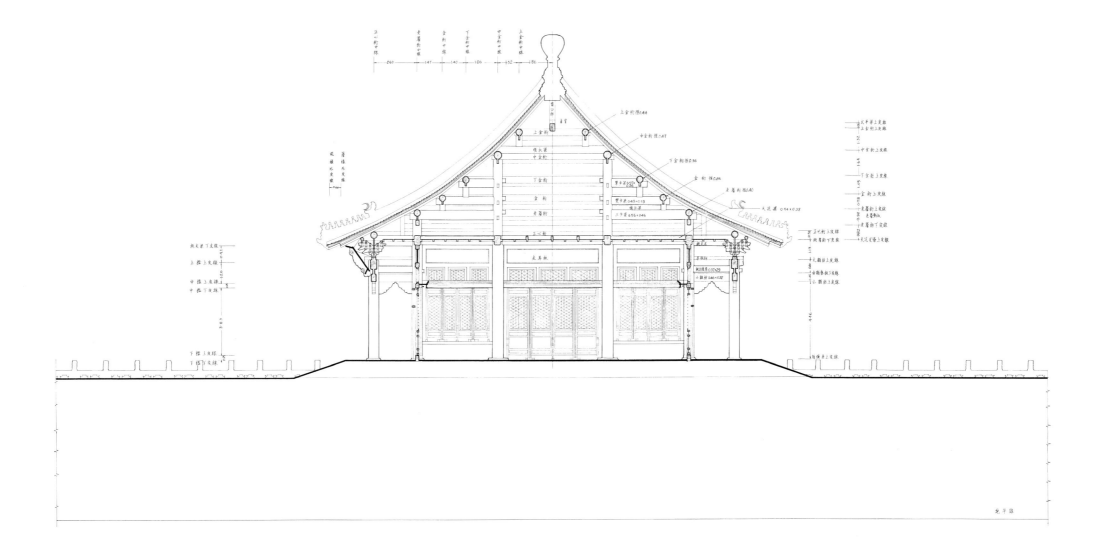

中和殿横剖面图

Cross Section of the Hall of Central Harmony

0 1 2 5 10m

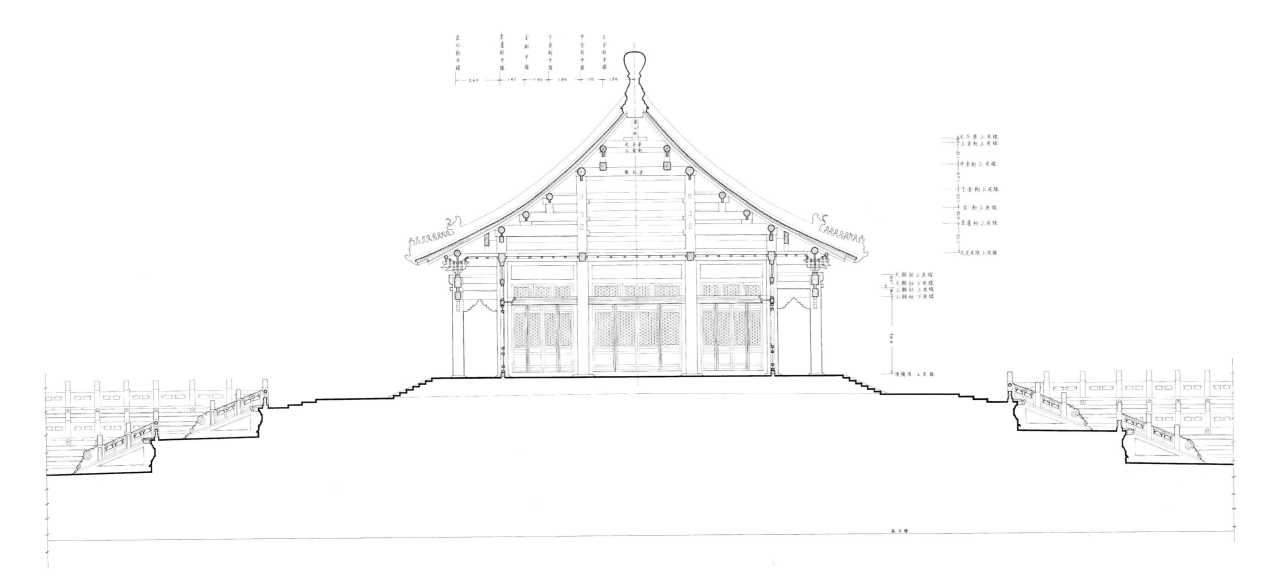

中和殿纵剖面图
Longitudinal Section of the Hall of Central Harmony

0 1 2 5 10m

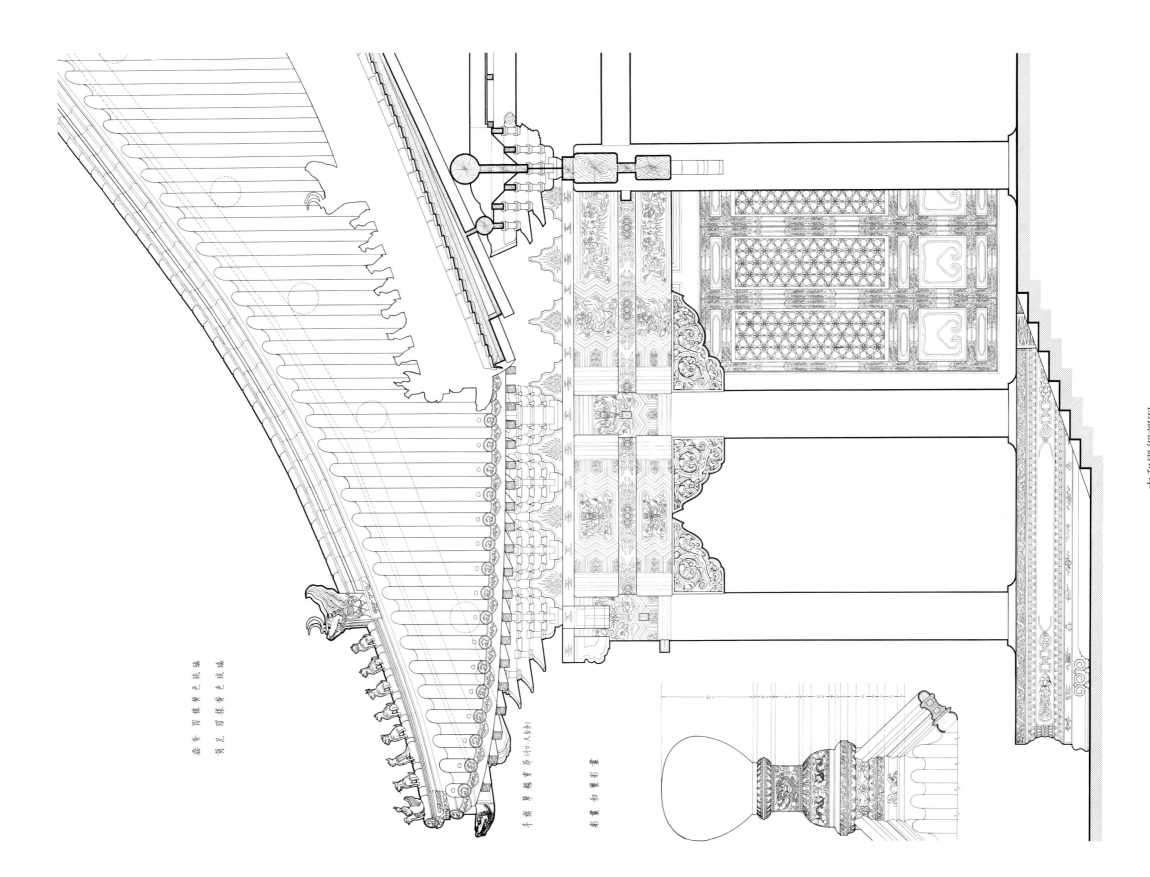

中和殿细部图

Detailed Drawing of the Hall of Central Harmony

0 0.1   0.5   1m

中和殿透视图
Perspective Drawing of the Hall of Central Harmony

保和殿
Hall of Preserving Harmony (*Baohe dian*)

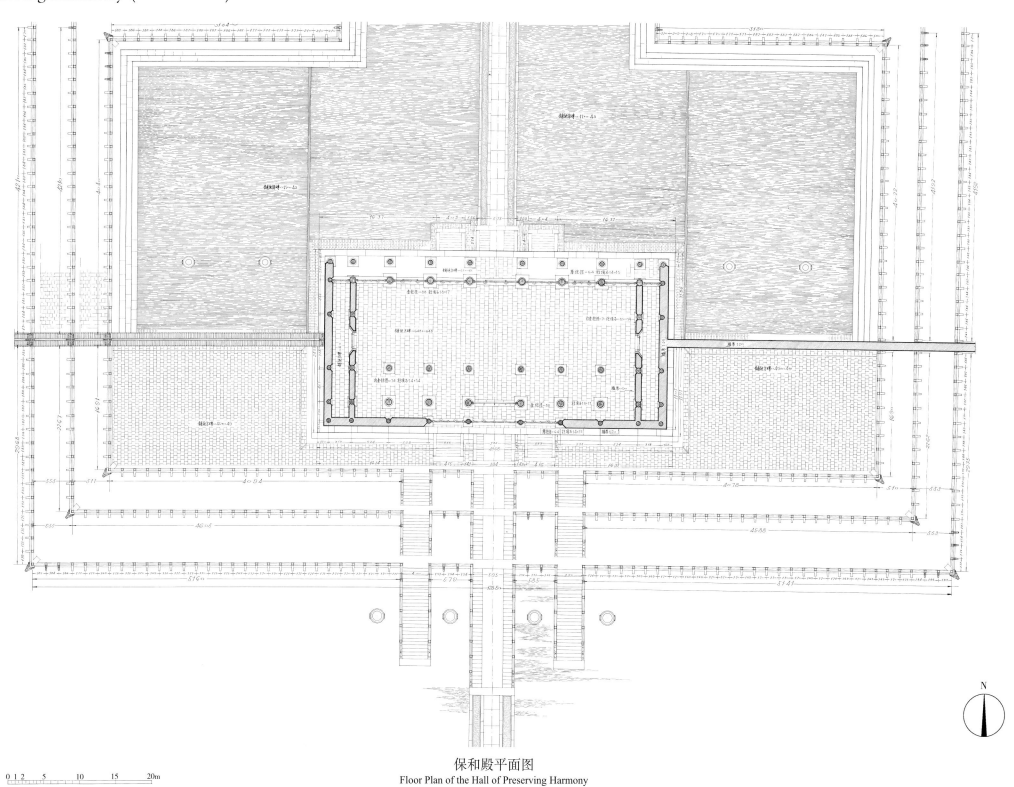

N

保和殿平面图
Floor Plan of the Hall of Preserving Harmony

0 1 2　　5　　　10　　　15　　　20m

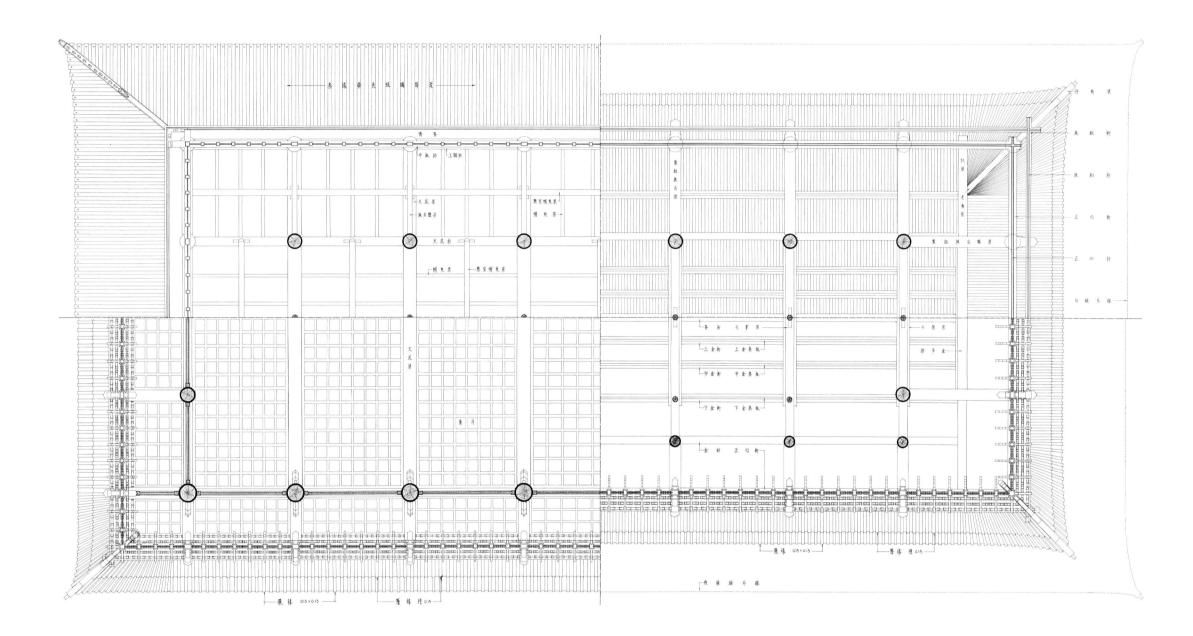

保和殿斗栱天花平面图
Bottom Views of the Brackets and Ceiling Panels, Hall of Preserving Harmony

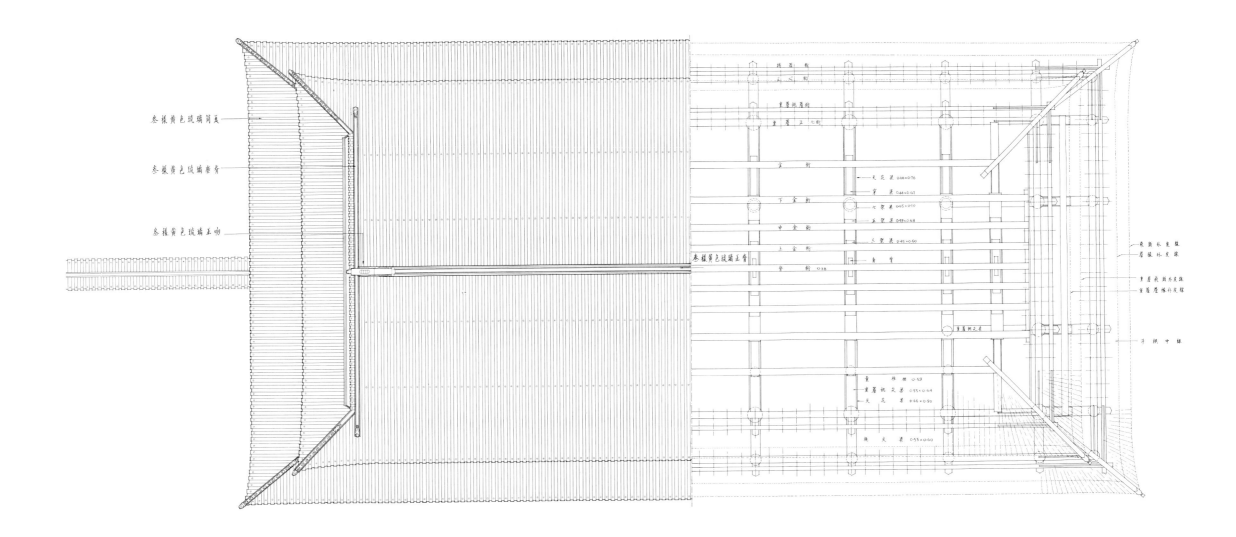

保和殿屋顶屋架平面图
Top Views of the Roof and Trusses, Hall of Preserving Harmony

0 1 2 5 10m

正吻 朵攒黄色玻璃

垂脊 朵攒黄色玻璃

盔脊 朵攒黄色玻璃

戗脊 肆攒黄色玻璃
筒瓦 朵攒黄色玻璃
重昂平身 单翘重昂(十四八含斗)
彩画 旋子彩画

斗栱 重昂(十八含斗)

墙身 青砖红主朱度

群房 青砖

保和殿

保和殿正立面图
Front Elevation of the Hall of Preserving Harmony

0　1　2　　5　　　　　10m

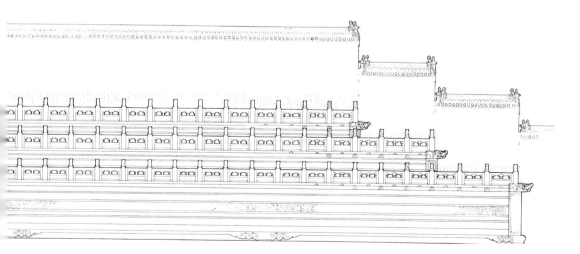

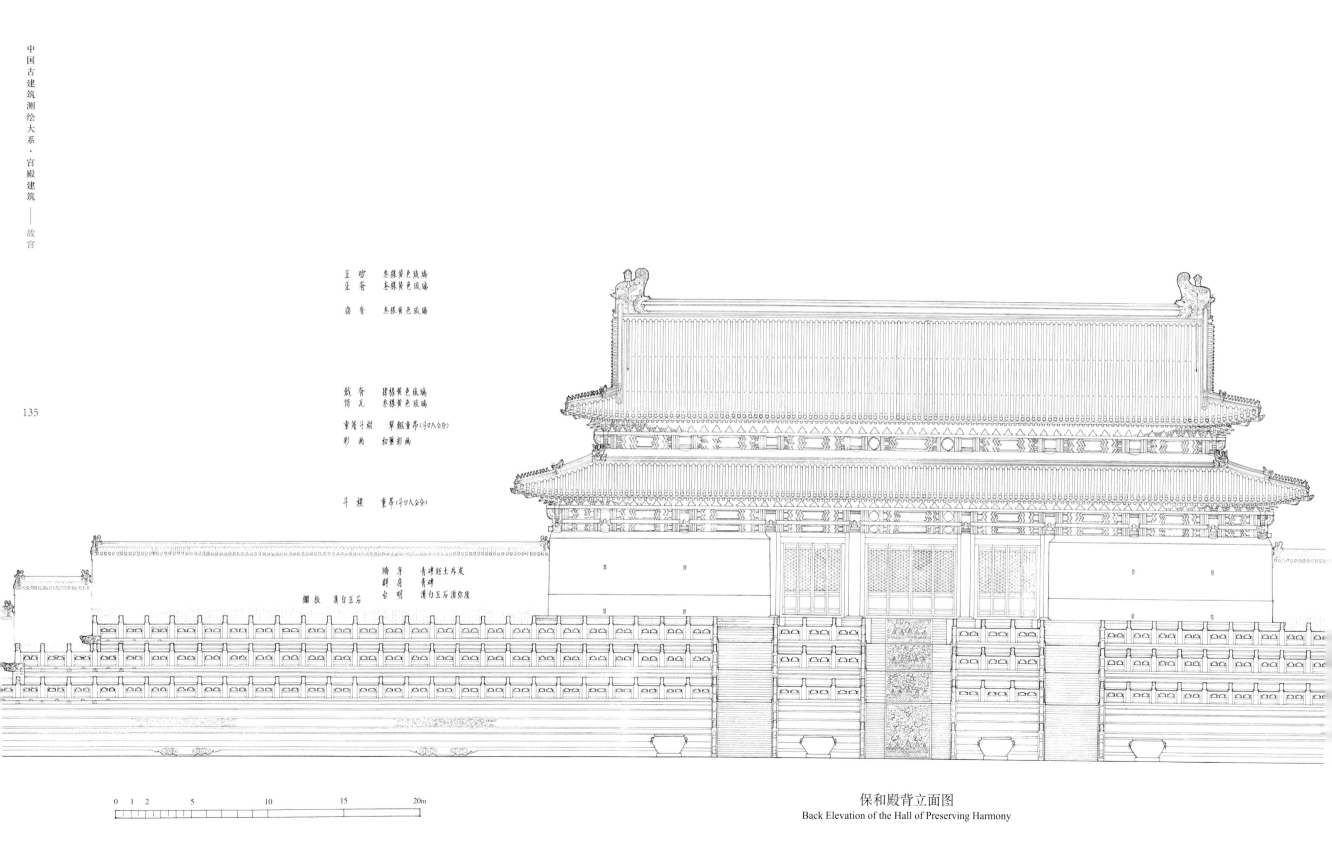

正　吻　叁样黄色琉璃
正　脊　叁样黄色琉璃

垂　脊　叁样黄色琉璃

戗　脊　肆样黄色琉璃
筒　瓦　叁样黄色琉璃
重檐斗栱　单翘重昂（斗口八公分）
彩　画　和玺彩画

斗　栱　重昂（斗口八公分）

墙　身　青砖红土外皮
裙　肩　青砖
台　明　汉白玉石须弥座

栏　板　汉白玉石

0 1 2　　5　　　10　　　15　　　20m

保和殿背立面图
Back Elevation of the Hall of Preserving Harmony

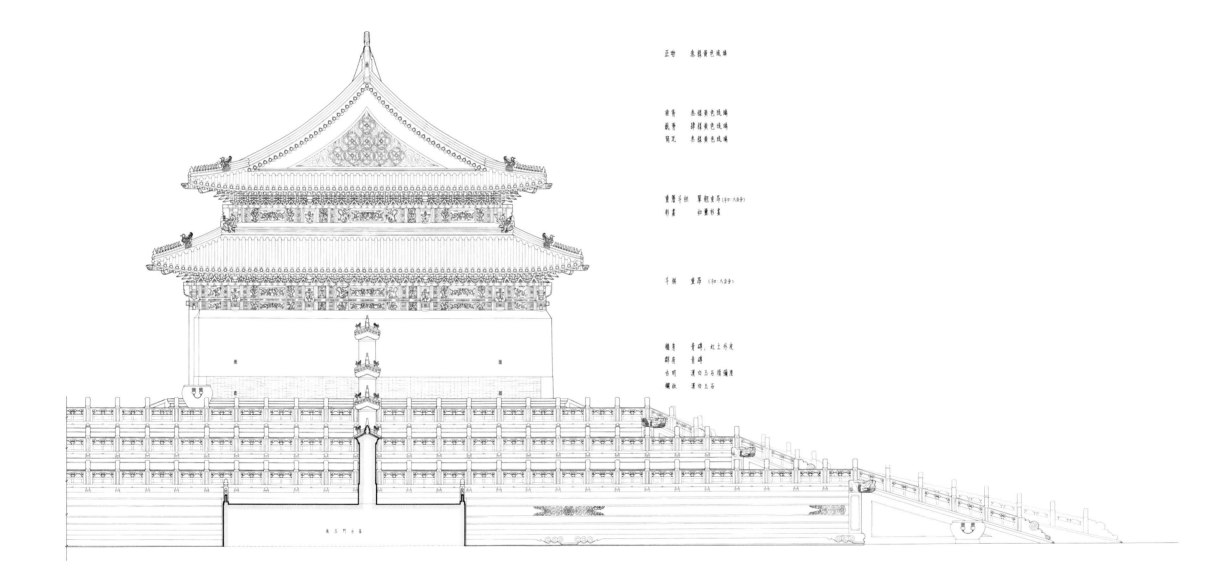

正吻　素摞黄色琉璃

垂兽　素摞黄色琉璃
戗兽　肆摞黄色琉璃
铜瓦　素摞黄色琉璃

重檐斗栱　單翘重昂(斗口八踩)
彩畫　扣重彩畫

斗栱　重昂(斗口八踩)

墙身　青磚，紅土外皮
群肩　青磚
台明　漢白玉石須彌座
螭級　漢白玉石

保和殿侧立面图
Side Elevation of the Hall of Preserving Harmony

0　1　2　　5　　　　　10m

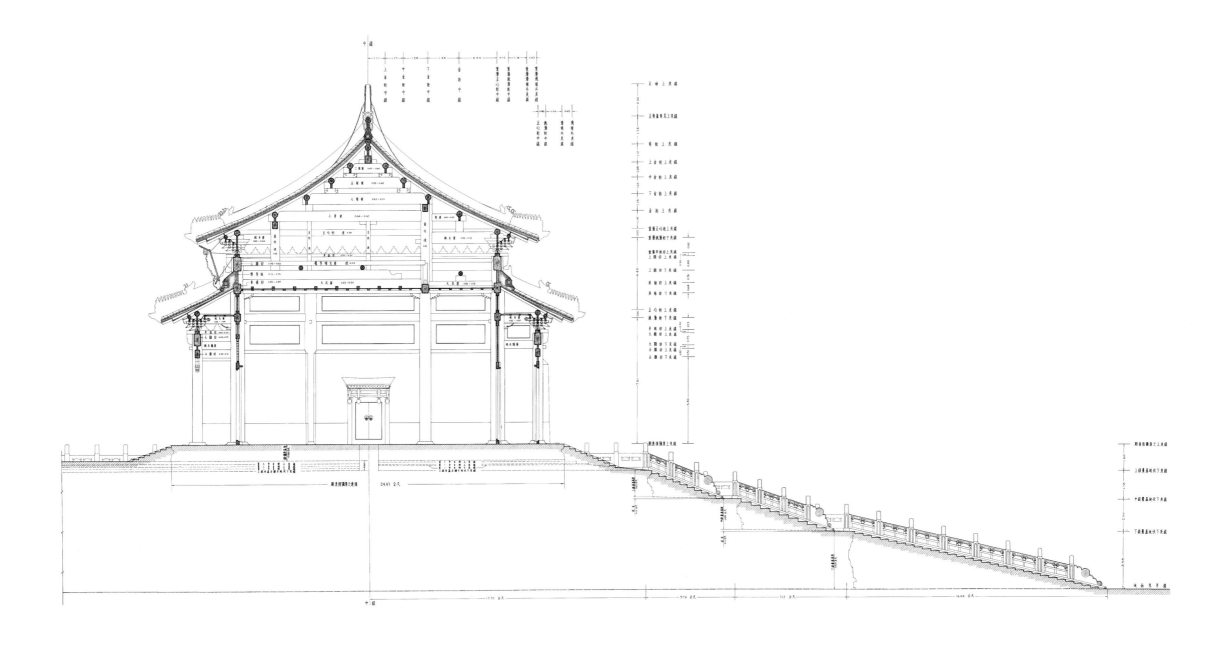

保和殿横剖面图
Cross Section of the Hall of Preserving Harmony

0 1 2 5 10m

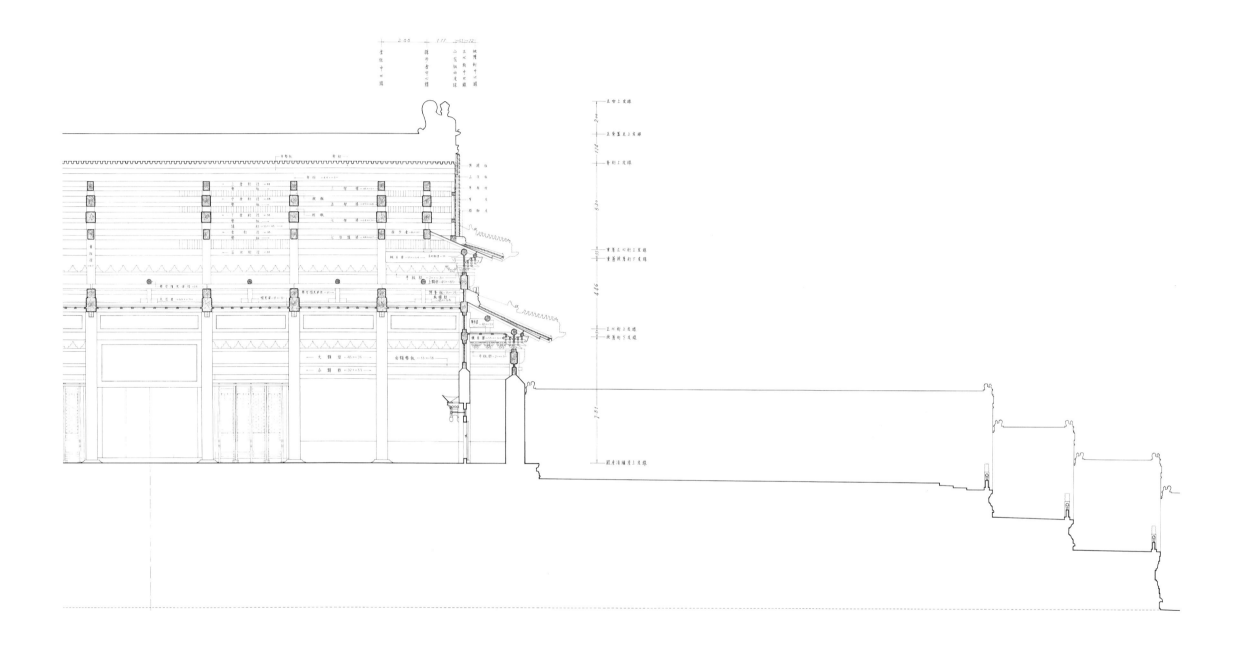

保和殿纵剖面图
Longitudinal Section of the Hall of Preserving Harmony

0 1 2   5   10m

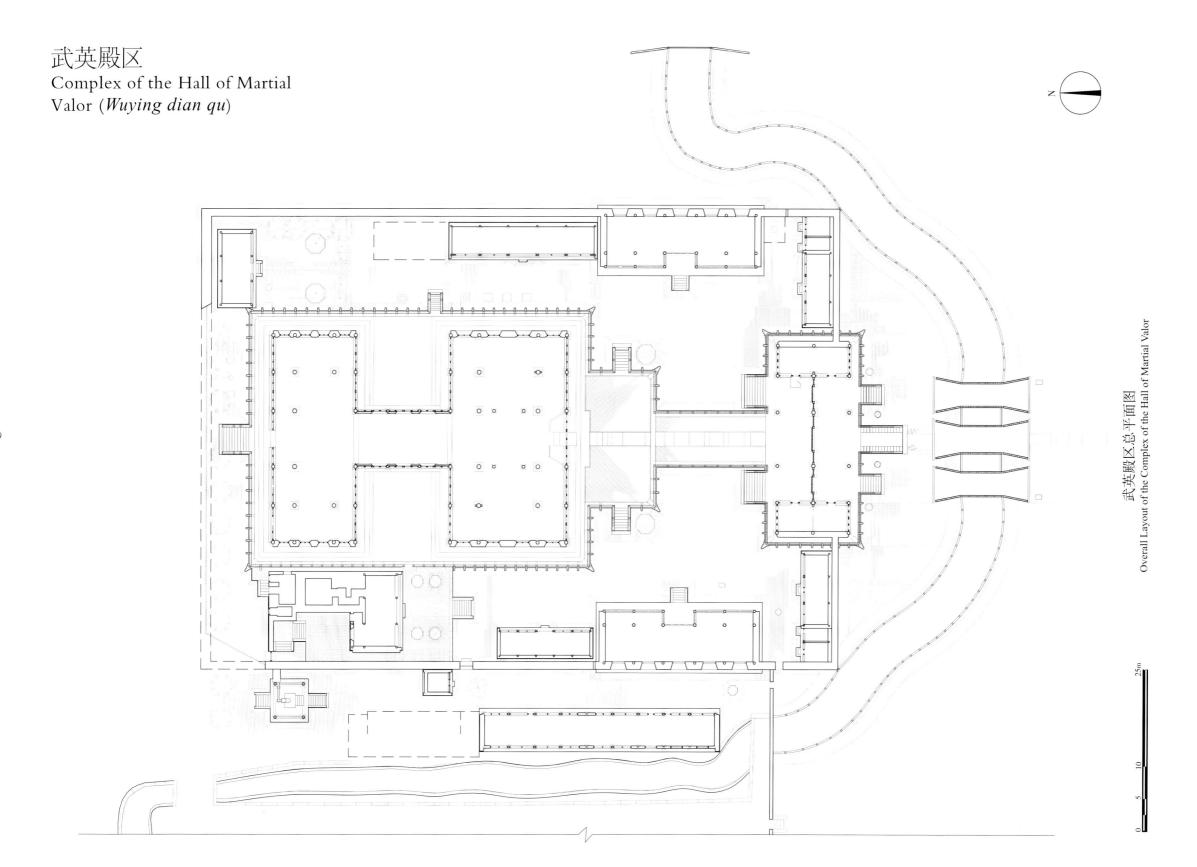

武英殿区
Complex of the Hall of Martial
Valor (*Wuying dian qu*)

中国古建筑测绘大系 · 宫殿建筑 —— 故宫

武英殿区总平面图
Overall Layout of the Complex of the Hall of Martial Valor

25m

10

5

0

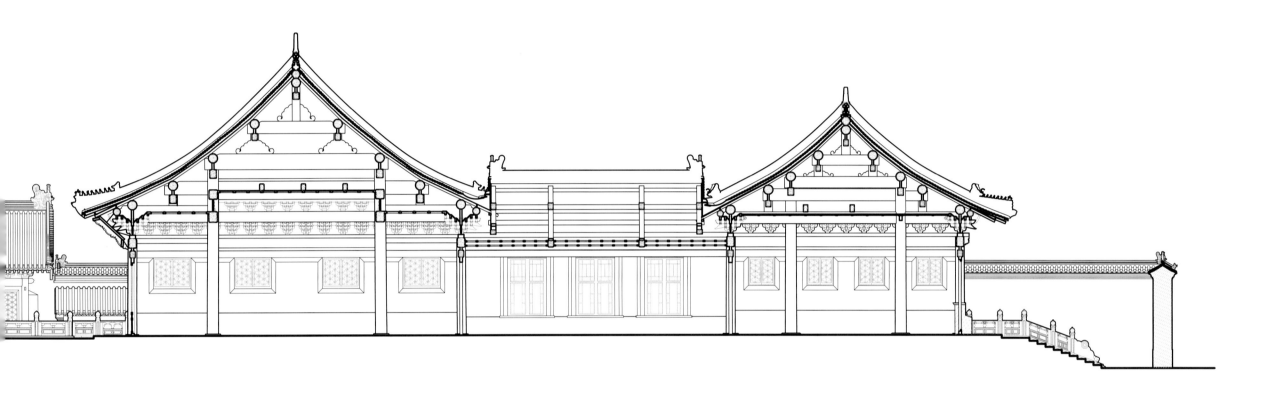

武英殿区总横剖面图
Overall Cross Section of the Complex of the Hall of Martial Valor

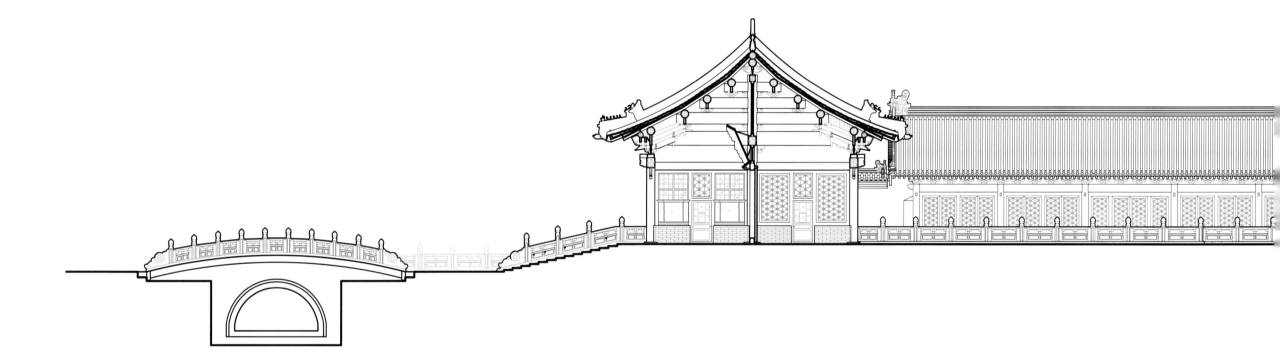

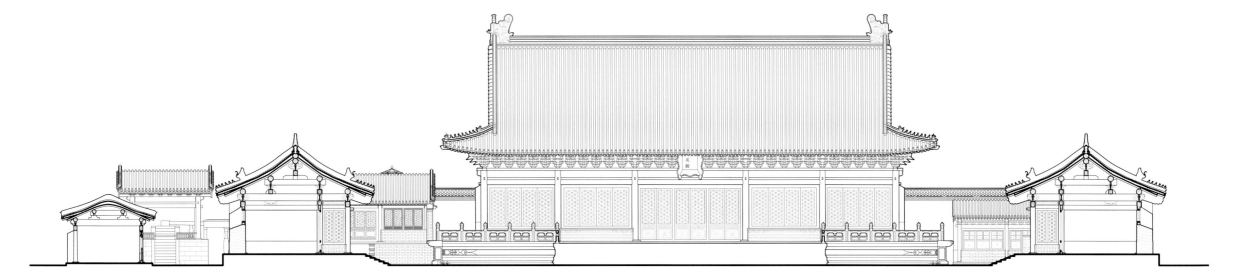

武英殿区总纵剖面图
Overall Longitudinal Section of the Complex of the Hall of Martial Valor

0 2 4   10m

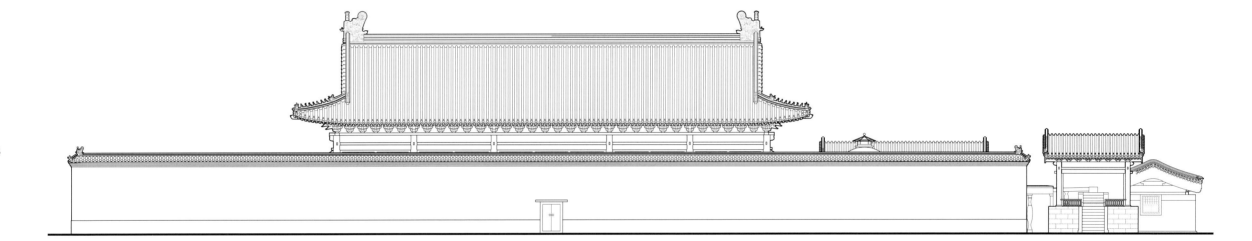

武英殿区总背立面图
Overall Back Elevation of the Complex of the Hall of Martial Valor

0 2 4   10m

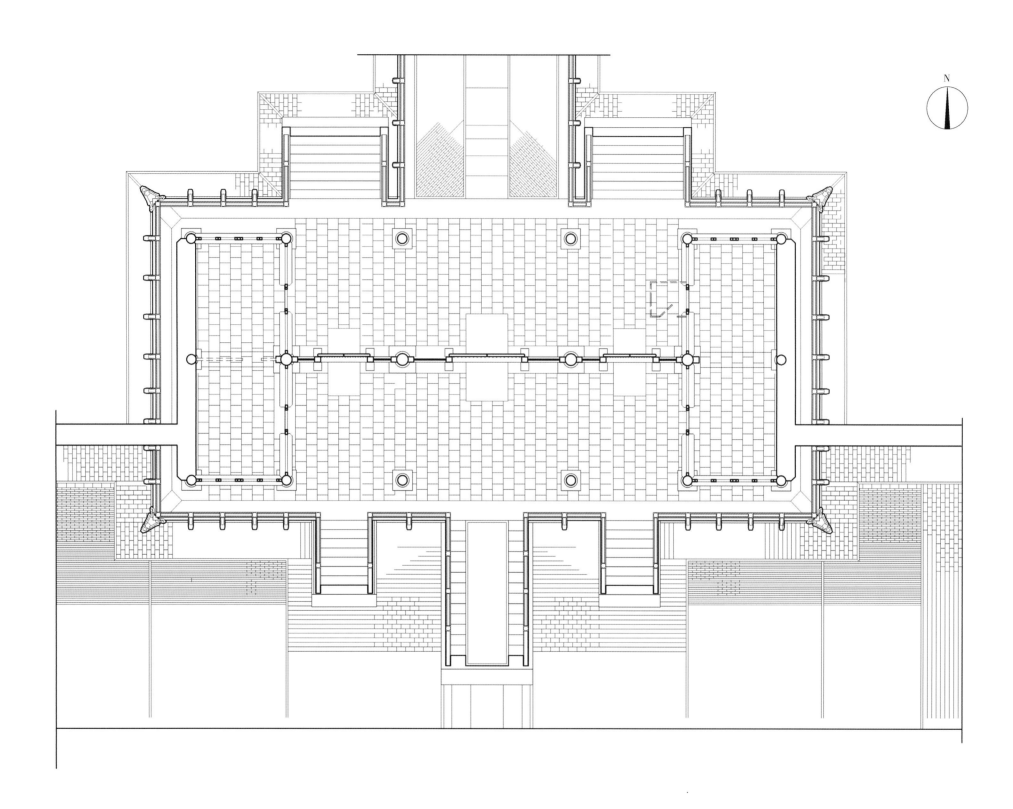

武英门平面图
Floor Plan of the Gate of Martial Valor

0　2　　5　　　　10m

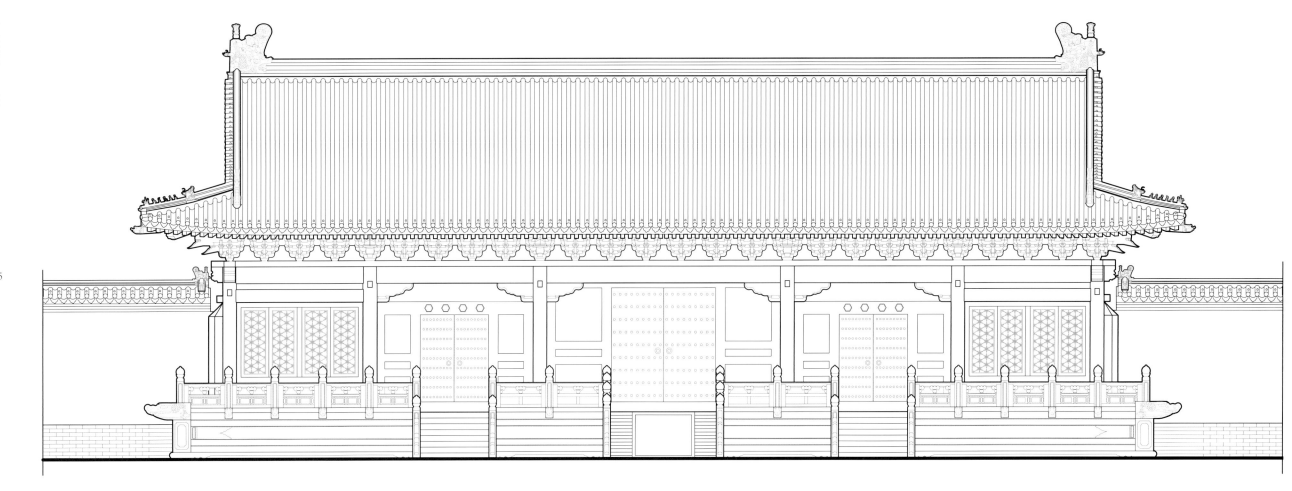

武英门正立面图
Front Elevation of the Gate of Martial Valor

0   2   5m

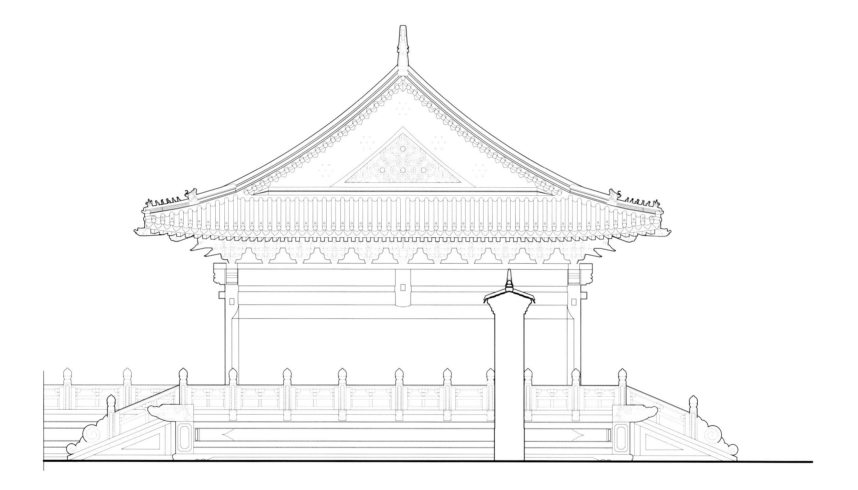

武英门东侧立面图
Eastern Elevation of the Gate of Martial Valor

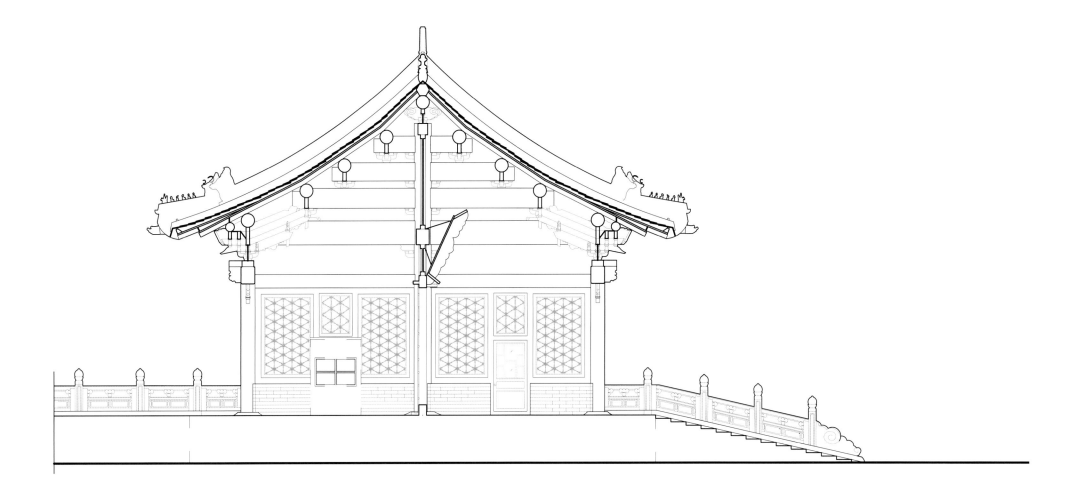

武英门明间横剖面图
Cross Section of the Central Bay of the Gate of Martial Valor

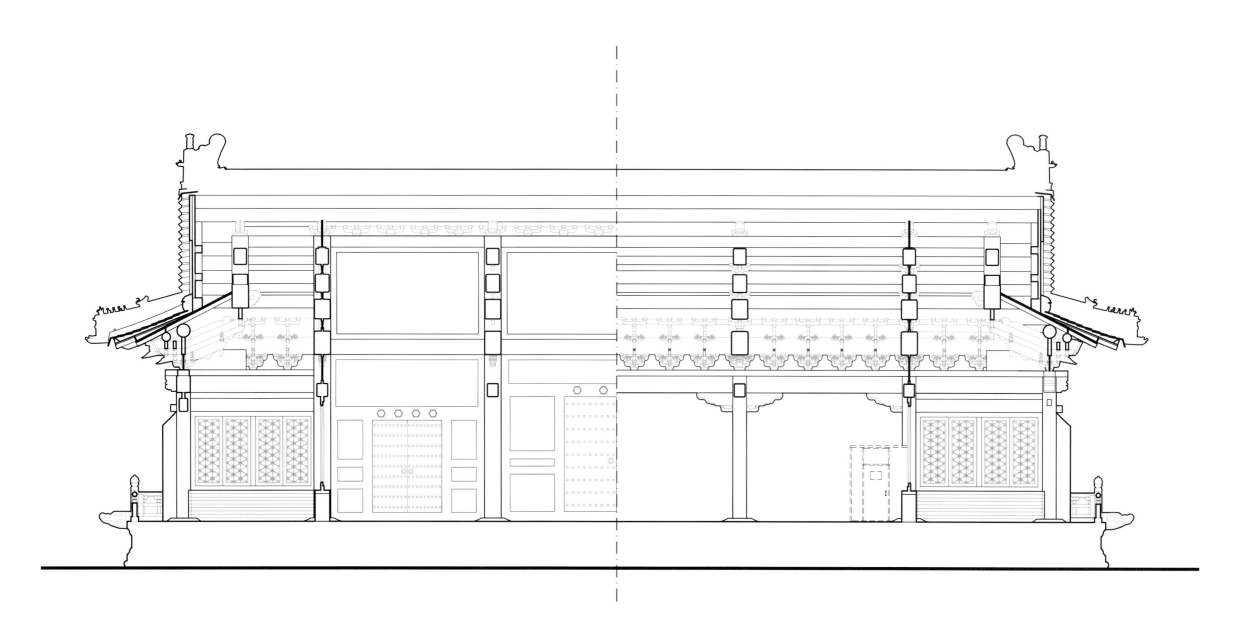

武英门纵剖面图
Longitudinal Section of the Gate of Martial Valor

0　　2　　5m

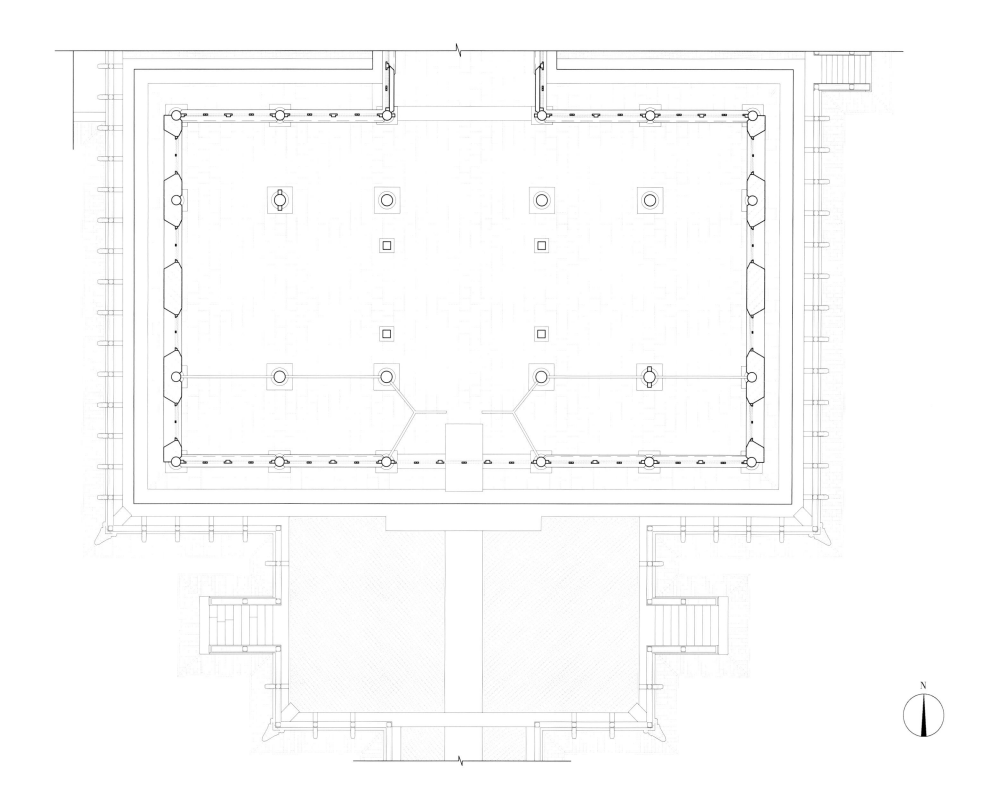

武英殿平面图
Floor Plan of the Hall of Martial Valor

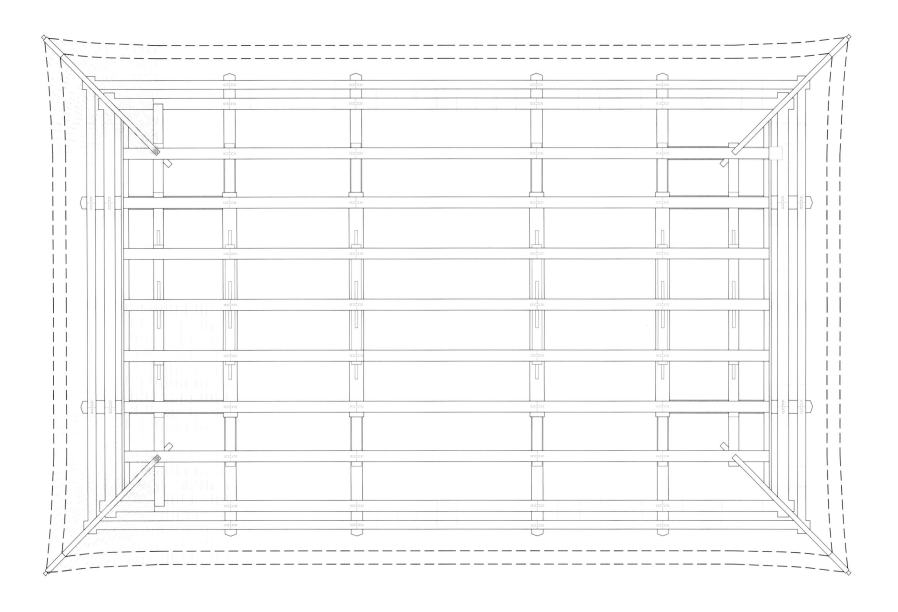

武英殿梁架俯视图
Top View of the Trusses, Hall of Martial Valor

0   2   5   10m

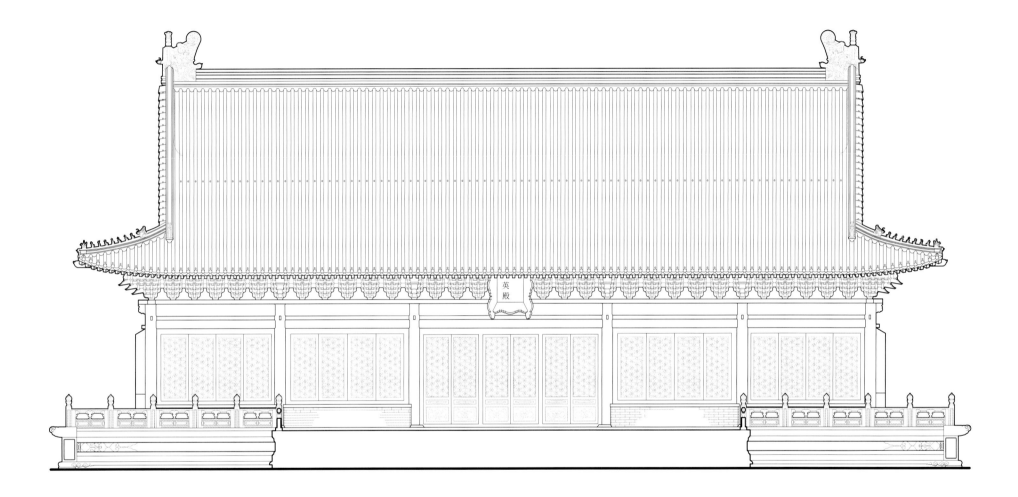

武英殿正立面图
Front Elevation of the Hall of Martial Valor

0   2   5   10m

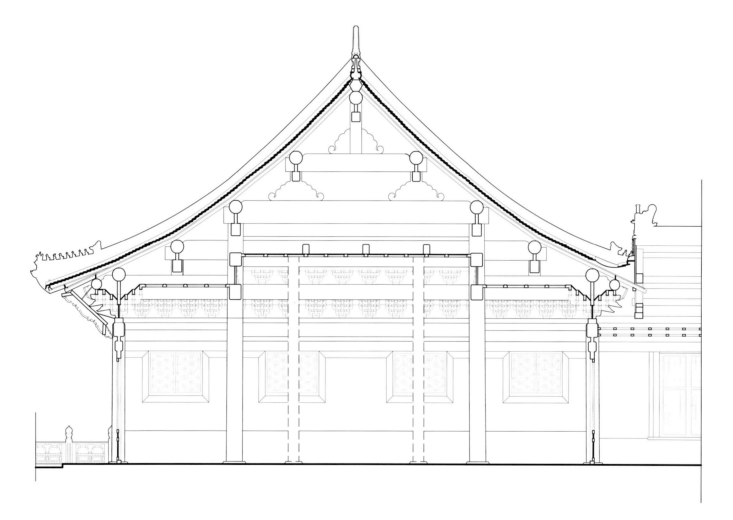

武英殿明间横剖面图
Cross Section of the Central Bay, Hall of Martial Valor

0　　2　　　5　　　　　　10m

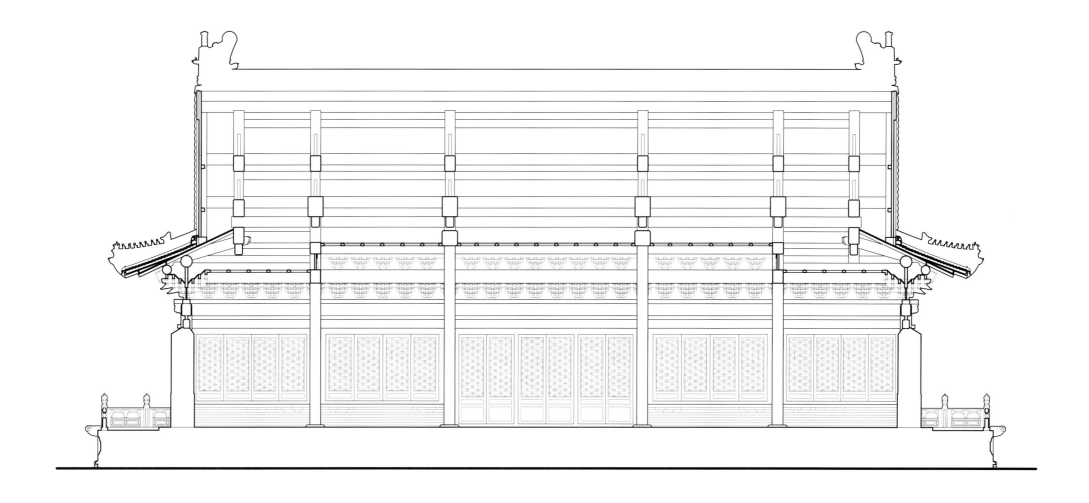

武英殿纵剖面图
Longitudinal Section of the Hall of Martial Valor

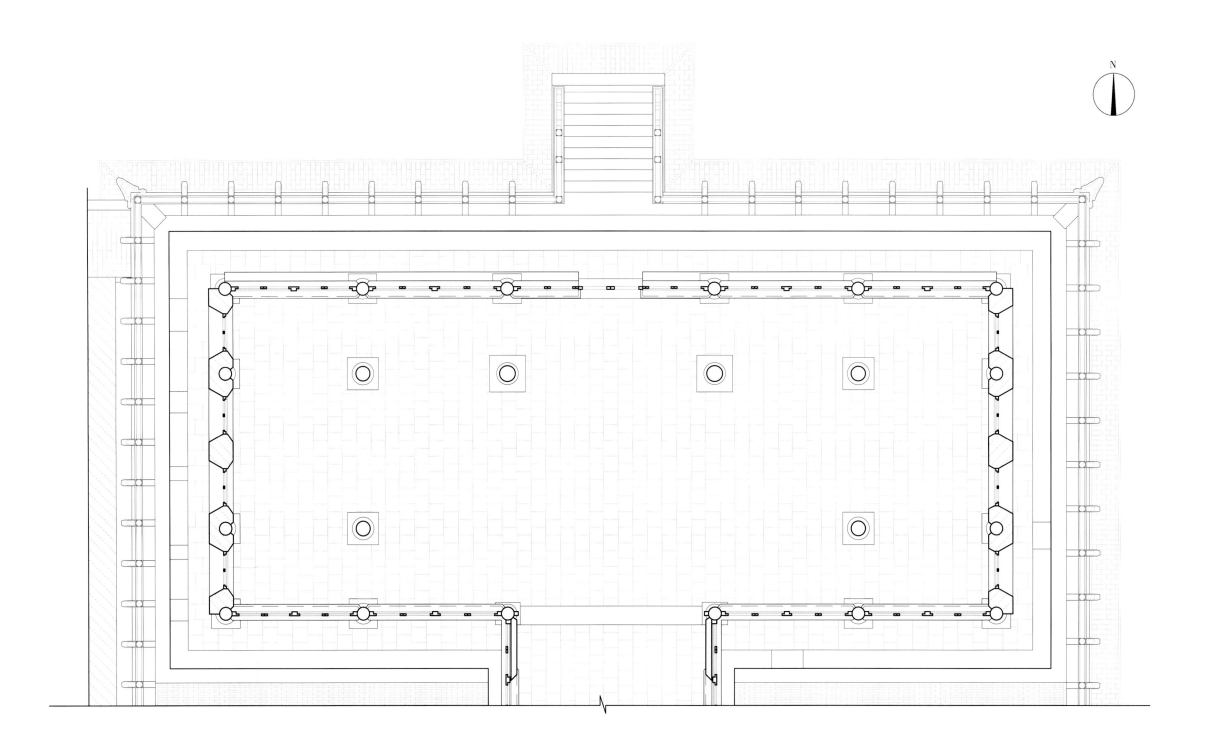

武英殿后殿平面图
Floor Plan of the Hall of Respectful Thoughts

0   2   5m

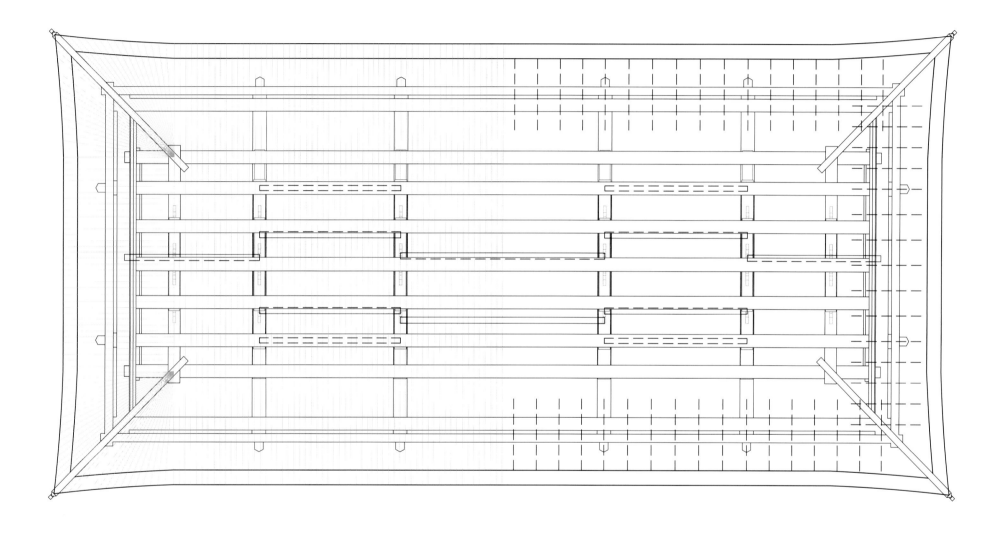

武英殿后殿梁架俯视图
Top View of the Trusses, Hall of Respectful Thoughts

0   2   5m

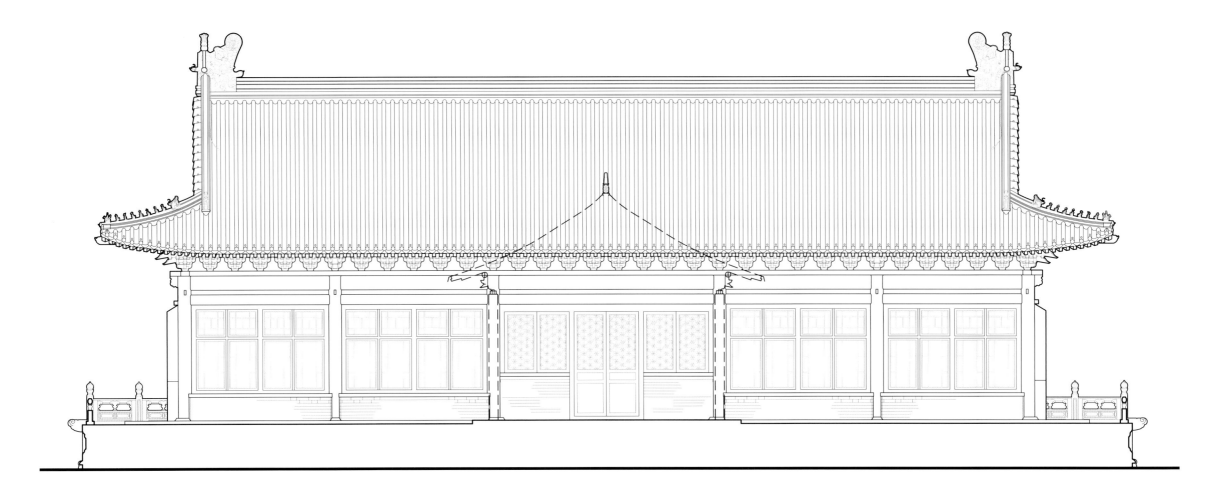

0 2 5m

武英殿后殿正立面图
Front Elevation of the Hall of Respectful Thoughts

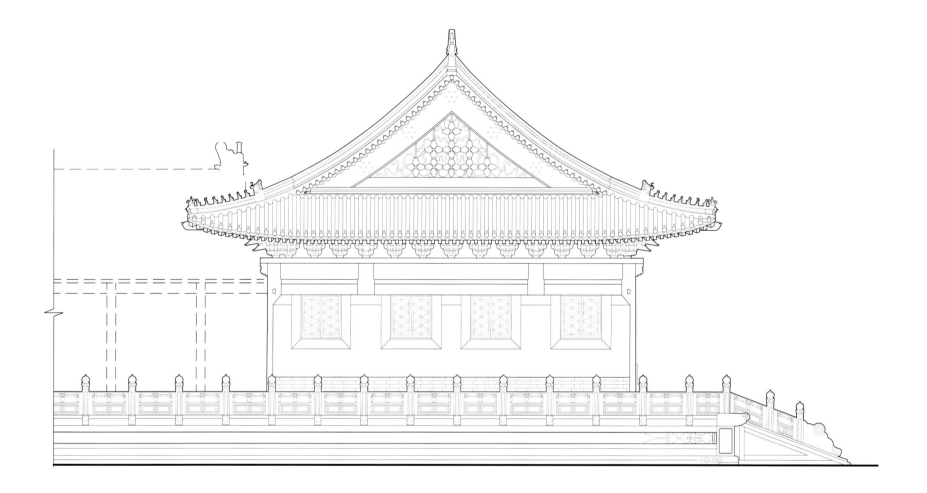

武英殿后殿侧立面图
Side Elevation of the Hall of Respectful Thoughts

0   2   5m

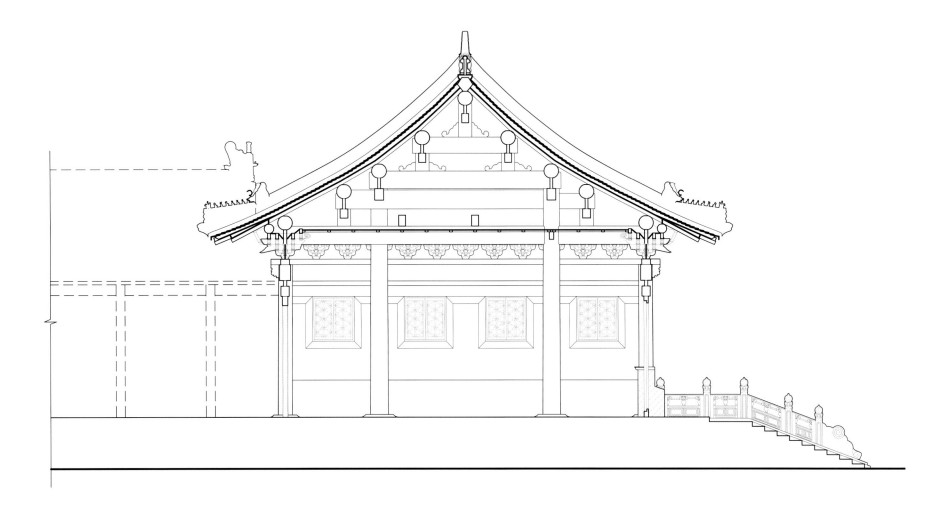

武英殿后殿明间横剖面图
Cross Section of the Central Bay, Hall of Respectful Thoughts

0 2 5m

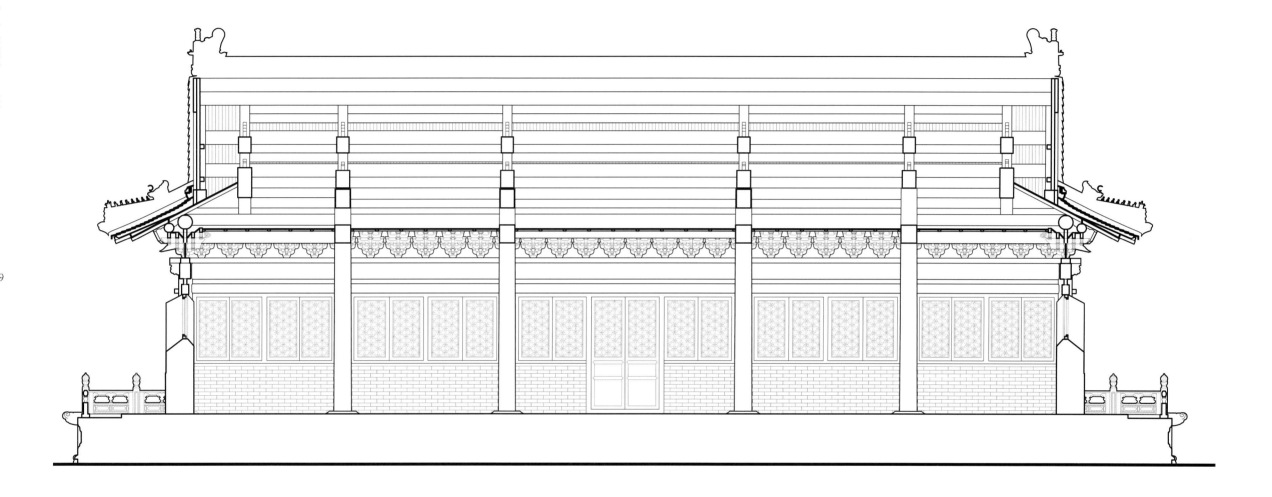

武英殿后殿纵剖面图

Longitudinal Section of the Hall of Respectful Thoughts

0   2   5m

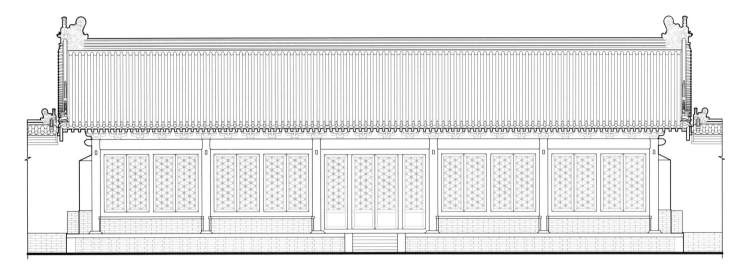

武英殿西配殿正立面图
Front Elevation of the Hall of Luminous Appeals

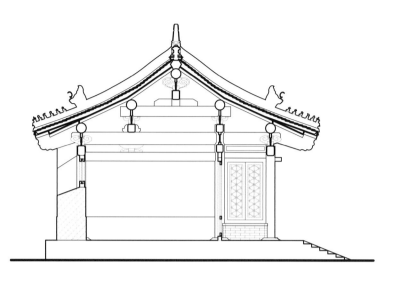

武英殿西配殿横剖面图
Cross Section of the Hall of Luminous Appeals

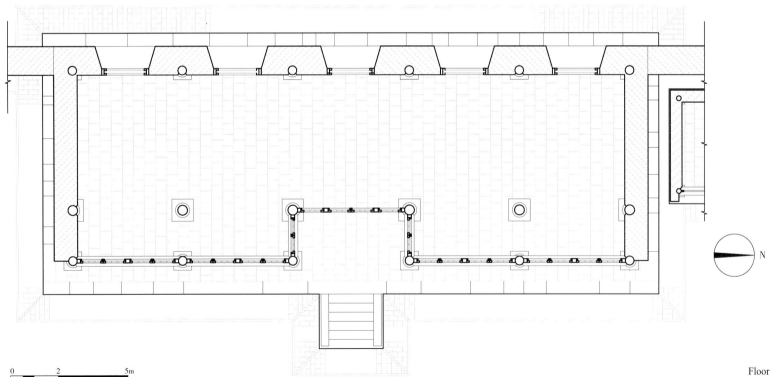

武英殿西配殿平面图
Floor Plan of the Hall of Luminous Appeals

0   2   5m

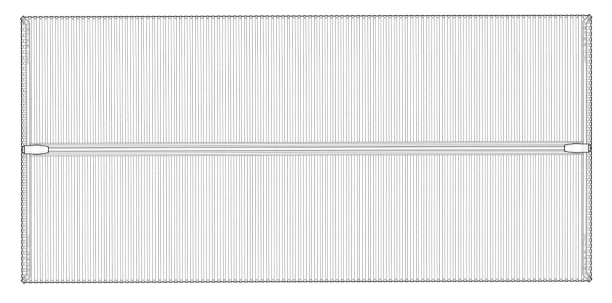

扣脊筒瓦
六样黄琉璃三连砖
压当条
正当沟
六样黄琉璃群色条

垂脊剖面（垂兽前）

六样黄琉璃垂脊
扣脊筒瓦
压当条
正当沟

垂脊剖面（垂兽后）

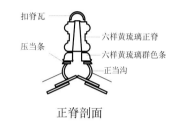

扣脊瓦
六样黄琉璃正脊
压当条
六样黄琉璃群色条
正当沟

正脊剖面

武英殿西配殿瓦顶俯视图
Top View of the Roofing Tiles, Hall of Luminous Appeals

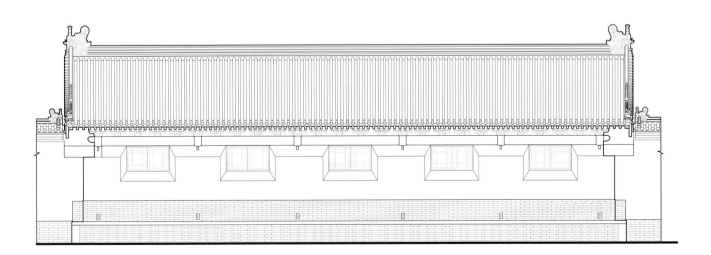

武英殿西配殿背立面图
Back Elevation of the Roofing Tiles, Hall of Luminous Appeals

0   2   5m

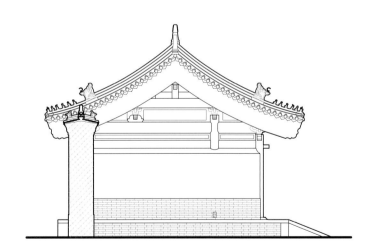

武英殿西配殿南侧立面图
Southern Elevation of the Roofing Tiles, Hall of Luminous Appeals

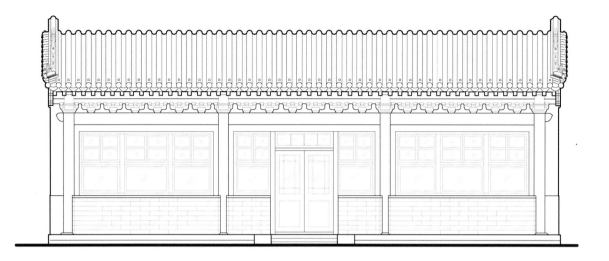

恒寿斋正立面图
Front Elevation of the Studio of Eternal Longevity

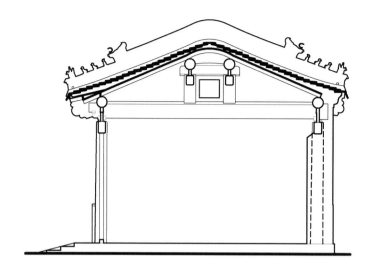

恒寿斋横剖面图
Cross Section of the Studio of Eternal Longevity

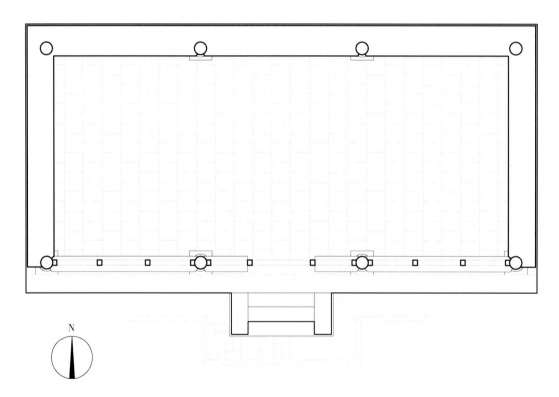

恒寿斋平面图
Floor Plan of the Studio of Eternal Longevity

0   1   2m

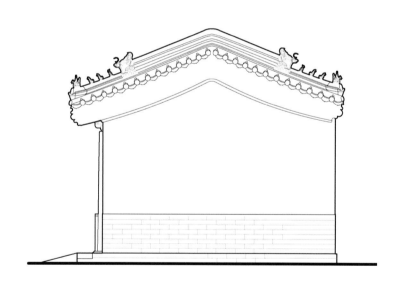

恒寿斋侧立面图
Side Elevation of the Studio of Eternal Longevity

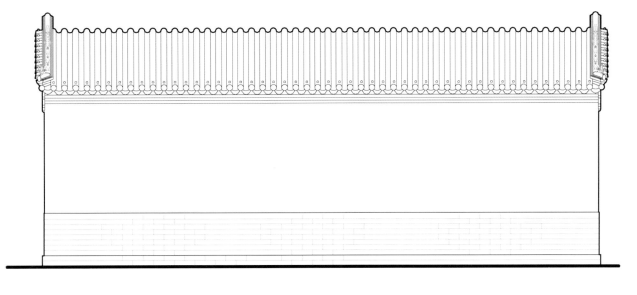

恒寿斋背立面图
Back Elevation of the Studio of Eternal Longevity

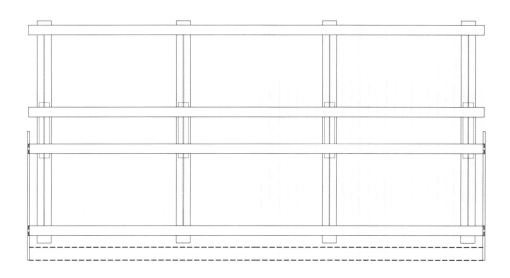

恒寿斋梁架俯视图
Top Views of the Trusses, Studio of Eternal Longevity

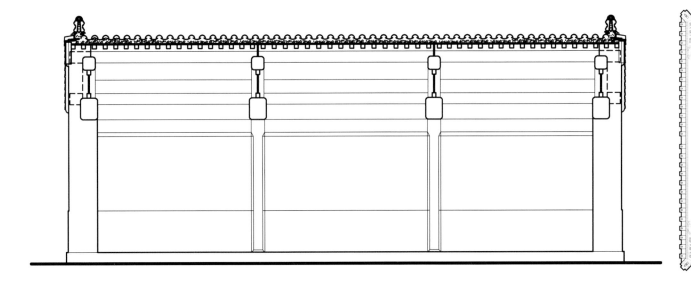

恒寿斋纵剖面图
Longitudinal Section of the Studio of Eternal Longevity

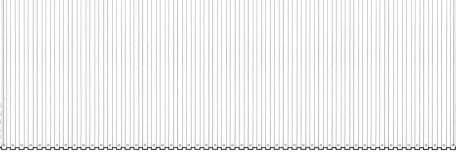

恒寿斋瓦顶俯视图
Top Views of the Roofing Tiles, Studio of Eternal Longevity

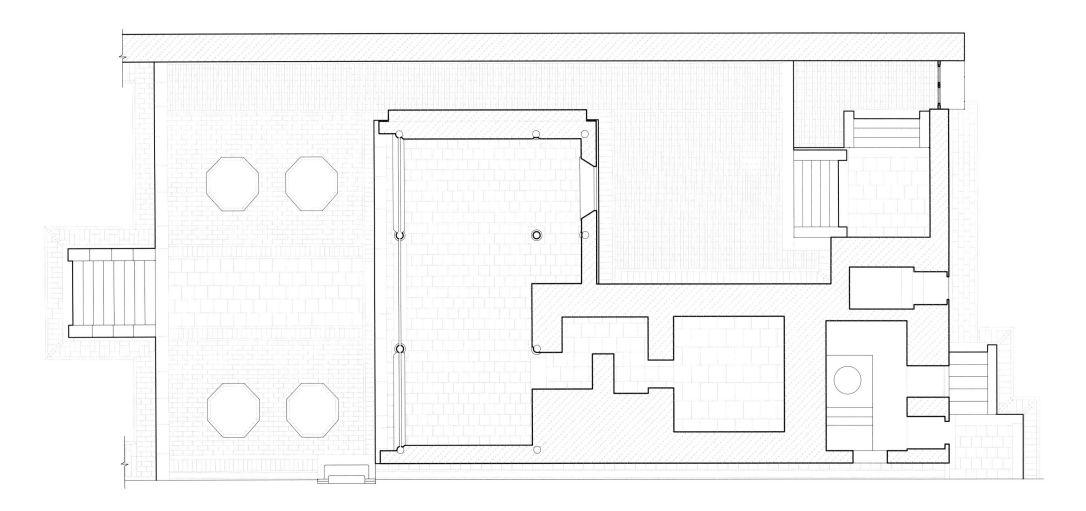

浴德堂平面图
Floor Plan of the Hall for Cultivating Virtues

0   2   5m

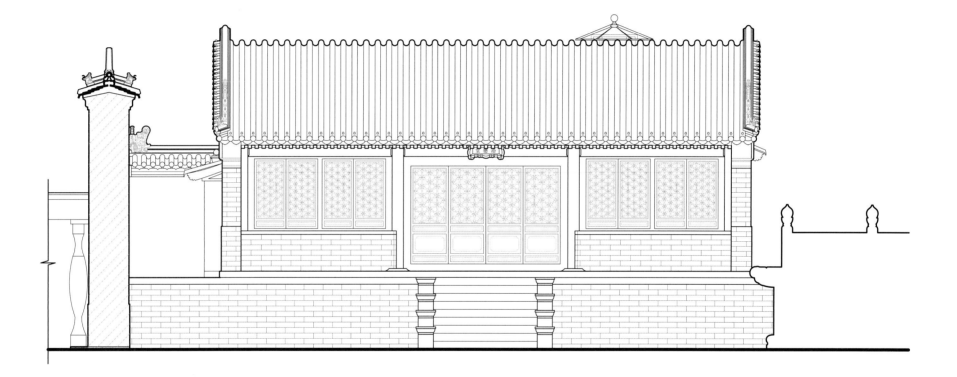

浴德堂正立面图
Front Elevation of the Hall for Cultivating Virtues

0 1 2 5m

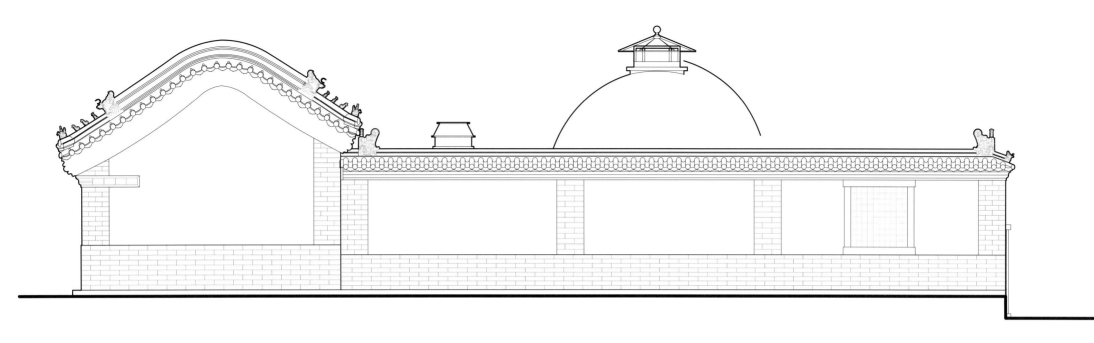

浴德堂东侧立面图
Eastern Elevations of the Hall for Cultivating Virtues

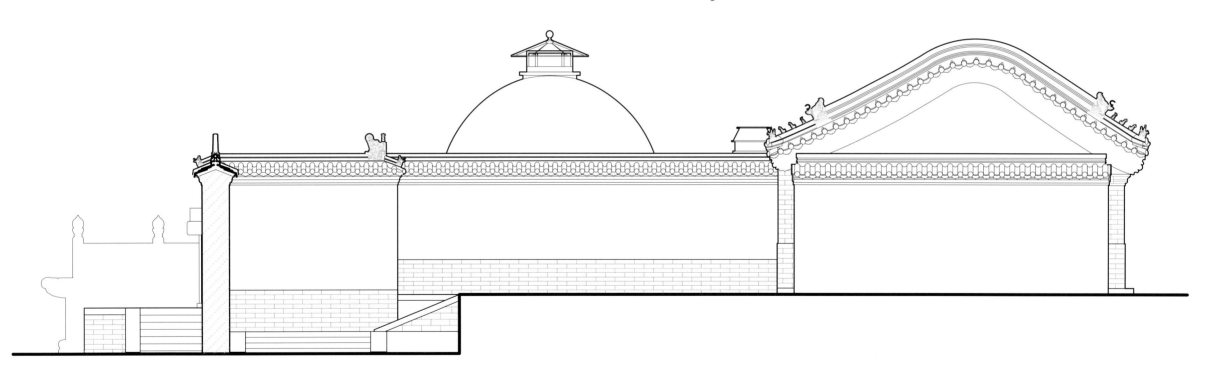

0 1 2   5m

浴德堂西侧立面图
Western Elevations of the Hall for Cultivating Virtues

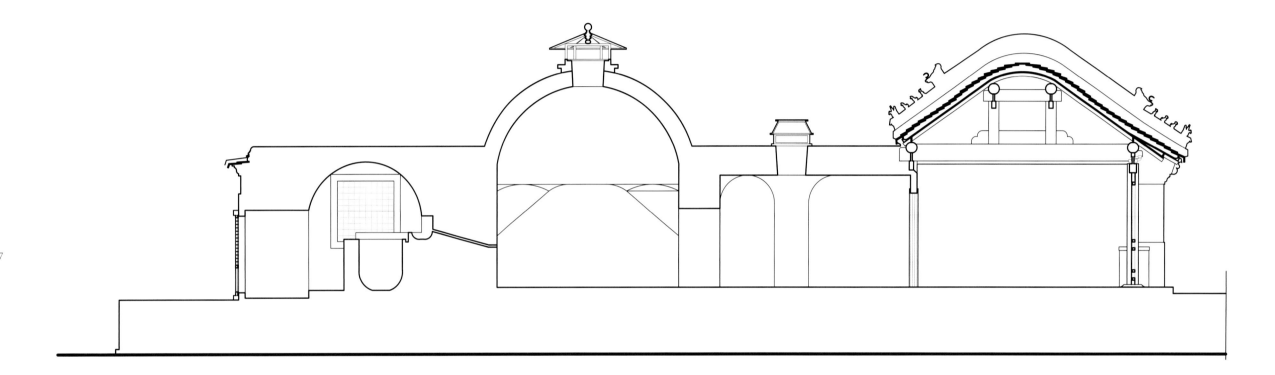

浴德堂明间横剖面图
Cross Section of the Central Bay, Hall for Cultivating Virtues

0   1   2   5m

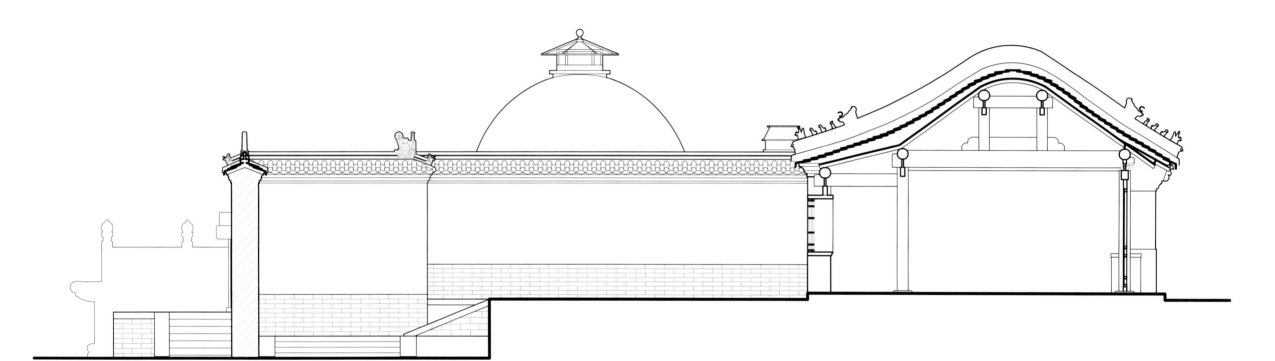

浴德堂西次间横剖面图
Cross Section of the Western Bay, Hall for Cultivating Virtues

0 1 2 5m

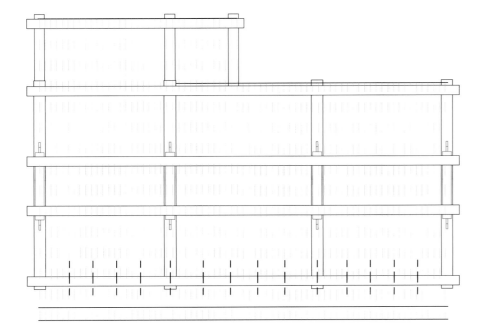

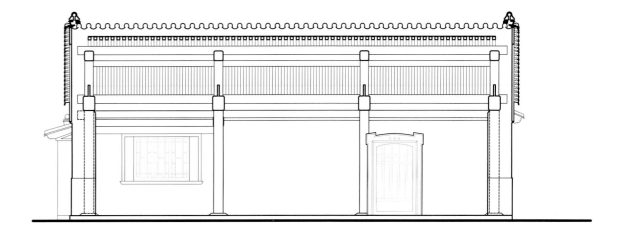

浴德堂梁架俯视图
Top View of the Trusses, Hall for Cultivating Virtues

0 1 2 5m

浴德堂纵剖面图
Longitudinal Section of the Hall for Cultivating Virtues

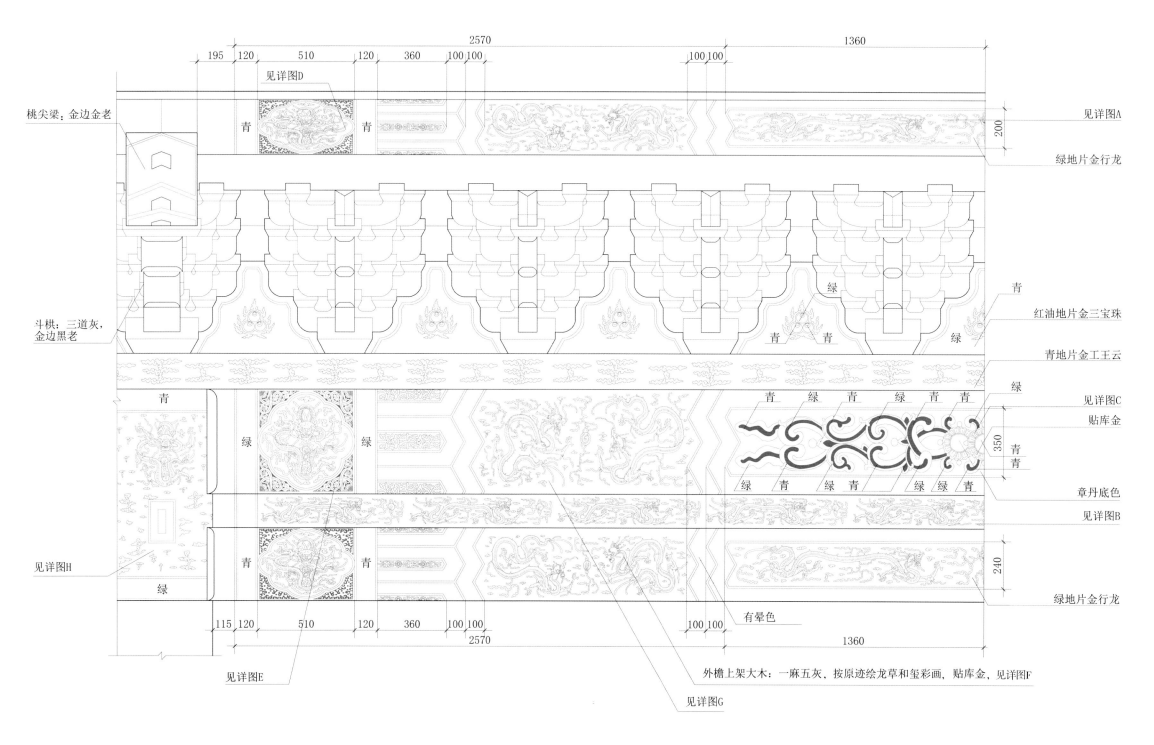

桃尖梁：金边金老

2570

1360

195 120 510 120 360 100 100 100 100

见详图D

青 青 见详图A

绿地片金行龙

200

斗栱：三道灰，金边黑老

红油地片金三宝珠

青 青 绿

青地片金工王云

青 绿 青 绿 青 青 绿 见详图C

贴库金

青 青

绿 青 绿 青 绿 绿 青 章丹底色

见详图B

240

青 青

见详图H

绿

绿地片金行龙

见详图E

115 120 510 120 360 100 100 100 100

2570 1360

有晕色

见详图G

外檐上架大木：一麻五灰，按原迹绘龙草和玺彩画、贴库金、见详图F

武英殿明间前外檐彩画设计图
Design Drawing of the Colored Painting of the Front Elevation's Central Bay, Hall of Martial Valor

绿地片金行龙

详图 A

详图 D

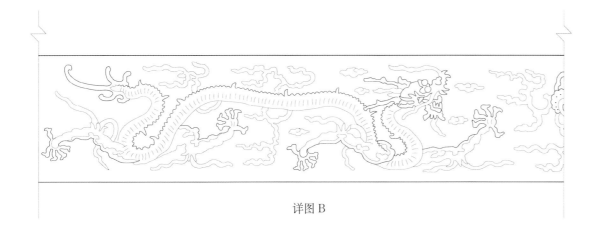

详图 B

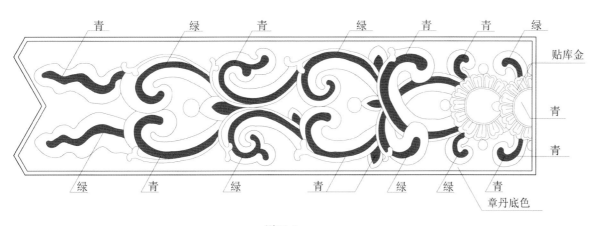

青　　绿　　青　　绿　　青　青　绿

绿　　青　　绿　　青　　绿　绿　青

贴库金

青

青

章丹底色

详图 C

详图 E

武英殿明间前外檐彩画设计图详图（一）
Detailed Drawing of Design Drawing of the Colored Painting, the Front Elevation's Central Bay, Hall of Martial Valor（Ⅰ）

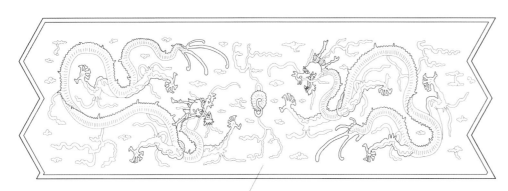

外檐上架大木：一麻五灰，按原迹绘龙草和玺彩画，贴库金

详图 F

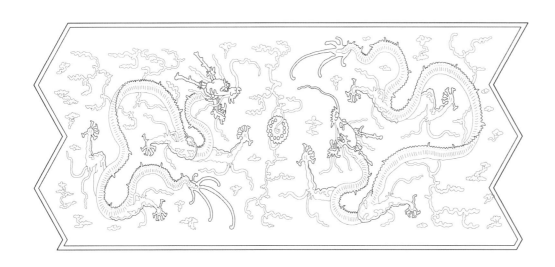

详图 G

详图 H

武英殿明间前外檐彩画设计图详图（二）
Detailed Drawing of Design Drawing of the Colored Painting, the Front Elevation's Central Bay, Hall of Martial Valor（Ⅱ）

片金西番莲

上架大木：一麻五灰，绘龙锦枋心墨线大点金旋子彩画，贴库金

1530

725

125 110 360 110 710 90

290

青 青

斗栱：三道灰、黑边做法

垫栱板：一布四灰、金线片金火焰三宝珠

31

260

110

绿 绿

250

绿 绿

220

落墨搭色异兽

110 360 110 20 60 720 70 80

90 1530 1450

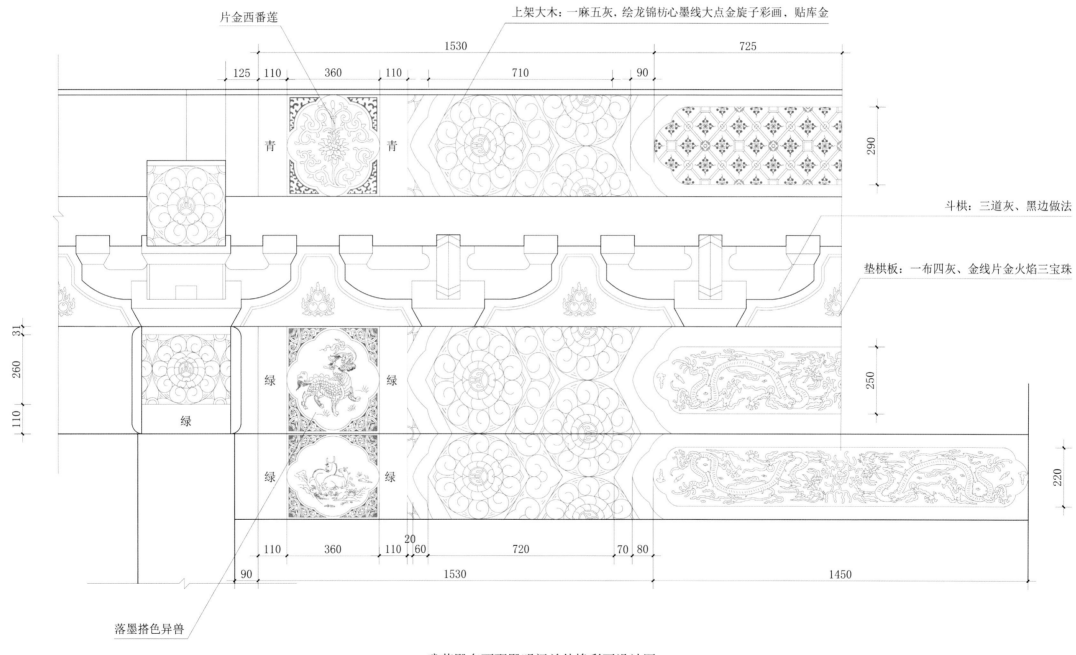

武英殿东西配殿明间前外檐彩画设计图
Design Drawing of the Colored Painting of the Front Elevation's Central Bay, Hall of Luminous Appeals

挑檐檩：做一麻五灰地仗，枋心内为青地（普照乾坤）

找头：绘一整两破加喜相逢

挑檐枋：做三道灰地仗，刷青色

梁头：做一麻五灰地仗，绘黑边黑老

斗栱：做三道灰地仗，绘黑边黑老

棋眼：做三道灰地仗，刷三道二朱色红油

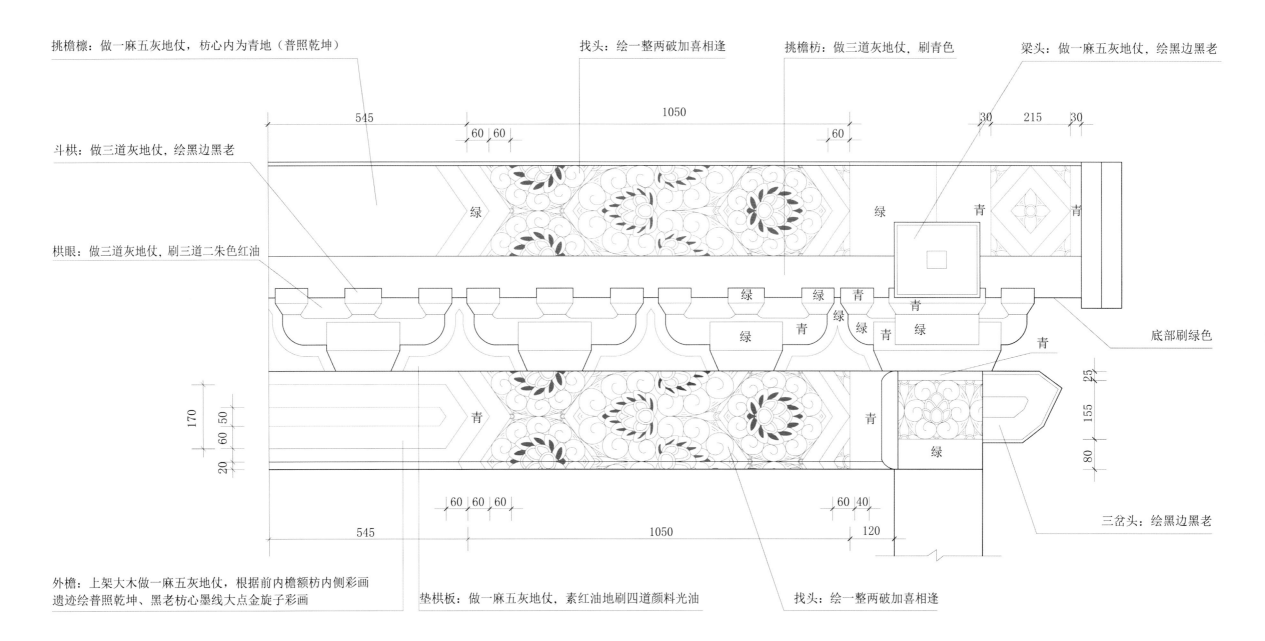

545

1050

30 215 30

60 60

60

绿   青   青

绿

绿 绿 青

青

绿 青 绿 绿

青

绿 青 绿

底部刷绿色

170

60 50

20

青

青

绿

155

25

80

545

60 60 60

1050

60 40

120

三岔头：绘黑边黑老

外檐：上架大木做一麻五灰地仗，根据前内檐额枋内侧彩画遗迹绘普照乾坤、黑老枋心墨线大点金旋子彩画

垫栱板：做一麻五灰地仗，素红油地刷四道颜料光油

找头：绘一整两破加喜相逢

恒寿斋次间前外檐彩画设计图
Design Drawing of the Colored Paintings of the Bays next to the Central Bay of the Front Elevation, Studio of Eternal Longevity

神武门
Gate of Divine Prowess (*Shenwu men*)

中国古建筑测绘大系·宫殿建筑——故宫

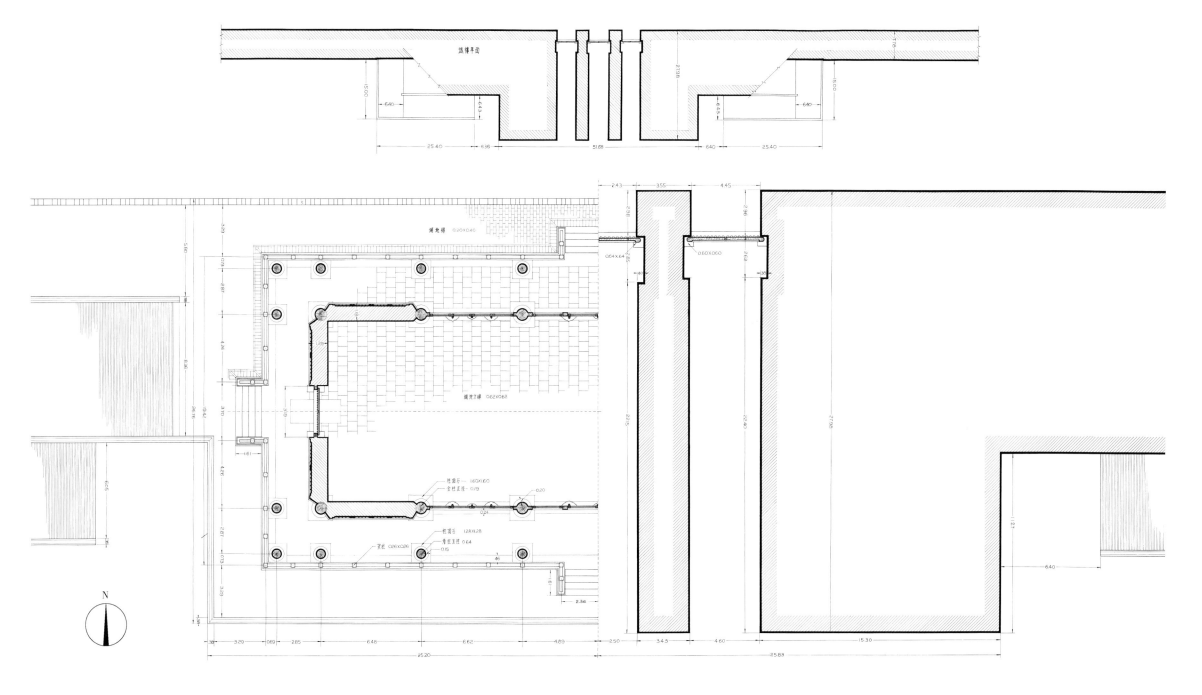

N

0 1 2 5m

神武门城台及城楼平面图
Layout of the Upper Tower and the Abutment, Gate of Divine Prowess

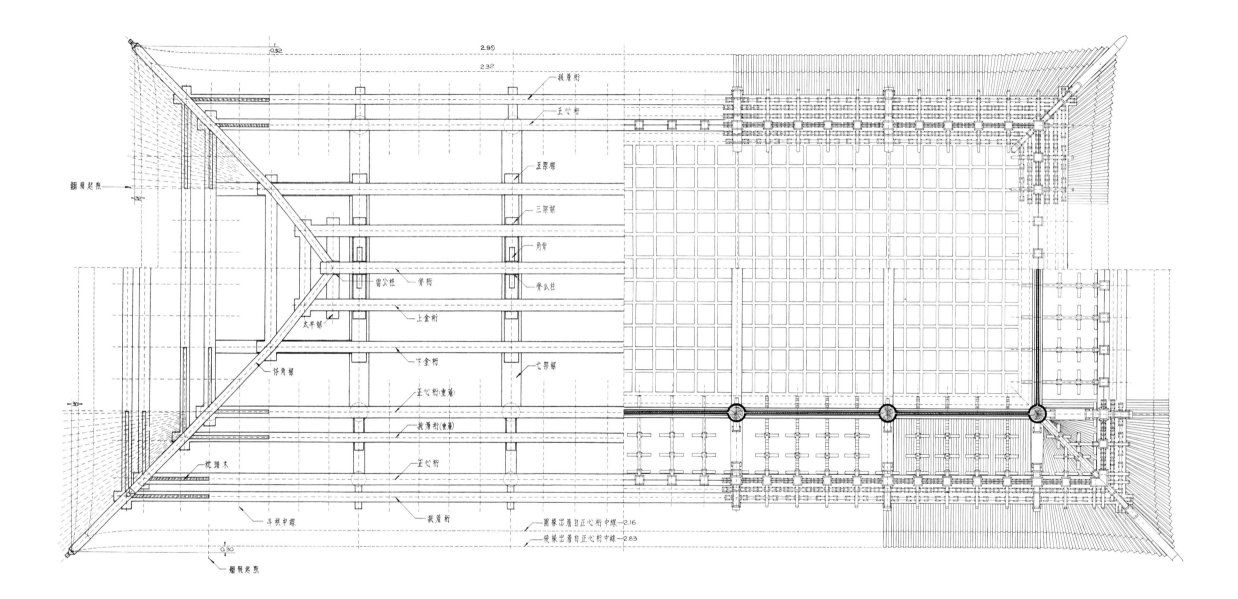

神武门天花屋架平面图
Bottom View of the Ceiling Panels and Top View of the Trusses, Gate of Divine Prowess

0 1 2 3 4 5m

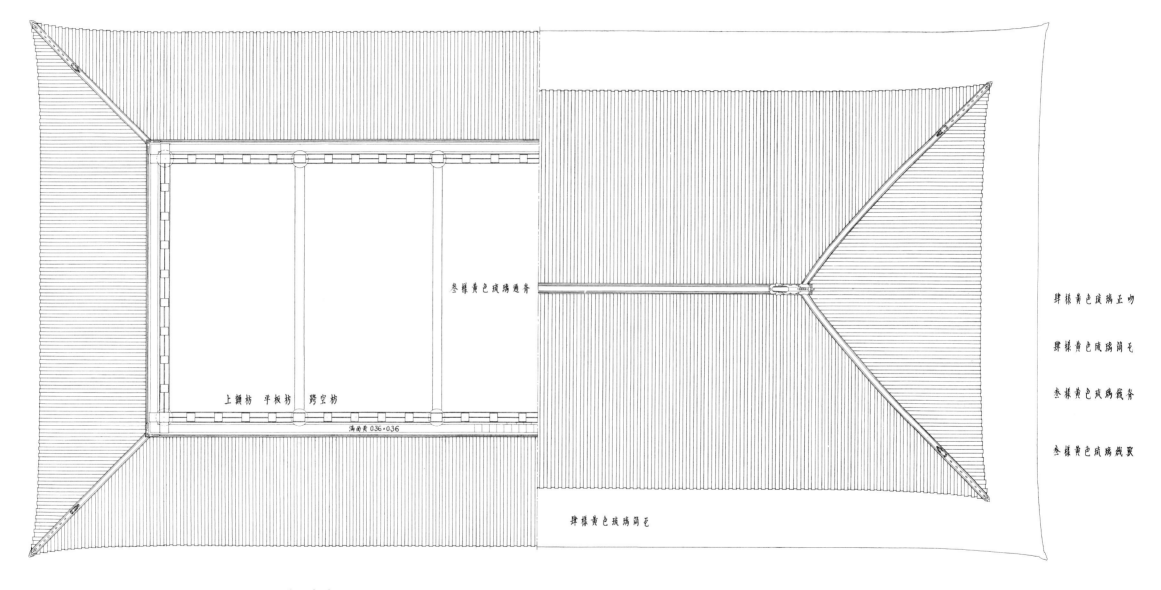

叁样黄色玻璃通脊

肆样黄色玻璃正吻

肆样黄色玻璃筒瓦

叁样黄色玻璃戗脊

叁样黄色玻璃戗兽

上額枋 平板枋 跨空枋

海墁黄 0.36×0.36

肆样黄色玻璃筒瓦

下層屋顶平面图

屋顶平面图

0 1 2 5 10m

神武门屋顶平面图
Top View of the Roof, Gate of Divine Prowess

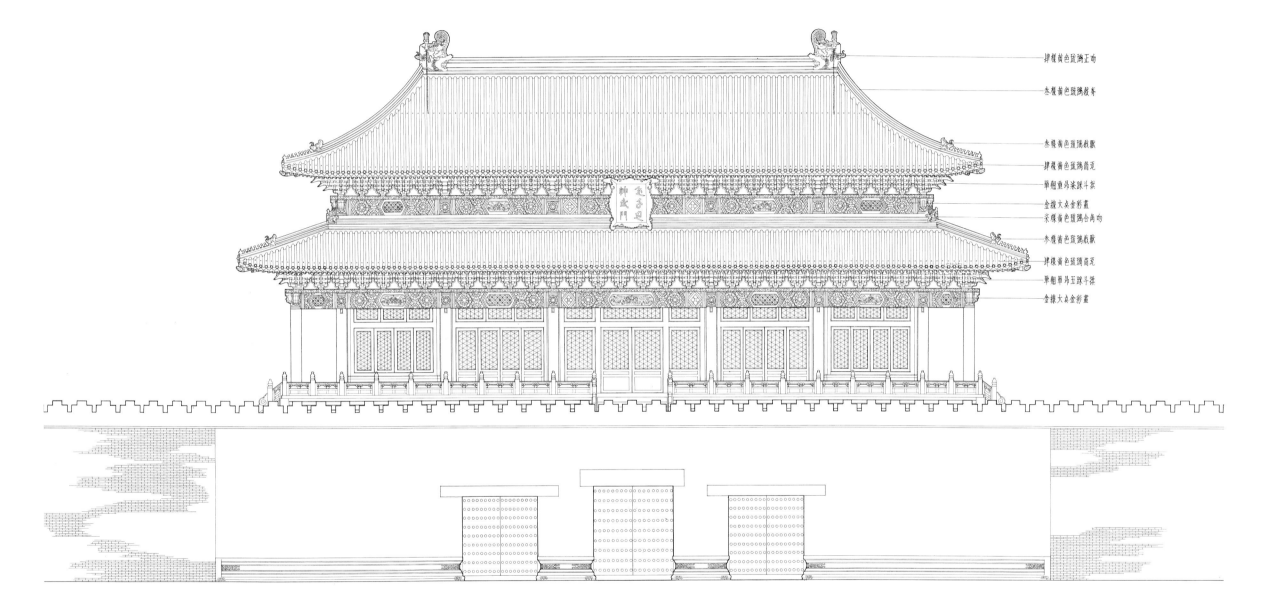

琉璃黄色琉璃正吻

杰檩黄色琉璃脊兽

杰檩黄色琉璃戗兽

琉璃黄色琉璃筒瓦

单翘重昂柒踩斗拱

金楼大点金彩画

杂檩黄色琉璃合角吻

杰檩黄色琉璃戗兽

琉璃黄色琉璃筒瓦

单翘单昂五踩斗拱

金楼大点金彩画

神武门正立面图
Front Elevation of the Gate of Divine Prowess

0 1 2   5m

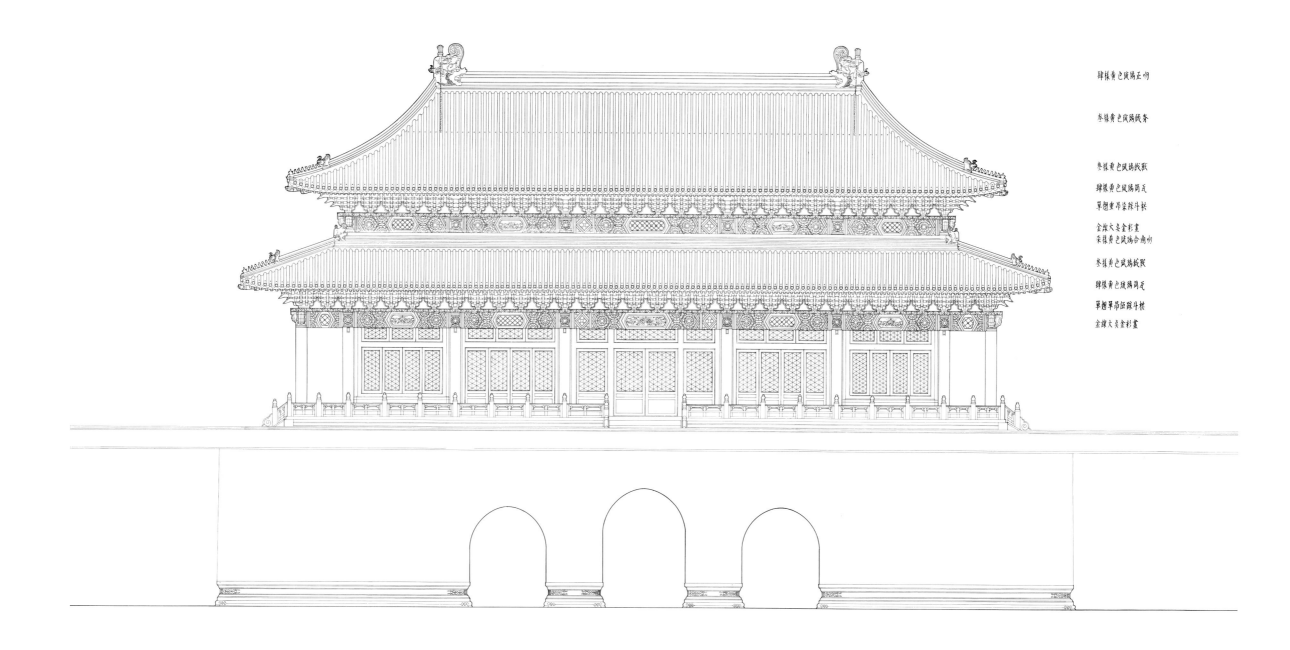

铺模黄色琉璃正吻

叁样黄色庑殿戗脊

叁样黄色琉璃戗兽

铺模黄色琉璃筒瓦

单翘重昂荣陡斗栱

金琢大点金彩画

叁样黄色琉璃合角吻

叁样黄色琉璃戗兽

铺模黄色琉璃筒瓦

单翘单昂五踩斗栱

金琢大点金彩画

神武门背立面图

Back Elevation of the Gate of Divine Prowess

0 1 2   5m

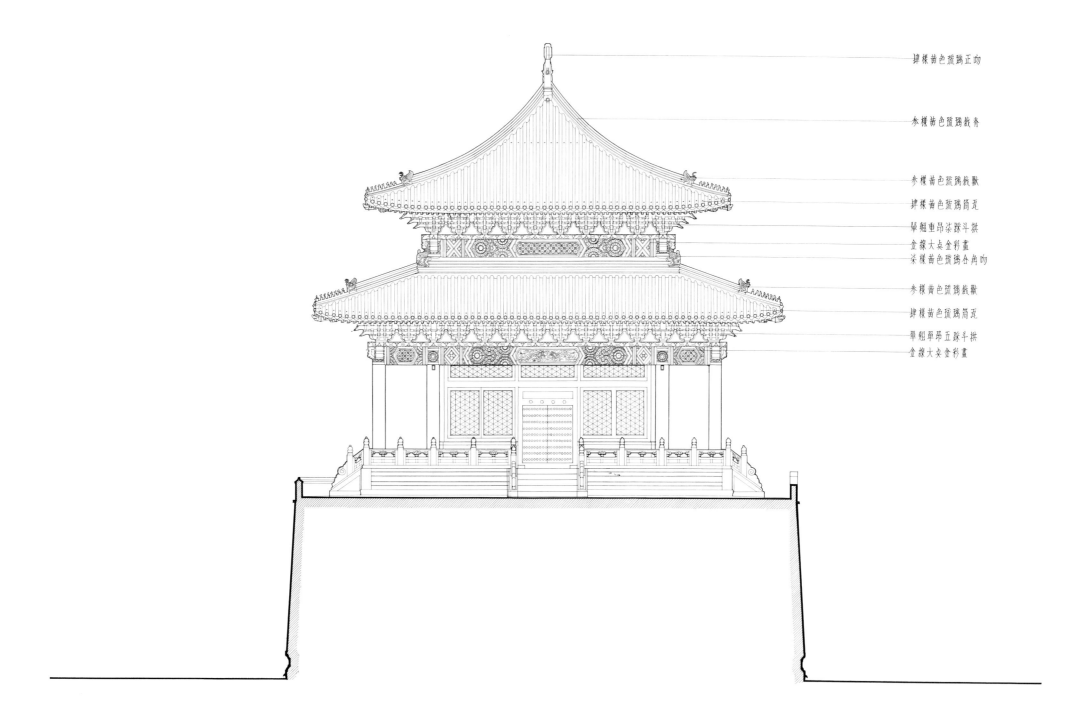

肆样黄色琉璃顶正吻

参样黄色琉璃戗脊

参样黄色琉璃戗兽
肆样黄色琉璃筒瓦
单翘重昂溜金斗拱
金线大点金彩画
柒样黄色琉璃合角吻

参样黄色琉璃戗兽
肆样黄色琉璃筒瓦
单翘单昂五踩斗拱
金线大点金彩画

神武门侧立面图
Side Elevation of the Gate of Divine Prowess

0 1 2   5m

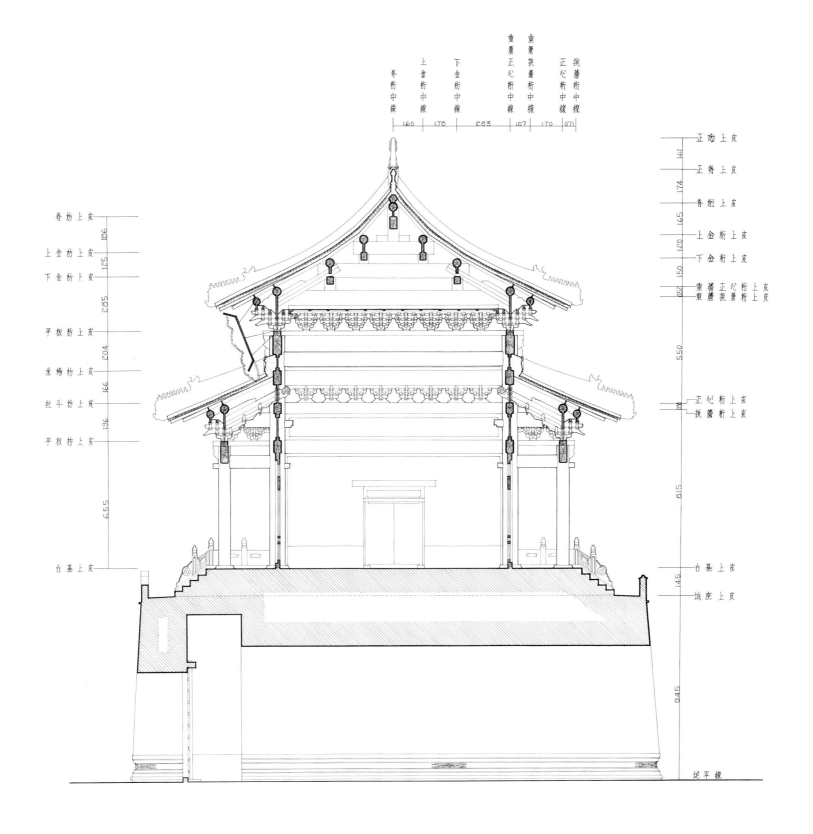

脊枋上皮 156

上金枋上皮 125

下金枋上皮 285

平板枋上皮 204

承椽枋上皮 166

扯斗枋上皮 136

平板枋上皮 655

白基上皮

重檐提檐桁中线
重檐正心桁中线
挑檐桁中线
正心桁中线

脊桁中线
上金桁中线
下金桁中线

160 178 283 107 170 071

正吻上皮 161
正脊上皮 174
脊桁上皮 165
上金桁上皮 120
下金桁上皮 150
重檐正心桁上皮 052
重檐挑檐桁上皮

正心桁上皮 102
挑檐桁上皮

白基上皮 615

白基上皮 145
城座上皮

845

地平线

0 1 2 5m

神武门横剖面图
Cross Section of the Gate of Divine Prowess

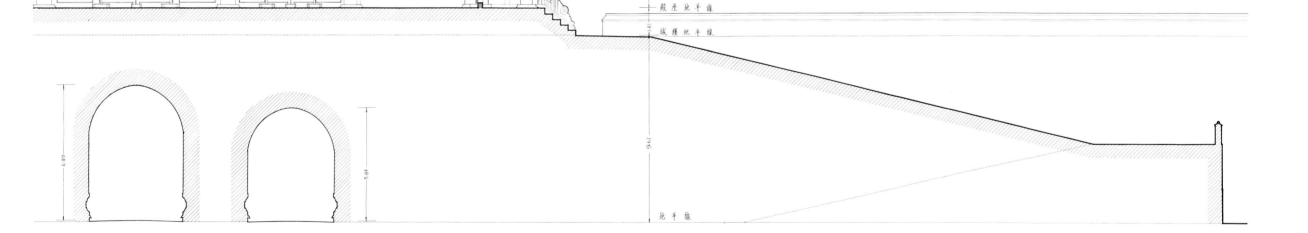

神武门纵剖面图

Longitudinal Section of the Gate of Divine Prowess

0 1 2 5 10m

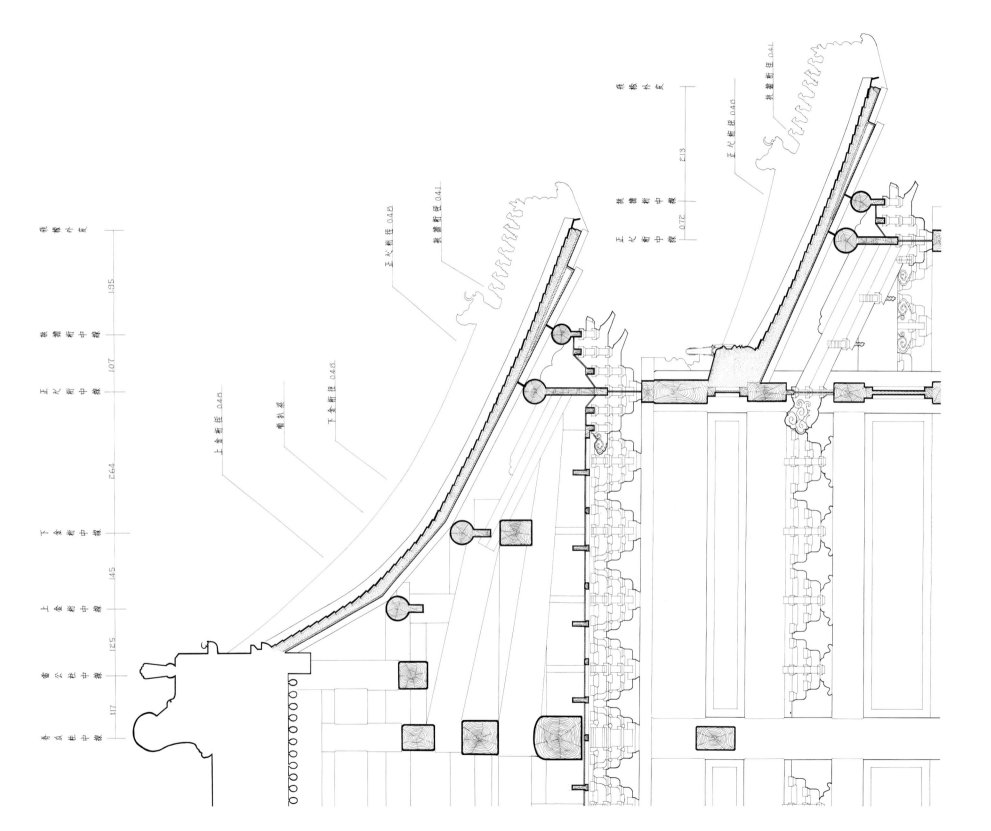

神武门细部图（一）

Detailed Drawing of the Gate of Divine Prowess（Ⅰ）

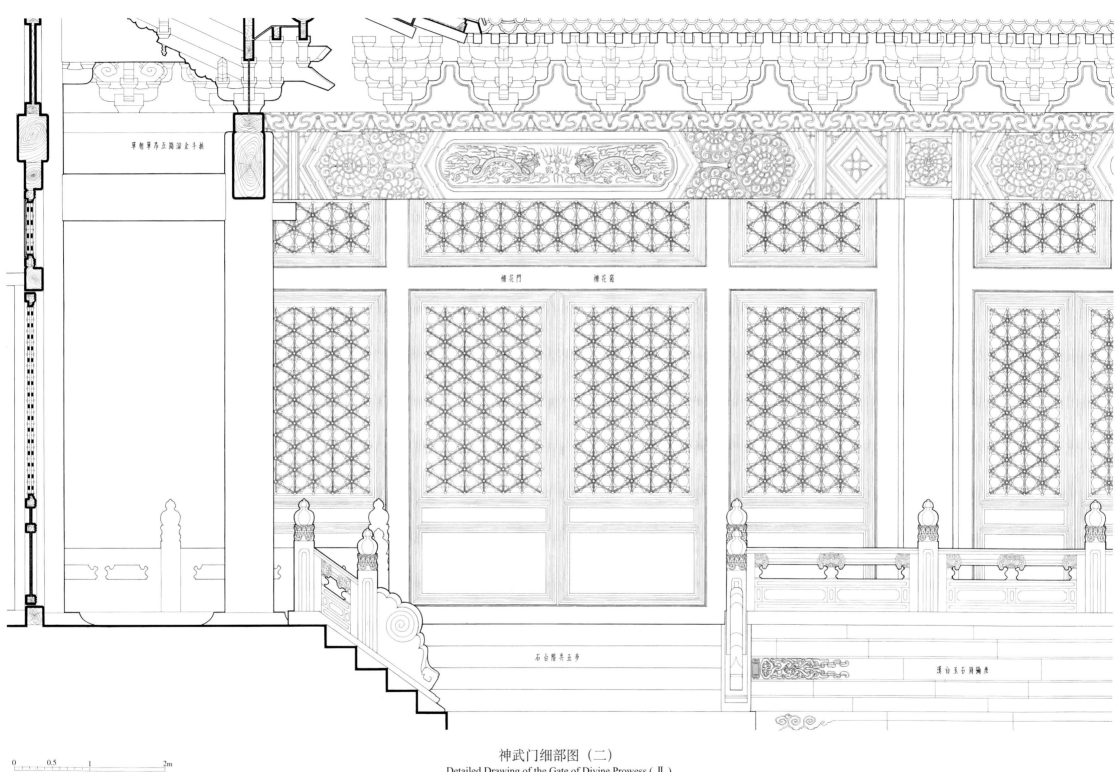

神武门细部图（二）
Detailed Drawing of the Gate of Divine Prowess（Ⅱ）

0 　0.5 　1 　　2m

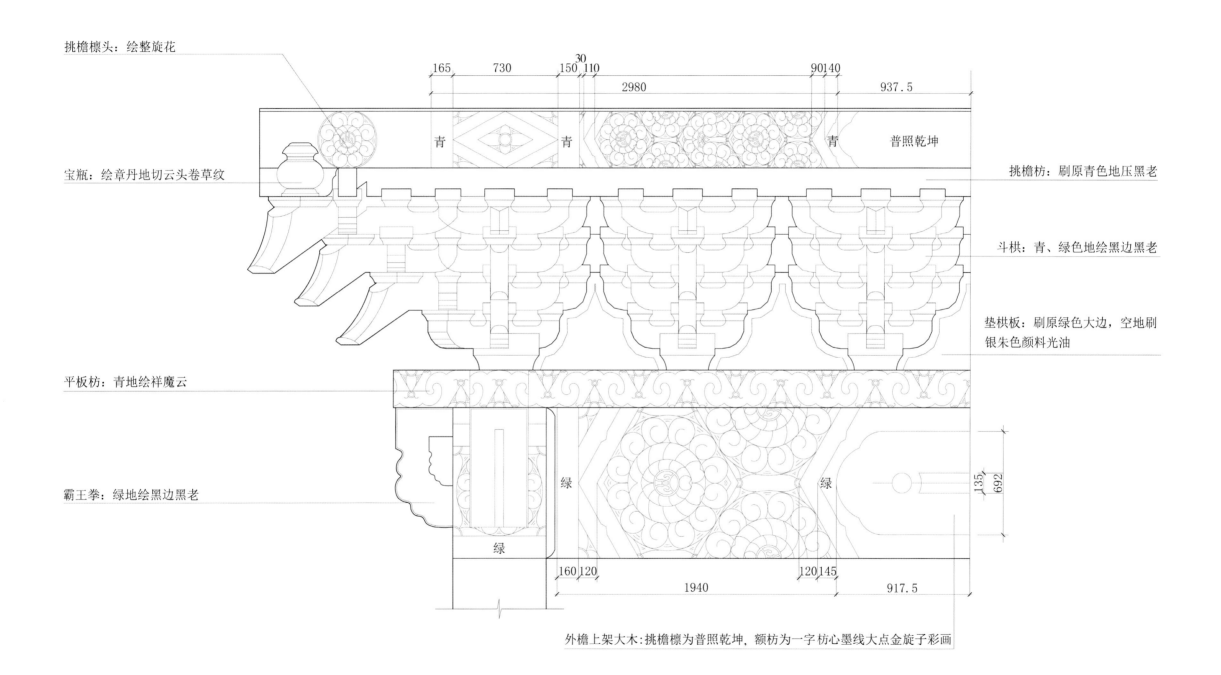

挑檐檩头：绘整旋花

宝瓶：绘章丹地切云头卷草纹

平板枋：青地绘祥魔云

霸王拳：绿地绘黑边黑老

挑檐枋：刷原青色地压黑老

斗栱：青、绿色地绘黑边黑老

垫栱板：刷原绿色大边，空地刷
银朱色颜料光油

165　730　150　110　30　90　140　2980　937.5

青　青　青　普照乾坤

绿　绿　绿

160　120　1940　120　145　917.5　135　692

外檐上架大木：挑檐檩为普照乾坤，额枋为一字枋心墨线大点金旋子彩画

神武门上檐梢间外檐彩画现状图

Present Condition of the Colored Paintings of the Front and Back Elevations' Westmost and Eastmost Bays under the Upper Eave, Gate of Divine Prowess

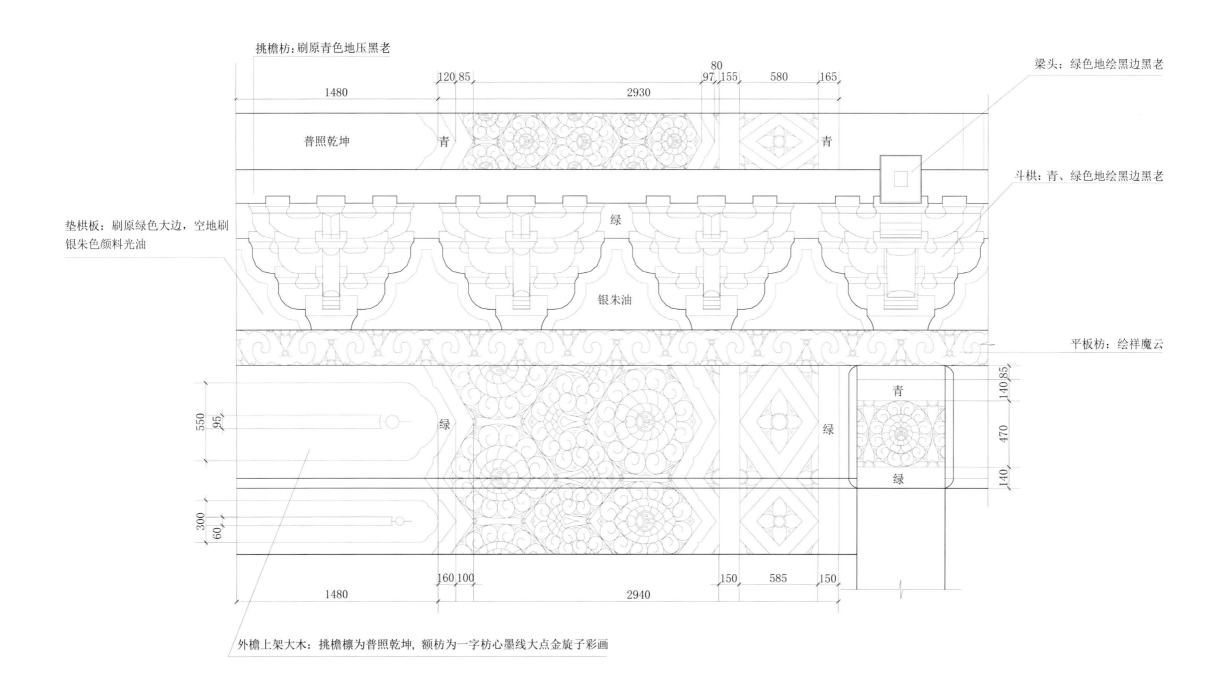

挑檐枋：刷原青色地压黑老

梁头：绿色地绘黑边黑老

斗栱：青、绿色地绘黑边黑老

垫栱板：刷原绿色大边，空地刷
银朱色颜料光油

平板枋：绘祥魔云

普照乾坤　　青　　　　　　　　　　　青

绿

银朱油

绿　　　　　　　　　　　绿　　青

绿

1480　　　120 85　　　2930　　80 97 155　580　165

550 95　　　300 60

140 85　470　140

1480　　160 100　　　2940　　150 585 150

外檐上架大木：挑檐檩为普照乾坤，额枋为一字枋心墨线大点金旋子彩画

神武门下檐明间外檐彩画现状图
Present Condition of the Colored Paintings of the Front and Back Elevations' Central Bays under the Lower Eave, Gate of Divine Prowess

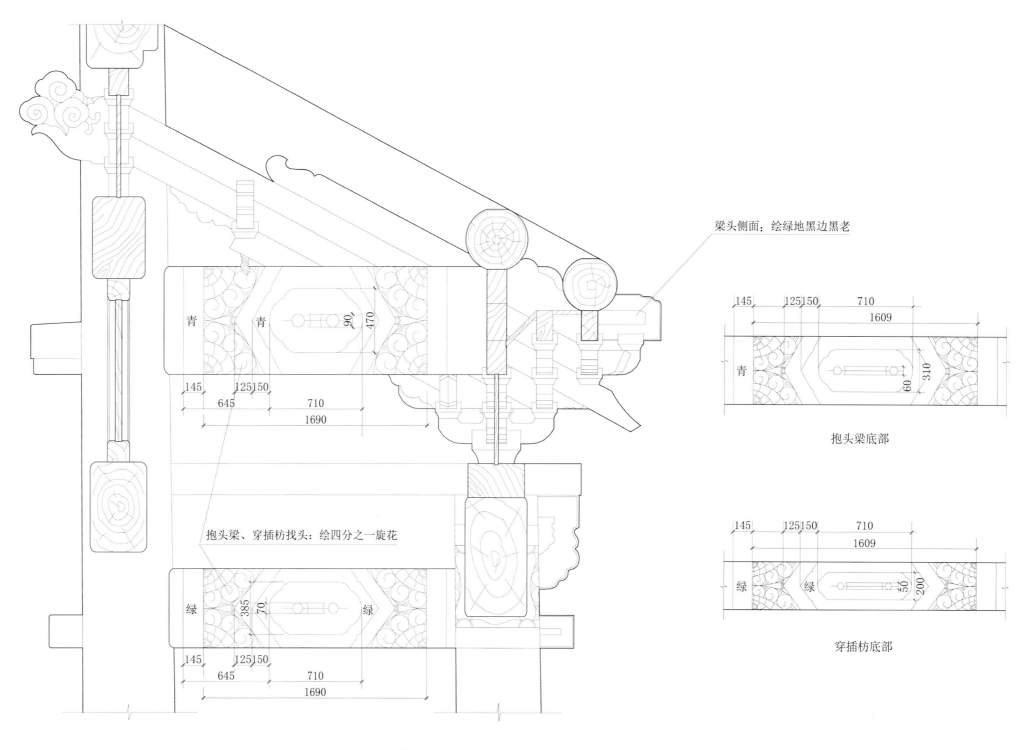

梁头侧面：绘绿地黑边黑老

青　青

青

抱头梁底部

抱头梁、穿插枋找头：绘四分之一旋花

绿　绿

绿　绿

穿插枋底部

神武门下檐抱头梁、穿插枋彩画现状图

Present Condition of the Colored Paintings on the Head Beams and Penetrating Ties under the Lower Eave, Gate of Divine Prowess

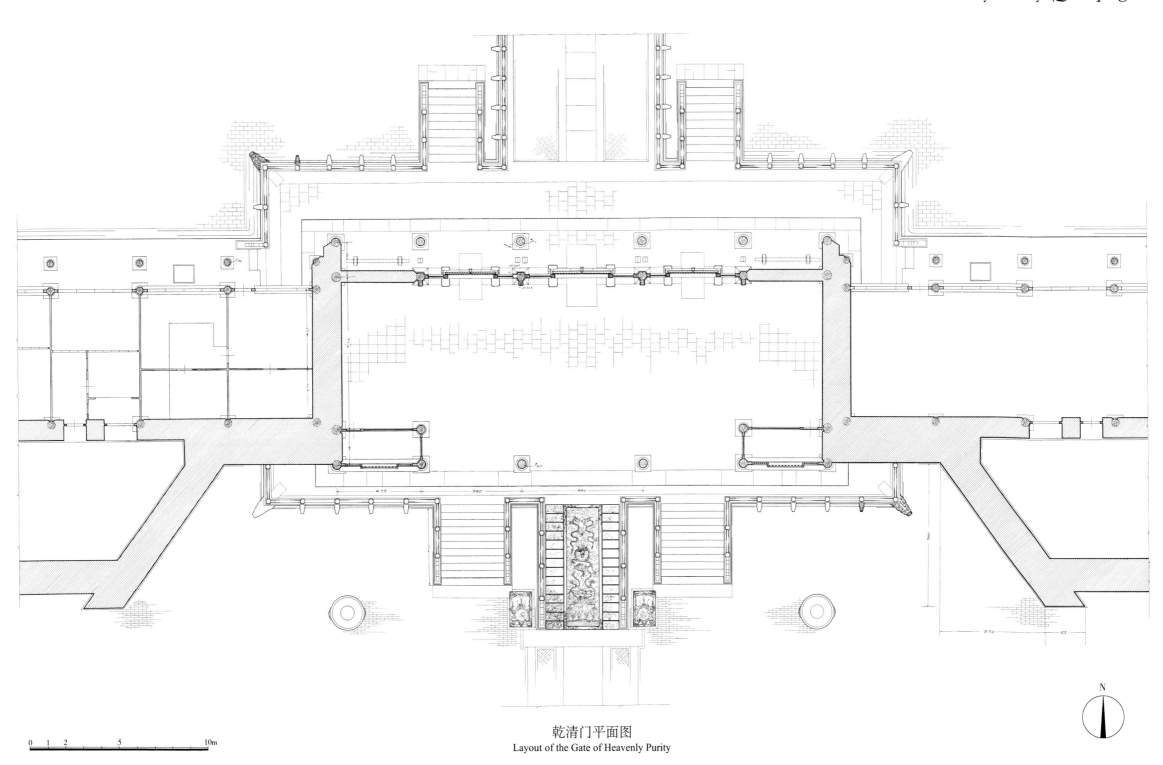

乾清门平面图
Layout of the Gate of Heavenly Purity

0 1 2 5 10m

N

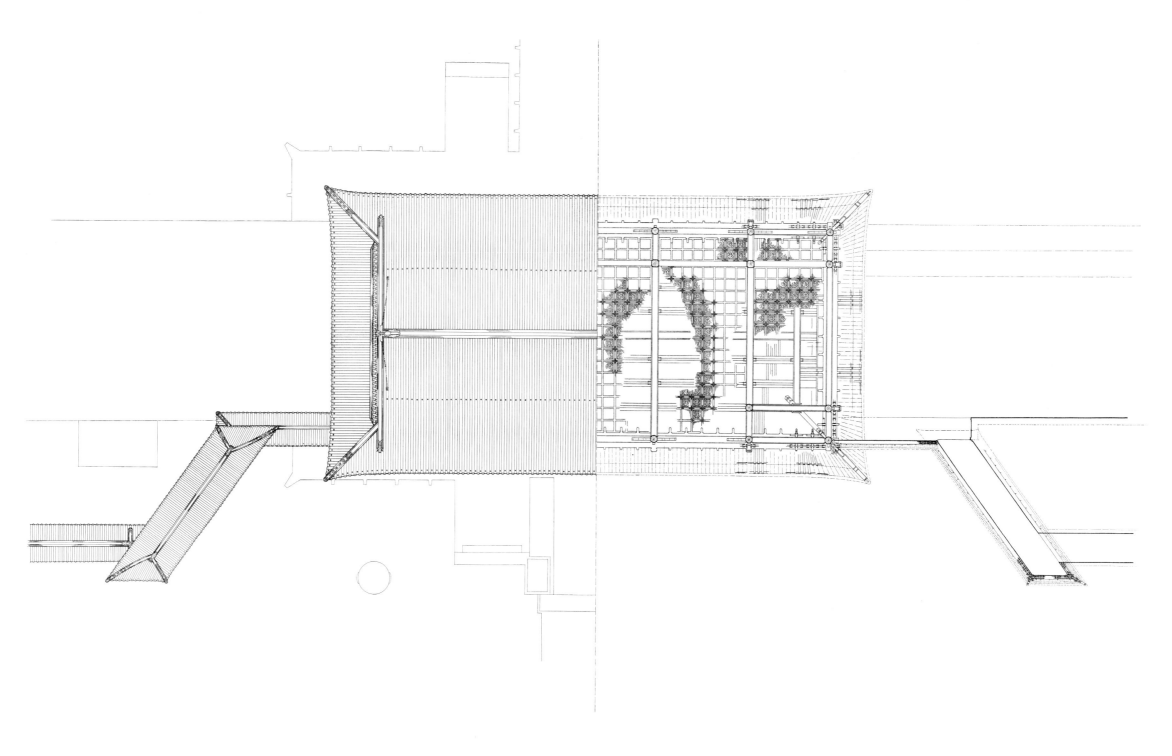

乾清门天花屋顶平面图
Bottom View of the Ceiling Panels and Top View of the Roof, Gate of Heavenly

0　2　4　6　8　10m

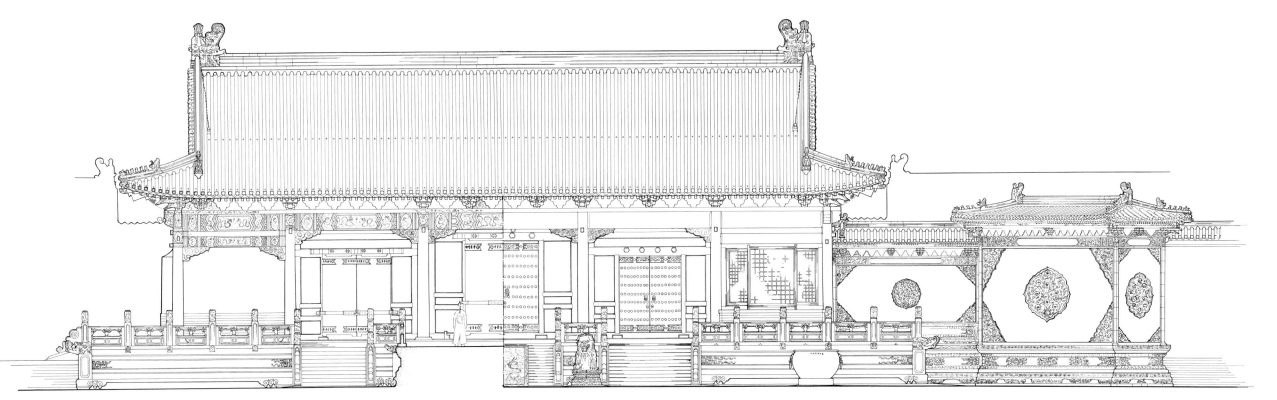

乾清门正立及背立面图
Front and Back Elevations of the Gate of Heavenly Purity

0 1 2 5 10m

191

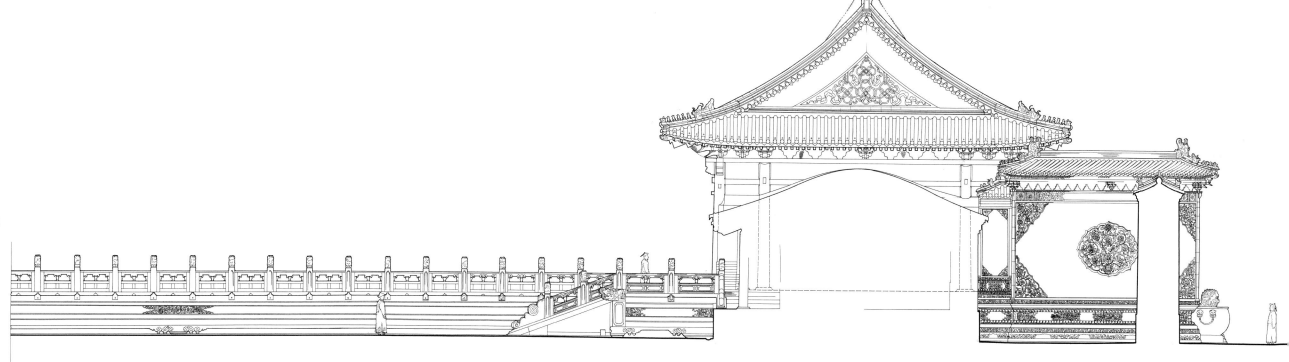

乾清门侧立面图

Side Elevation of the Gate of Heavenly Purity

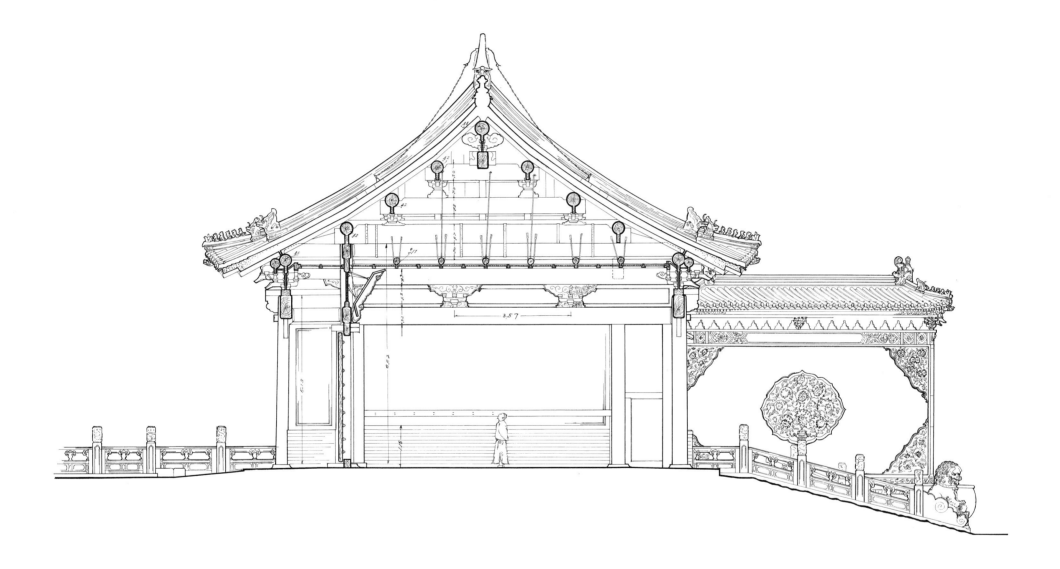

乾清门纵剖、横剖面图
Longitudinal Section of the Gate of Heavenly Purity、Cross Section of the Gate of Heavenly Purity

0 1 2 5m

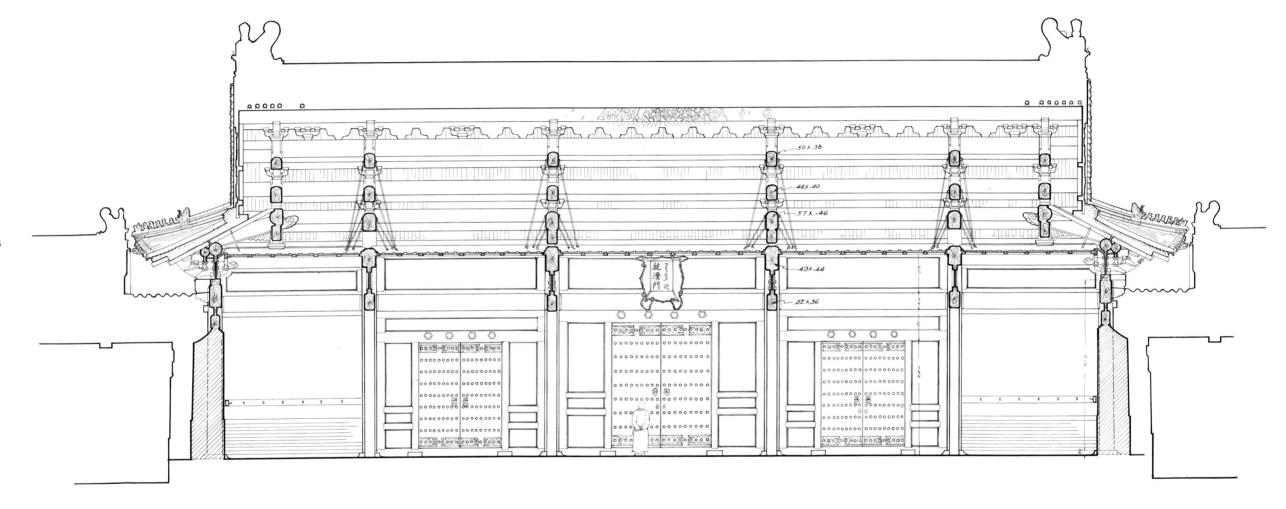

乾清门纵剖、横剖面图
Longitudinal Section of the Gate of Heavenly Purity、 Cross Section of the Gate of Heavenly Purity

0 1 2 5m

注：经核验，原图比例尺单位"公尺"有误，应为"公寸"（dm）。

乾清门屋顶山花板详图
Detailed Drawing of the Pediments, Gate of Heavenly Purity

乾清门前铜狮子详图
Detailed Drawing of the Lions in Front of the Gate of Heavenly Purity

0　0.1　0.2　　0.5　　　　　1m

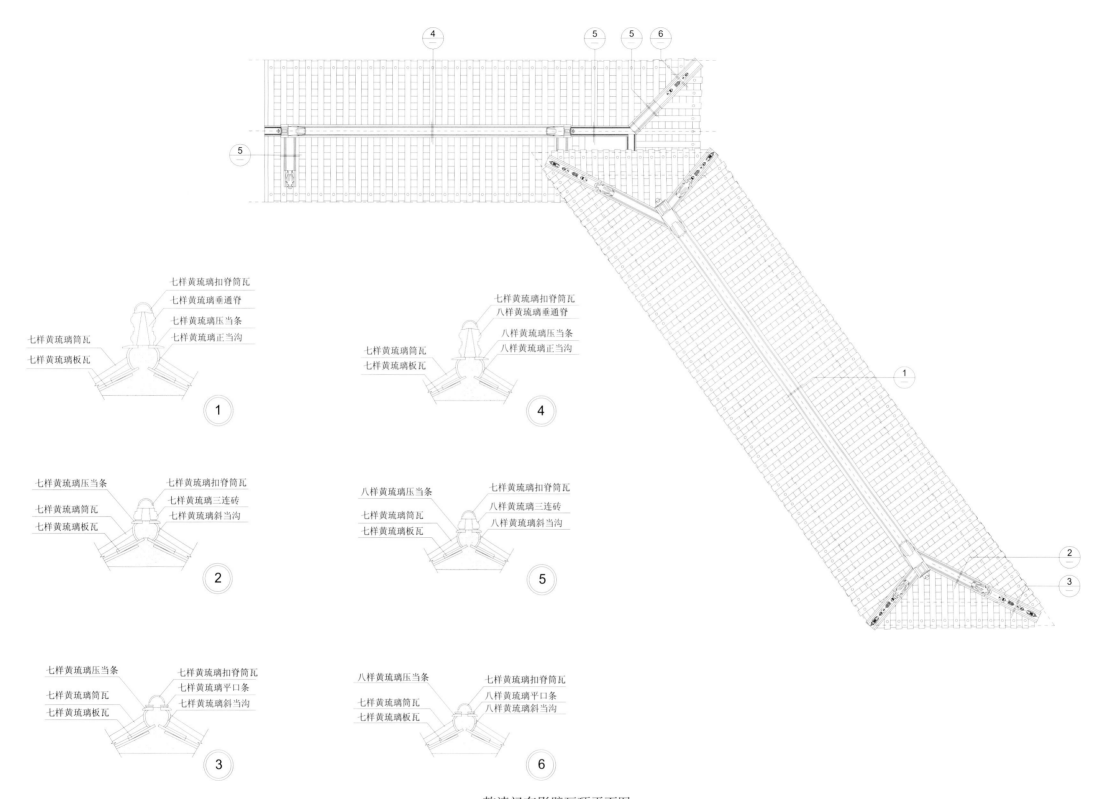

七样黄琉璃筒瓦
七样黄琉璃板瓦

七样黄琉璃扣脊筒瓦
七样黄琉璃垂通脊
七样黄琉璃压当条
七样黄琉璃正当沟

1

七样黄琉璃压当条
七样黄琉璃筒瓦
七样黄琉璃板瓦

七样黄琉璃扣脊筒瓦
七样黄琉璃三连砖
七样黄琉璃斜当沟

2

七样黄琉璃压当条
七样黄琉璃筒瓦
七样黄琉璃板瓦

七样黄琉璃扣脊筒瓦
七样黄琉璃平口条
七样黄琉璃斜当沟

3

七样黄琉璃筒瓦
七样黄琉璃板瓦

七样黄琉璃扣脊筒瓦
八样黄琉璃垂通脊
八样黄琉璃压当条
八样黄琉璃正当沟

4

八样黄琉璃压当条
七样黄琉璃筒瓦
七样黄琉璃板瓦

七样黄琉璃扣脊筒瓦
八样黄琉璃三连砖
八样黄琉璃斜当沟

5

八样黄琉璃压当条
七样黄琉璃筒瓦
七样黄琉璃板瓦

七样黄琉璃扣脊筒瓦
八样黄琉璃平口条
八样黄琉璃斜当沟

6

乾清门东影壁瓦顶平面图
Top View of the Roofing Tiles, Eastern Part of the Splayed Glaze-tile Screens, Gate of Heavenly Purity

0   1   2m

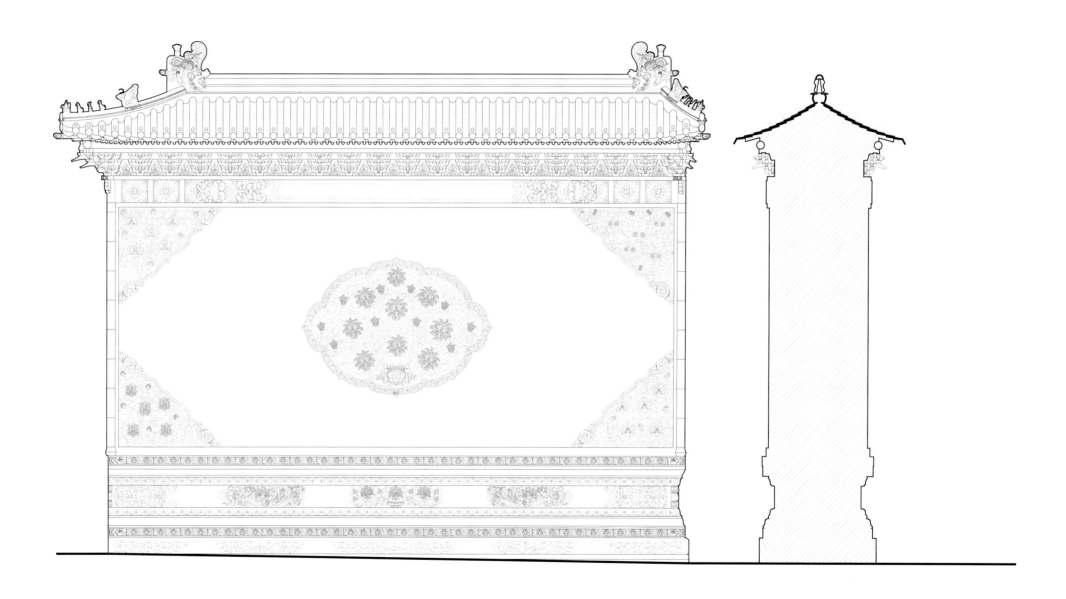

东影壁八字部分正立面图
Front Elevation of the Diagonal Screen, Eastern Part of the Splayed Glaze-tile

东影壁八字部分剖面图
Section of the Diagonal Screen, Eastern Part of the Splayed Glaze-tile Screens

0　　　　1　　　　2m

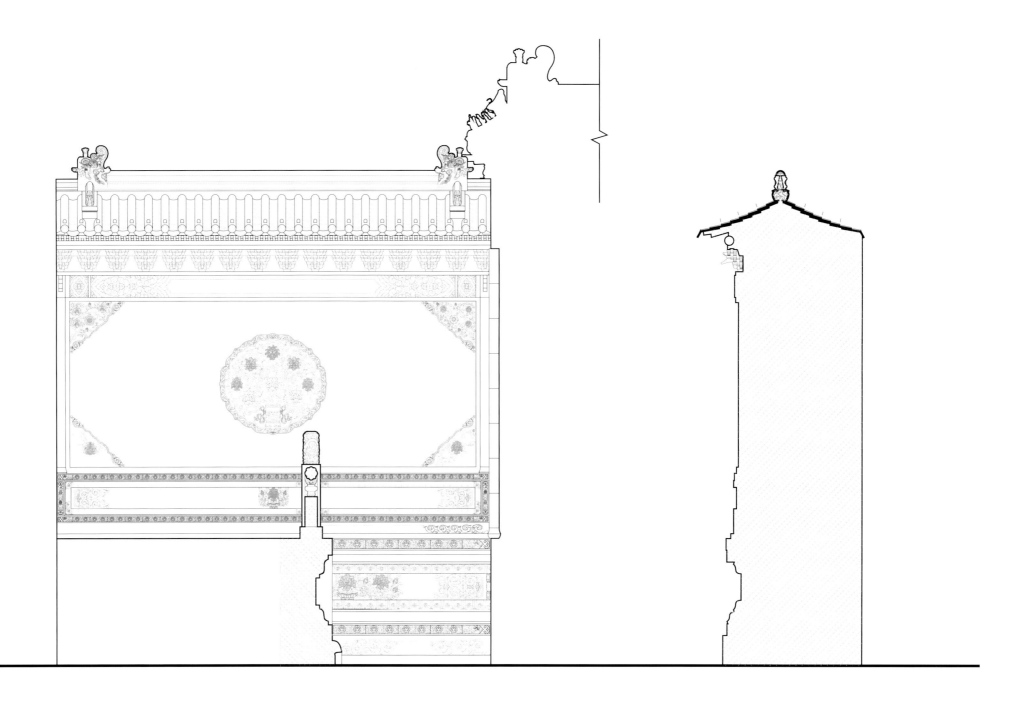

东影壁一字部分正立面图
Front Elevation of the Southfacing Screen, Eastern Part
of the Splayed Glaze-tile

0　　　　1　　　　2m

东影壁一字部分剖面图
Section of the Southfacing Screen, Eastern Part of the
Splayed Glaze-tile Screens

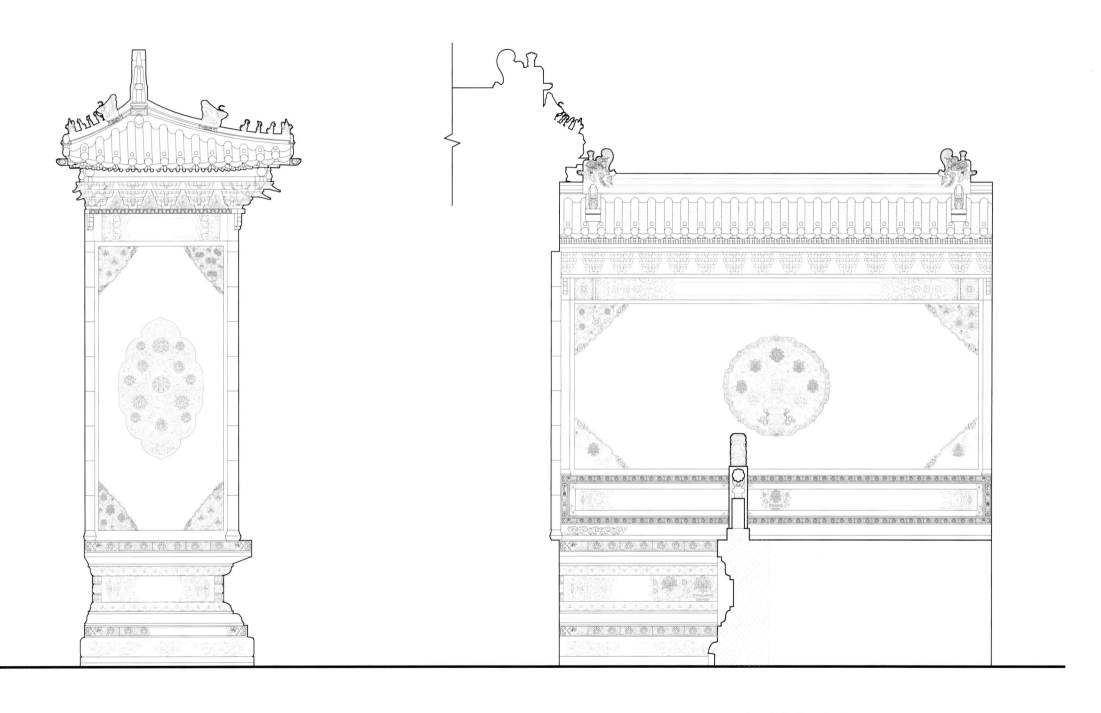

东影壁八字部分侧立面图
Side Elevation of the Diagonal Screen, Eastern Part of
the Splayed Glaze-tile

西影壁一字部分正立面图
Front Elevation of the Southfacing Screen, Western Part
of the Splayed Glaze-tile

0   1   2m

西影壁八字部分侧立面图
Side Elevation of the Diagonal Screen, Western Part of the
Splayed Glaze-tile

西影壁八字部分正立面图
Front Elevation of the Diagonal Screen, Western Part of the
Splayed Glaze-tile

0   1   2m

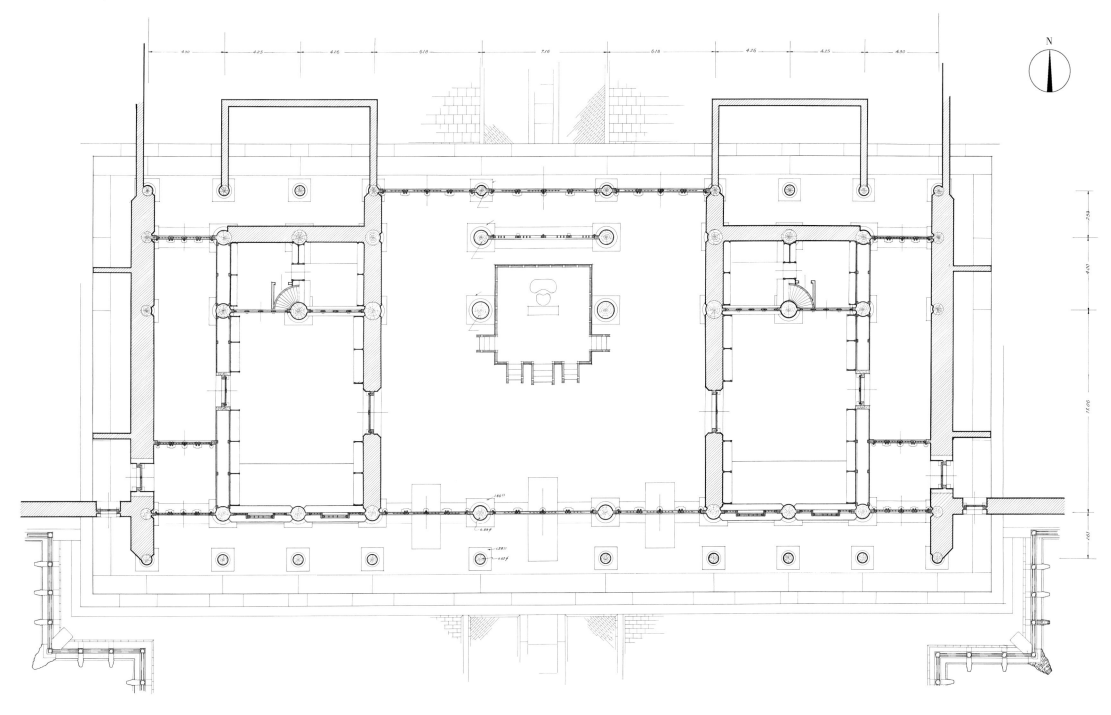

N

0 1 2 5 10m

乾清宫平面图
Floor Plan of the Palace of Heavenly Purity

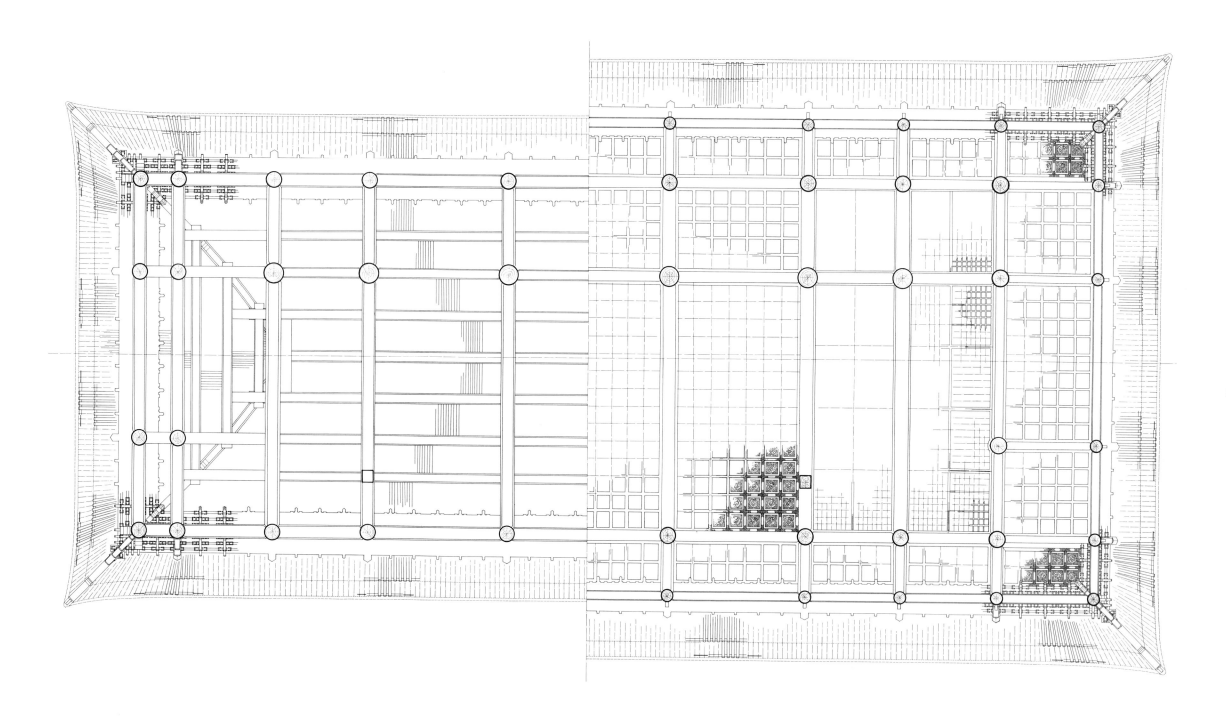

乾清宫天花平面图
Bottom View of the Ceiling Panels, Palace of Heavenly Purity

0　1　2　　　5　　　　　　10m

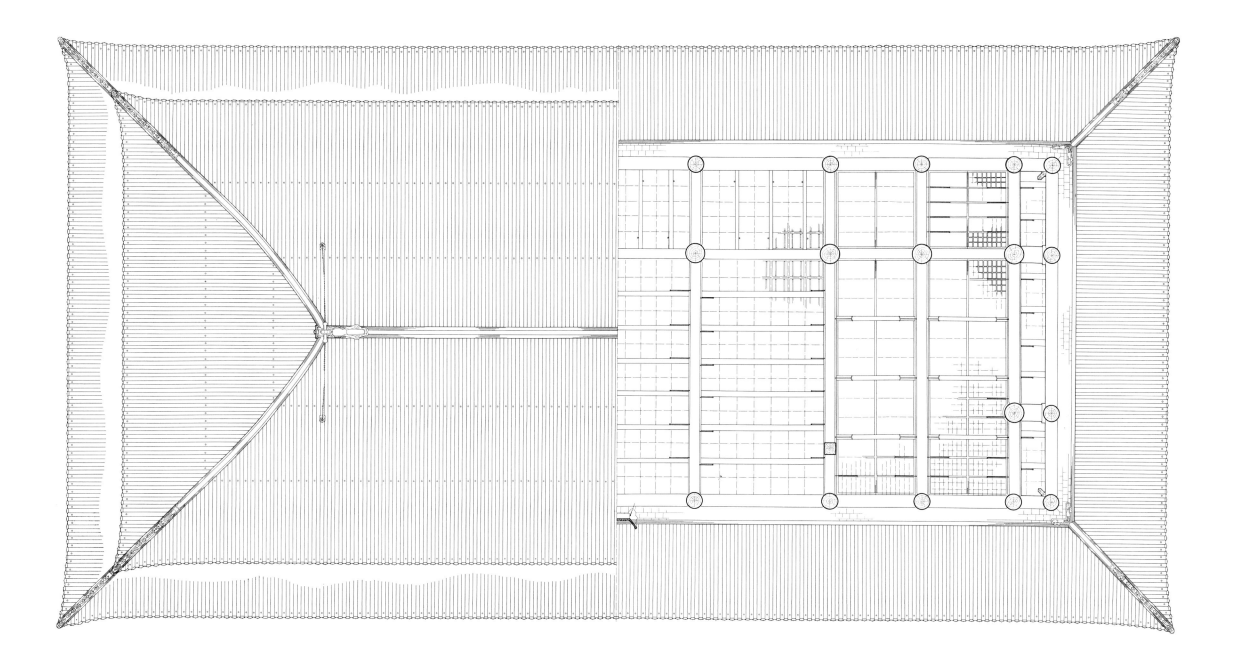

乾清宫屋顶平面图
Top View of the Roof, Palace of Heavenly Purity

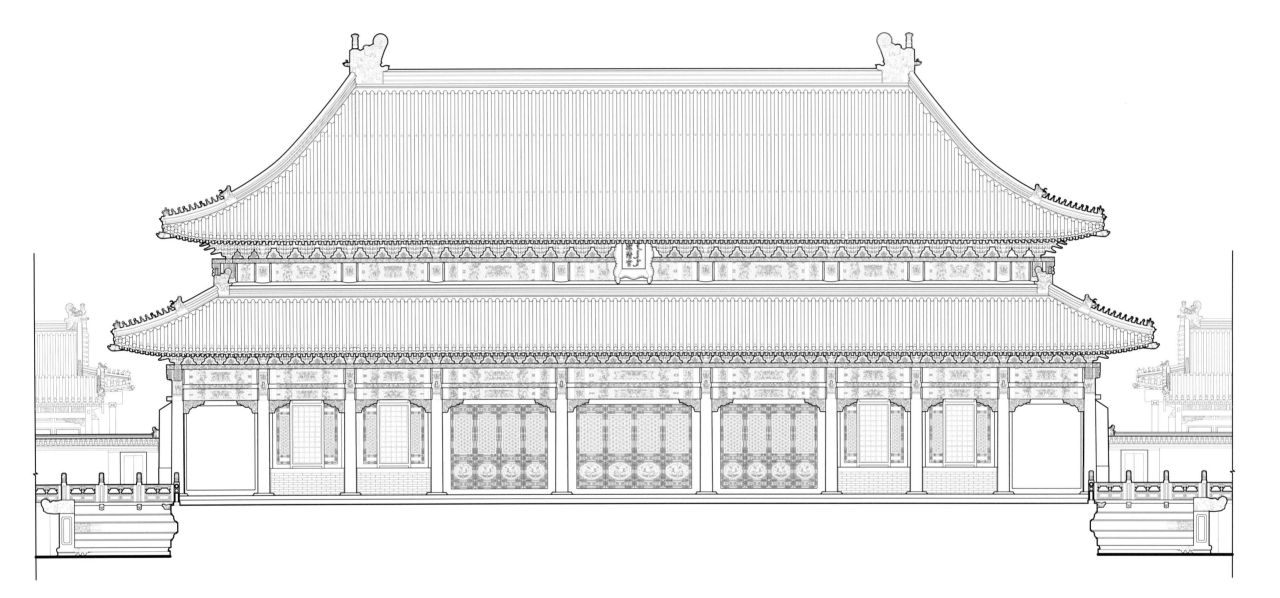

0　2　4　　　　10m

乾清宫正立面图
Front Elevation of the Palace of Heavenly Purity

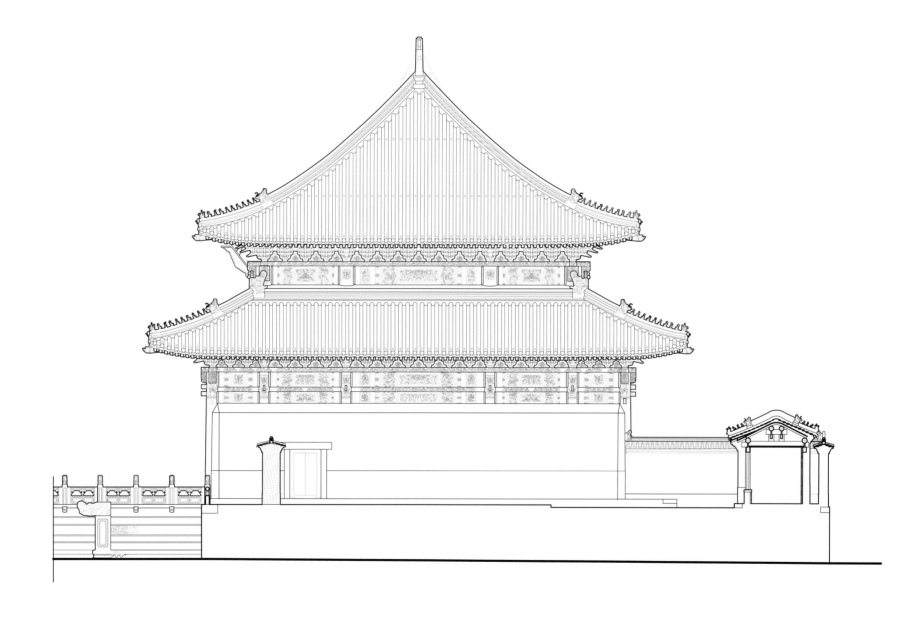

乾清宫侧立面图
Side Elevation of the Palace of Heavenly Purity

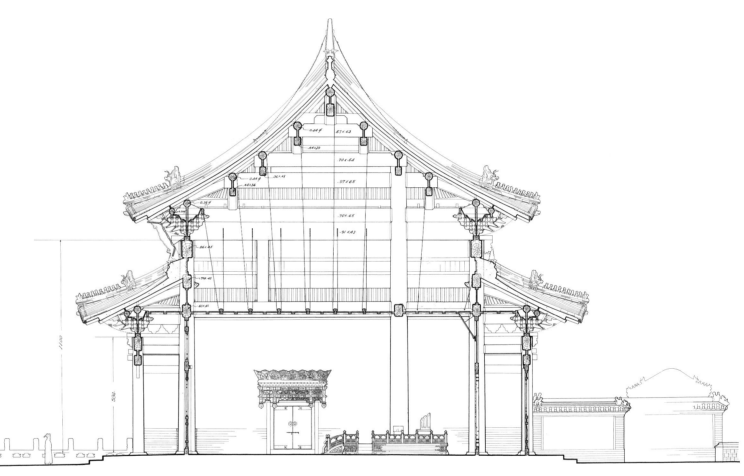

乾清宫横剖面图
Cross Section of the Palace of Heavenly Purity

0 1 3 5 7 9m

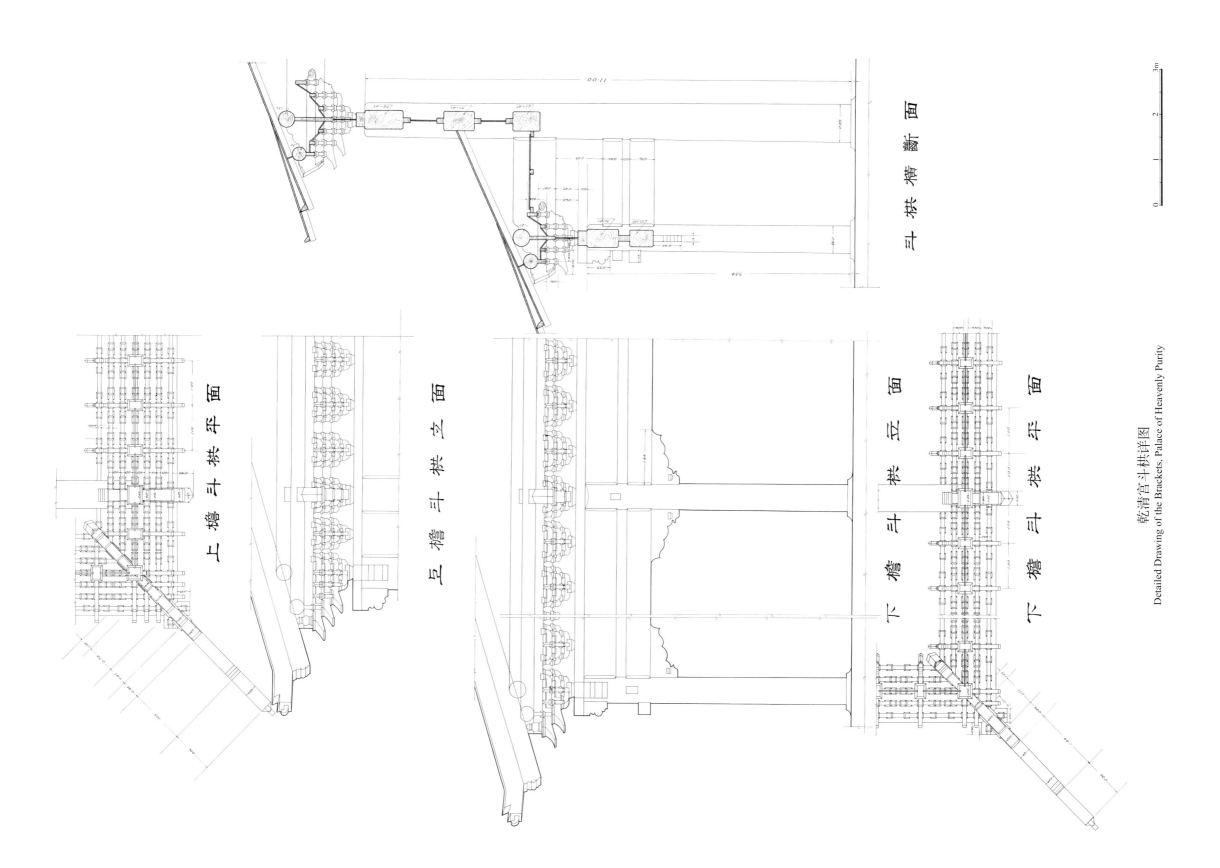

斗栱横断面

上檐斗栱平面

正檐斗栱立面

下檐斗栱立面

下檐斗栱平面

乾清宫斗栱详图

Detailed Drawing of the Brackets, Palace of Heavenly Purity

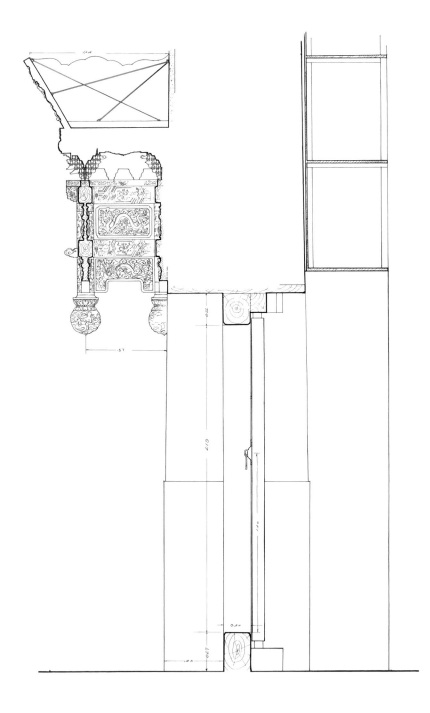

乾清宫内檐装修详图
Detailed Drawing of the Interior Decorations, Palace of Heavenly Purity

0　　　0.5　　　1　　　　　2m

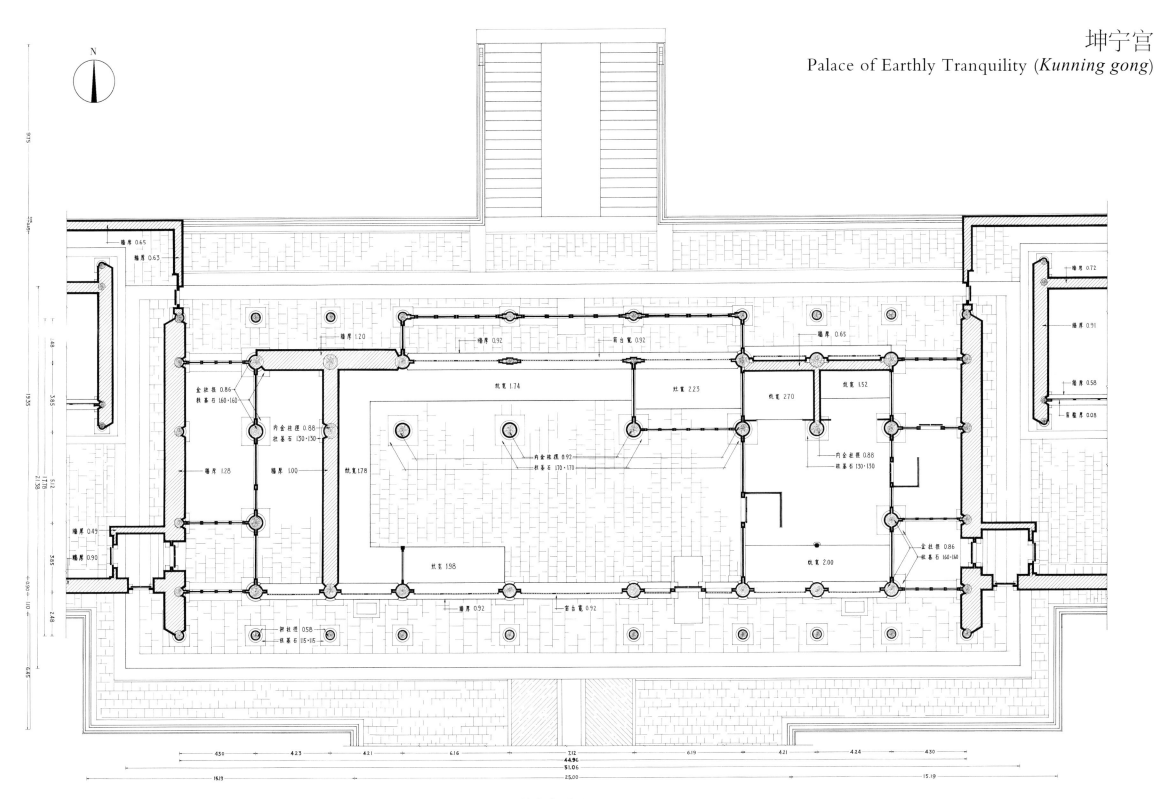

坤宁宫平面图
Floor Plan of the Palace of Earthly Tranquility

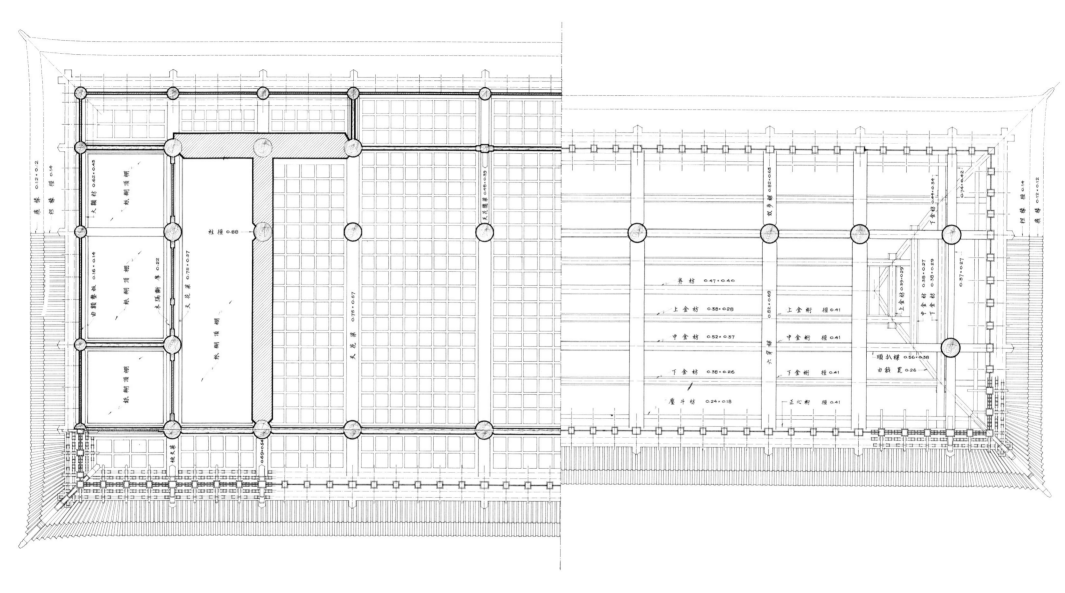

天 花 仰 视 平 面　　　　　　　　　　　重 簷 屋 架 仰 视 平 面

坤宁宫天花屋架平面图
Bottom View of the Ceiling Panels and Top View of the Trusses, Palace of Earthly Tranquility

0　1　2　　　5m

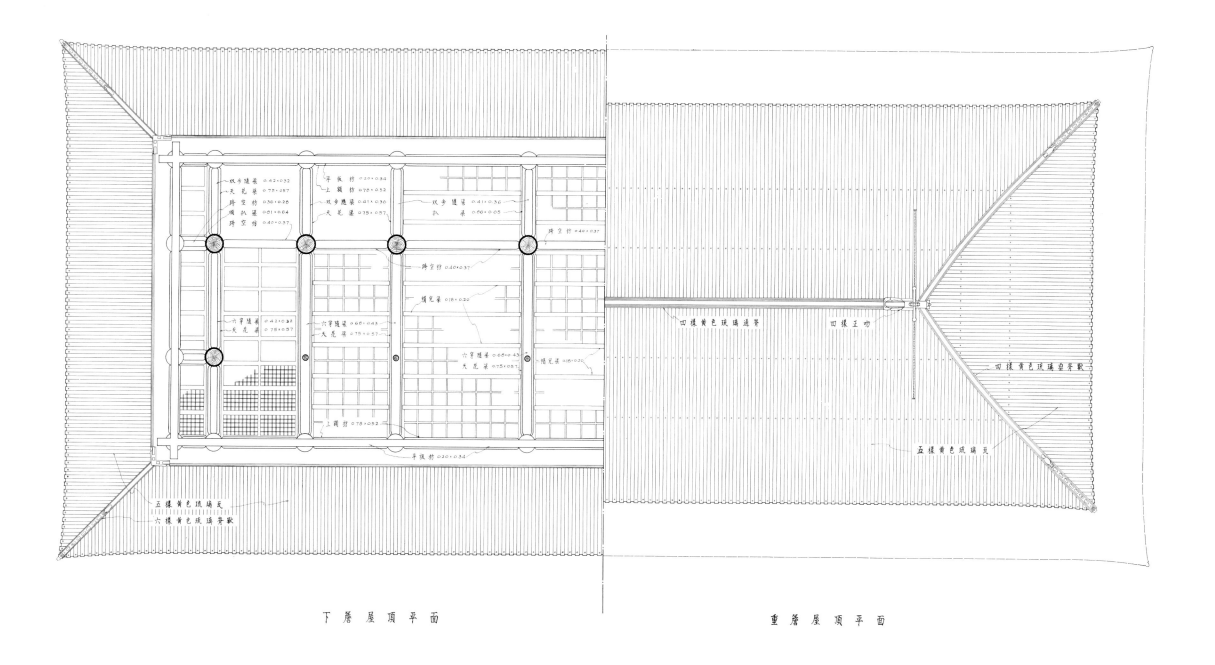

下 層 屋 頂 平 面

重 簷 屋 頂 平 面

坤宁宫屋顶平面图
Top View of the Roof, Palace of Earthly Tranquility

0 1 2 5m

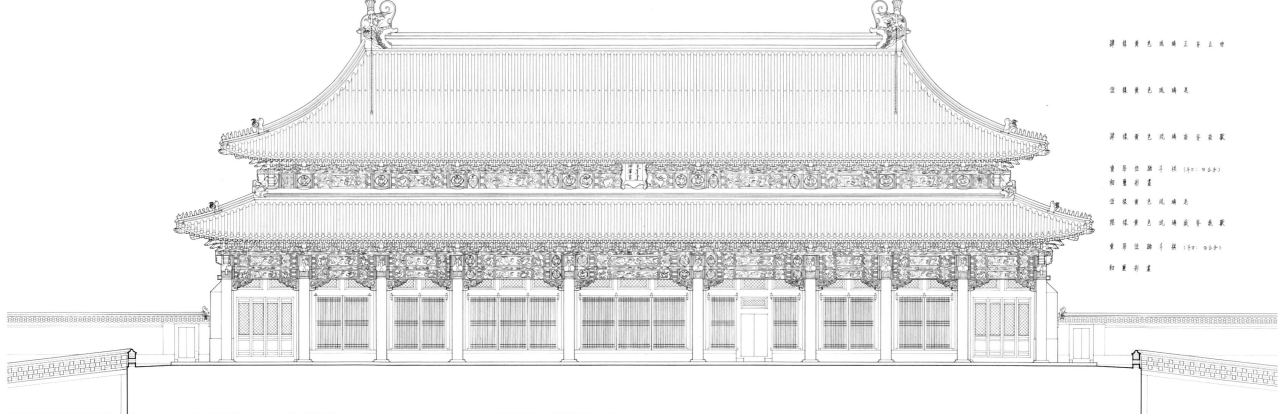

坤宁宫正立面图
Front Elevation of the Palace of Earthly Tranquility

0 1 2 5m

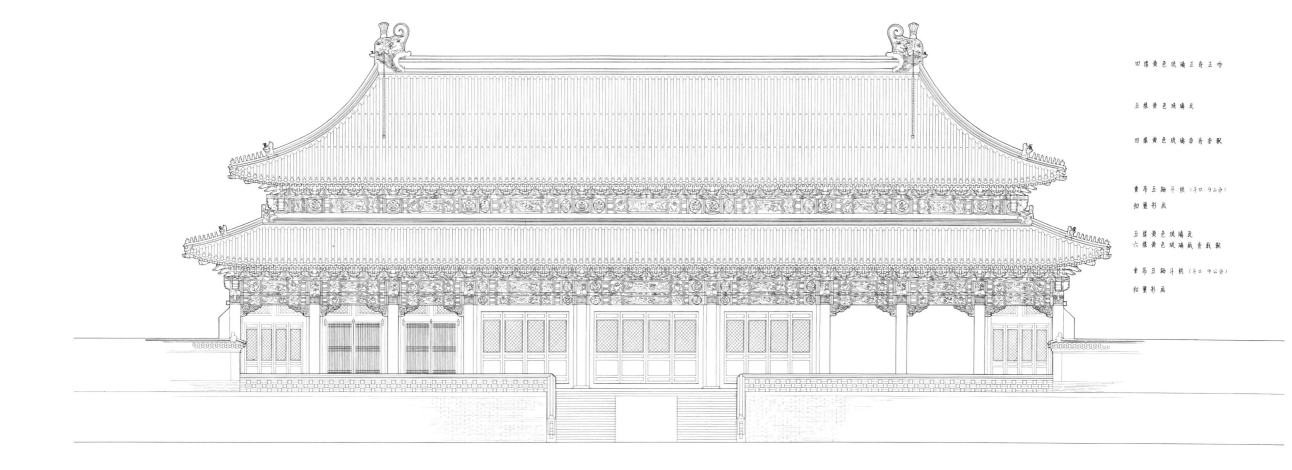

四樣黄色玻璃正脊正吻

五樣黄色玻璃瓦

四樣黄色玻璃合脊吞兽

重昂五踩斗栱（斗口：9公分）
扣置彩画

五樣黄色玻璃瓦
六樣黄色玻璃截脊戗兽

重昂五踩斗栱（斗口：9公分）
扣置彩画

坤宁宫背立面图
Back Elevation of the Palace of Earthly Tranquility

0 1 2 5m

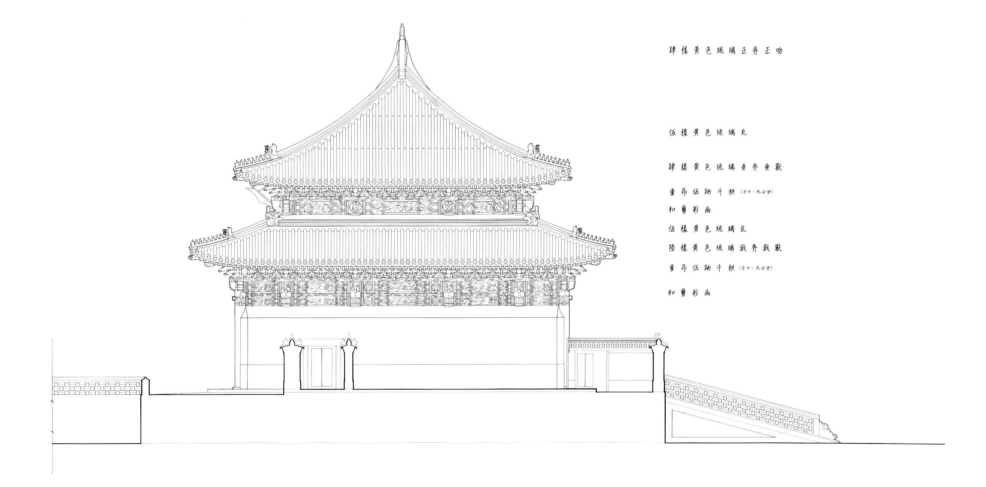

肆样黄色琉璃正脊正吻

伍样黄色琉璃瓦

肆样黄色琉璃垂脊垂兽
重昂伍踩斗栱（斗口：九公分）
和玺彩画
伍样黄色琉璃瓦
陆样黄色琉璃戗脊戗兽
重昂伍踩斗栱（斗口：九公分）

和玺彩画

坤宁宫侧立面图
Side Elevation of the Palace of Earthly Tranquility

0　1　2　　5m

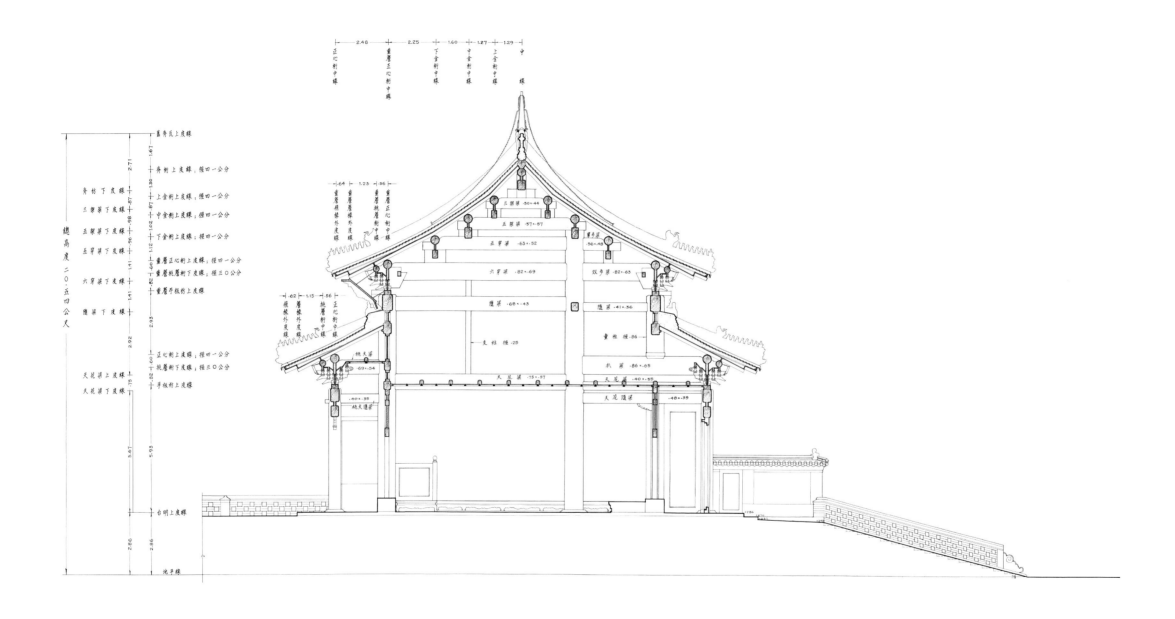

坤宁宫横剖面图
Cross Section of the Palace of Earthly Tranquility

0 1 2 5m

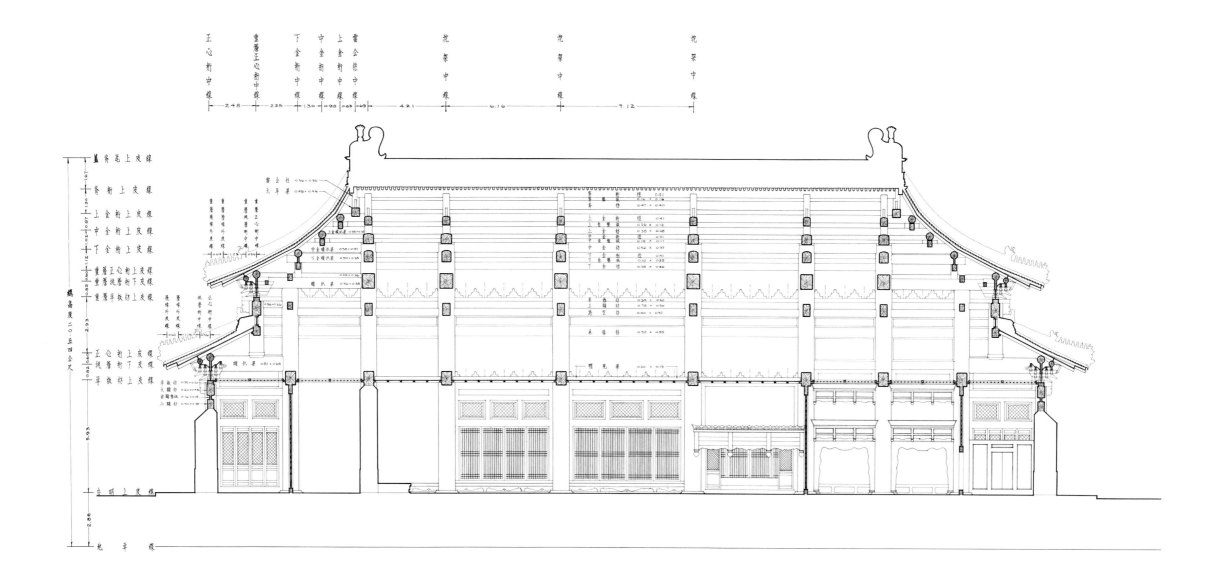

坤宁宫纵剖面图
Longitudinal Section of the Palace of Earthly Tranquility

0　1　2　　　5m

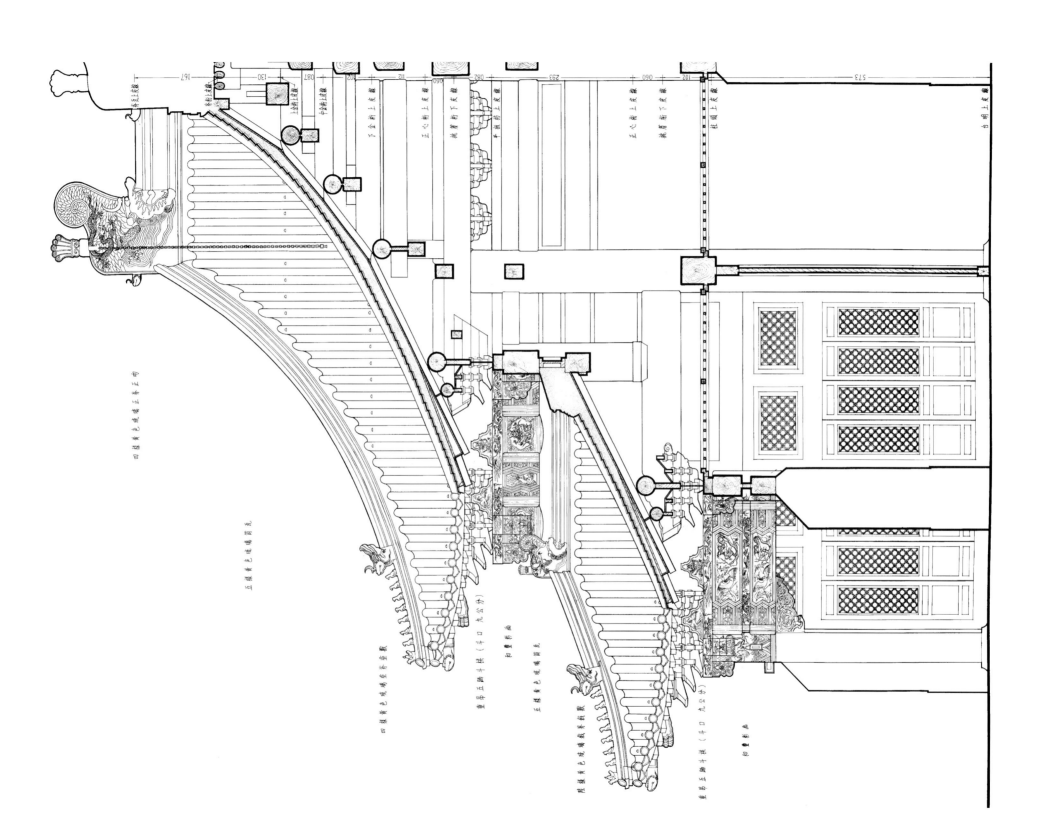

坤宁宫细部图（一）

Detailed Drawing of the Palace of Earthly Tranquility（Ⅰ）

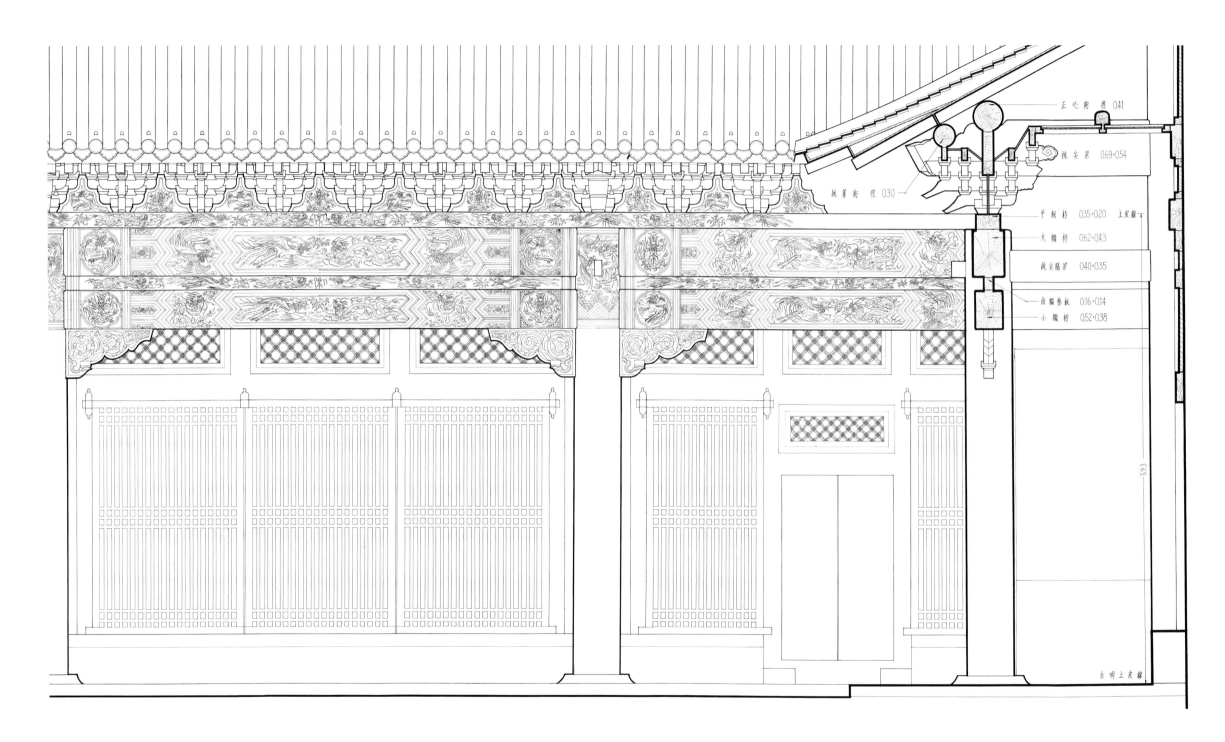

正心枯径 0.41

挑尖梁 0.69·0.54

挑檐枯径 0.30

平板枋 0.35·0.20 上发檐丁

大额枋 0.62·0.43

挑尖随梁 0.40·0.35

由额垫板 0.16·0.14

小额枋 0.52·0.38

台明上皮雄

坤宁宫细部图（二）
Detailed Drawing of the Palace of Earthly Tranquility（Ⅱ）

0 0.2 0.4 ___ 1m

长春宫
Palace of Eternal Spring (*Changchun gong*)

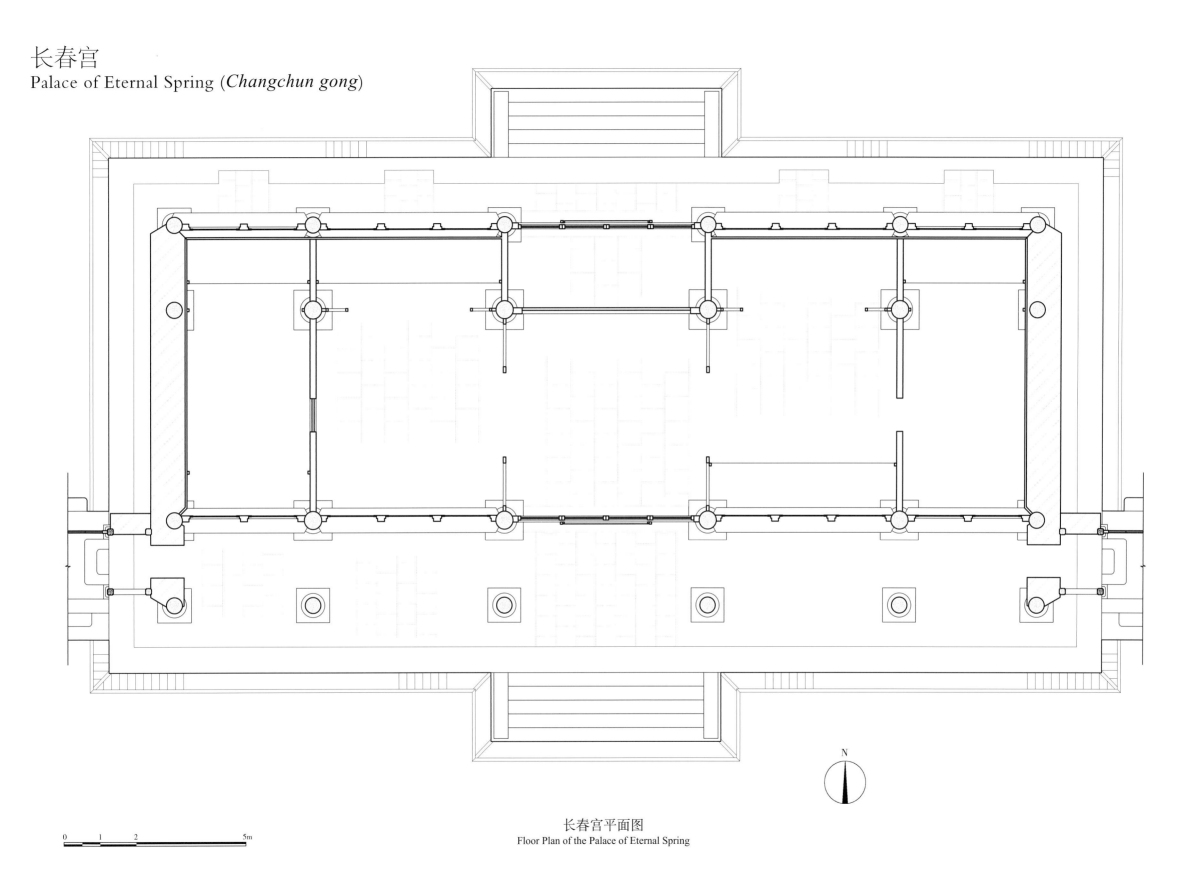

N

长春宫平面图
Floor Plan of the Palace of Eternal Spring

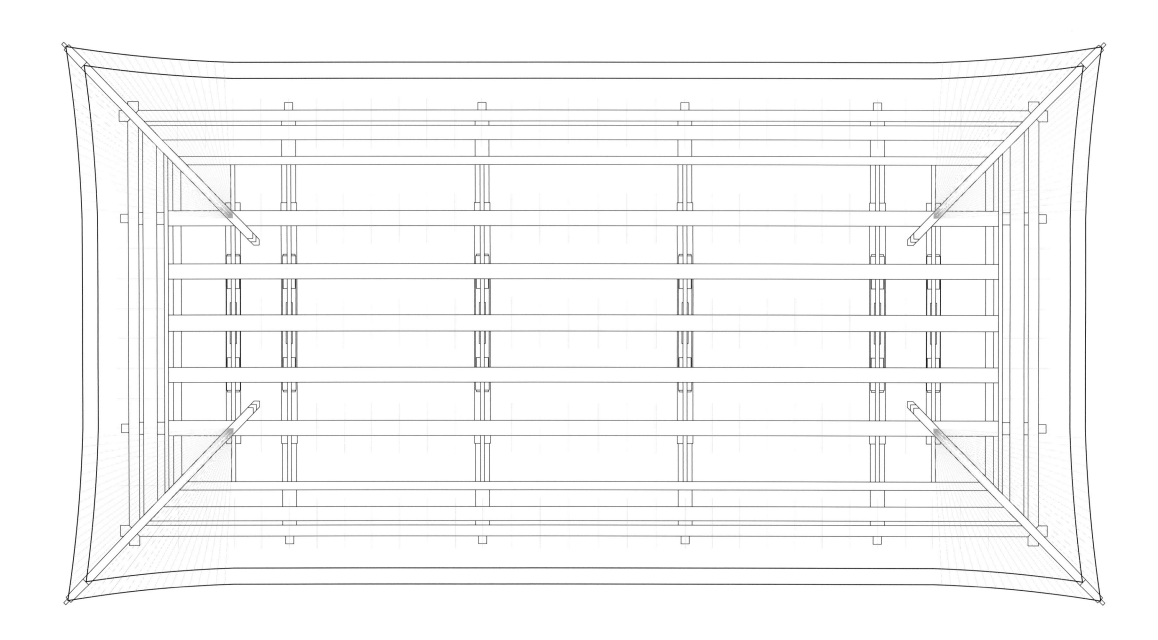

长春宫梁架俯视图
Top View of the Trusses, Palace of Eternal Spring

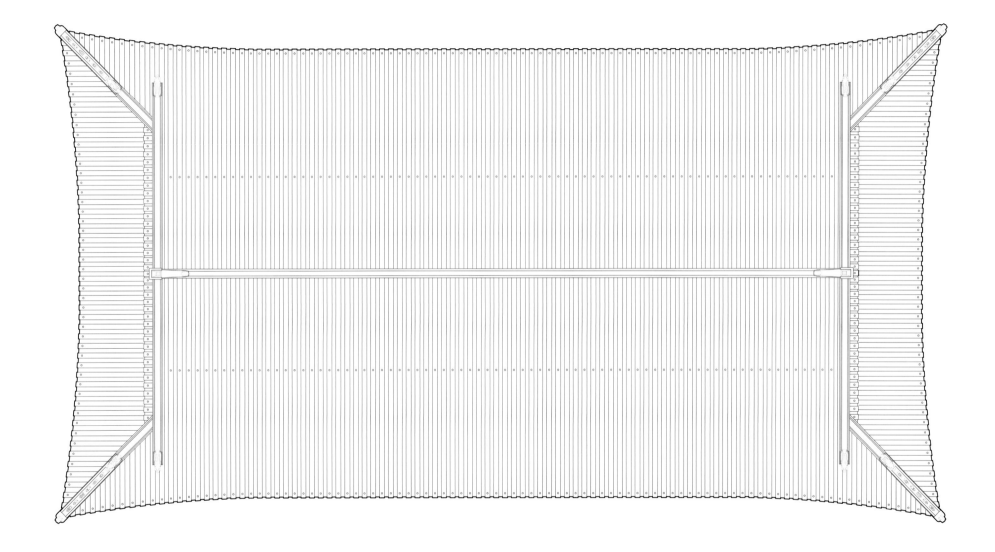

长春宫瓦顶俯视图
Top View of the Roofing Tiles, Palace of Eternal Spring

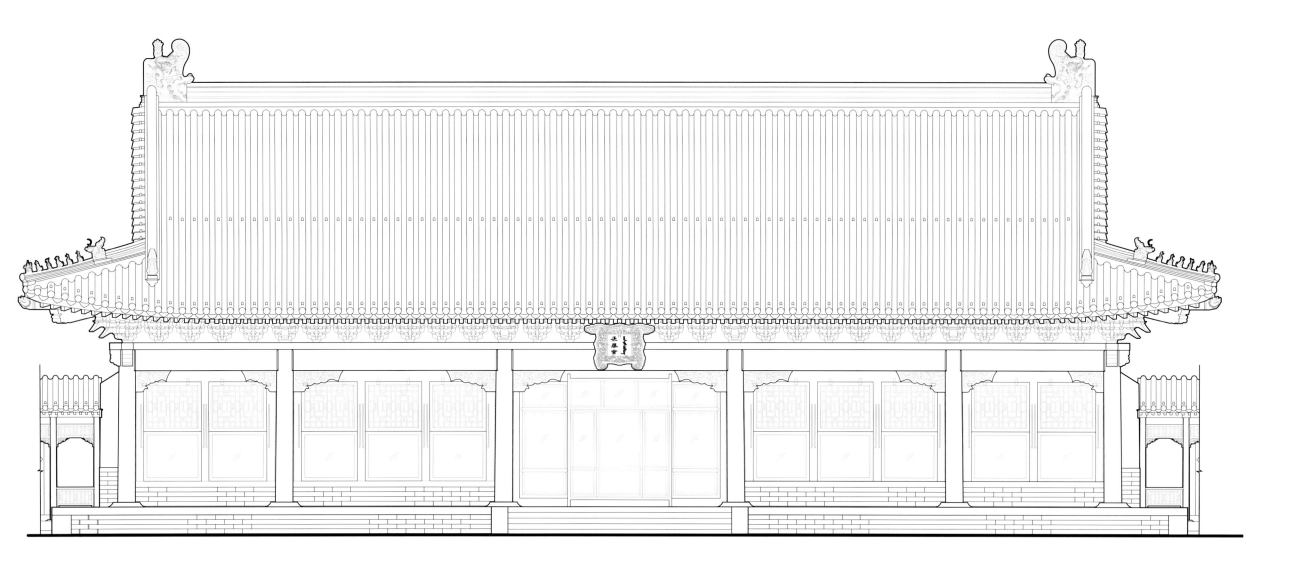

长春宫正立面图
Front Elevation of the Palace of Eternal Spring

长春宫背立面图

Back Elevation of the Palace of Eternal Spring

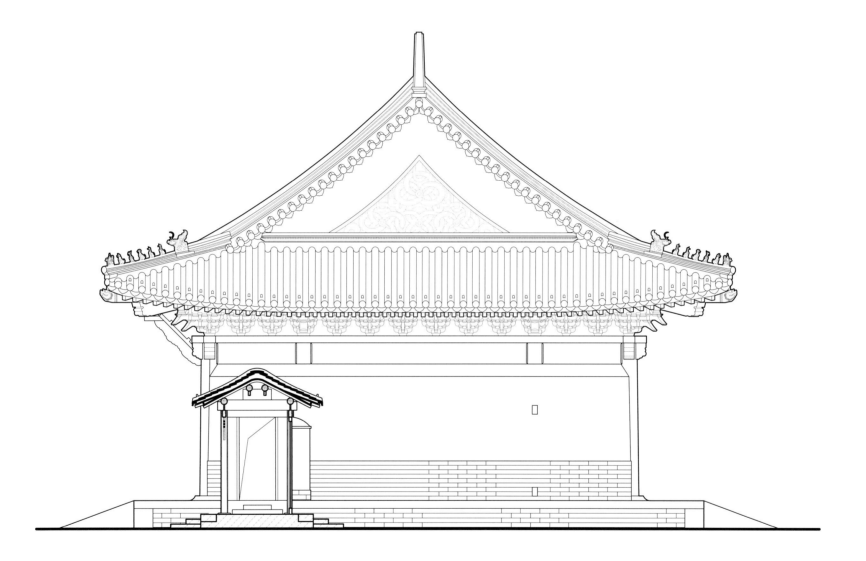

长春宫东侧立面图
Eastern Elevation of the Palace of Eternal Spring

0   1   2   5m

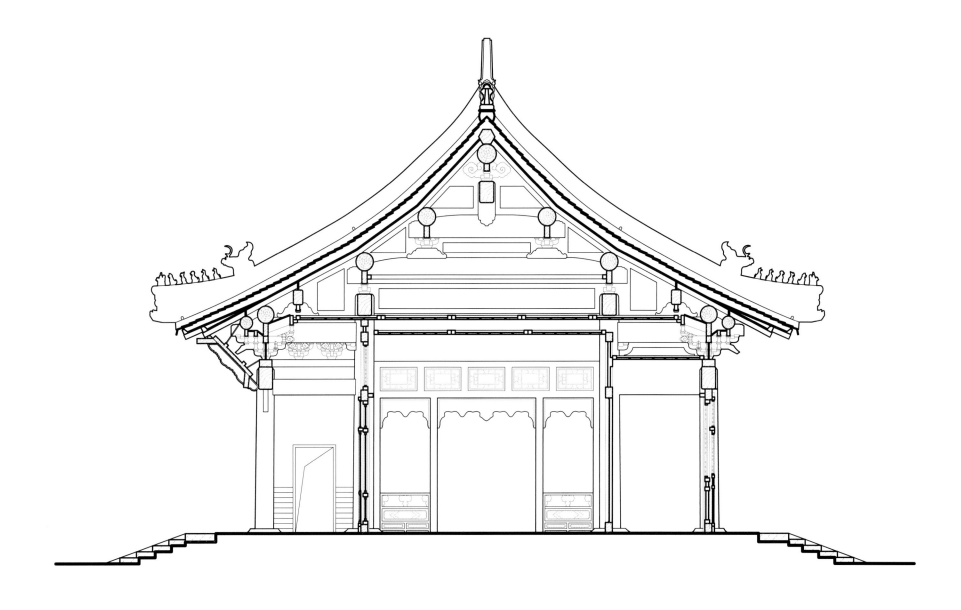

长春宫明间横剖面图
Cross Section of the Central Bay, Palace of Eternal Spring

0　1　2　　　　5m

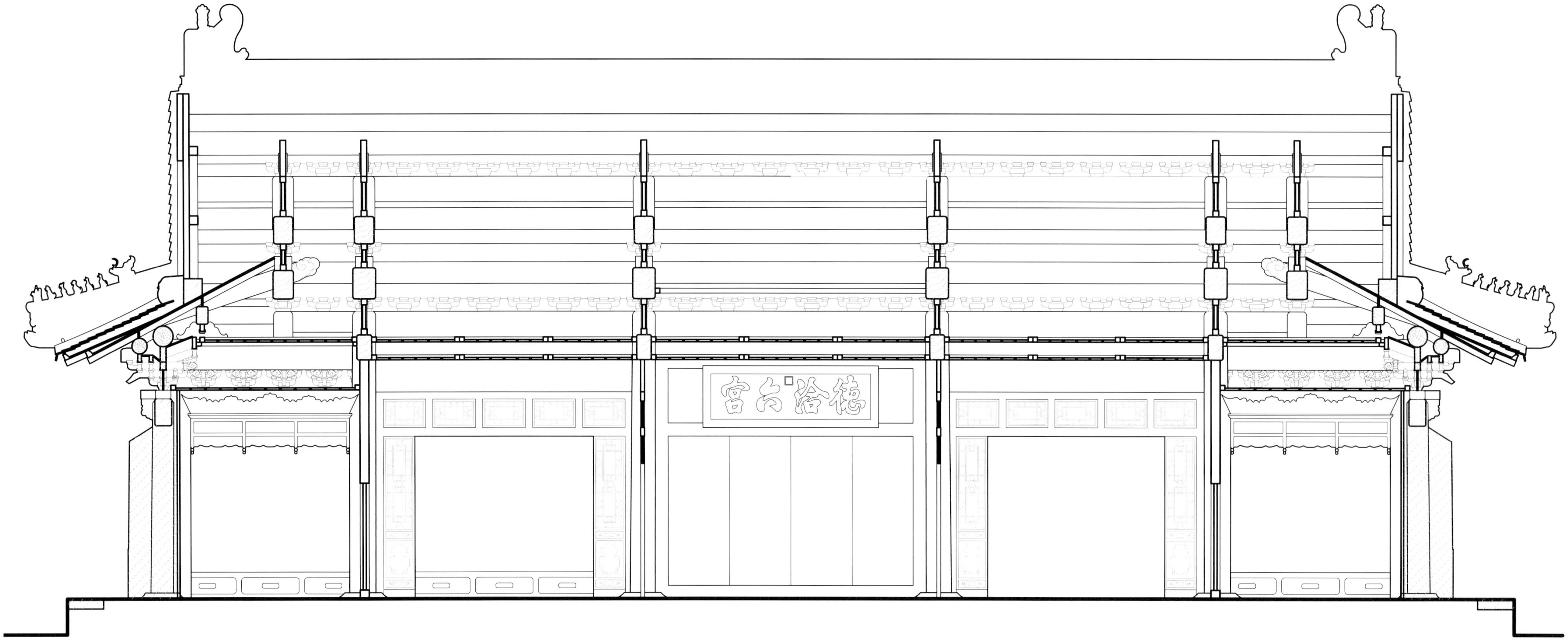

宫右洽德

长春宫纵剖面图
Longitudinal Section of the Palace of Eternal Spring

0　　1　　2　　　　　5m

寿康宫
Palace of Longevity and Health (*Shoukang gong*)

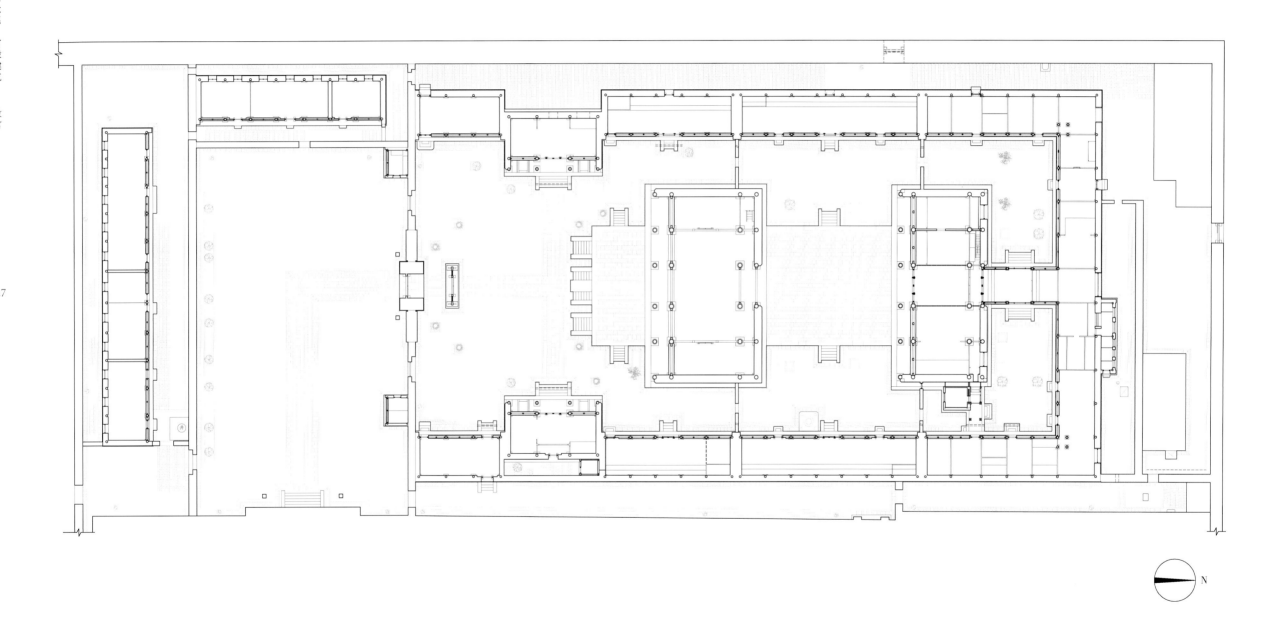

0   5   10m

寿康宫区总平面图
Overall Layout of the Complex of the Palace of Longevity and Health

N

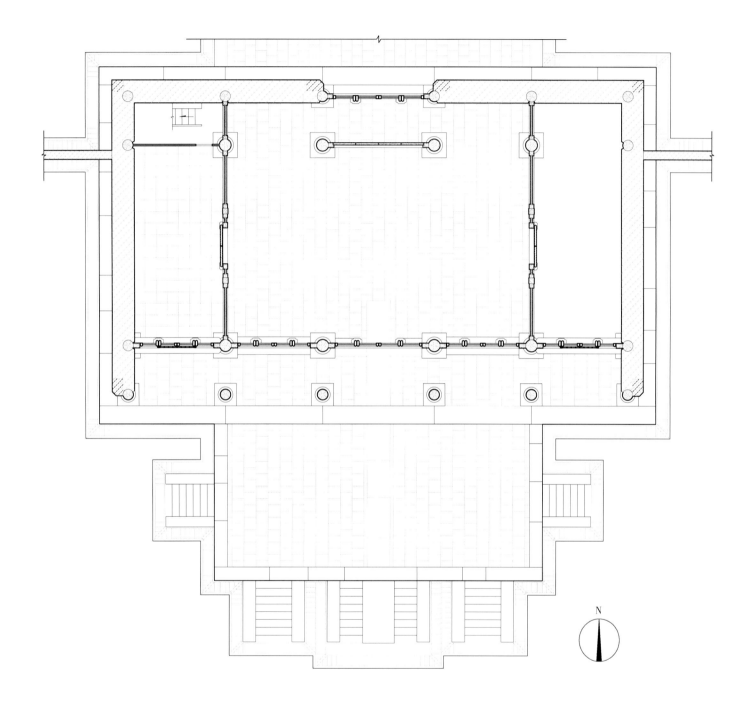

寿康宫平面图
Floor Plan of the Palace of Longevity and Health

0 1 2   5m

N

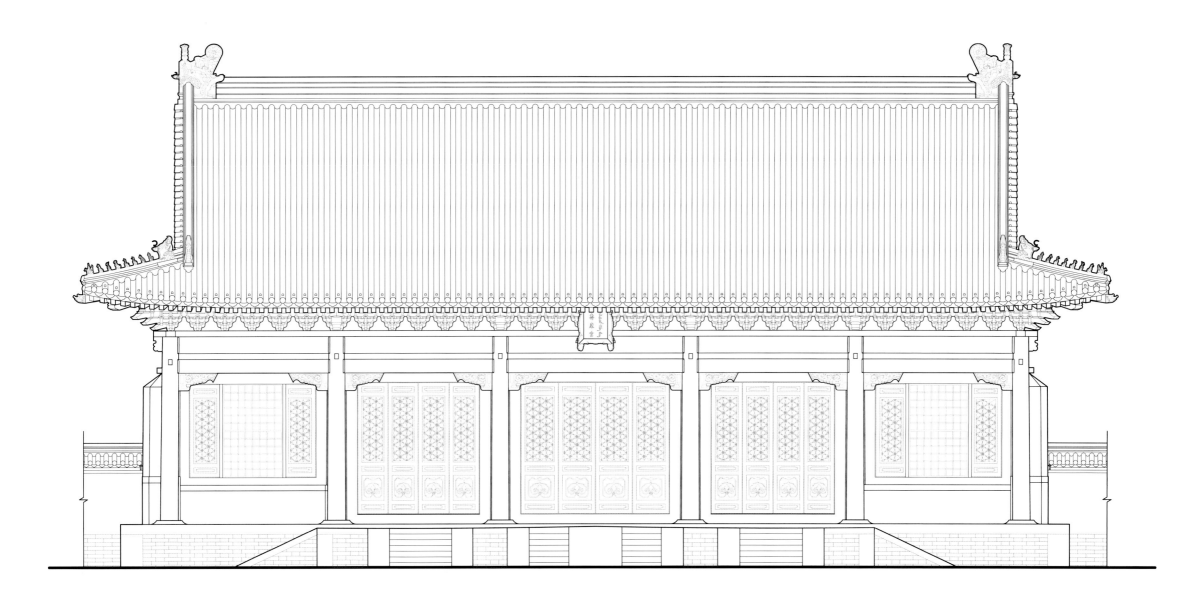

寿康宫正立面图
Front Elevation of the Palace of Longevity and Health

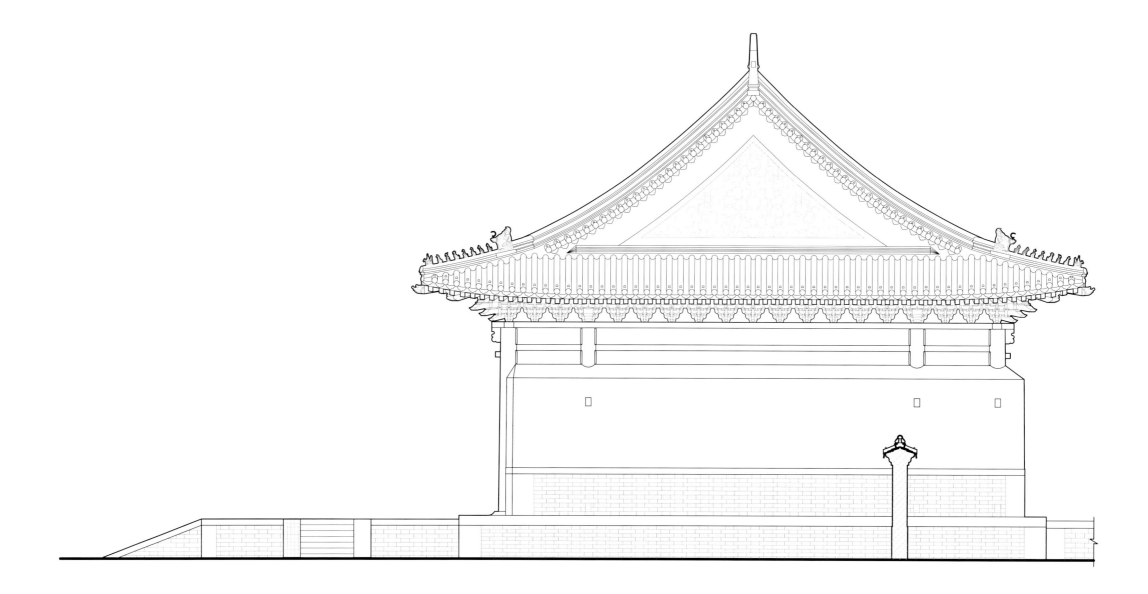

寿康宫东侧立面图
Eastern Elevation of the Palace of Longevity and Health

0 1 2 5m

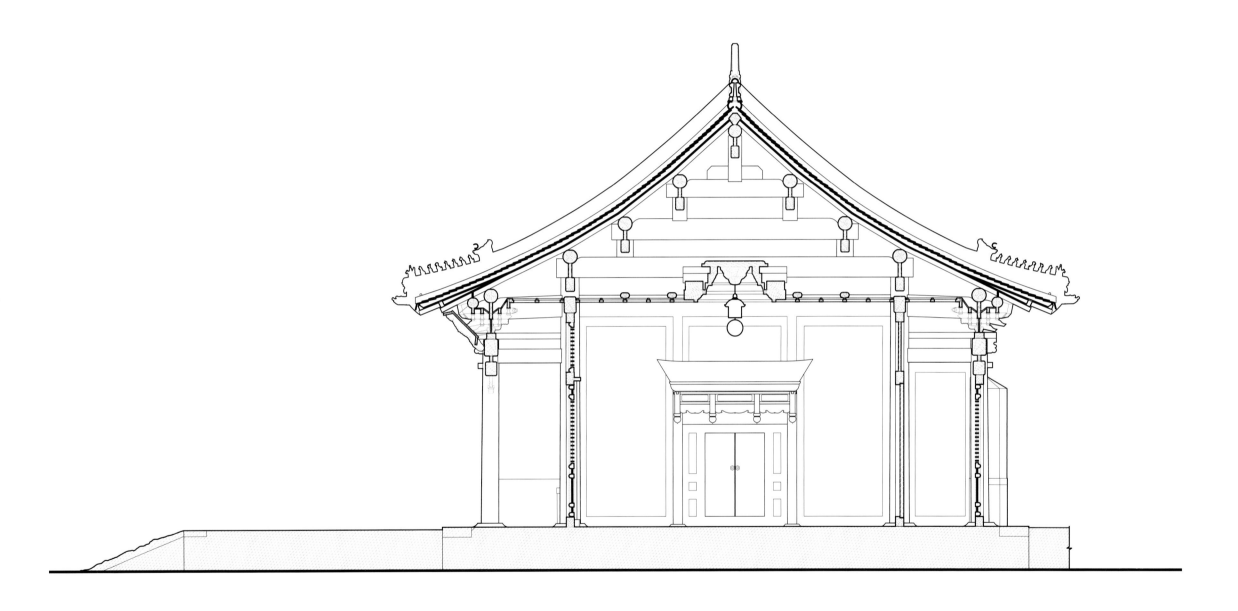

寿康宫明间横剖面图
Cross Section of the Central Bay, Palace of Longevity and Health

0 1 2 5m

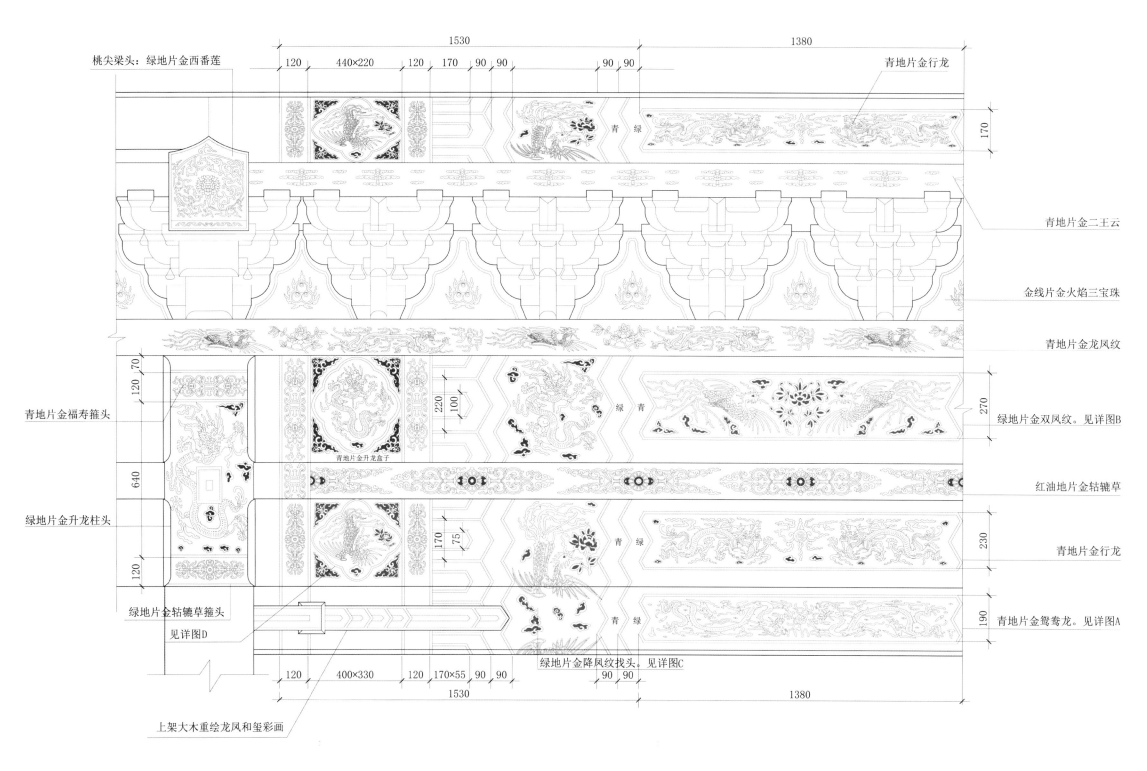

桃尖梁头：绿地片金西番莲

1530 1380

120 440×220 120 170 90 90 90 90

青地片金行龙

青地片金二王云

金线片金火焰三宝珠

青地片金龙凤纹

青地片金福寿箍头

青 绿

绿地片金双凤纹。见详图B

青地片金升龙盒子

绿 青

红油地片金轱辘草

绿地片金升龙柱头

青 绿

青地片金行龙

绿地片金轱辘草箍头

见详图D

青 绿

青地片金鸳鸯龙。见详图A

120 400×330 120 170×55 90 90

绿地片金降凤纹找头。见详图C

90 90

1530 1380

上架大木重绘龙凤和玺彩画

寿康宫明间前后外檐彩画设计图

Design Drawing of the Colored Paintings of the Front and Back Elevations' Central Bays, Palace of Longevity and Health

青

青地片金鸳鸯龙

详图 A

绿

绿地片金双凤纹

详图 B

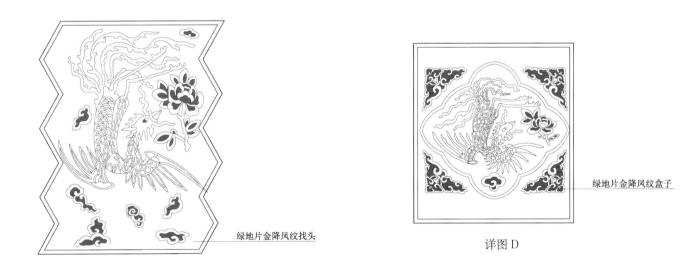

绿地片金降凤纹找头

绿地片金降凤纹盒子

详图 C

详图 D

寿康宫明间前后外檐彩画设计图详图
Detailed Drawing of Design Drawing of the Colored Paintings, the Front and Back Elevations' Central Bays, Palace of Longevity and Health

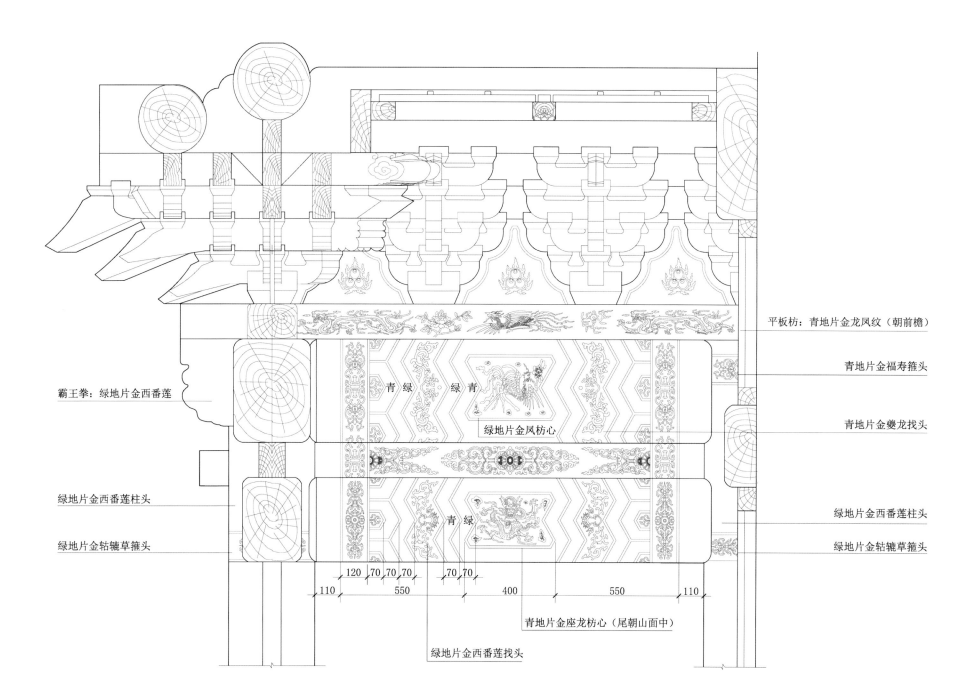

平板枋：青地片金龙凤纹（朝前檐）

青地片金福寿箍头

青地片金夔龙找头

绿地片金西番莲柱头

绿地片金轱辘草箍头

霸王拳：绿地片金西番莲

绿地片金西番莲柱头

绿地片金轱辘草箍头

青绿　绿青

绿地片金凤枋心

青绿

青地片金座龙枋心（尾朝山面中）

绿地片金西番莲找头

120 70 70 70　70 70

110　550　400　550　110

寿康宫两山面南次间内檐彩画设计图
Design Drawing of the Colored Paintings on the Interior Sides of the Gable Walls' Southmost Bays, Palace of Longevity and Health

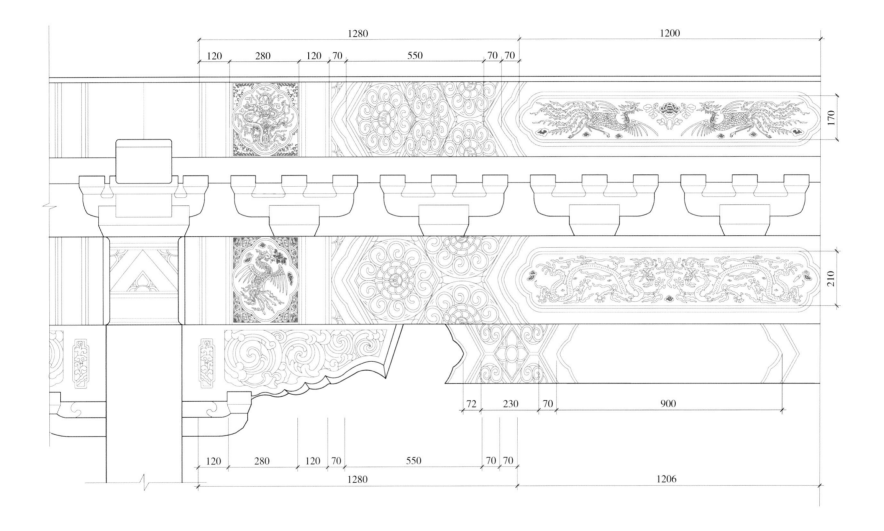

寿康宫东西配殿明间前外檐彩画设计图

Design Drawing of the Colored Paintings of the Central Bays of the Western and Eastern Side Halls' Front Elevations, Palace of Longevity and Health

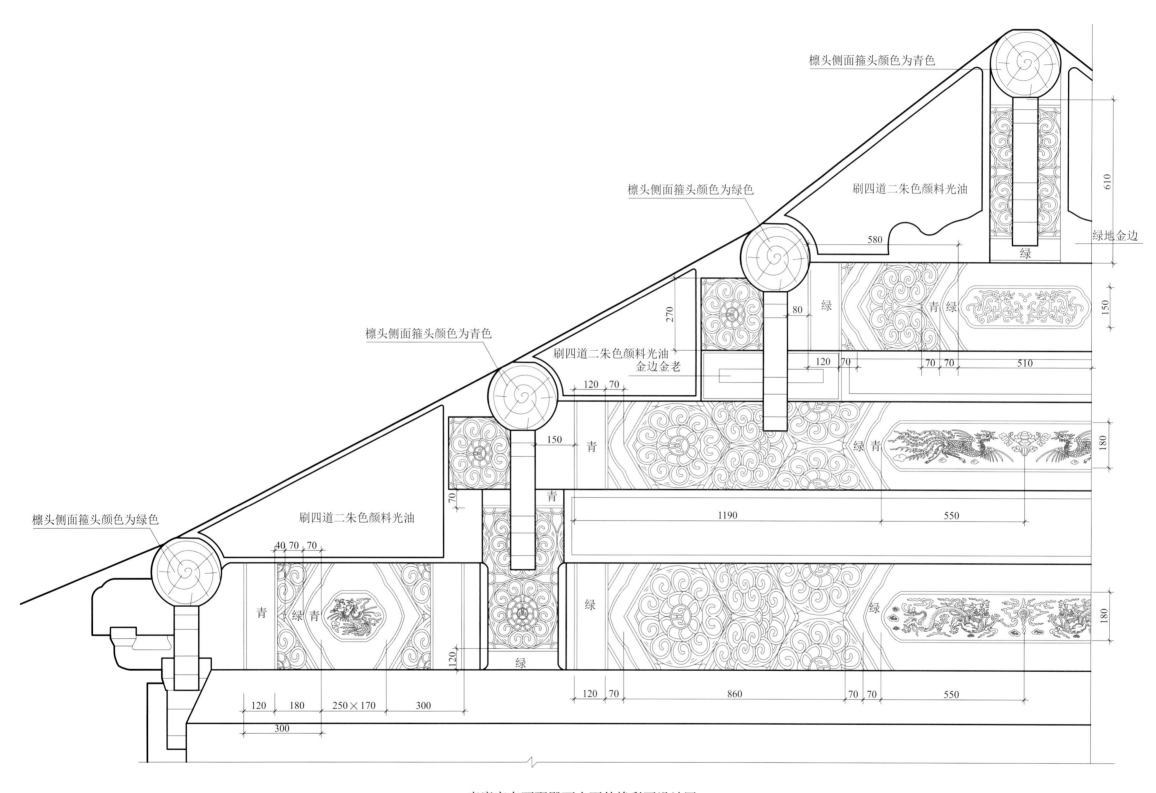

檩头侧面箍头颜色为青色

檩头侧面箍头颜色为绿色

刷四道二朱色颜料光油

绿地金边

610

580

270

150

绿

青绿

檩头侧面箍头颜色为青色

刷四道二朱色颜料光油
金边金老

80

绿

120 70

70 70

510

150

青

150

120 70

180

70

青

绿青

1190

550

檩头侧面箍头颜色为绿色

刷四道二朱色颜料光油

40 70 70

青

绿 青

120

绿

绿

180

120 70

860

70 70

550

120 180 250×170 300

300

寿康宫东西配殿两山面外檐彩画设计图

Design Drawing of the Colored Paintings of the Side Elevations of the Western and Eastern Side Halls, Palace of Longevity and Health

慈宁宫花园
Garden of Compassion and Tranquility
(*Cininggong huayuan*)

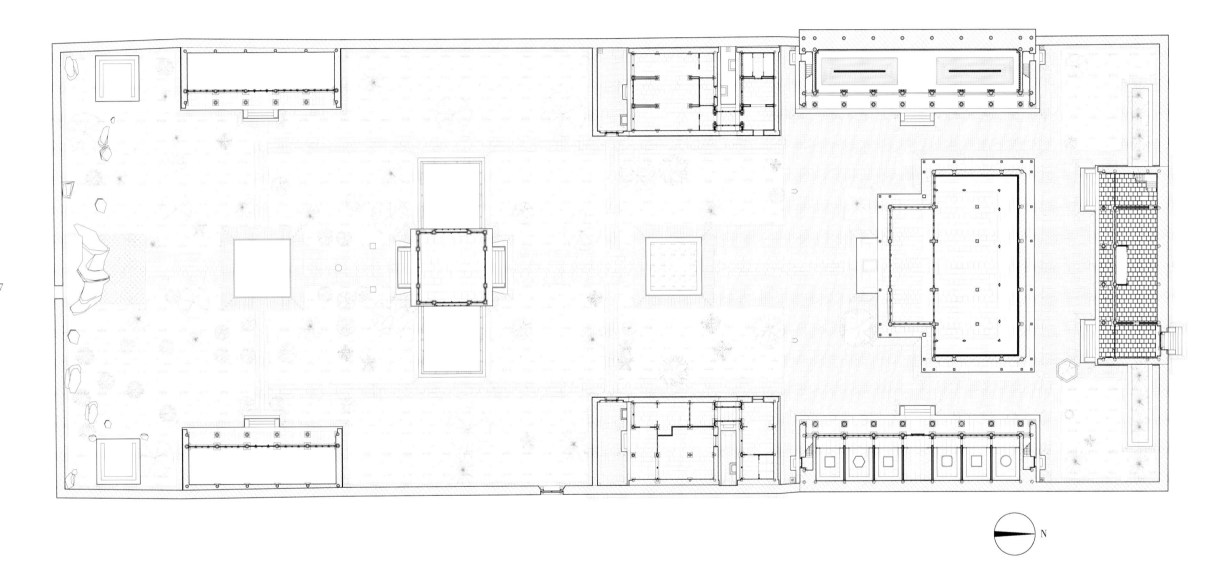

0 2 4   10   20m

慈宁宫花园总平面图
Overall Layout of the Garden of Compassion and Tranquility

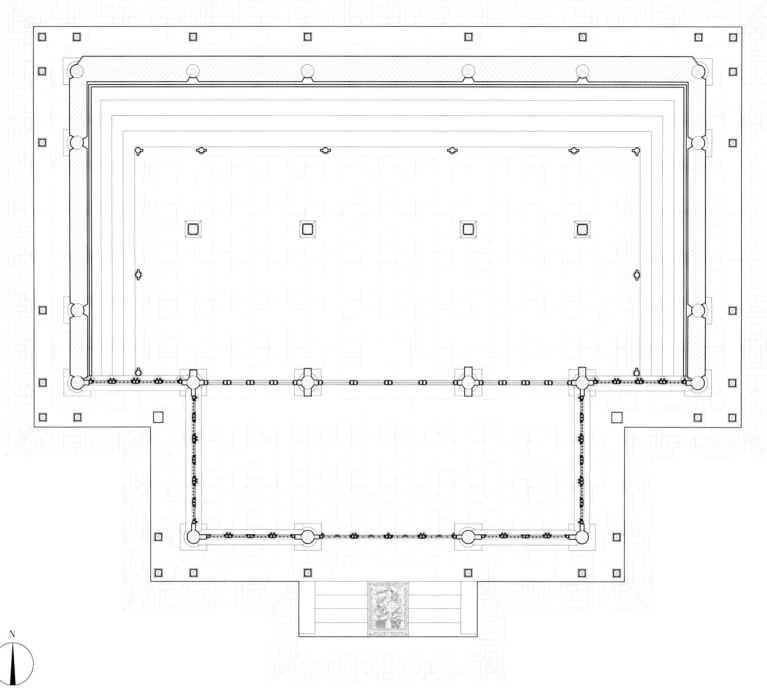

N

咸若馆平面图
Floor Plan of the Studio of Understanding and Bringing Peace

0 1 2 5m

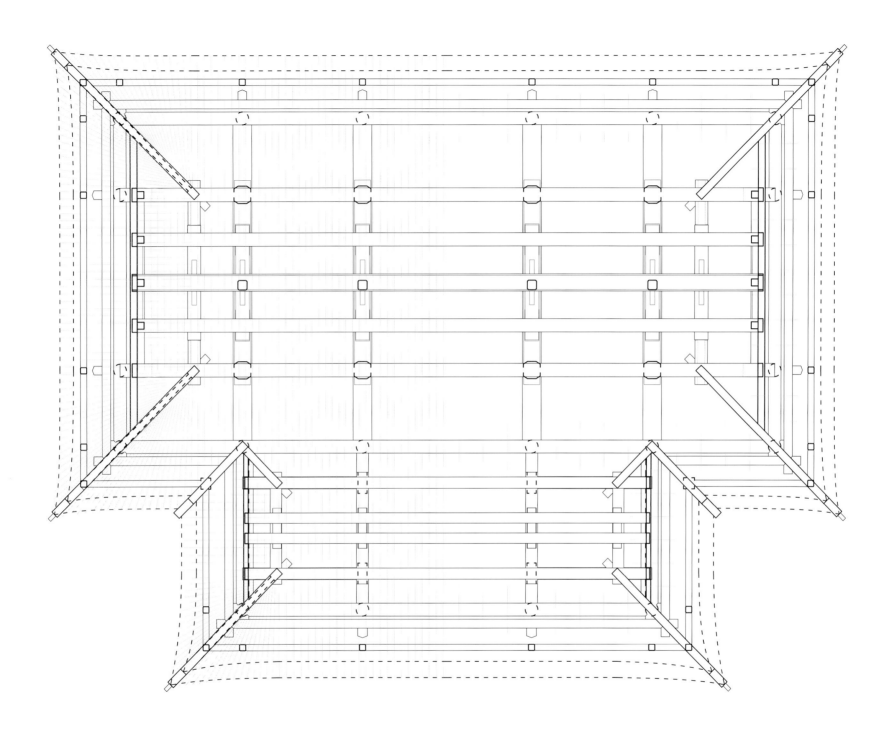

咸若馆梁架俯视图
Top View of the Trusses, Studio of Understanding and Bringing Peace

0   1   2   5m

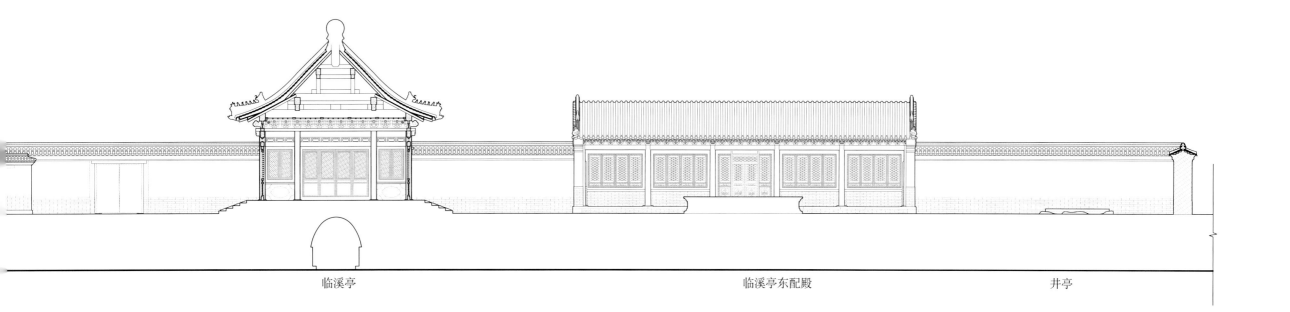

临溪亭　　　　　　　　　　　　　临溪亭东配殿　　　　　　　　　井亭

慈宁宫花园总横剖面图
Overall Cross Section of the Garden of Compassion and Tranquility

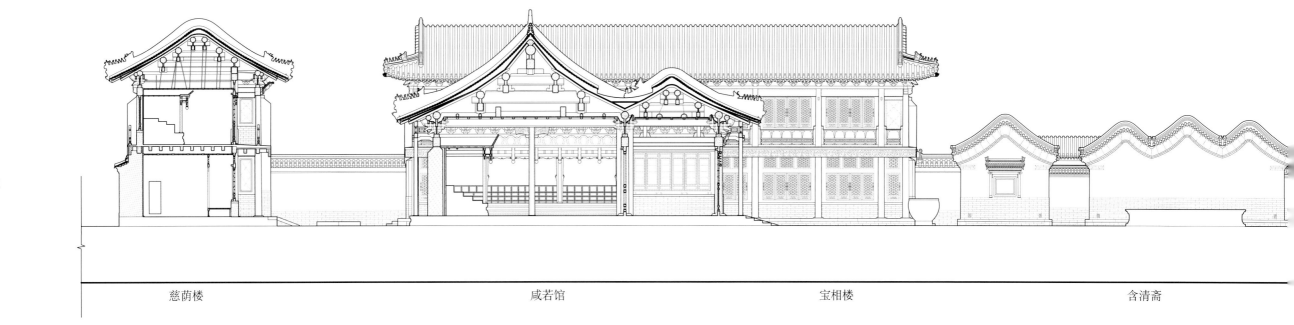

慈荫楼　　　　　　　　　　　　　　　　　　咸若馆　　　　　　　　　　　宝相楼　　　　　　　　　　　含清斋

0　　2　　4　　　　　　10m

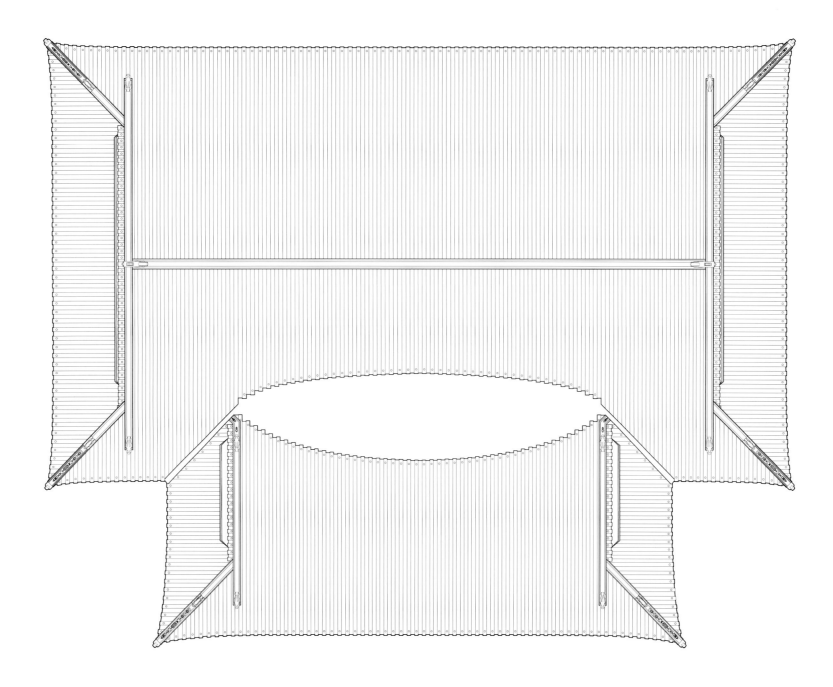

咸若馆瓦顶俯视图
Top View of the Roofing Tiles, Studio of Understanding and Bringing Peace

0 1 2   5m

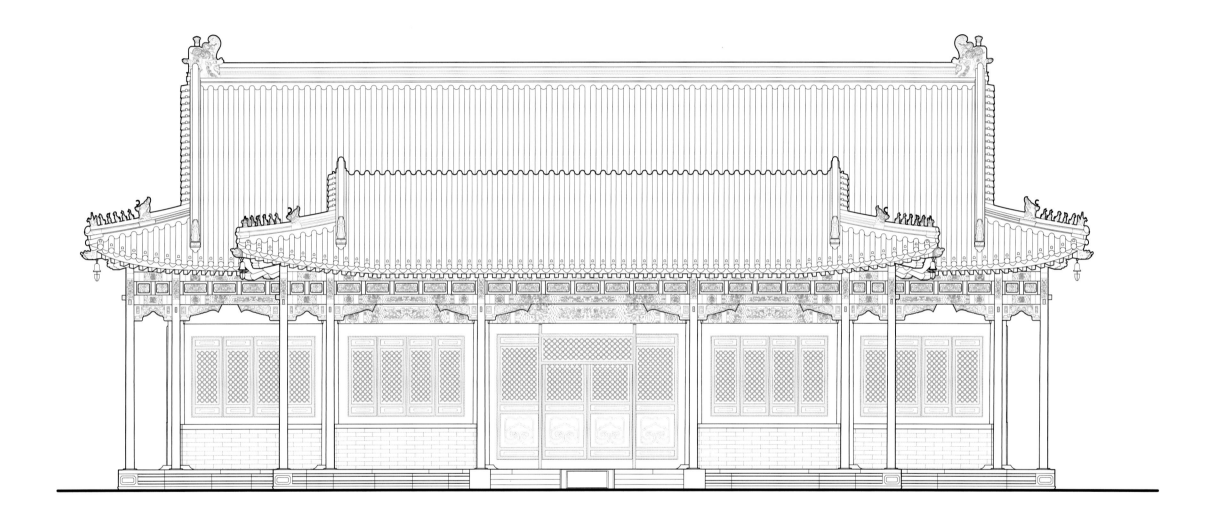

咸若馆正立面图
Front Elevation of the Studio of Understanding and Bringing Peace

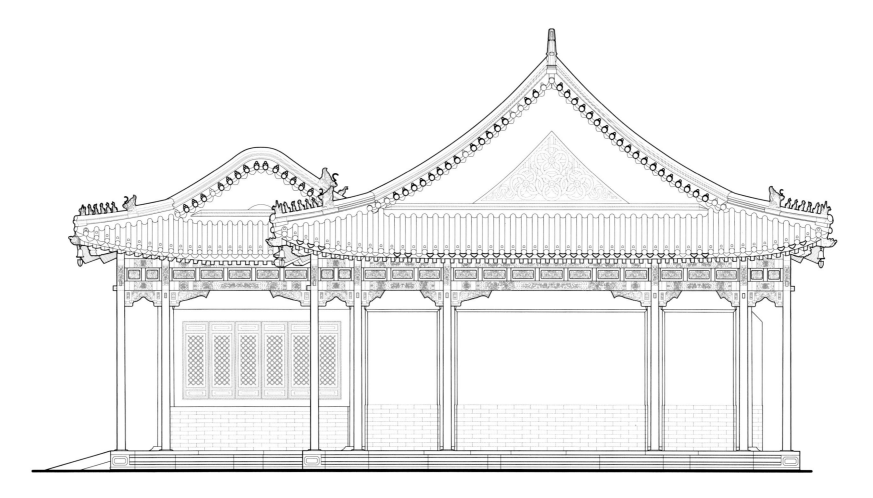

咸若馆东侧立面图
Eastern Elevation of the Studio of Understanding and Bringing Peace

0 1 2   5m

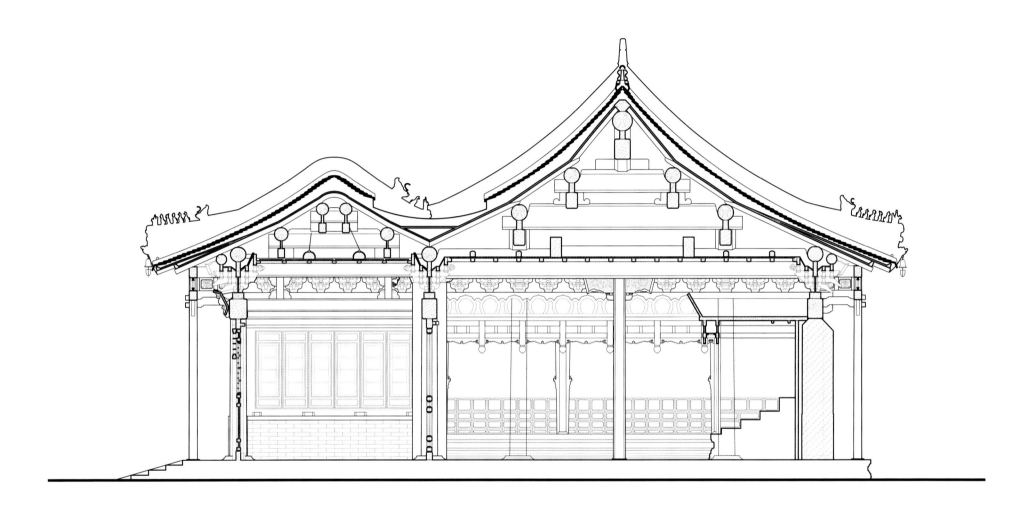

咸若馆明间横剖面图
Cross Section of the Central Bay, Studio of Understanding and Bringing Peace

0   1   2   5m

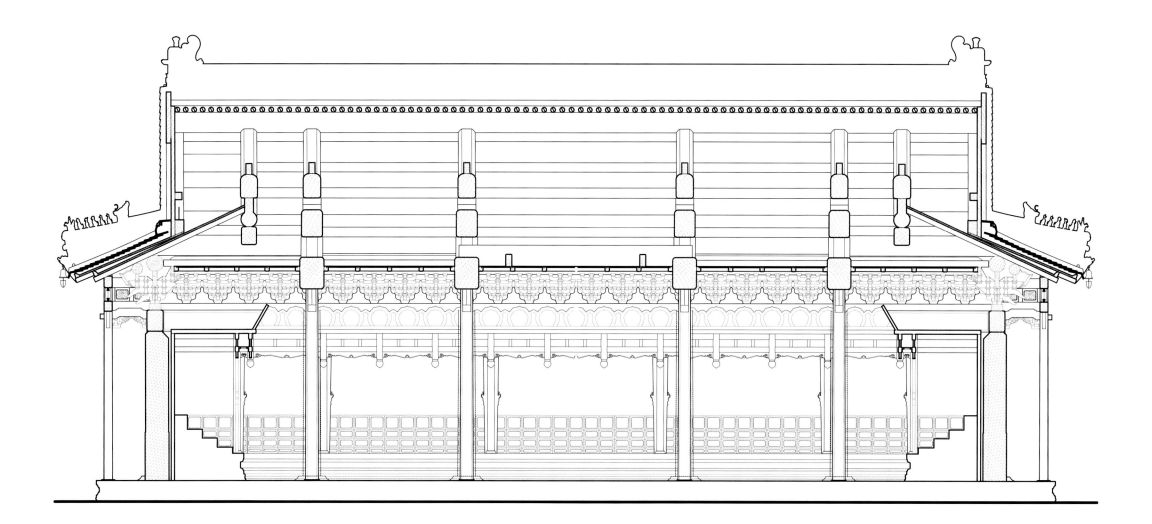

咸若馆正殿纵剖面图
Longitudinal Section of the Studio of Understanding and Bringing Peace

0 1 2 5m

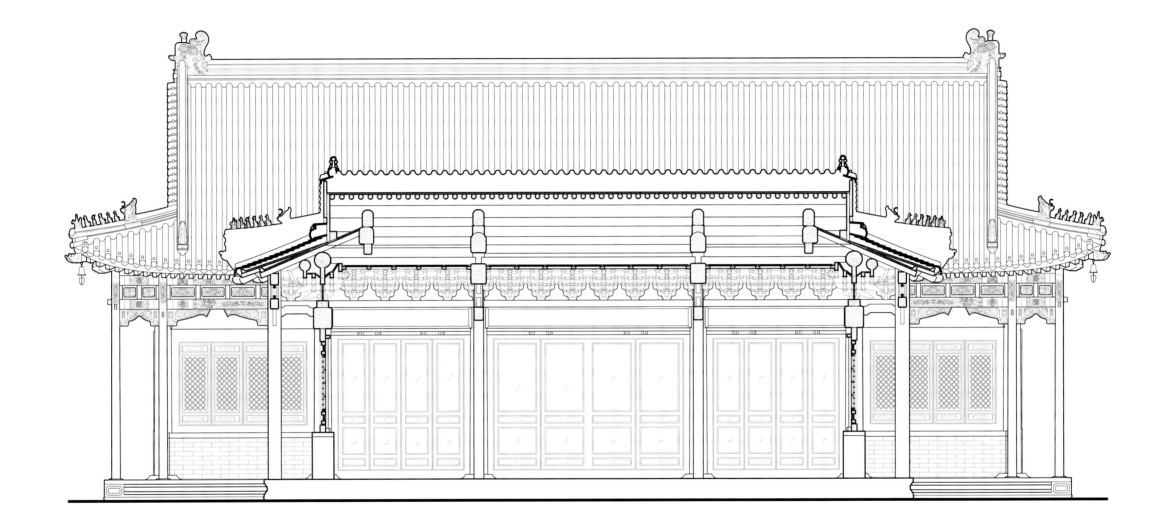

咸若馆抱厦纵剖面图
Longitudinal Section of the Protruding Facet, Studio of Understanding and Bringing

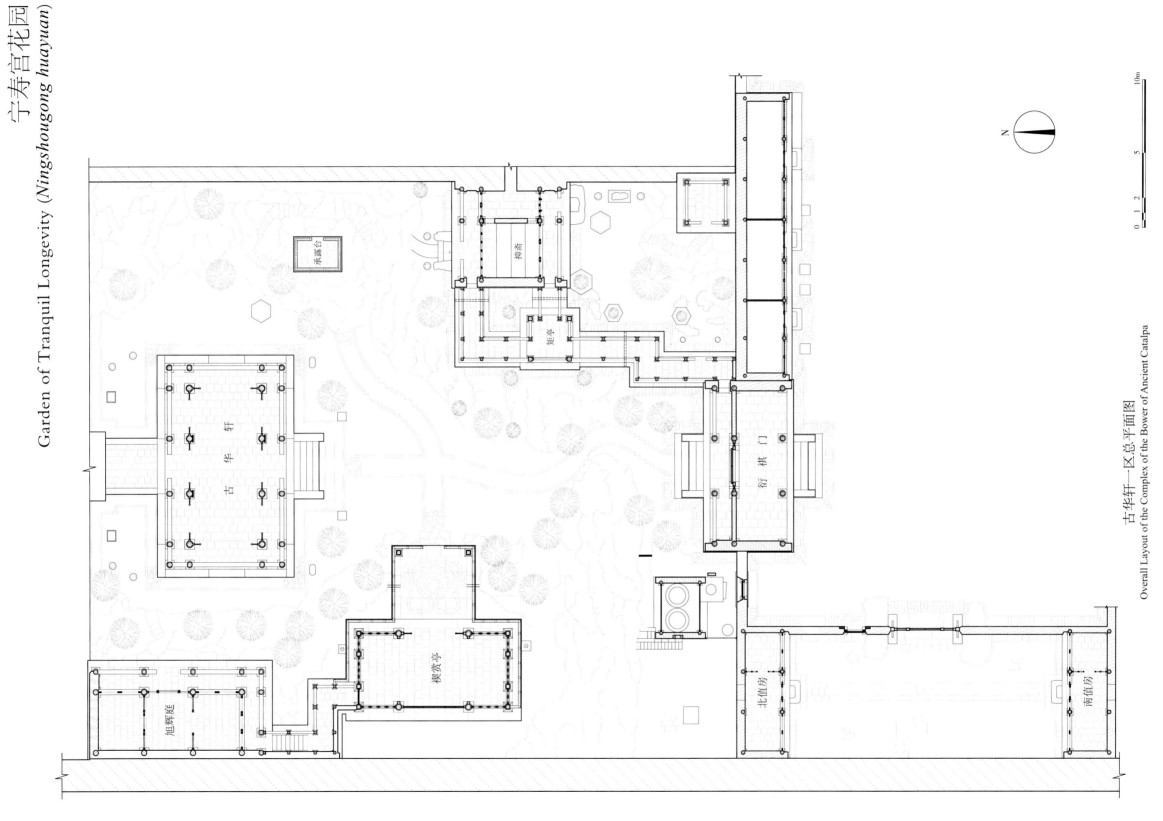

古华轩

古华轩一区总平面图

Overall Layout of the Complex of the Bower of Ancient Catalpa

承露台

抑斋

矩亭

衍祺门

禊赏亭

旭辉庭

北值房

南值房

N

0 1 2 5 10m

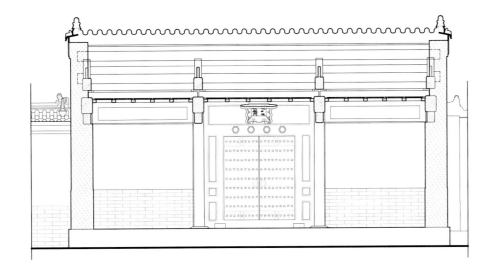

衍祺门纵剖面图
Longitudinal Section of the Gate of Extending Auspiciousness

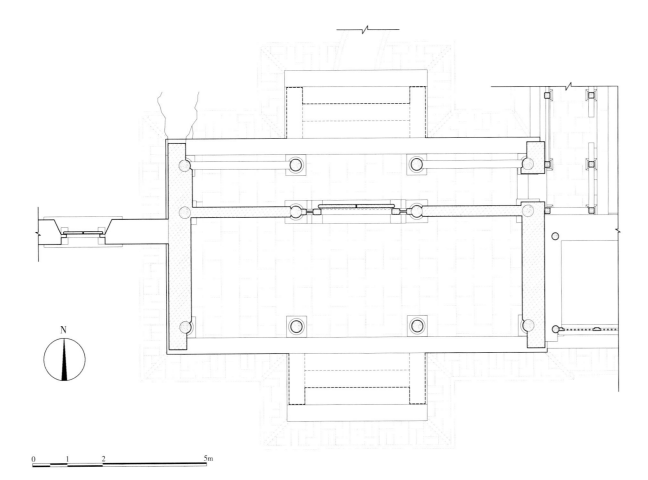

N

0　1　2　　　　5m

衍祺门平面图
Layout of the Gate of Extending Auspiciousness

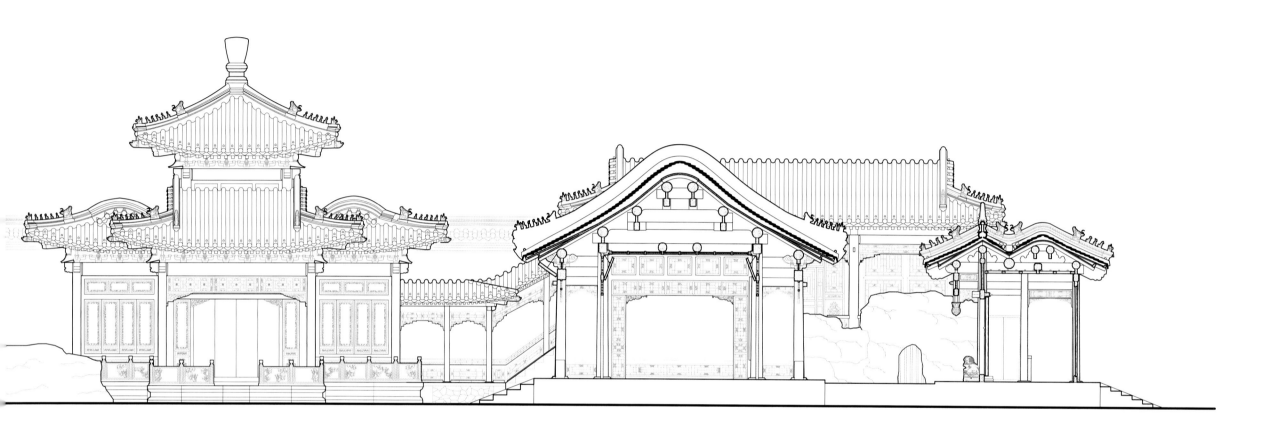

古华轩一区总剖面图
Overall Section of the Complex of the Bower of Ancient Catalpa

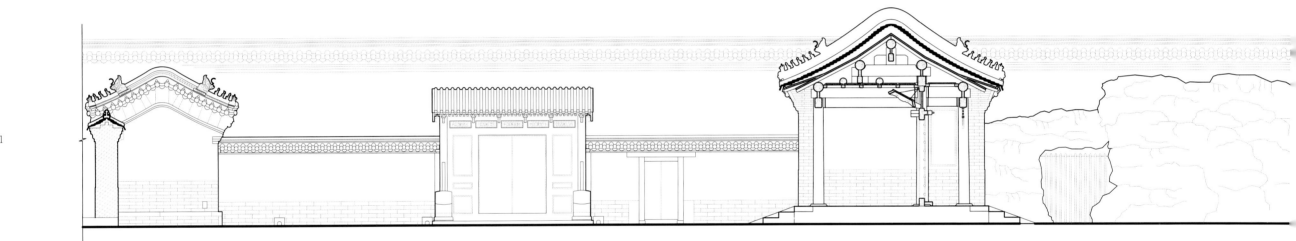

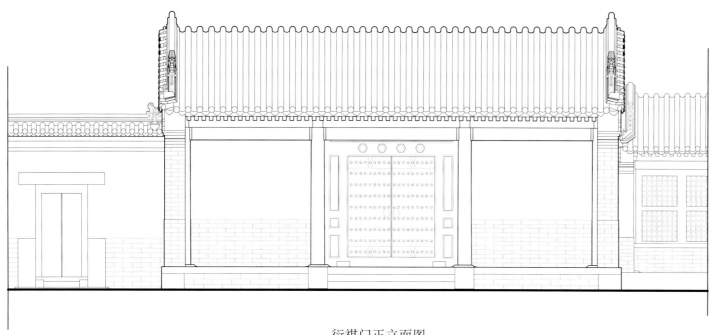

衍祺门正立面图
Front Elevations of the Gate of Extending Auspiciousness

衍祺门东侧立面图
Eastern Elevations of the Gate of Extending Auspiciousness

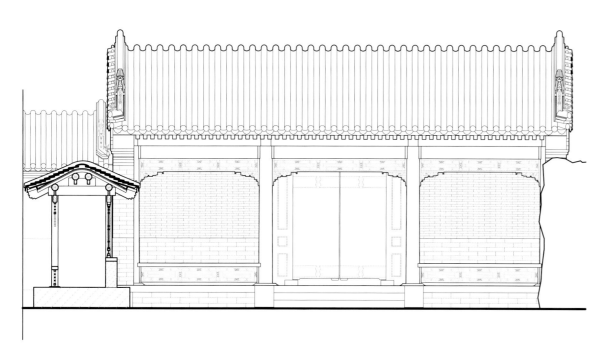

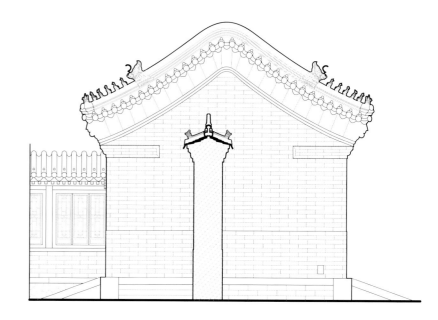

衍祺门背立面图
Back Elevations of the Gate of Extending Auspiciousness

衍祺门西侧立面图
Western Elevations of the Gate of Extending Auspiciousness

0   1   2m

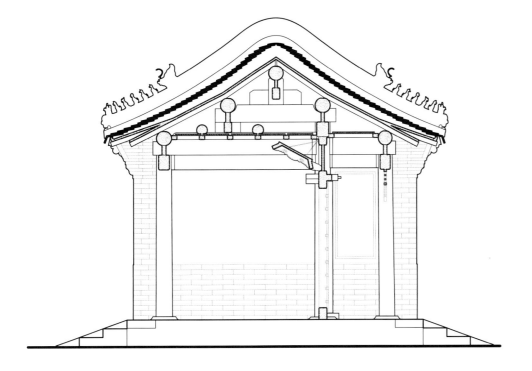

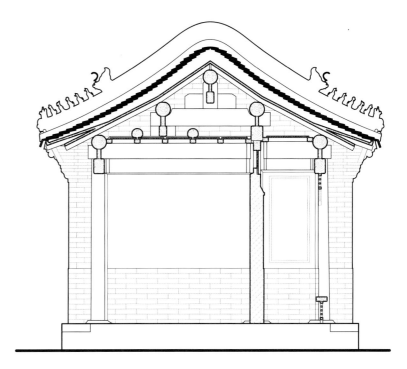

衍祺门明间横剖面图
Cross Sections of the Central Bay, Gate of Extending Auspiciousness

0　　1　　2m

衍祺门次间横剖面图
Cross Sections of the Western Bay, Gate of Extending Auspiciousness

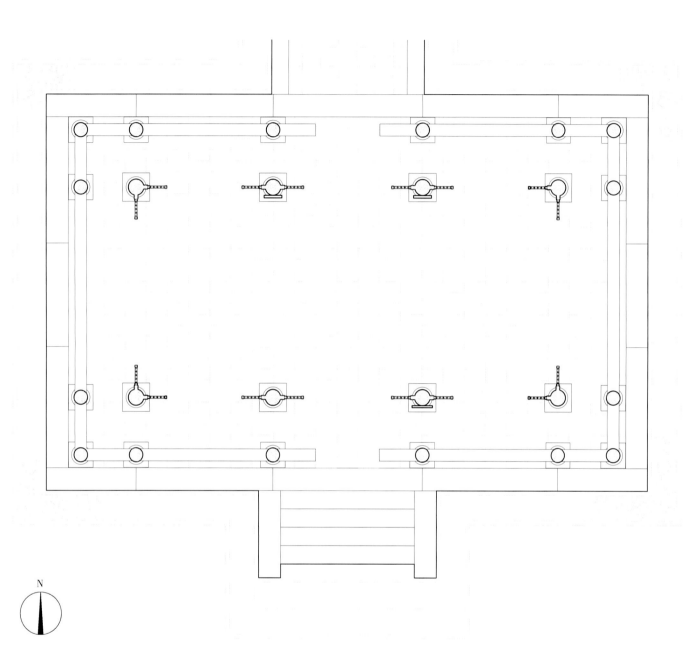

N

0 1 2m

古华轩平面图
Layout of the Bower of Ancient Catalpa

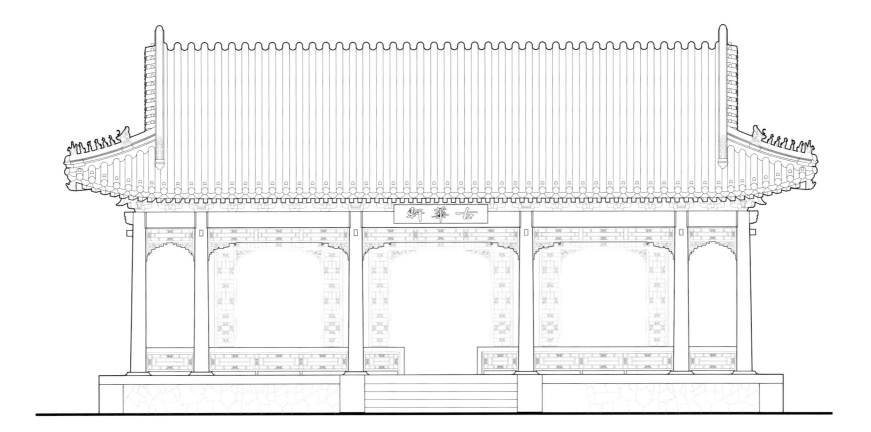

古华轩正立面图
Front Elevations of the Bower of Ancient Catalpa

0　　1　　2m

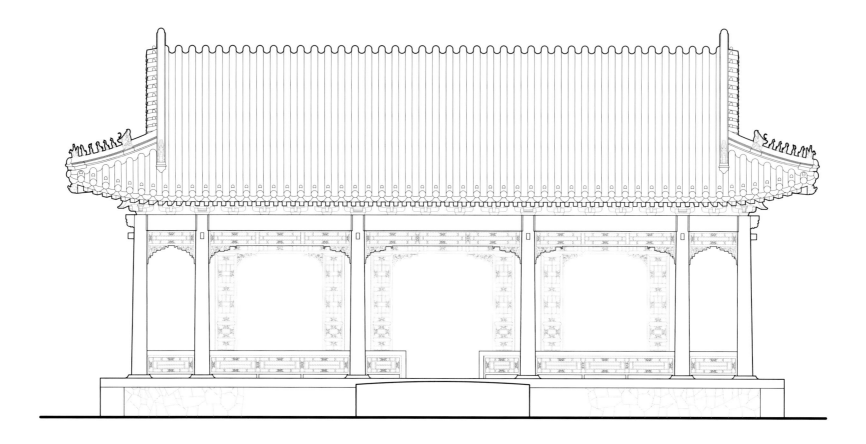

0   1   2m

古华轩背立面图

Back Elevations of the Bower of Ancient Catalpa

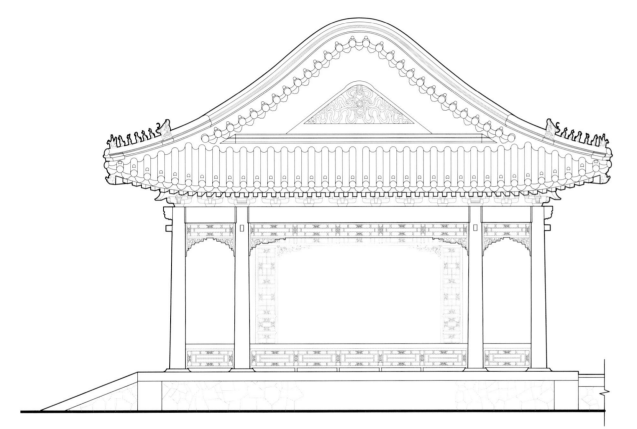

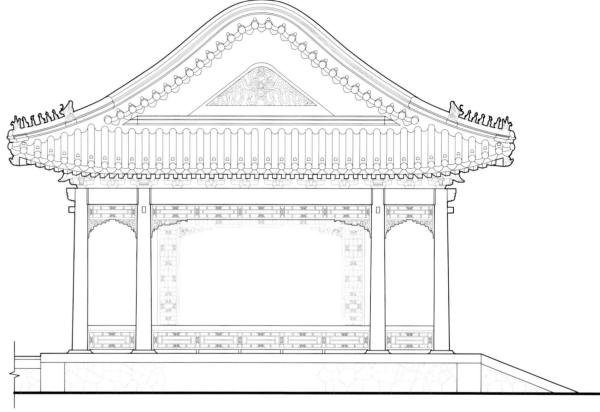

古华轩东侧立面图
Eastern Elevations of the Bower of Ancient Catalpa

0   1   2m

古华轩西侧立面图
Western Elevations of the Bower of Ancient Catalpa

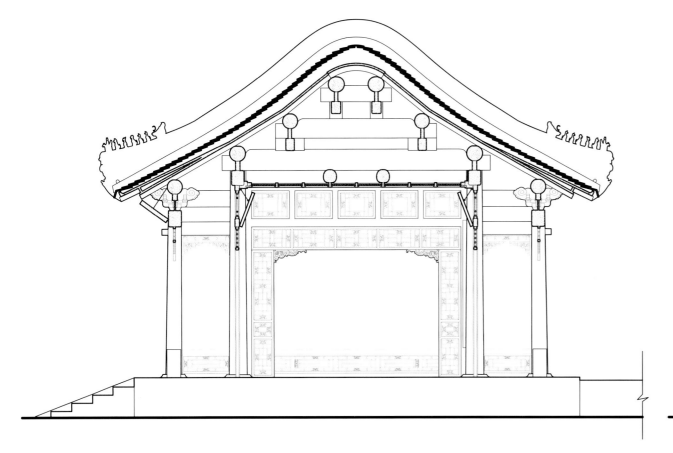

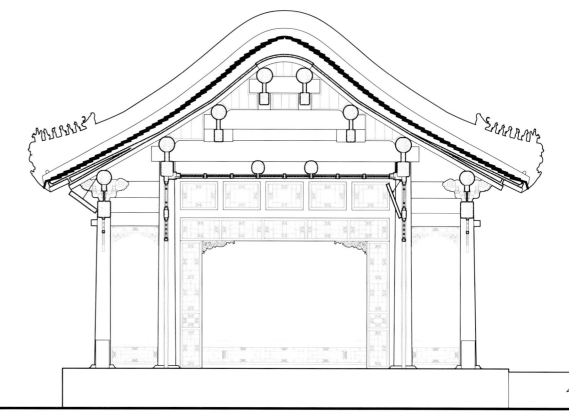

古华轩明间横剖面图
Cross Sections of the Central Bay, Bower of Ancient Catalpa

0　1　2m

古华轩次间横剖面图
Cross Sections of the Western Bay, Bower of Ancient Catalpa

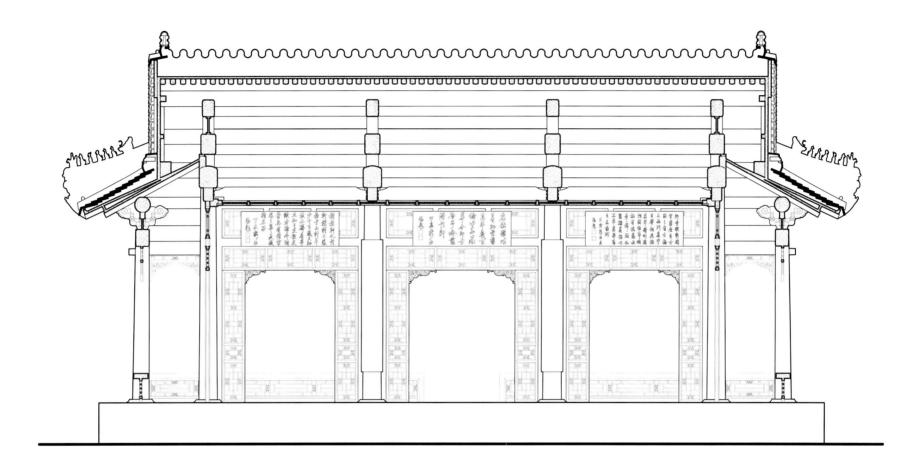

古华轩纵剖面图
Longitudinal Section of the Bower of Ancient Catalpa

0　　　1　　　2m

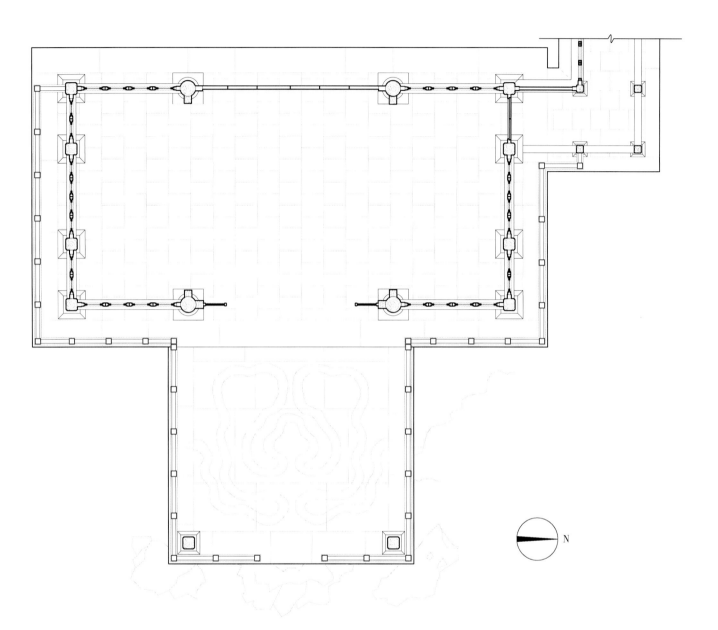

N

禊赏亭平面图
Floor Plan of the Pavilion of the Purification Ceremony

0 1 2m

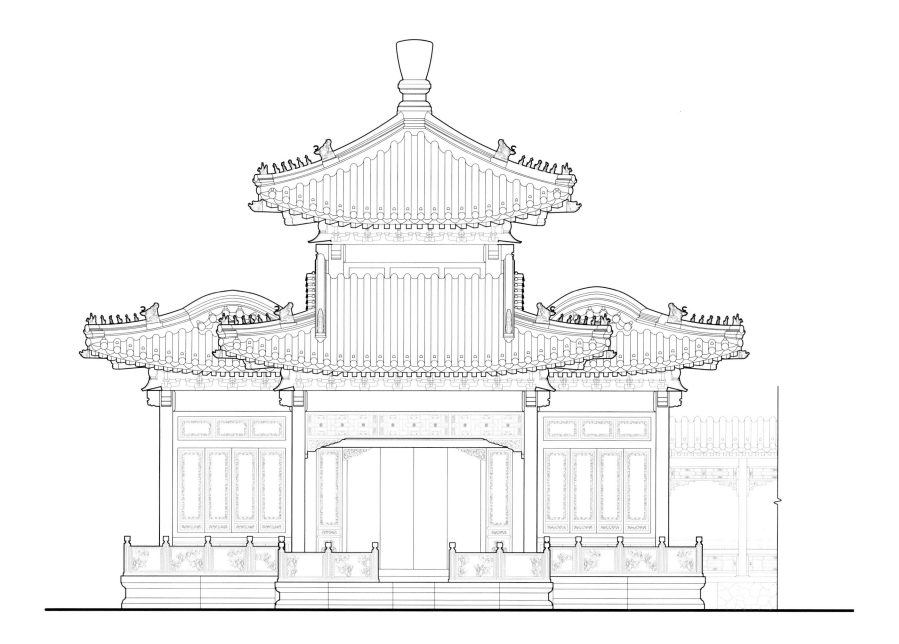

0   1   2m

禊赏亭正立面图
Front Elevation of the Pavilion of the Purification Ceremony

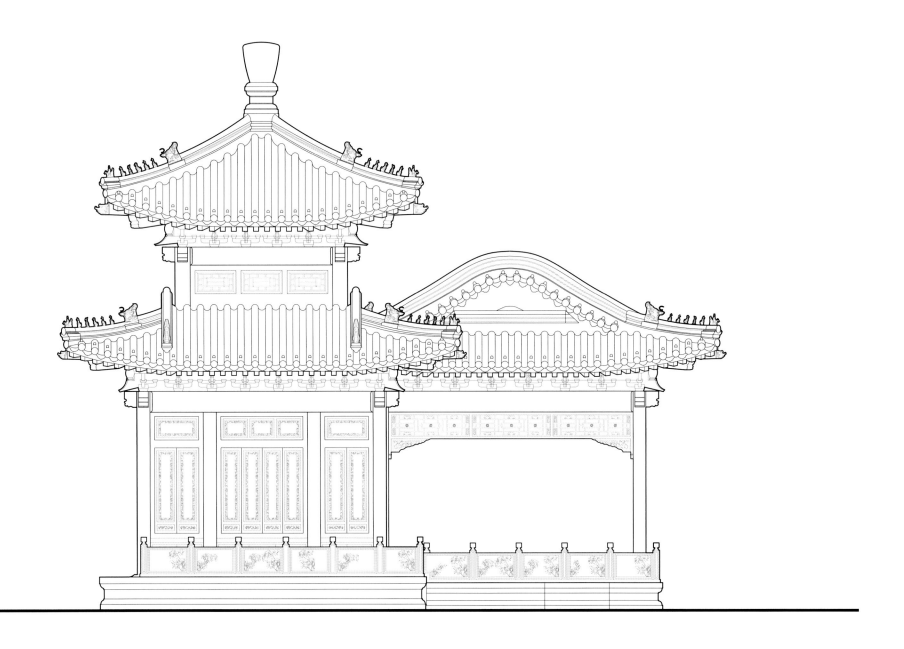

禊赏亭南侧立面图
Southern Elevation of the Pavilion of the Purification Ceremony

0　　1　　2m

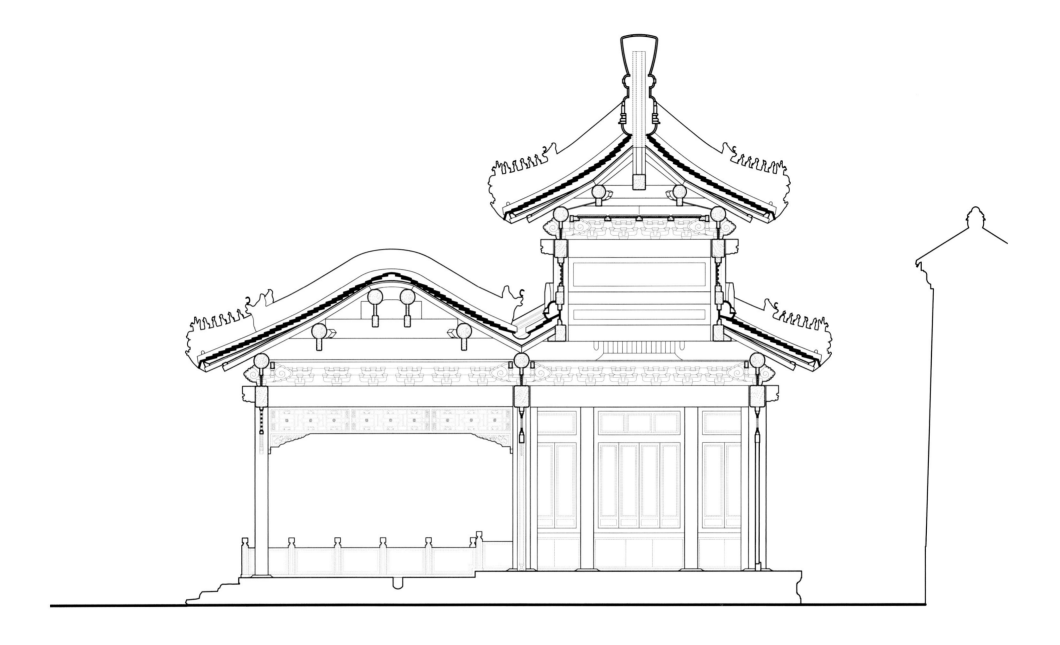

禊赏亭横剖面图
Cross Section of the Pavilion of the Purification Ceremony

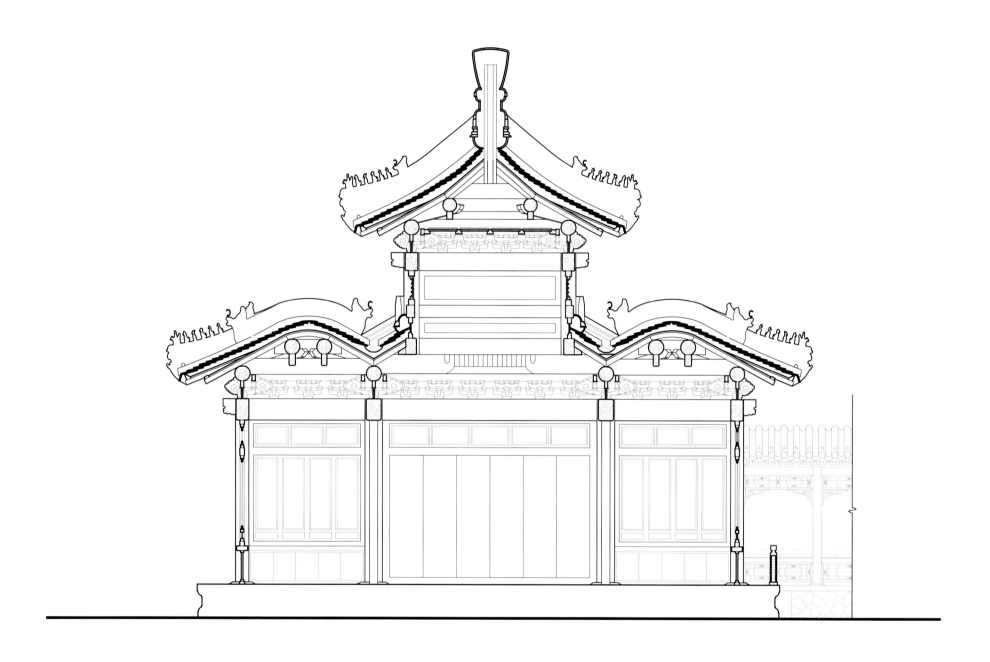

禊赏亭纵剖面图
Longitudinal Section of the Pavilion of the Purification Ceremony

0　　1　　2m

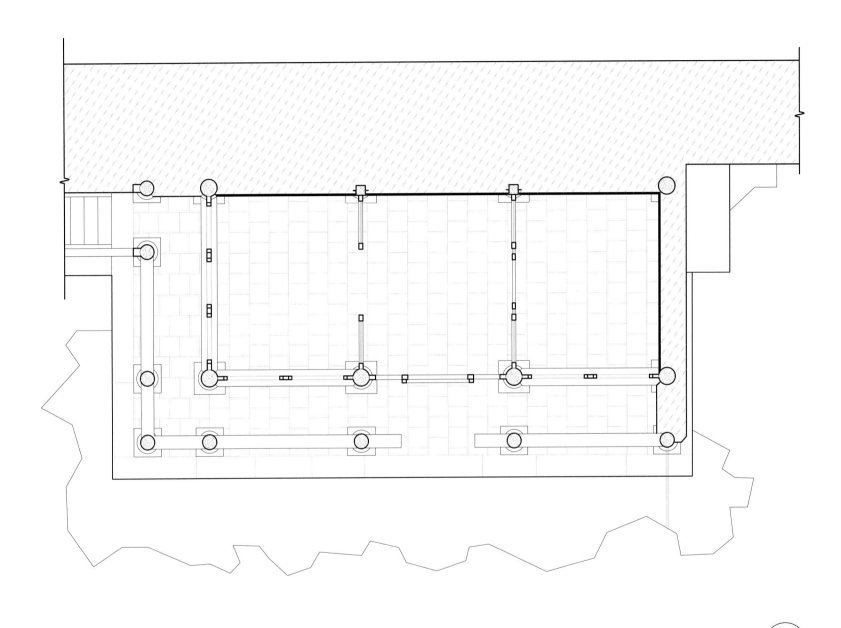

旭辉庭平面图
Layout of the Pavilion for Greeting the Rising Sun

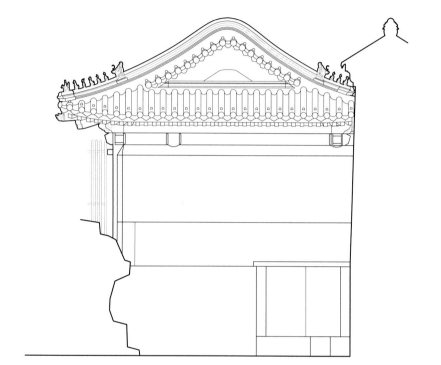

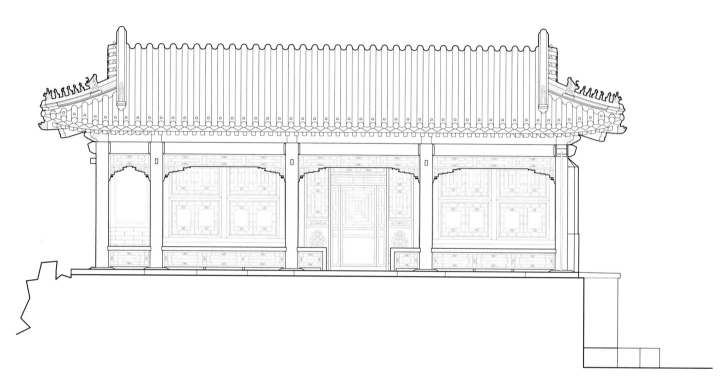

旭辉庭北侧立面图
Front Elevations of the Pavilion for Greeting the Rising Sun

0 1 2m

旭辉庭正立面图
Northern Elevations of the Pavilion for Greeting the Rising Sun

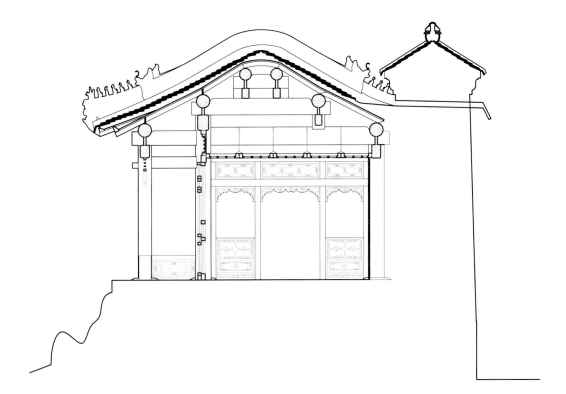

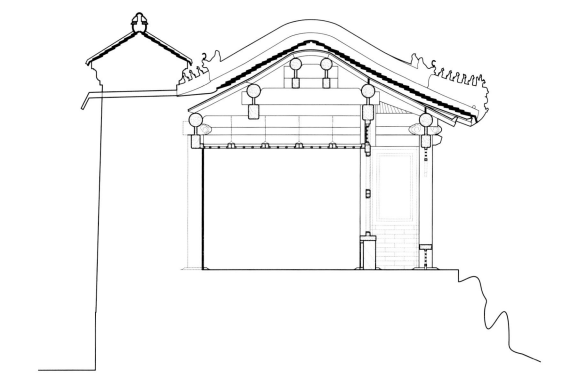

旭辉庭横剖面图 1−1

1-1 Cross Section of the Pavilion for Greeting the Rising Sun

0　　　1　　　2m

旭辉庭横剖面图 2−2

2-2 Cross Section of the Pavilion for Greeting the Rising Sun

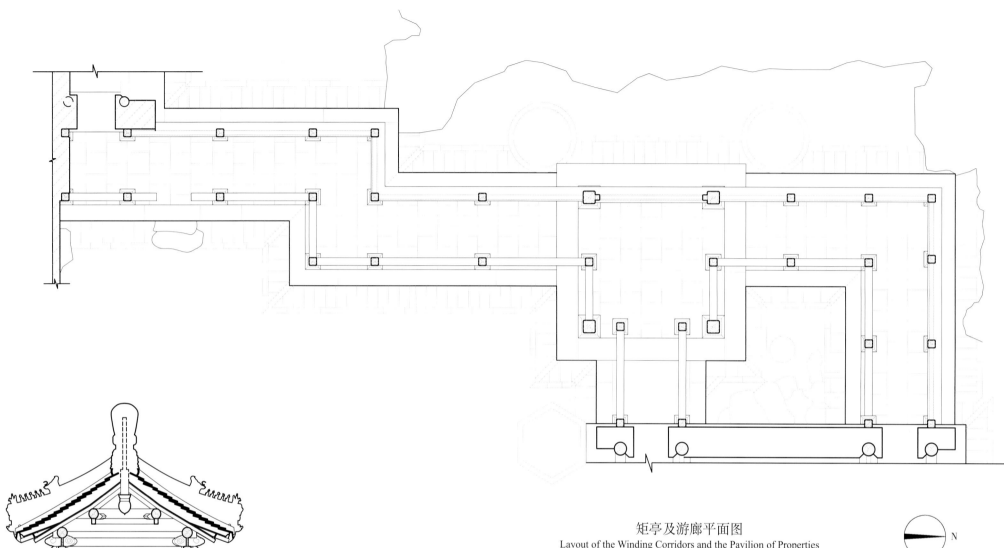

矩亭及游廊平面图
Layout of the Winding Corridors and the Pavilion of Properties

N

矩亭剖面图
Section of the Pavilion of Properties

0   1   2m

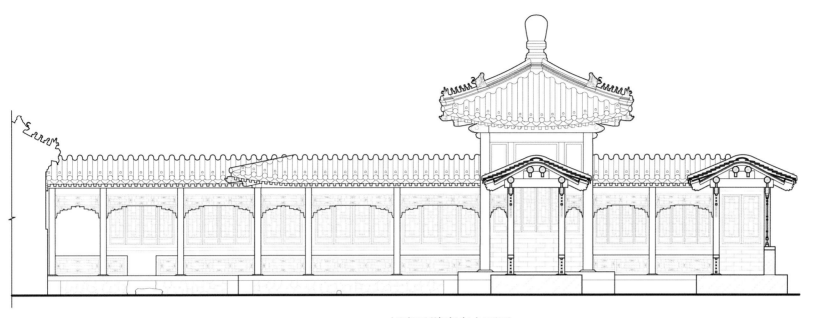

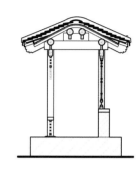

矩亭及游廊东立面图
Eastern Elevation of the Winding Corridors and the Pavilion of Properties

游廊横剖面图
Cross Section of the Winding Corridors and
the Pavilion of Properties

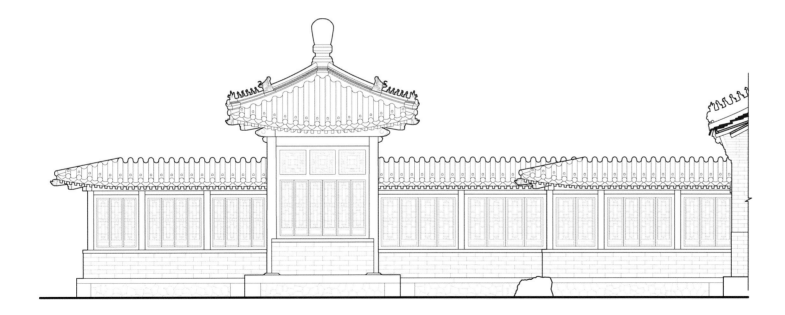

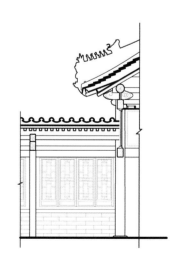

0   1   2m

矩亭及游廊西立面图
Western Elevation of the Winding Corridors and the Pavilion of Properties

游廊纵剖面图
Longitudinal Section of the Winding Corridors and the
Pavilion of Properties

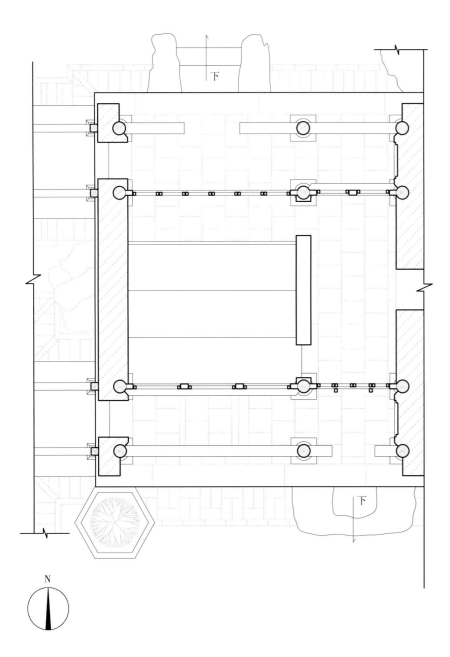

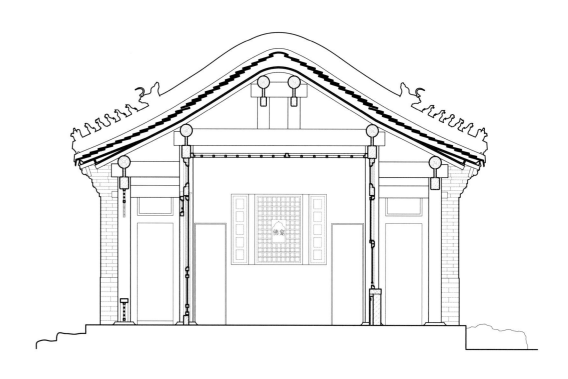

抑斋平面图
Layout of the Studio of Self Restraint

0　　1　　2m

抑斋横剖面图
Cross Section of the Studio of Self Restraint

N

下

下

佛堂

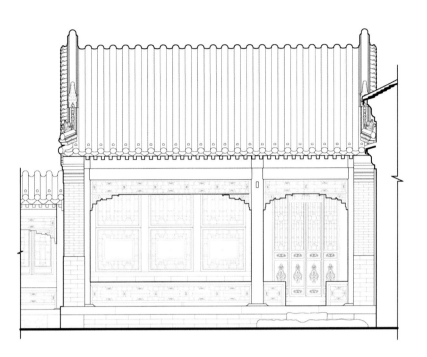

抑斋正立面图
Front Elevations of the Studio of Self Restraint

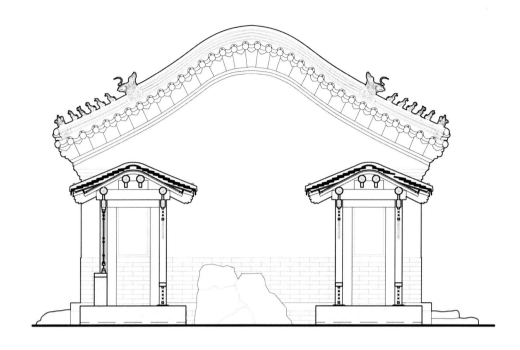

抑斋西侧立面图
Western Elevations of the Studio of Self Restraint

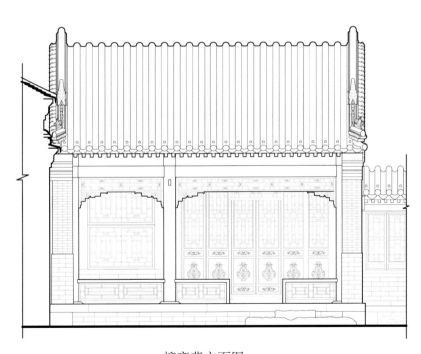

抑斋背立面图
Back Elevations of the Studio of Self Restraint

0   1   2m

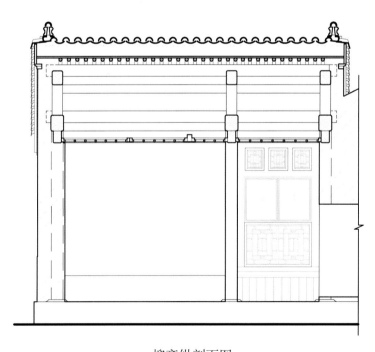

抑斋纵剖面图
Longitudinal Section of the Studio of Self Restraint

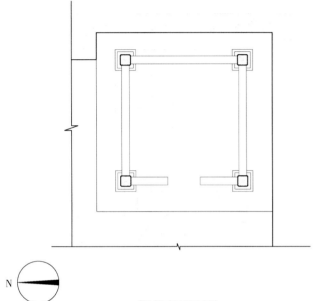

撷芳亭平面图
Layout of the Pavilion of Plucking Fragrance

N

0   1   2m

撷芳亭正立面图
Front Elevation of the Pavilion of Plucking Fragrance

撷芳亭剖面图
Section of the Pavilion of Plucking Fragrance

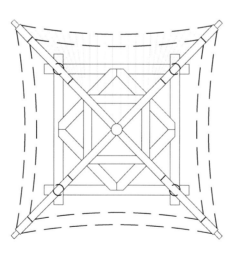

撷芳亭梁架俯视图
Top View of the Trusses, Pavilion of Plucking Fragrance

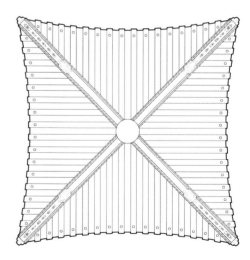

撷芳亭瓦顶俯视图
Top View of the Roofing Tiles, Pavilion of Plucking Fragrance

N

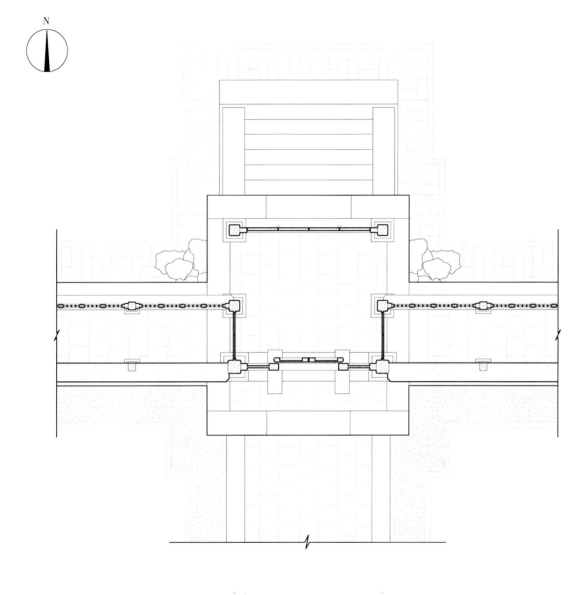

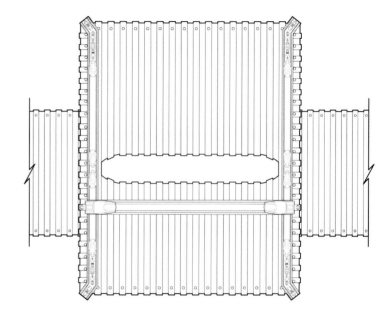

垂花门平面图
Layout of the Floral-pendant Gate

0   1   2m

垂花门瓦顶俯视图
Top View of the Roofing Tiles, Floral-pendant Gate

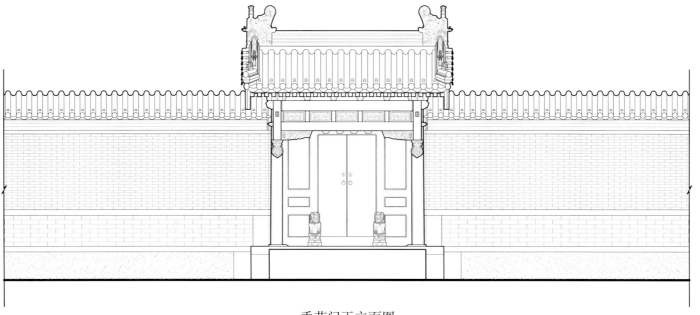

垂花门正立面图
Front Elevations of the Floral-pendant Gate

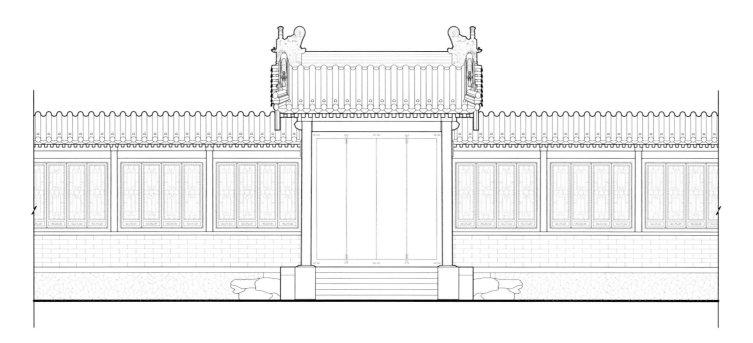

0　　1　　2m

垂花门背立面图
Back Elevations of the Floral-pendant Gate

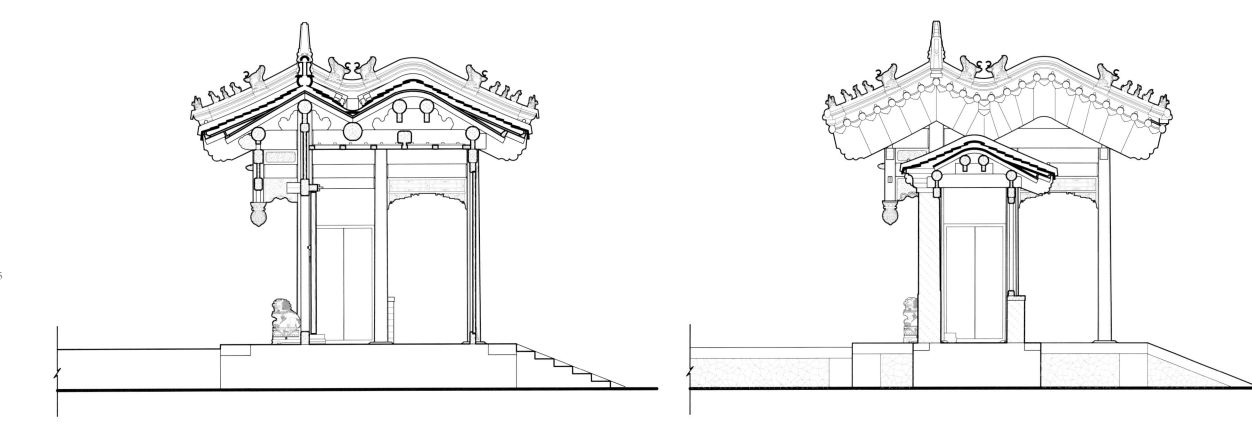

垂花门横剖面图
Cross Section of the Floral-pendant Gate

0   1   2m

垂花门东侧立面图
Eastern Elevation of the Floral-pendant Gate

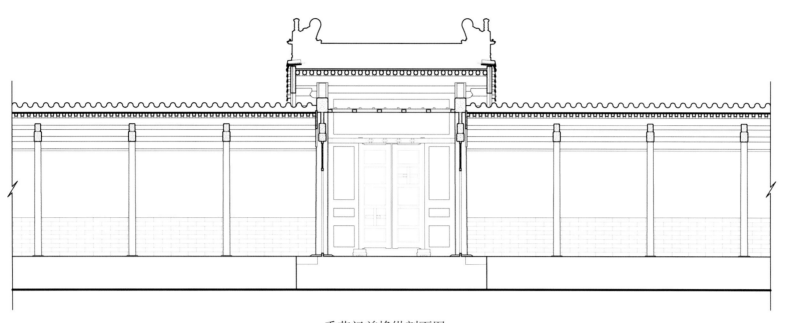

垂花门前檐纵剖面图
Longitudinal Section of the Front Eave, Floral-pendant Gate

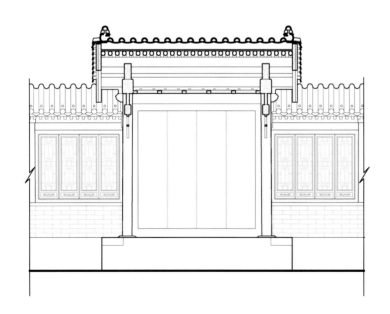

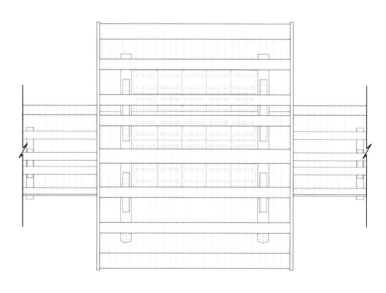

垂花门后檐纵剖面图
Longitudinal Section of the Back Eave, Floral-pendant Gate

0 1 2m

垂花门梁架俯视图
Top View of the Trusses, Floral-pendant Gate

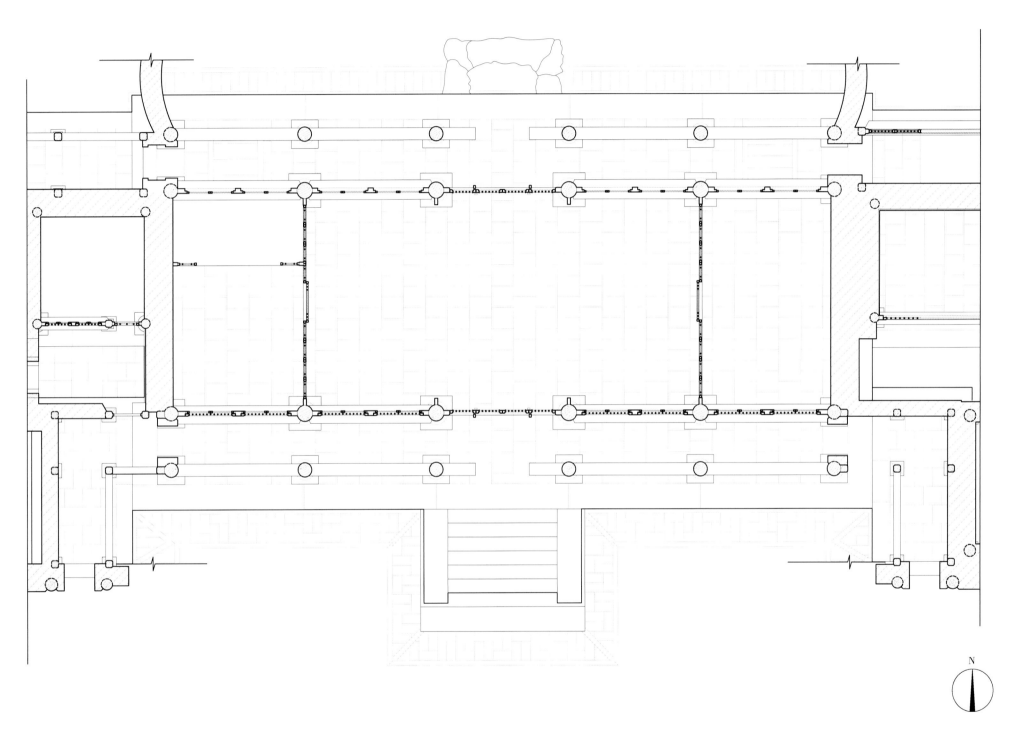

遂初堂平面图
Floor Plan of the Hall of Fulfilling Original Wishes

N

0   1   2m

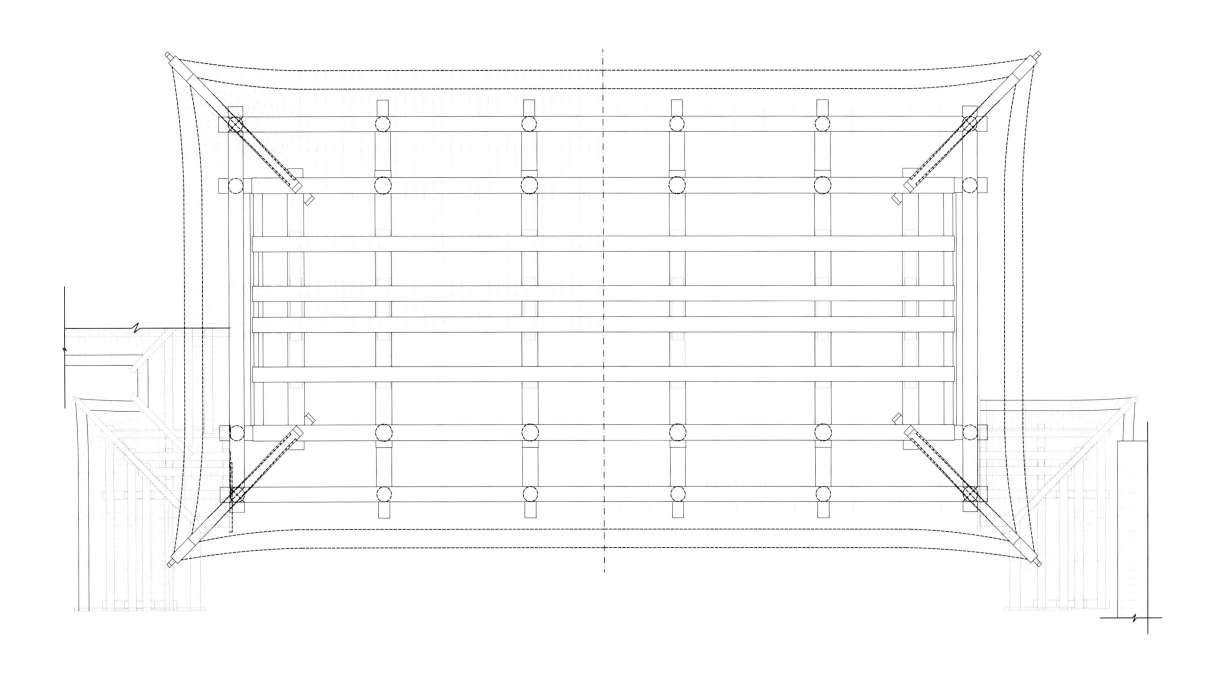

遂初堂梁架俯视图
Top View of the Trusses, Hall of Fulfilling Original Wishes

0   1   2m

遂初堂瓦顶俯视图
Top View of the Roofing Tiles, Hall of Fulfilling Original Wishes

0 1 2m

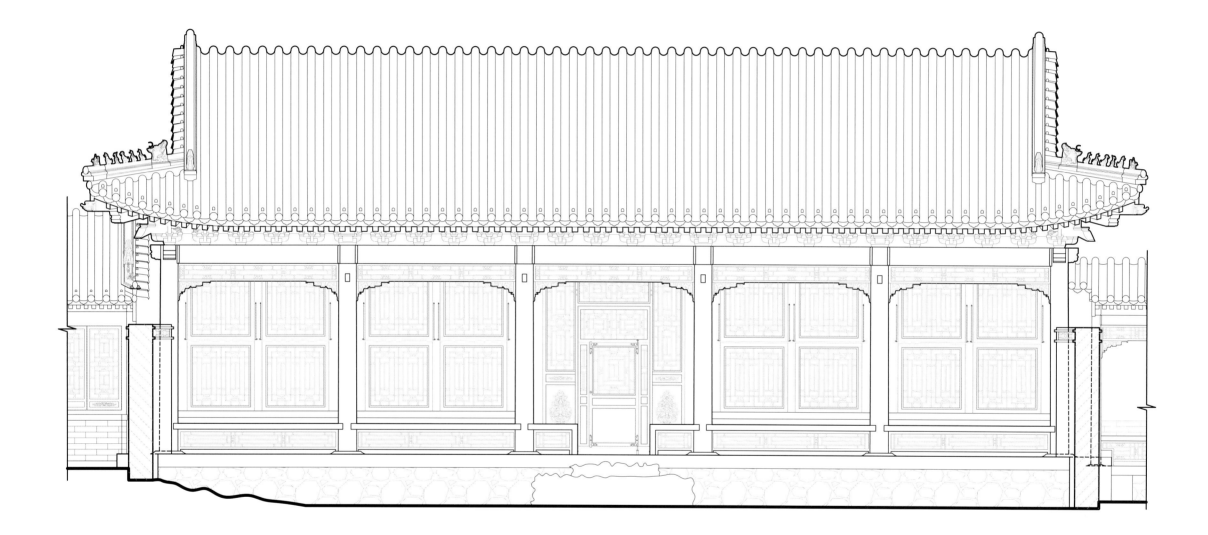

遂初堂背立面图
Back Elevations of the Hall of Fulfilling Original Wishes

0　　1　　2m

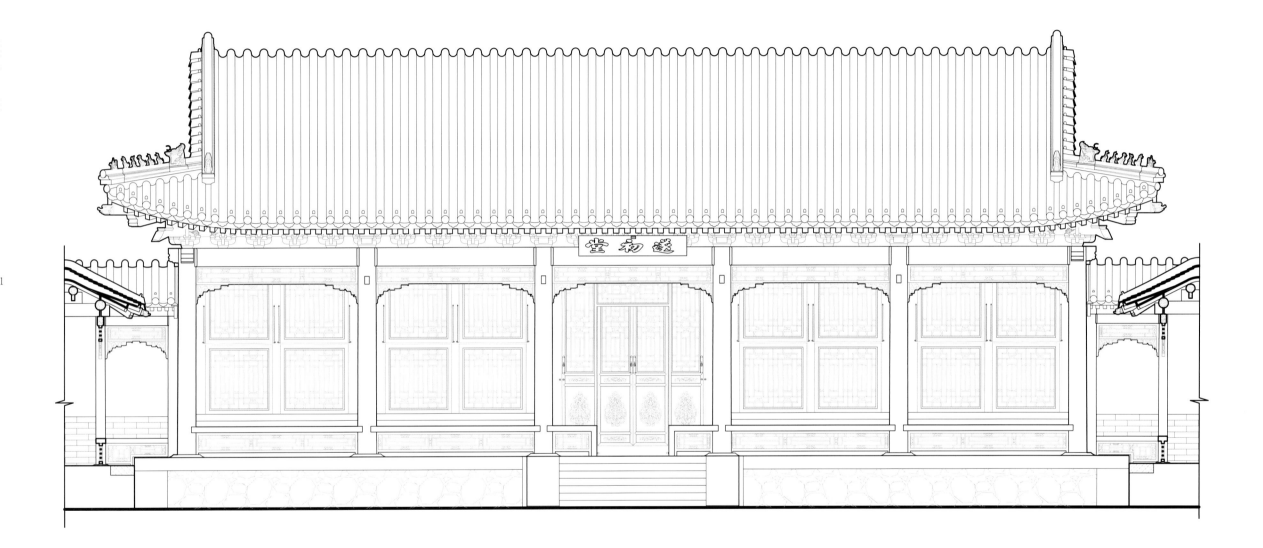

遂初堂正立面图

Front Elevations of the Hall of Fulfilling Original Wishes

0　　1　　2m

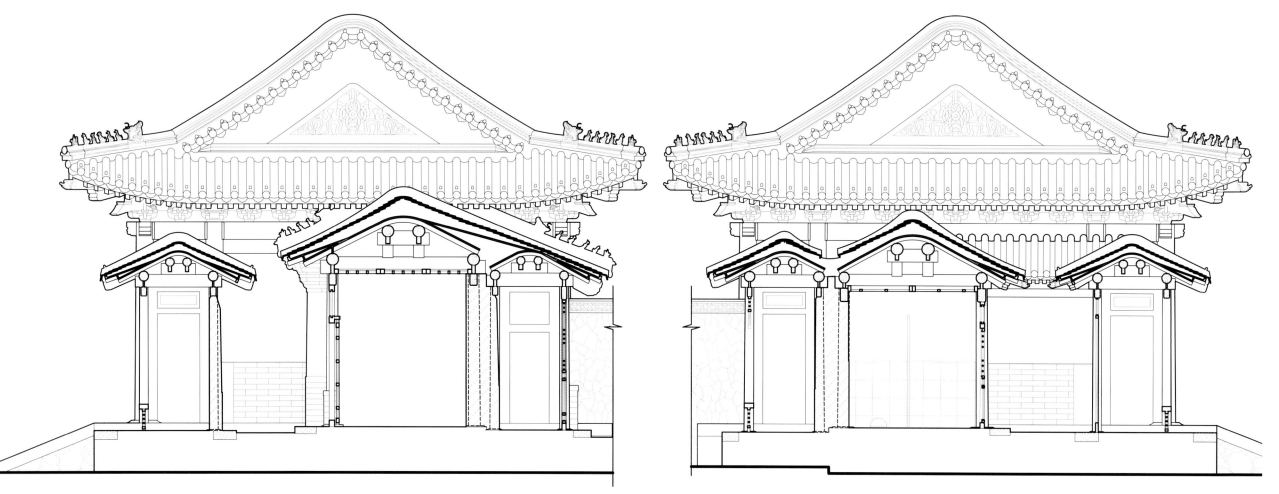

遂初堂东侧立面图
Eastern Elevations of the Hall of Fulfilling Original Wishes

遂初堂西侧立面图
Western Elevations of the Hall of Fulfilling Original Wishes

0　　　1　　　2m

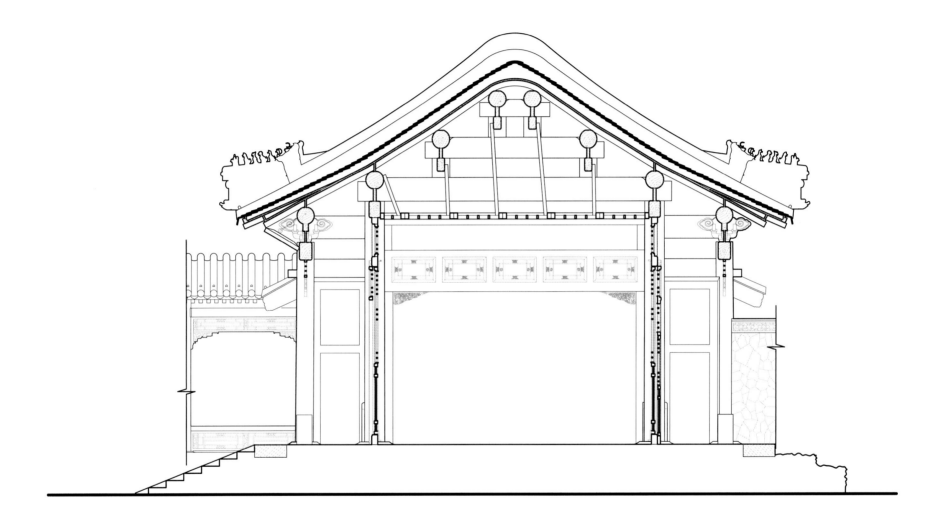

遂初堂明间横剖面图
Cross Section of the Central Bay, Hall of Fulfilling Original Wishes

0   1   2m

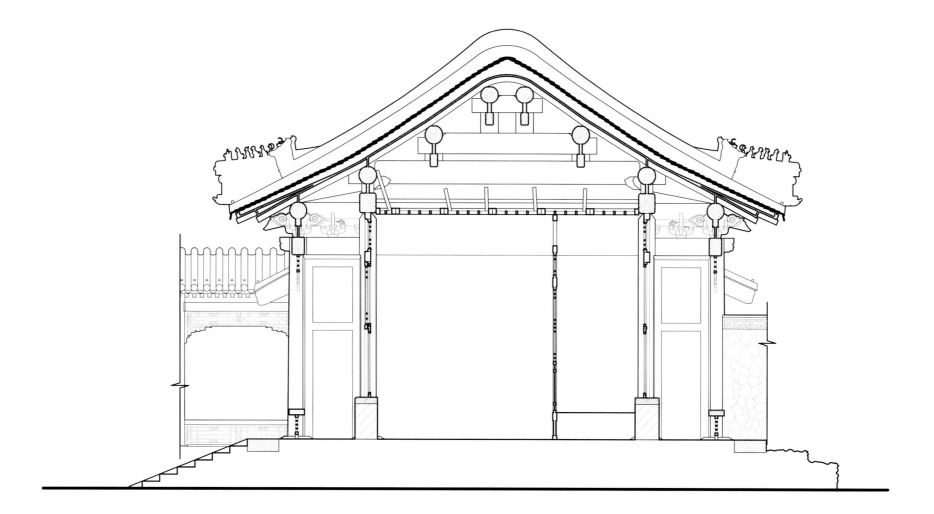

遂初堂西梢间横剖面图
Cross Section of the Westmost Bay, Hall of Fulfilling Original Wishes

0   1   2m

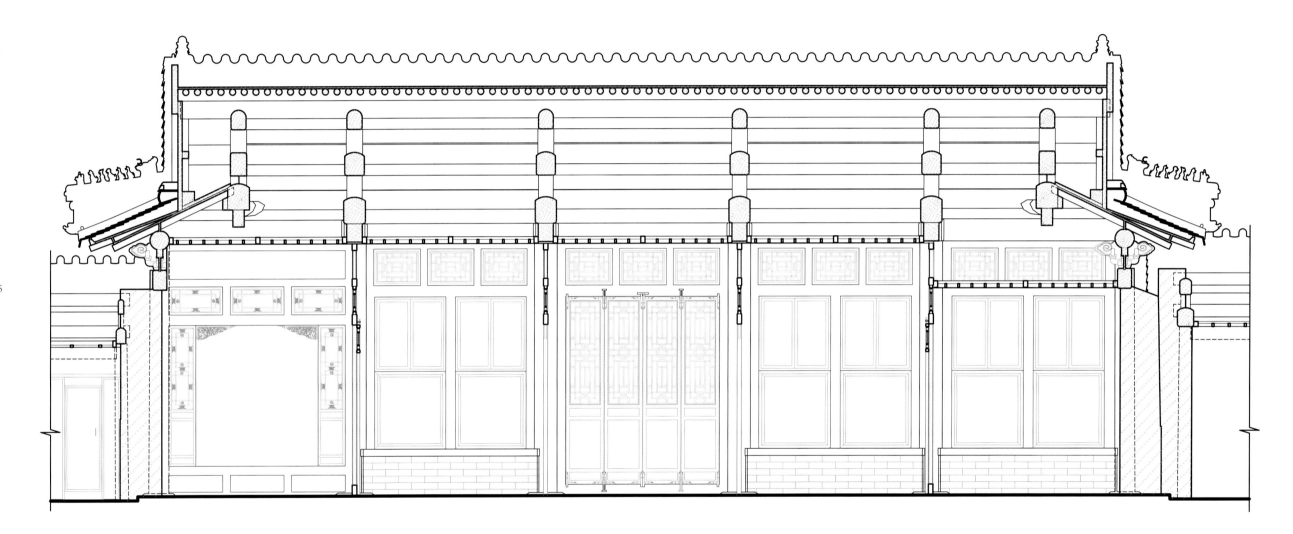

遂初堂纵剖面图
Longitudinal Section of the Hall of Fulfilling Original Wishes

0   1   2m

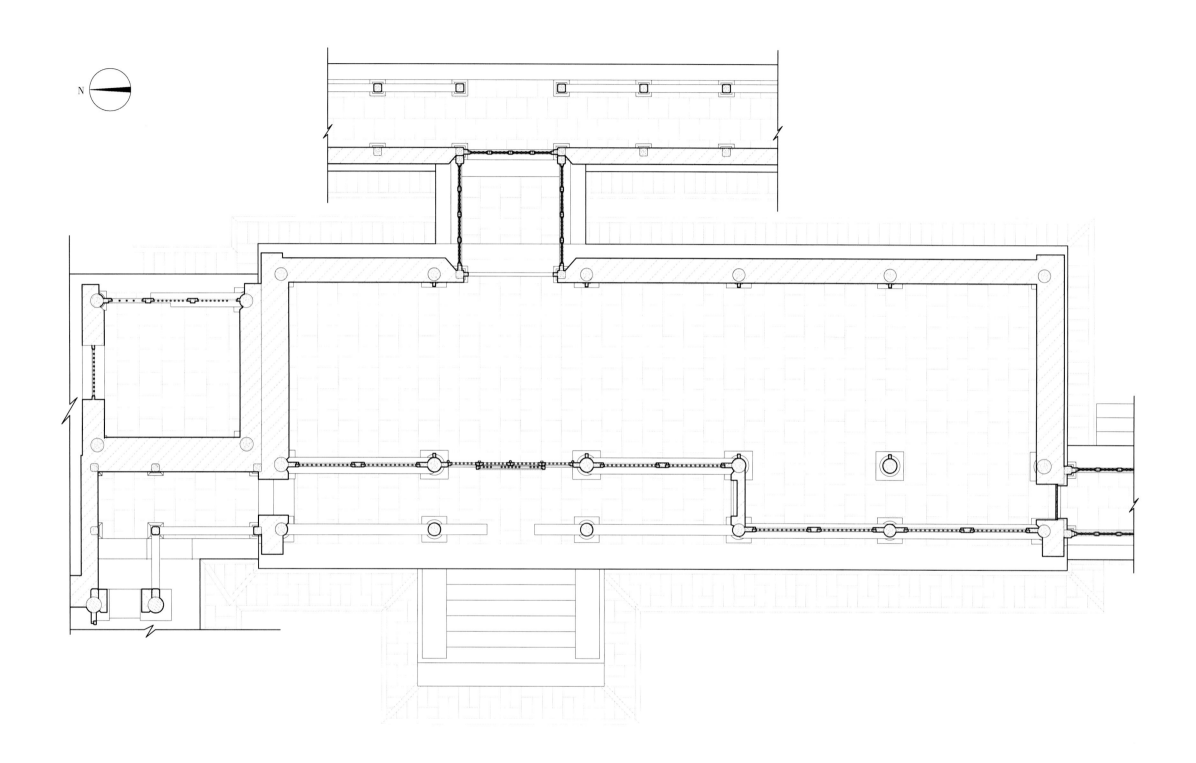

N

东配殿及工字廊平面图
Floor Plan of the Eastern Side Hall, Hall of Fulfilling Original Wishes and its

0   1   2m

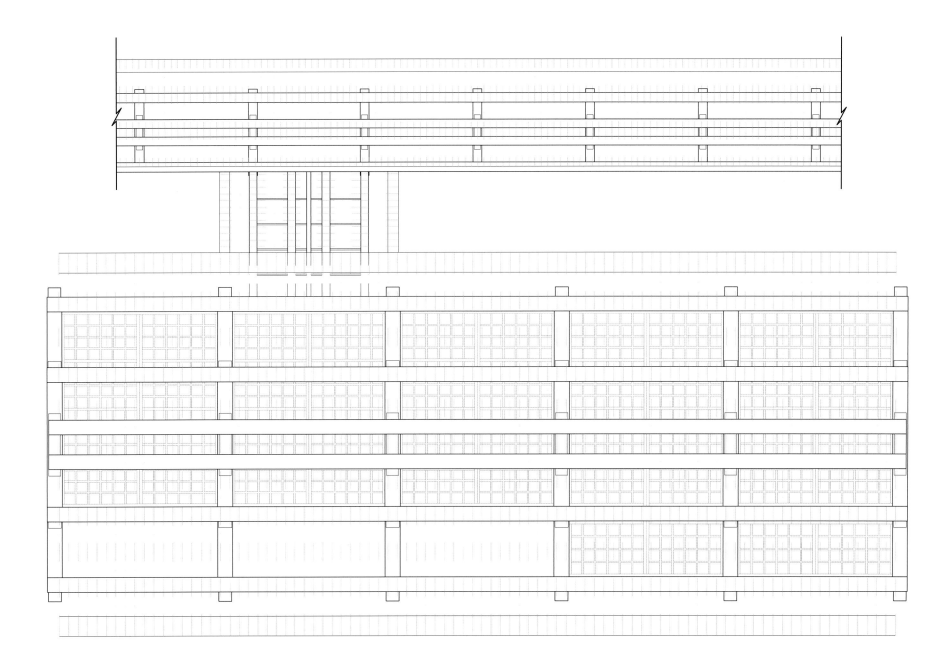

东配殿及工字廊梁架俯视图

Top View of the Trusses of the Eastern Side Hall, Hall of Fulfilling Original Wishes and its Corridors

0   1   2m

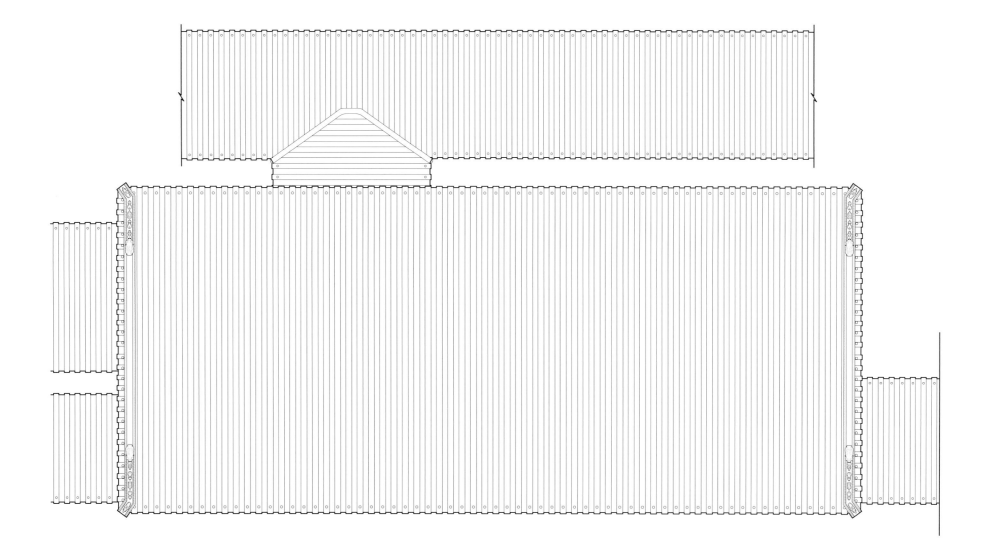

东配殿及工字廊瓦顶俯视图
Top View of the Roofing Tiles of the Eastern Side Hall, Hall of Fulfilling Original Wishes and its Corridors

0 1 2m

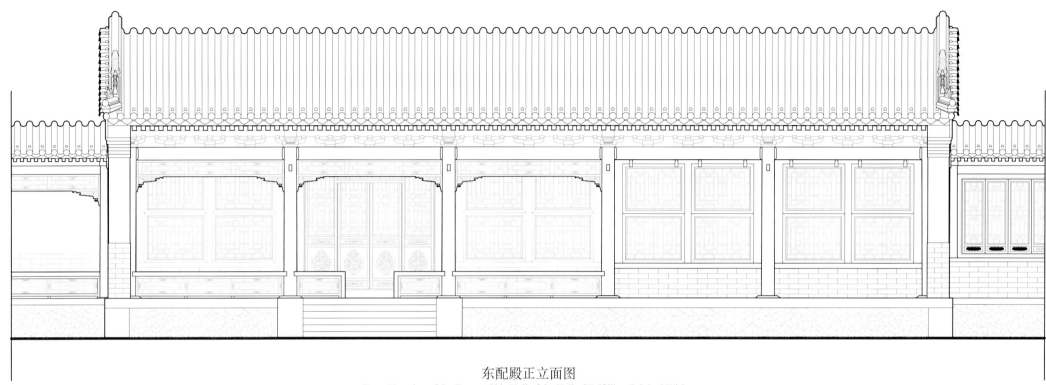

东配殿正立面图

Front Elevation of the Eastern Side Hall of the Hall of Fulfilling Original Wishes

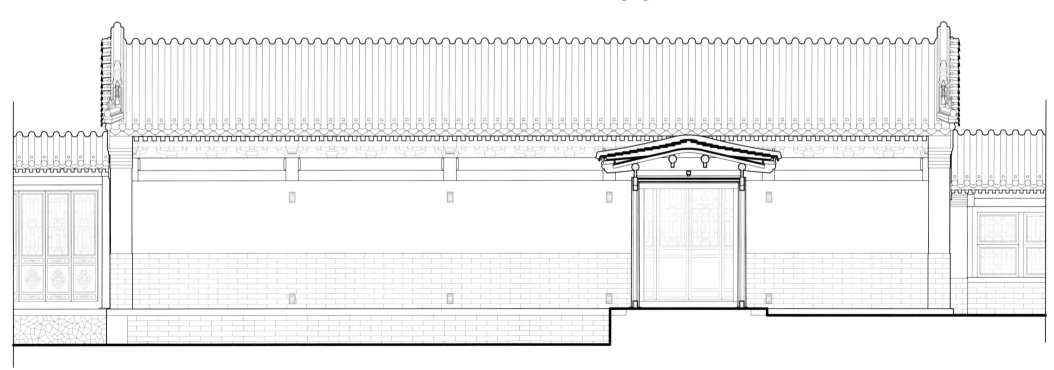

东配殿背立面及工字廊横剖面图

Back Elevation of the Eastern Side Hall and Cross Section of Corridors, Hall of Fulfilling Original Wishes

0　　1　　2m

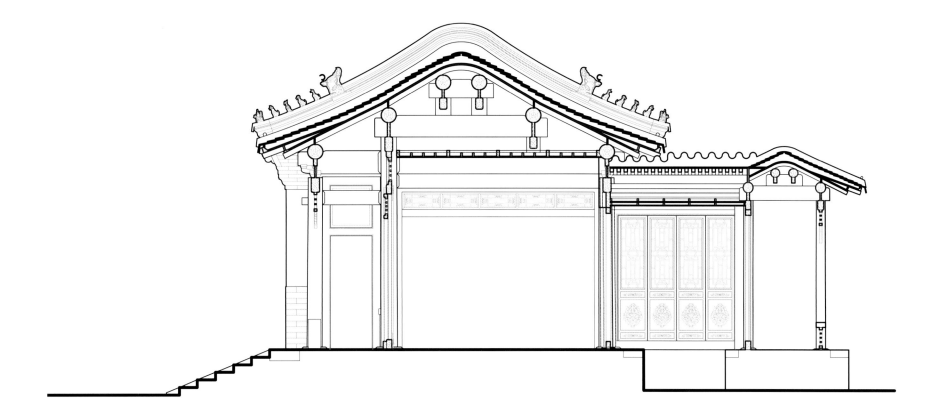

东配殿北次间横剖面及工字廊纵剖面图
Cross Section of the Bay on the north of the Central Bay of the Eastern Side Hall and Longitudinal Section of the Corridors, Hall of Fulfilling Original Wishes

0　　1　　2m

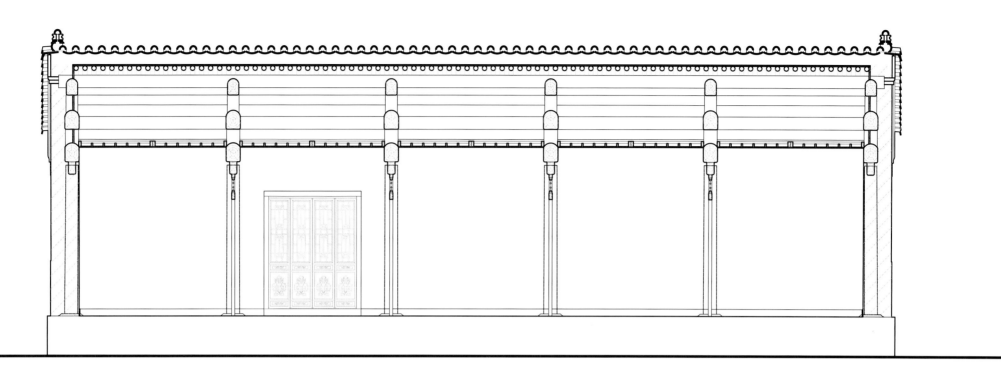

东配殿纵剖面图

Longitudinal Section of the Eastern Side Hall, Hall of Fulfilling Original Wishes

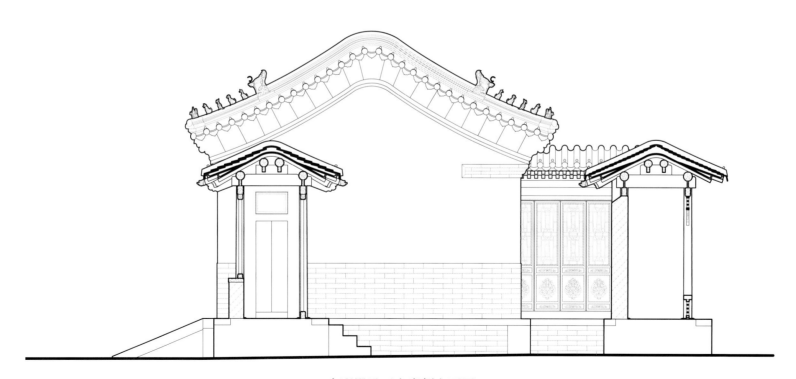

0　　1　　2m

东配殿及工字廊侧立面图

Side Elevation of the Eastern Side Hall of the Hall of Fulfilling Original Wishes and its Corridors

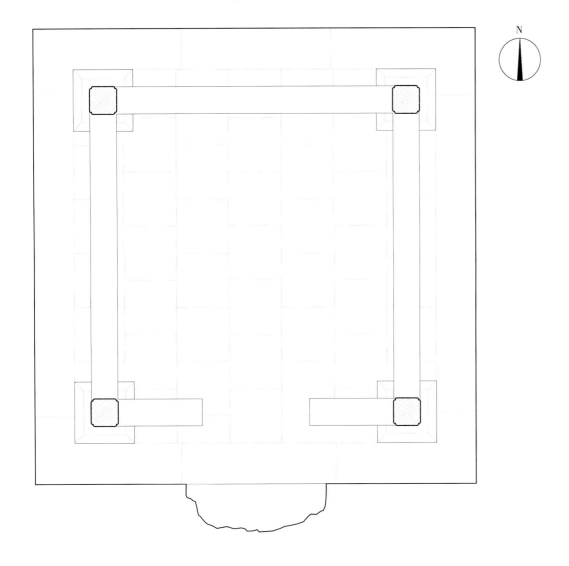

耸秀亭平面图
Floor Plan of the Pavilion of Lofty Elegance

耸秀亭横剖面图
Cross Section of the Pavilion of Lofty Elegance

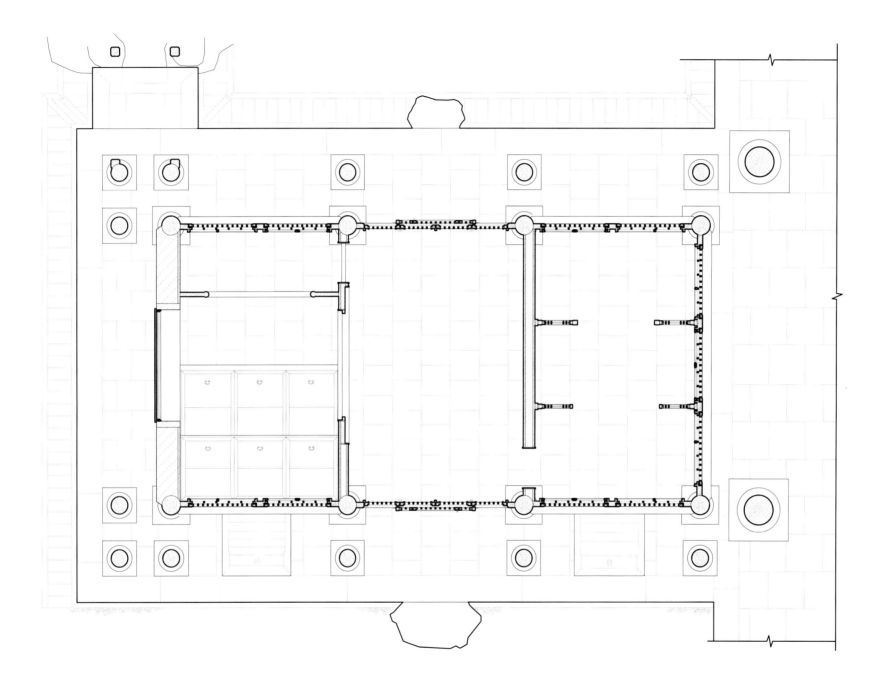

三友轩平面图
Floor Plan of the Bower of Three Friends

0　　　　1　　　　2m

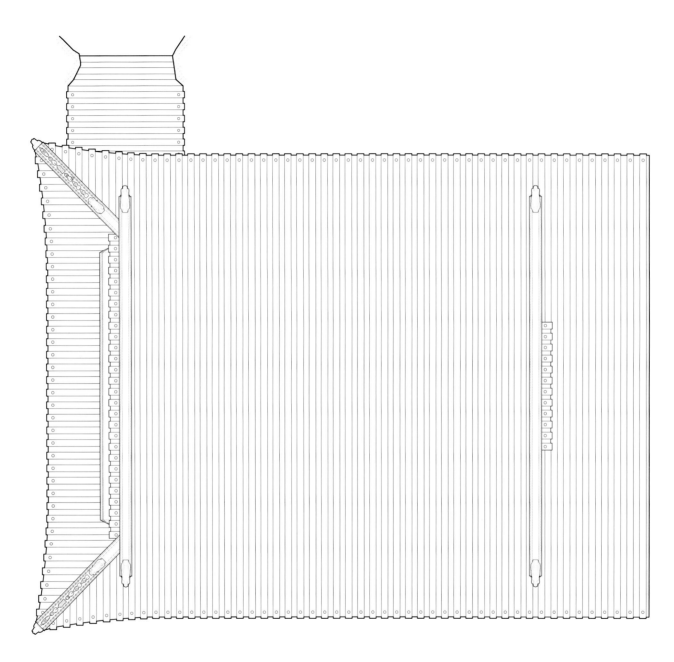

三友轩瓦顶俯视图
Top View of the Roofing Tiles, Bower of Three Friends

0 1 2m

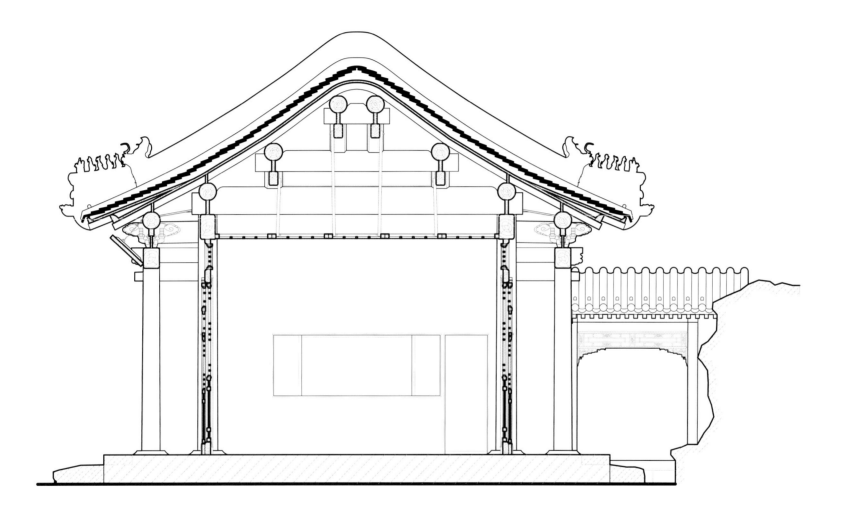

三友轩明间横剖面图
Cross Section of the Central Bay, Bower of Three Friends

0   1   2m

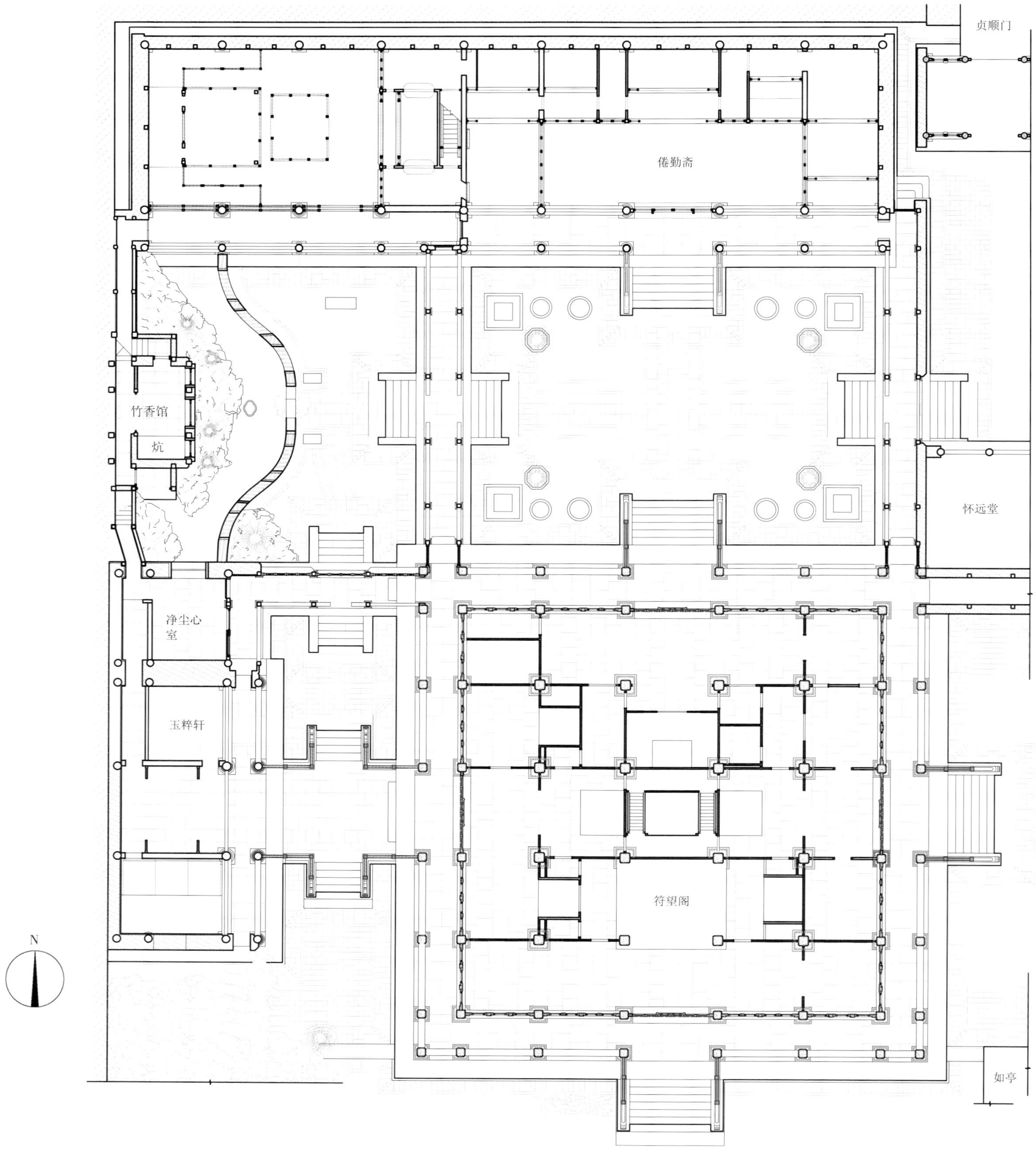

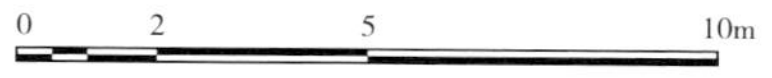

贞顺门

林远堂

倦勤斋

符望阁

竹香馆

净尘心室

玉粹轩

如亭

符望阁一区总平面图
Overall Layout of the Complex of the Belvedere of Viewing Achievements

0　2　5　10m

N

符望阁一区总瓦顶俯视图
Top View of the Overall Roofing Tiles, the Complex of the Belvedere of Viewing Achievements

符望阁一区总瓦顶俯视图
Top View of the Overall Roofing Tiles, the Complex of the Belvedere of Viewing Achievements

0   2   5   10m

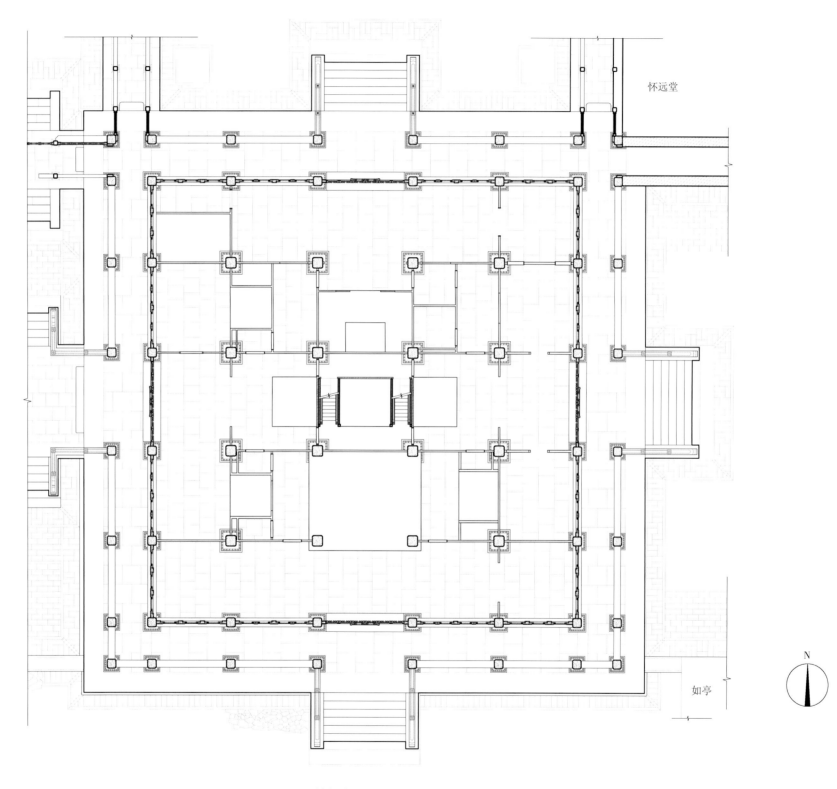

怀远堂

如亭

N

符望阁一层平面图
First Floor of the Belvedere of Viewing Achievements

0　　2　　5m

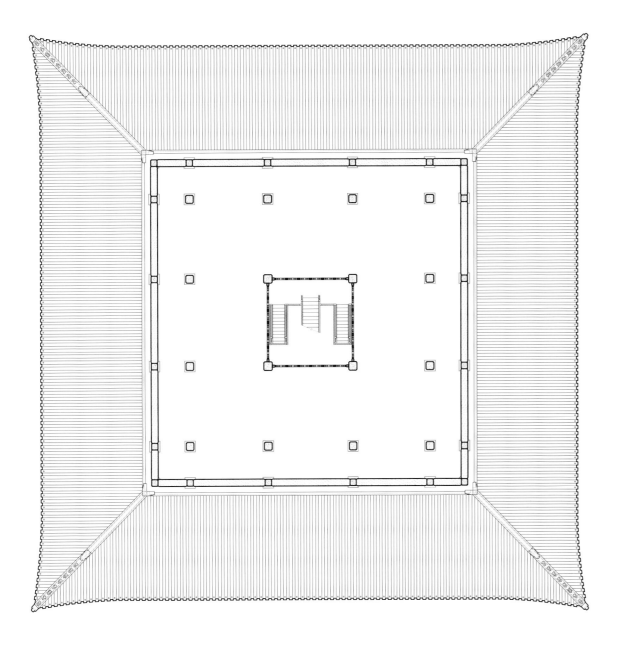

符望阁平坐层平面图

Mezzanine Floor of the Belvedere of Viewing Achievements

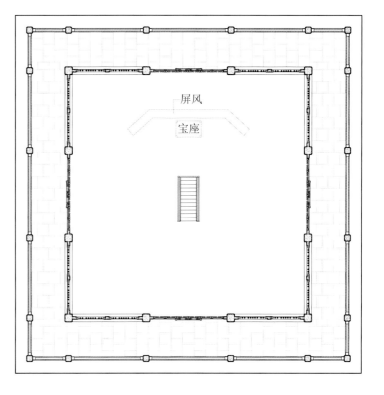

屏风

宝座

符望阁三层平面图

The Third Floor of the Belvedere of Viewing Achievements

0　　2　　5m

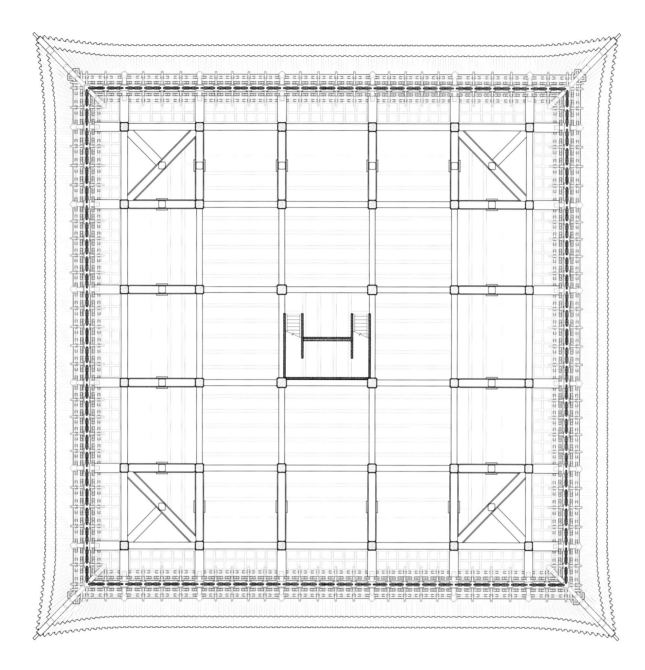

符望阁下檐天花仰视图

Bottom View of the Ceiling Panels, the Lower Eave of the Belvedere of Viewing Achievements

0　　2　　　　5m

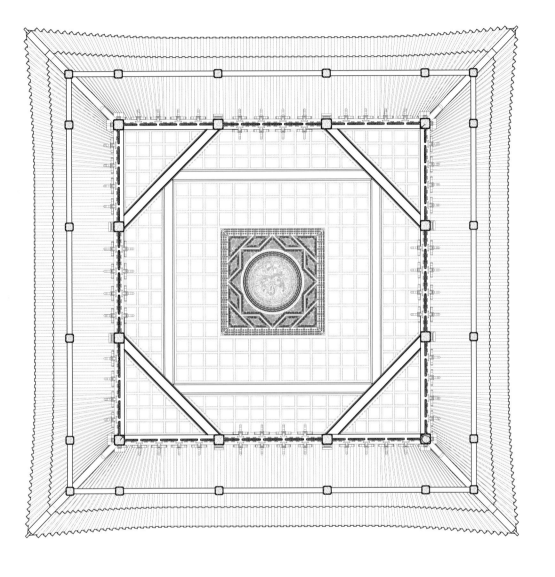

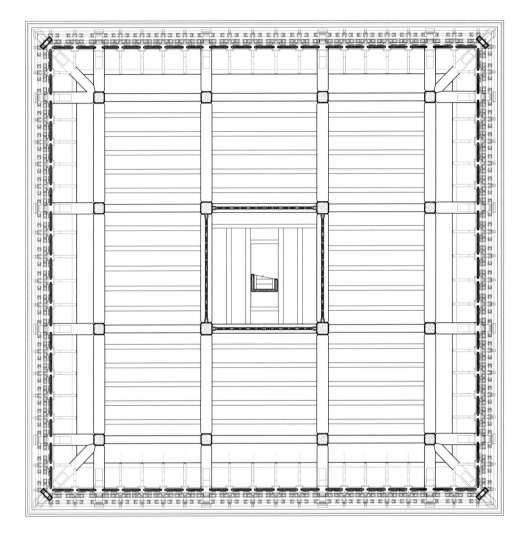

符望阁上檐天花仰视图
Bottom Views of the Ceiling Panels, the Upper Eave of the Belvedere of Viewing Achievements

0 2 5m

符望阁平坐层天花仰视图
Bottom Views of the Ceiling Panels, the Mezzanine Story of the Belvedere of Viewing Achievements

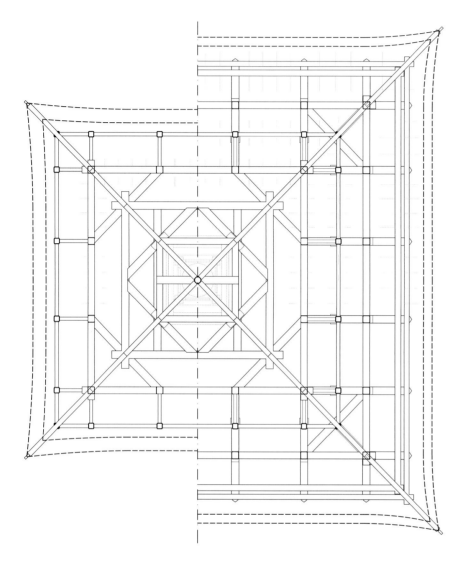

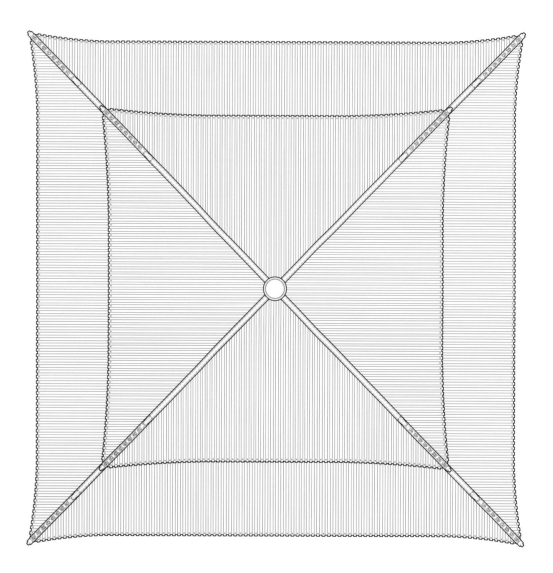

符望阁梁架俯视图
Top Views of the Trusses, Belvedere of Viewing Achievements

符望阁瓦顶俯视图
Top Views of the Roofing Tiles, Belvedere of Viewing Achievements

0　2　5m

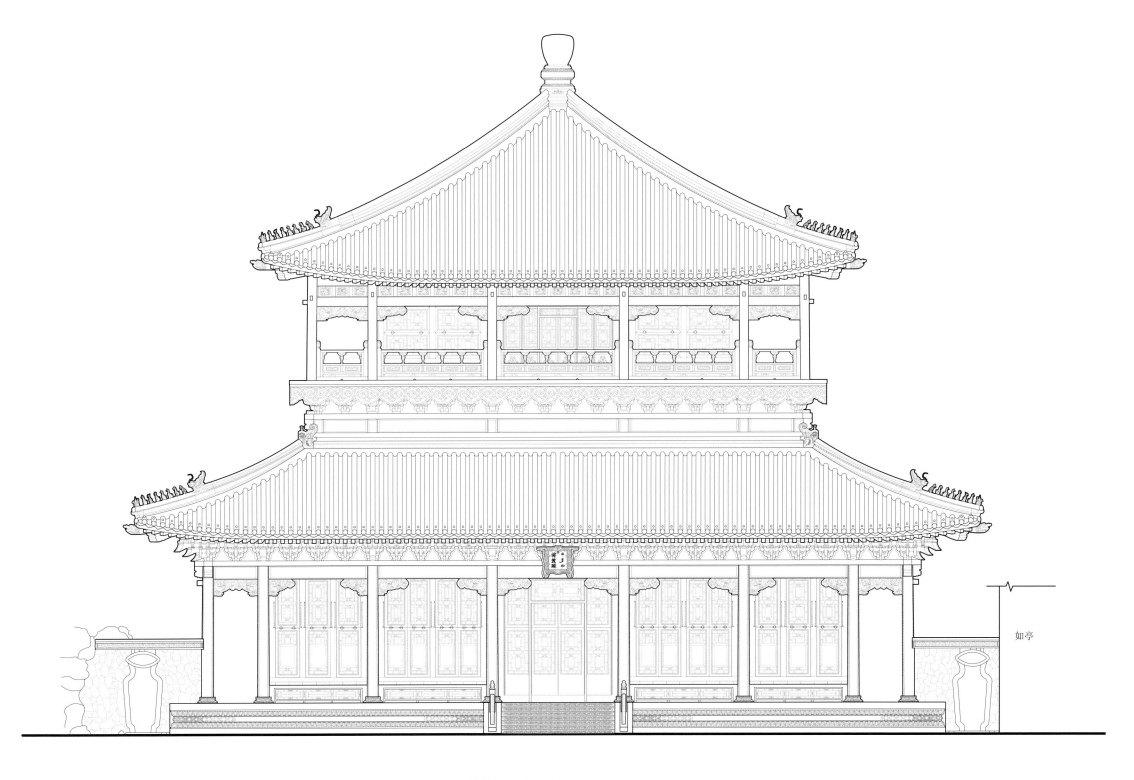

如亭

符望阁正立面图
Front Elevation of the Belvedere of Viewing Achievements

0　　　2　　　　5m

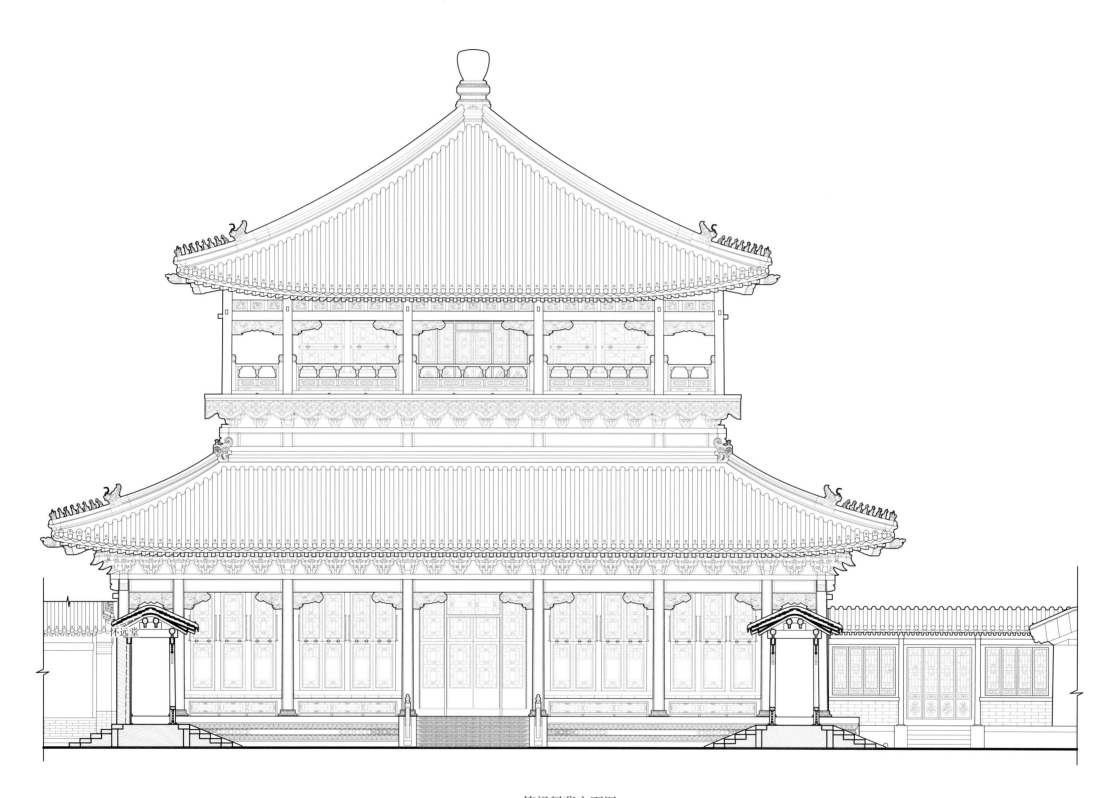

符望阁背立面图
Back Elevation of the Belvedere of Viewing Achievements

0   2   5m

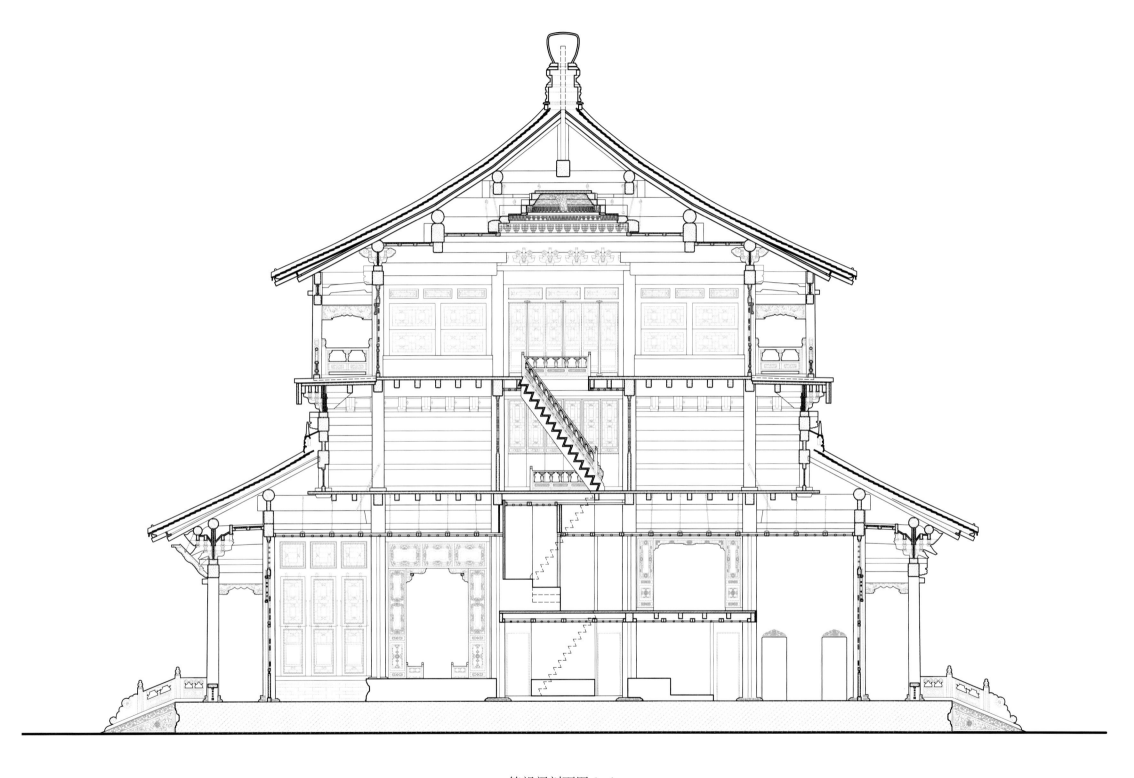

符望阁剖面图 1-1
1-1 Section of the Belvedere of Viewing Achievements

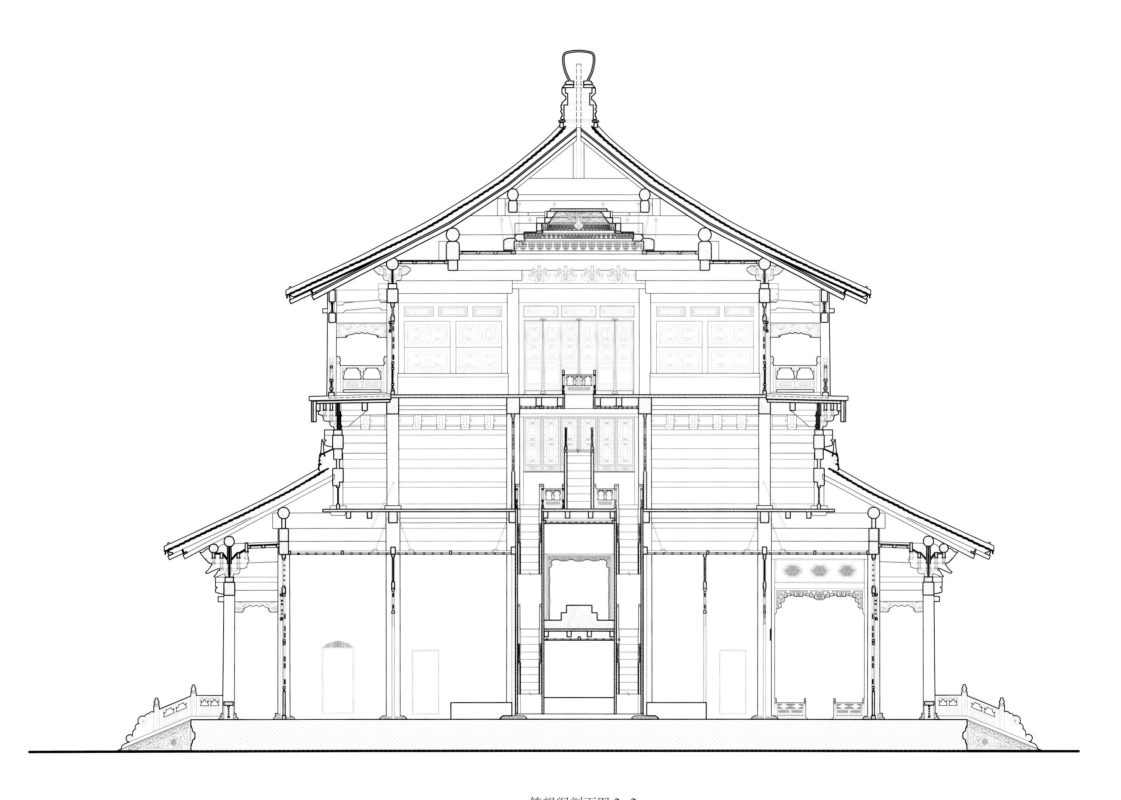

符望阁剖面图 2-2
2-2 Section of the Belvedere of Viewing Achievements

0　　　　2　　　　　5m

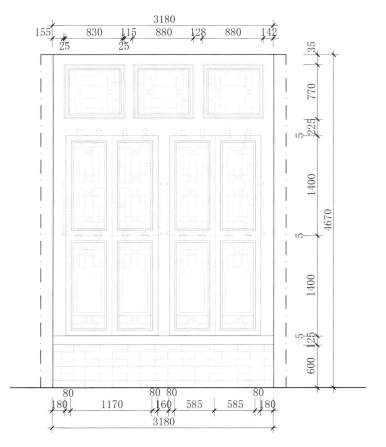

下檐一次间隔扇立面

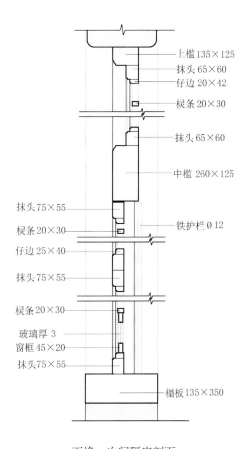

下檐一次间隔扇剖面

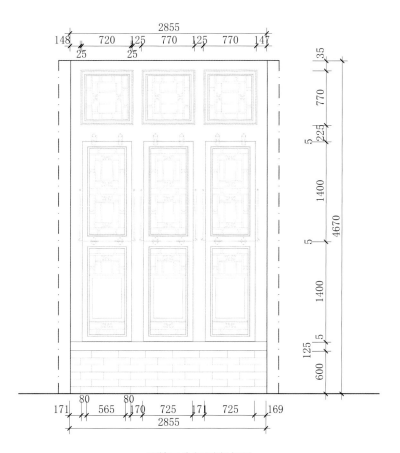

下檐二次间隔扇立面

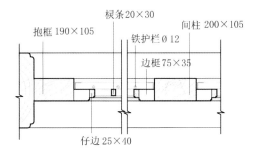

下檐一次间隔扇平面

符望阁下檐外檐装修详图
Detailed Drawing of the Exterior Decorations under the Lower Eave, Belvedere of Viewing Achievements

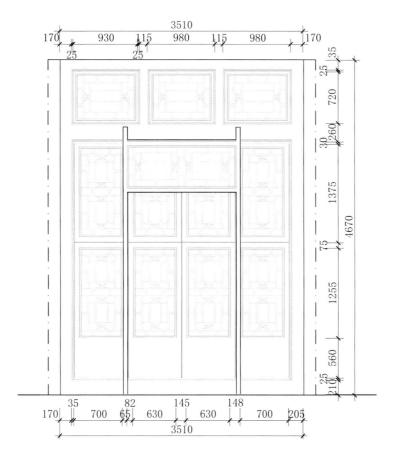

上檐明间带帘架隔扇立面

上檐明间带帘架隔扇剖面

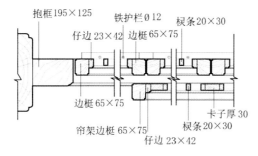

上檐明间带帘架隔扇平面

符望阁上檐外檐装修详图
Detailed Drawing of the Exterior Decorations Under the Upper Eave, Belvedere of Viewing Achievements

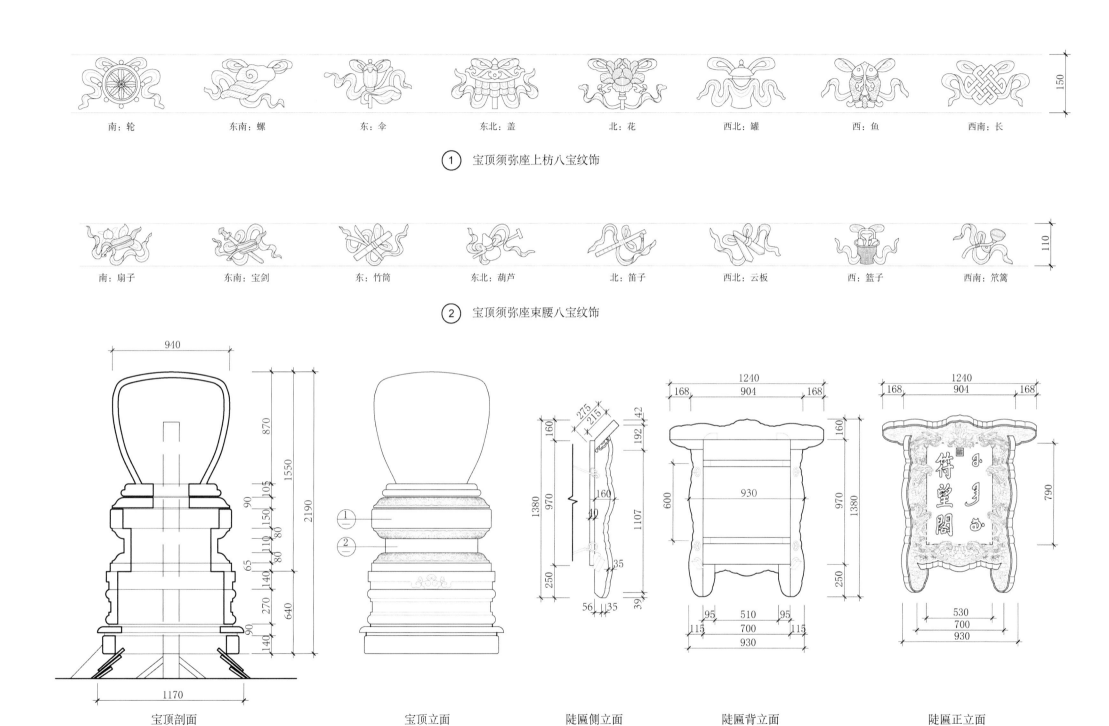

南：轮　　东南：螺　　东：伞　　东北：盖　　北：花　　西北：罐　　西：鱼　　西南：长

① 宝顶须弥座上枋八宝纹饰

南：扇子　　东南：宝剑　　东：竹筒　　东北：葫芦　　北：笛子　　西北：云板　　西：篮子　　西南：笊篱

② 宝顶须弥座束腰八宝纹饰

宝顶剖面　　　　宝顶立面　　　　陡匾侧立面　　　　陡匾背立面　　　　陡匾正立面

符望阁宝顶、陡匾详图

Detailed Drawings of the Spherical Finial and the Inscribed Panel, Belvedere of Viewing Achievements

符望阁藻井俯视图
Top View of the Caisson Ceiling, Belvedere of Viewing Achievements

符望阁藻井仰视图
Bottom View of the Caisson Ceiling, Belvedere of Viewing Achievements

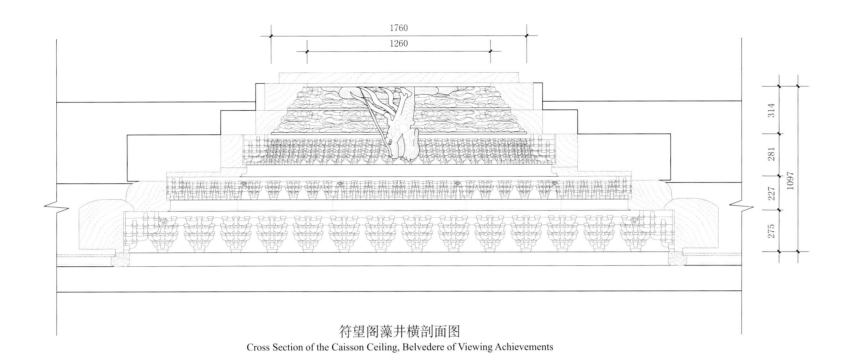

符望阁藻井横剖面图
Cross Section of the Caisson Ceiling, Belvedere of Viewing Achievements

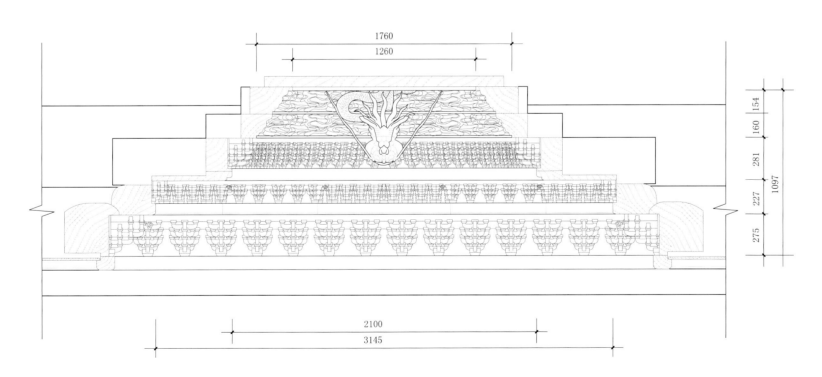

符望阁藻井纵剖面图
Longitudinal Section of the Caisson Ceiling, Belvedere of Viewing Achievements

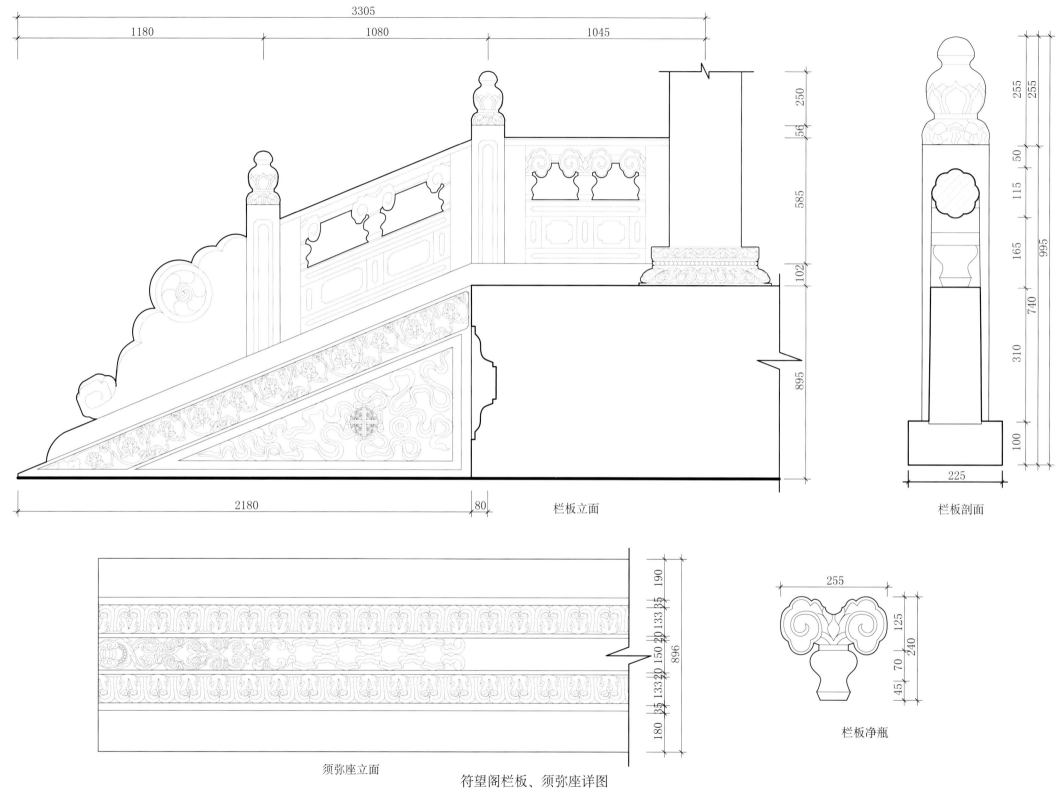

栏板立面

栏板剖面

须弥座立面

栏板净瓶

符望阁栏板、须弥座详图
Detailed Drawings of the Balustrades and Sumeru-seat, Belvedere of Viewing Achievements

下檐角科斗栱尺寸表

斗口：75

名称＼部位	上宽	下宽	上深	下深	耳	腰	底	总高
坐斗	255	195	255	195	60	30	60	150
三才升	115	75	120	90	30	15	30	75
槽升子	115	75	150	120	30	15	30	75
上平盘斗	220	220	350	300				45
中平盘斗	185	185	300	250				45
下平盘斗	160	160	260	210				45

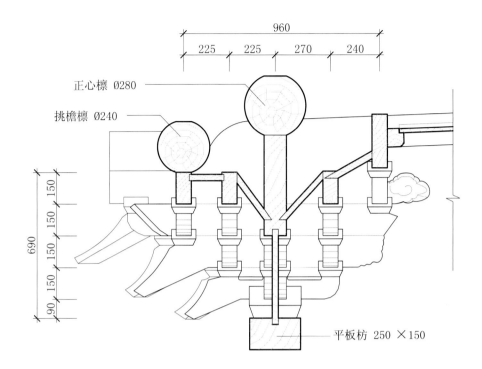

正心檩 Ø280
挑檐檩 Ø240
平板枋 250×150

下檐角科斗栱侧立面

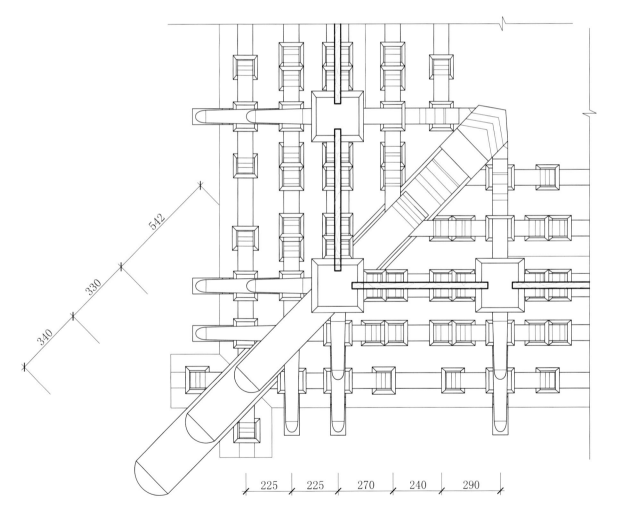

角科斗栱仰视

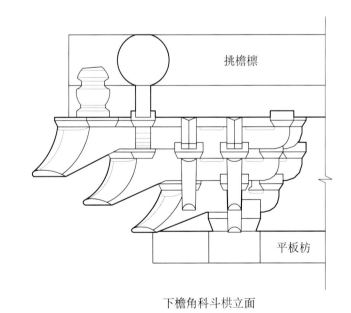

挑檐檩
平板枋

下檐角科斗栱立面

符望阁下檐角科斗栱详图

Detailed Drawings of the Corner Brackets under the Lower Eave, Belvedere of Viewing Achievements

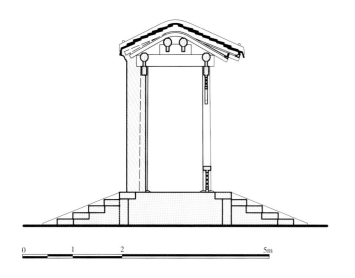

符望阁北面东游廊横剖面图
Cross Section of the Eastern Corridors on the north of the Belvedere of
Viewing Achievements

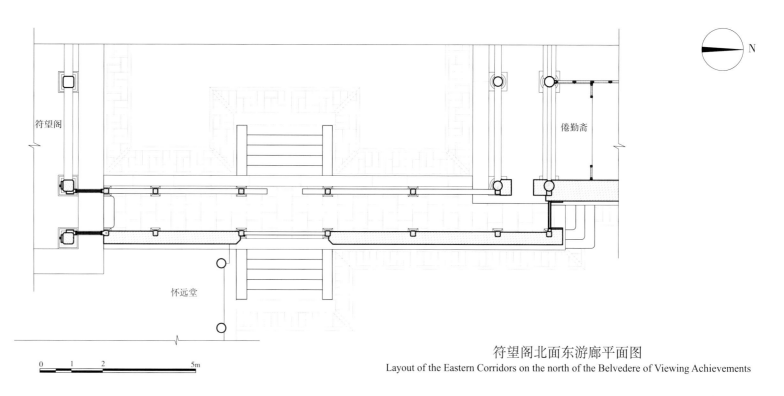

符望阁北面东游廊平面图
Layout of the Eastern Corridors on the north of the Belvedere of Viewing Achievements

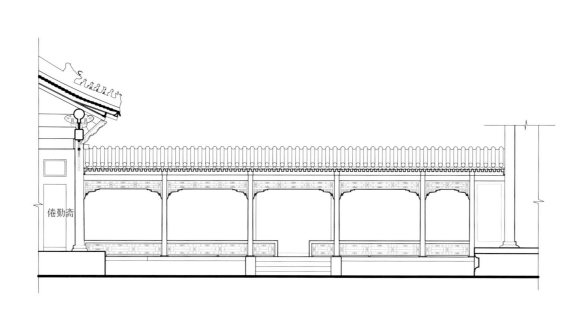

符望阁北面东游廊西立面图
Elevation of the Eastern Corridors on the north of the Belvedere of Viewing Achievements

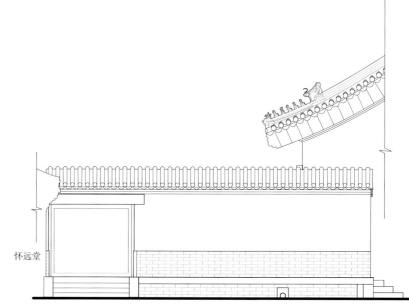

符望阁北面东游廊东立面图
Elevation of the Eastern Corridors on the north of the Belvedere of Viewing Achievements

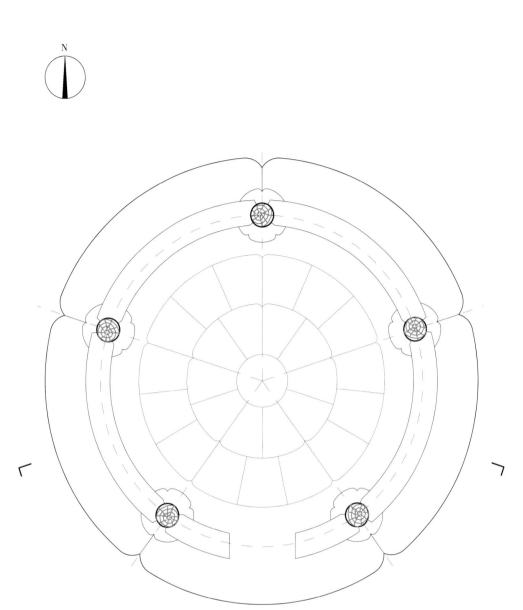

碧螺亭平面图
Floor Plan of the Pavilion of Jade-green Conch

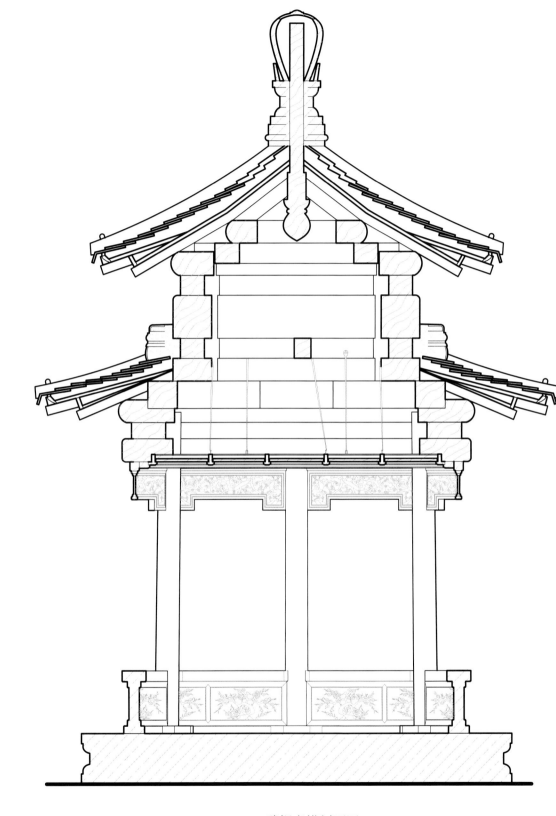

碧螺亭横剖面图
Cross Section of the Pavilion of Jade-green Conch

0　　　　　　1　　　　　　2m

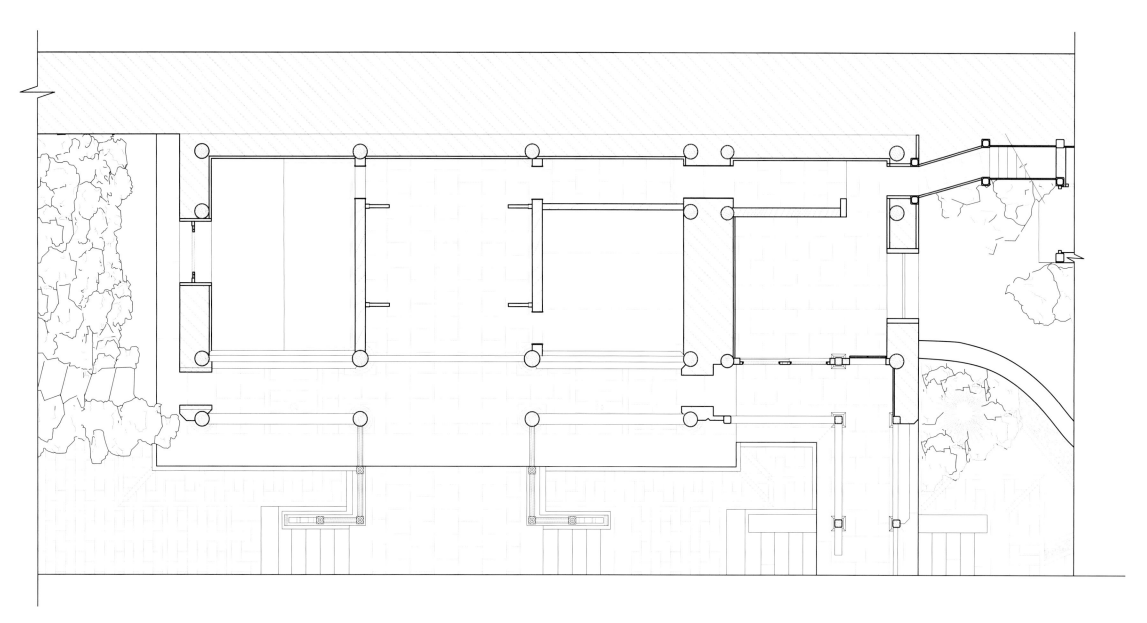

玉粹轩平面图
Floor Plan of the Bower of Purest Jade

0   1   2m

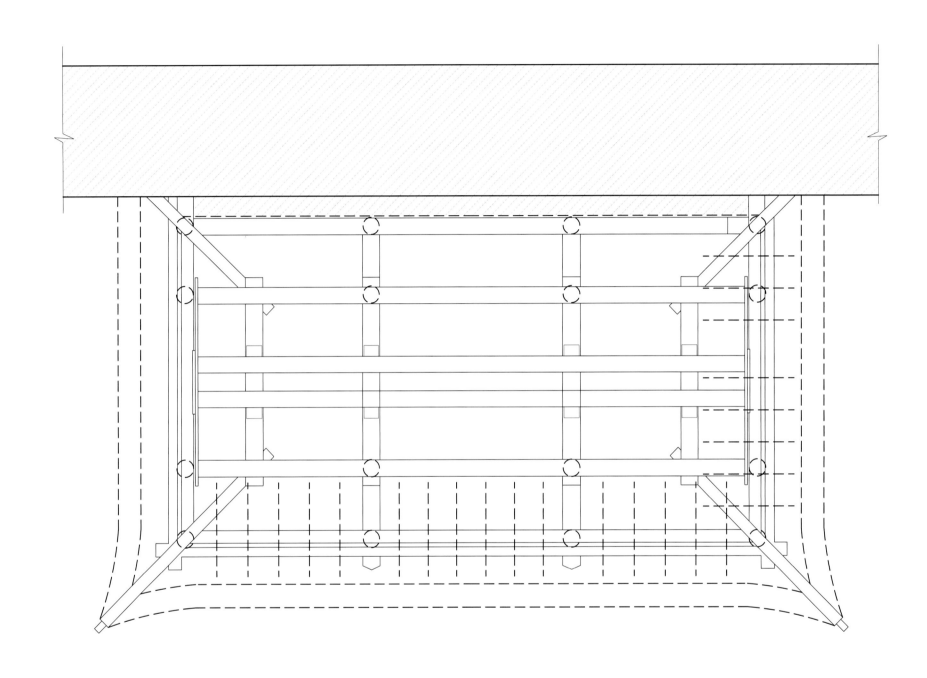

玉粹轩梁架俯视图
Top View of the Trusses, Bower of Purest Jade

0   1   2m

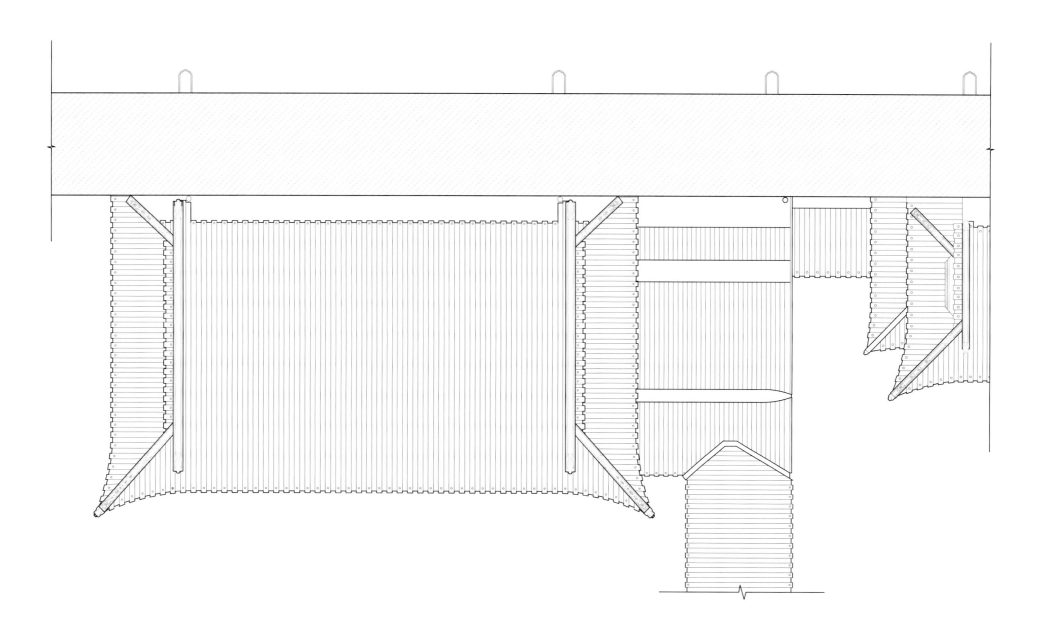

玉粹轩瓦顶俯视图
Top View of the Roofing Tiles, Bower of Purest Jade

0 1 2m

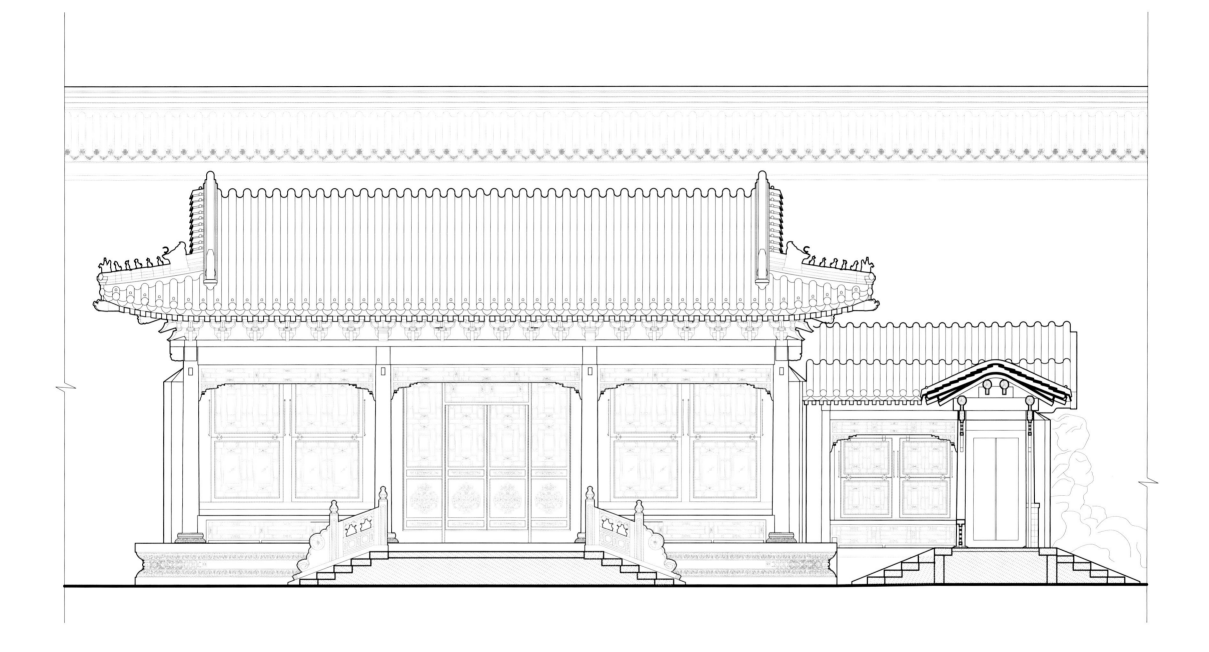

玉粹轩正立面图

Front Elevation of the Bower of Purest Jade

0　　　1　　　2m

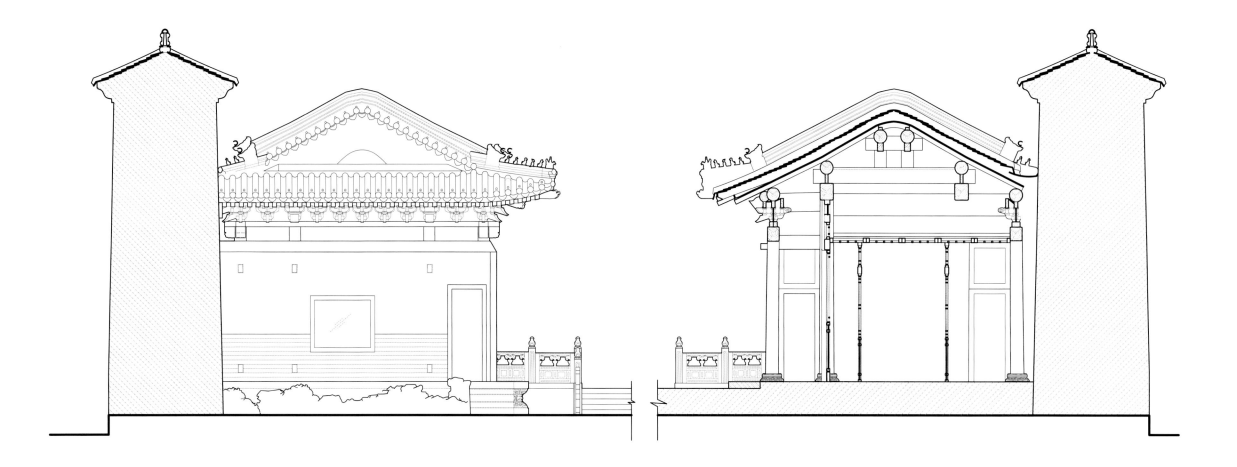

玉粹轩南侧立面图
Southern Elevation of the Central Bay, Bower of Purest Jade

0 1 2m

玉粹轩明间横剖面图
Cross Section of the Central Bay, Bower of Purest Jade

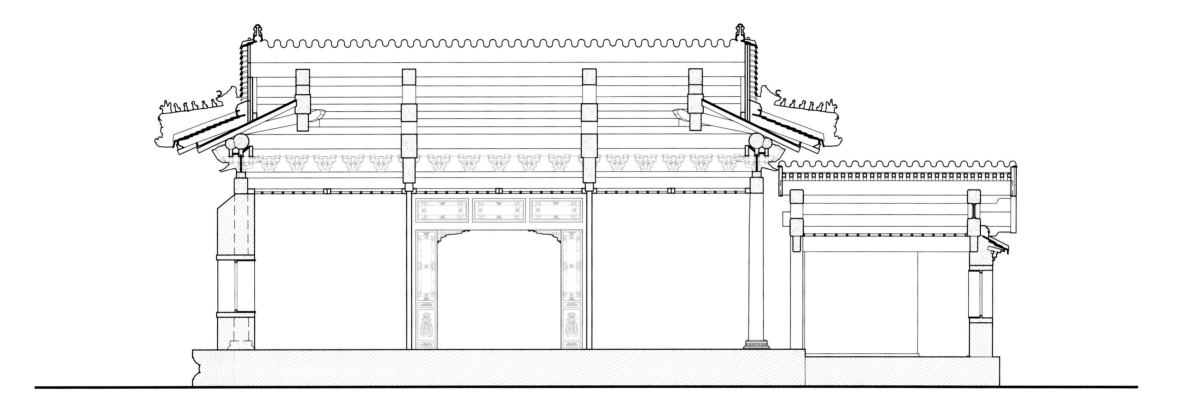

玉粹轩纵剖面图
Longitudinal Section of the Bower of Purest Jade

0   1   2m

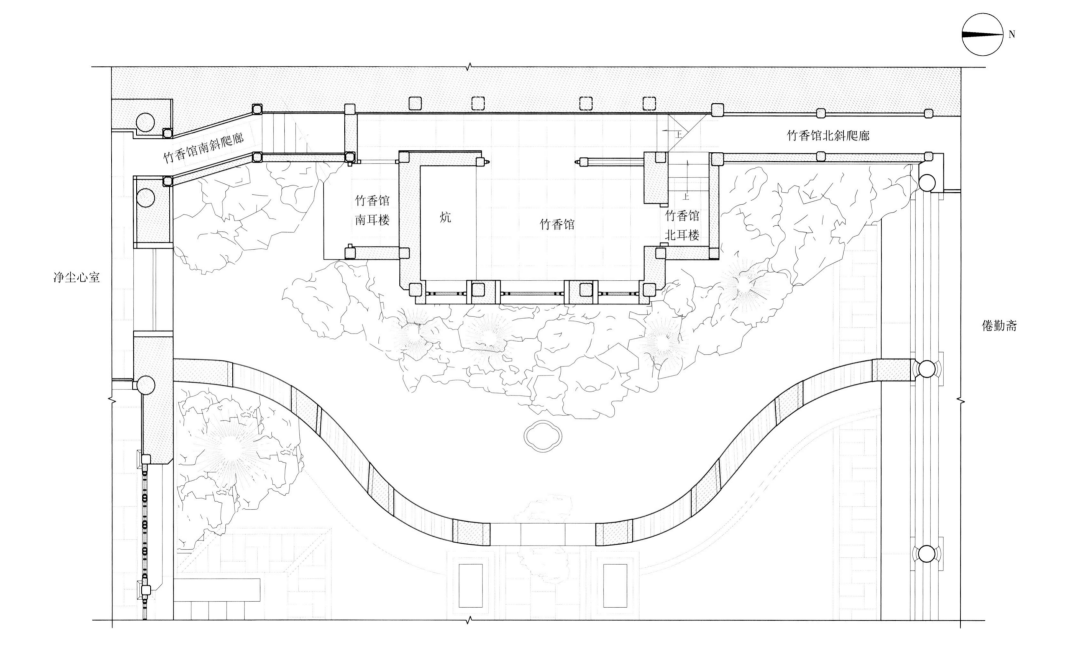

净尘心室

倦勤斋

竹香馆南斜爬廊

竹香馆北斜爬廊

竹香馆
南耳楼

炕

竹香馆

竹香馆
北耳楼

上

上

N

0 1 2m

竹香馆总平面图
Overall Layout of the Complex of the Lodge of Bamboo Fragrant

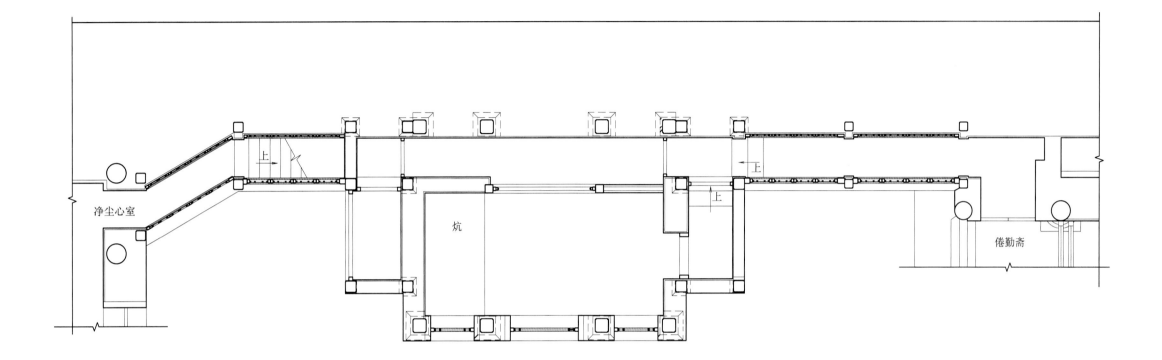

净尘心室

炕

倦勤斋

竹香馆一层平面图
First Floor of the Lodge of Bamboo Fragrant

N

0   1   2m

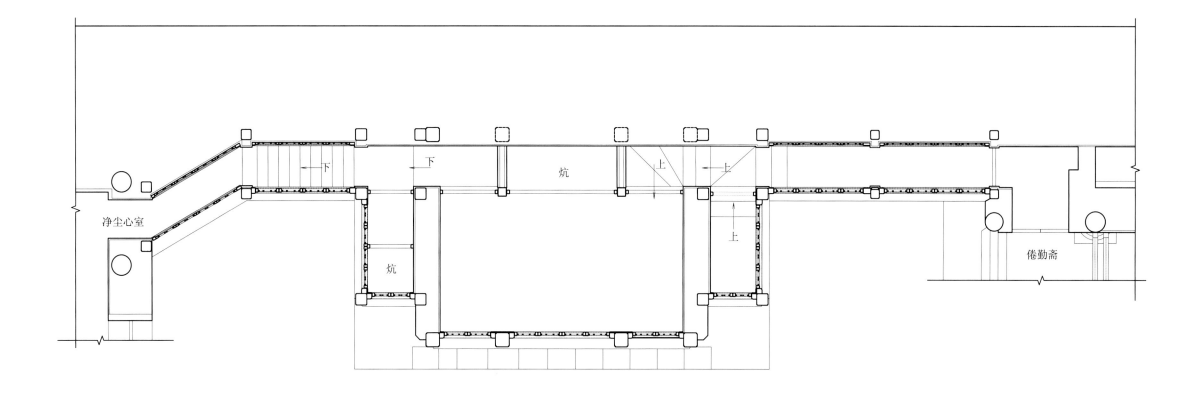

净尘心室

炕

下

下

炕

上

上

上

倦勤斋

0　　1　　2m

竹香馆二层平面图
Second Floor of the Lodge of Bamboo Fragrant

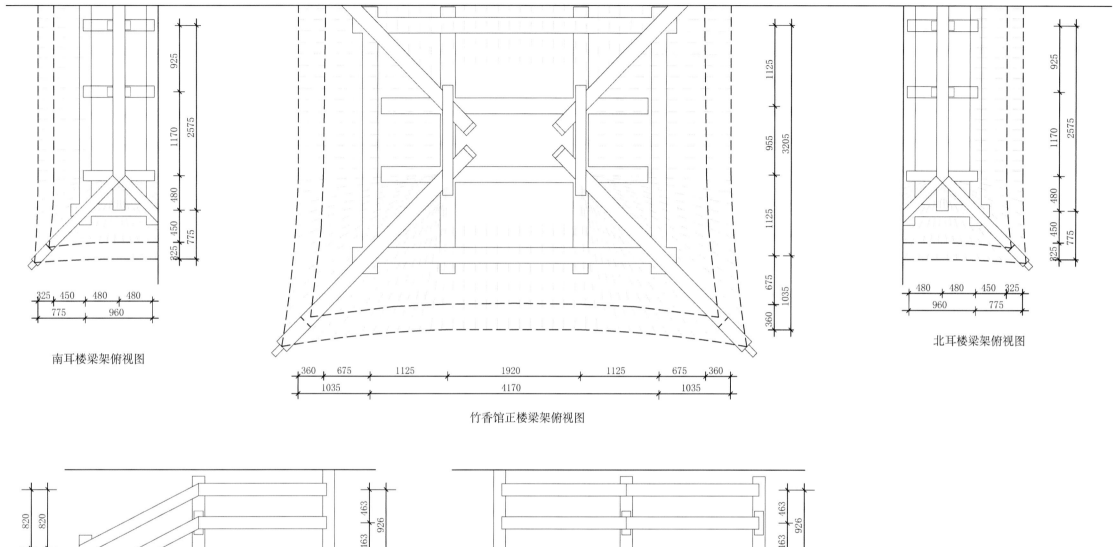

南耳楼梁架俯视图

竹香馆正楼梁架俯视图

北耳楼梁架俯视图

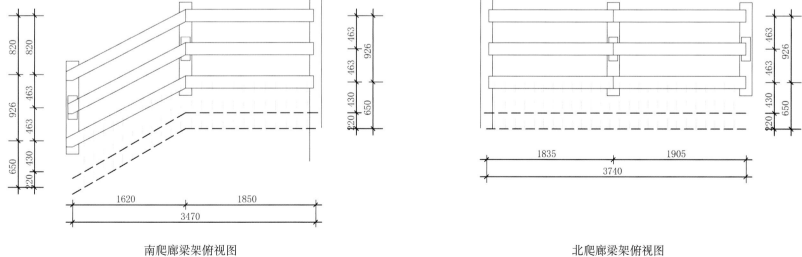

南爬廊梁架俯视图

北爬廊梁架俯视图

竹香馆梁架俯视图
Top View of the Trusses, Lodge of Bamboo Fragrant

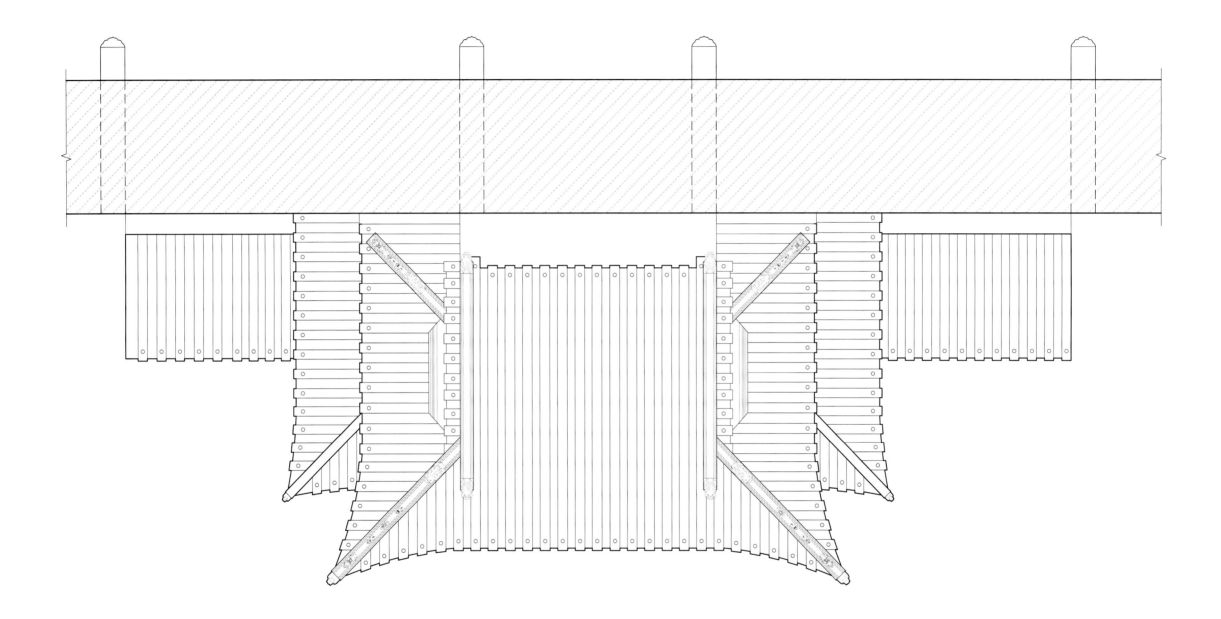

竹香馆瓦顶俯视图
Top View of the Roofing Tiles, Lodge of Bamboo Fragrant

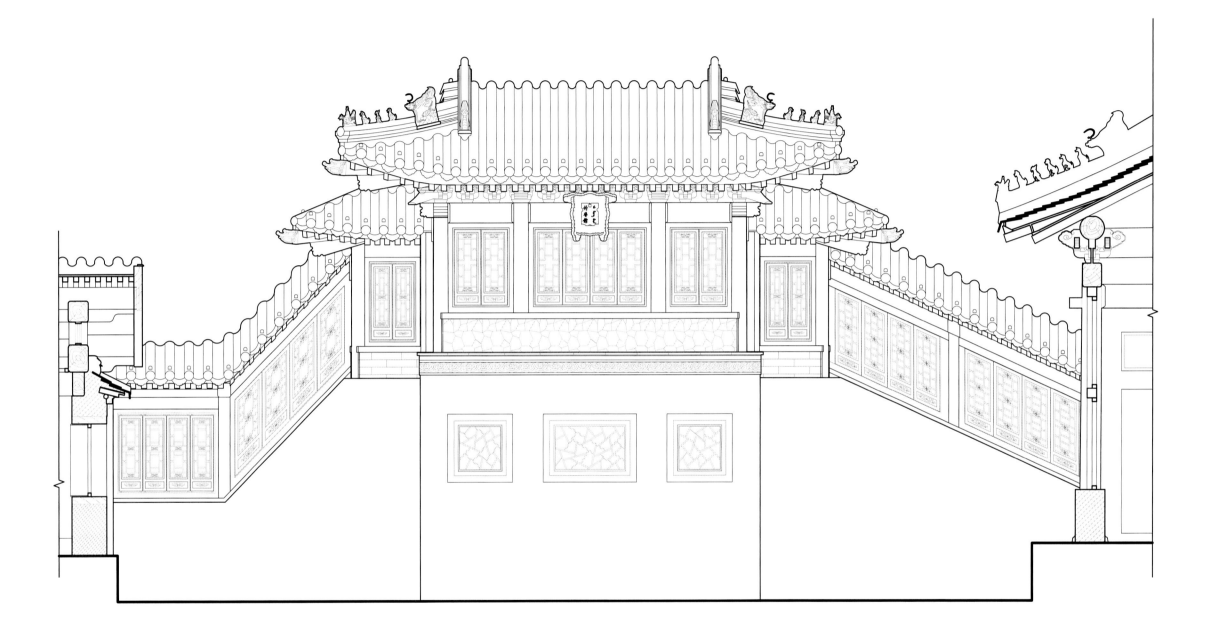

竹香馆正立面图
Front Elevation of the Lodge of Bamboo Fragrant

0   0.5   1   3m

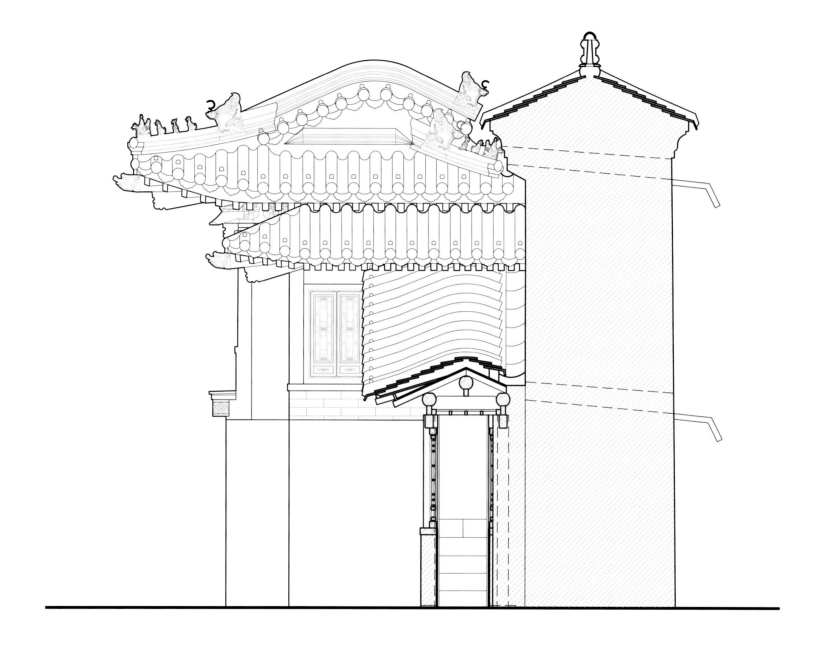

竹香馆北侧立面图
Northern Elevation of the Lodge of Bamboo Fragrant

0　　　　　1　　　　　2m

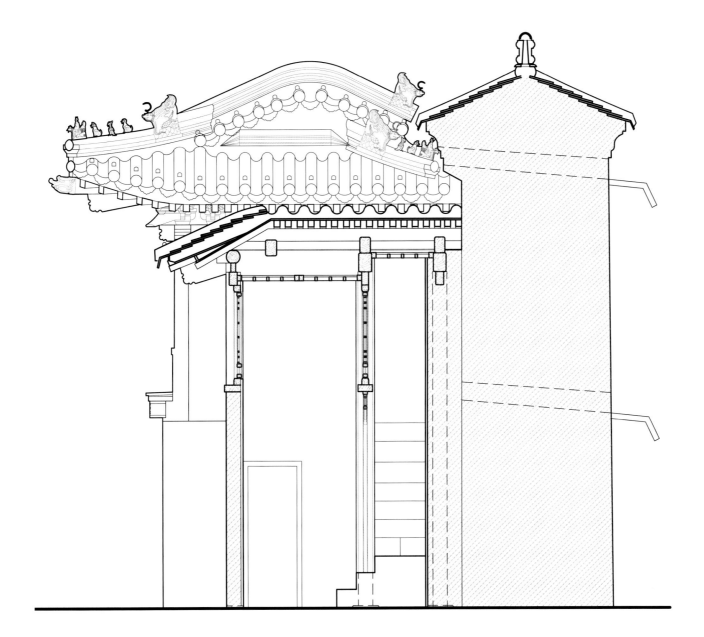

竹香馆北耳楼横剖面图
Cross Section of the Northern Side Room, Lodge of Bamboo Fragrant

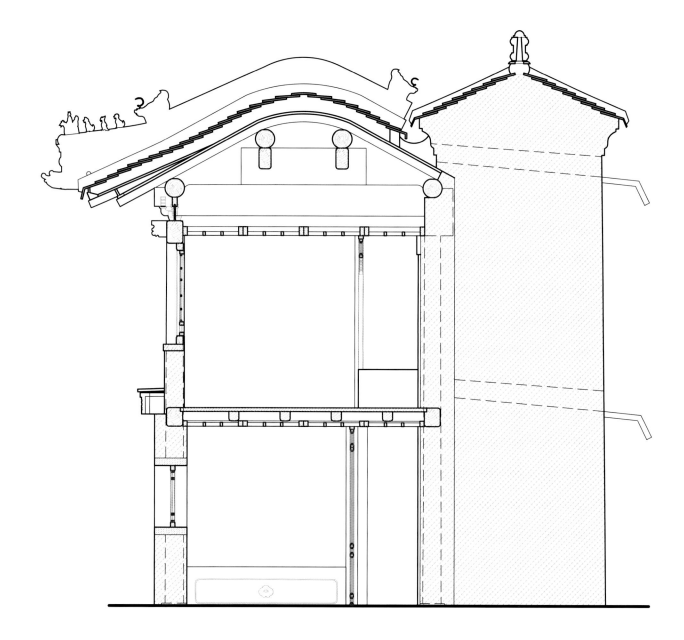

竹香馆横剖面图
Cross Section of the Lodge of Bamboo Fragrant

0　　　　1　　　　2m

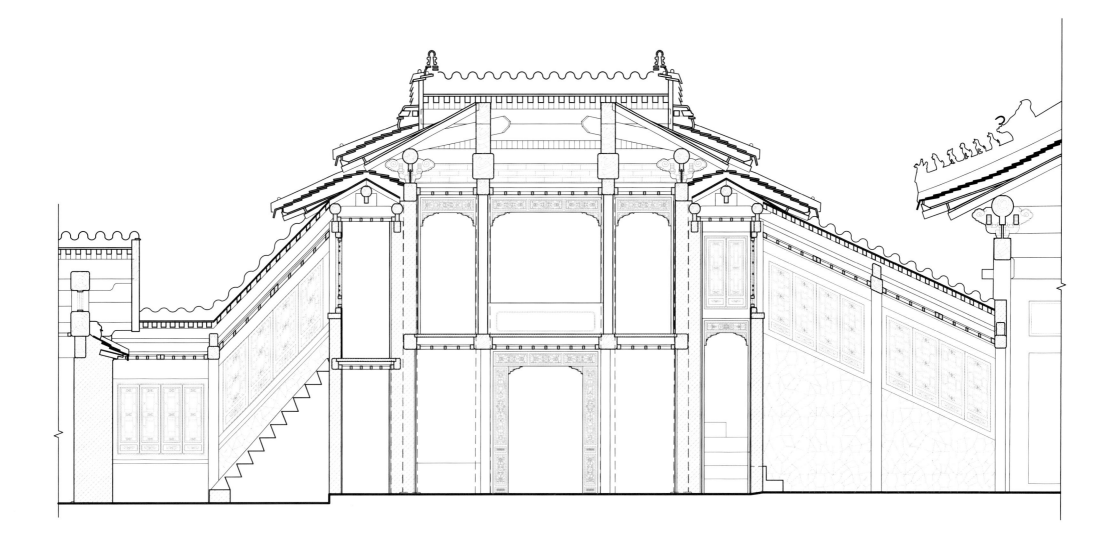

竹香馆纵剖面图
Longitudinal Section of the Lodge of Bamboo Fragrant

0   1   2m

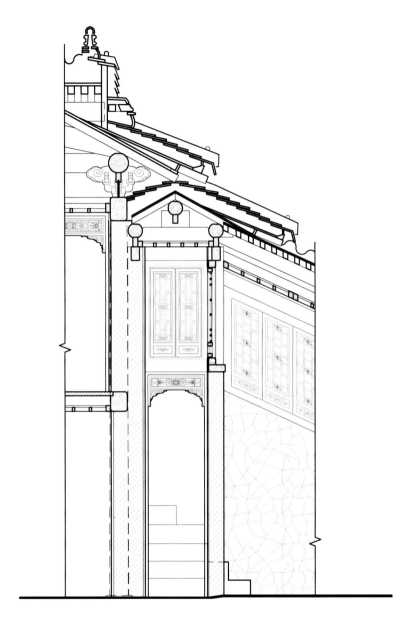

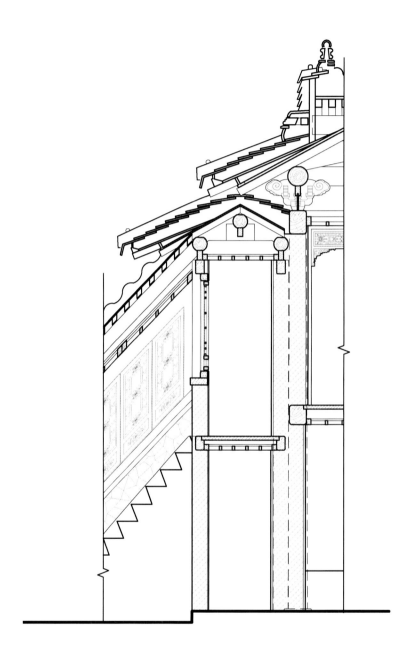

竹香馆北耳楼纵剖面图
Longitudinal Sections of the Northern Side Rooms, Lodge of Bamboo Fragrant

0   1   2m

竹香馆南耳楼纵剖面图
Longitudinal Sections of the Southern Side Rooms, Lodge of Bamboo Fragrant

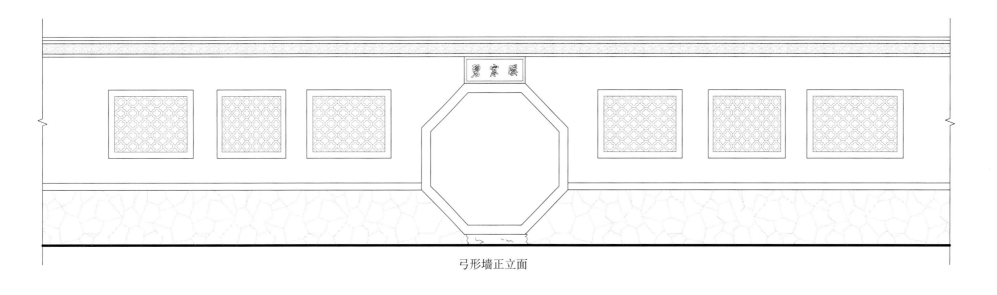
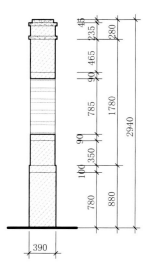

弓形墙正立面

弓形墙剖面

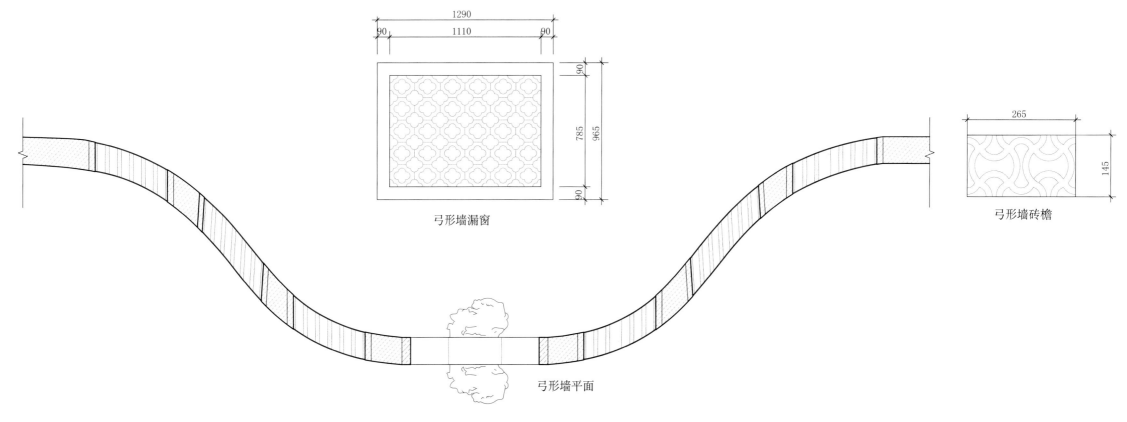

弓形墙漏窗

弓形墙砖檐

弓形墙平面

竹香馆弓形墙详图
Detailed Drawing of the Arced Wall, Lodge of Bamboo Fragrant

上架大木：绘夔龙、真龙方心，片金西番莲、窝金地花卉，盒子金线苏画

枋心：青地绘金琢墨拽退夔龙纹，夔龙纹颜色为硝红色拽紫红色

找头：绘蝠鹤锦纹

盒子：窝金地绘写生花卉，岔角青地切卷草

压斗枋：青地金边

斗栱：青绿地绘金边黑老

垫栱板：红油地绘金线片金西番莲纹

平板枋：青地绘金片金西番莲纹，东面明间北端补绘，南端保留

东面明间大额枋北端补绘，南端保留

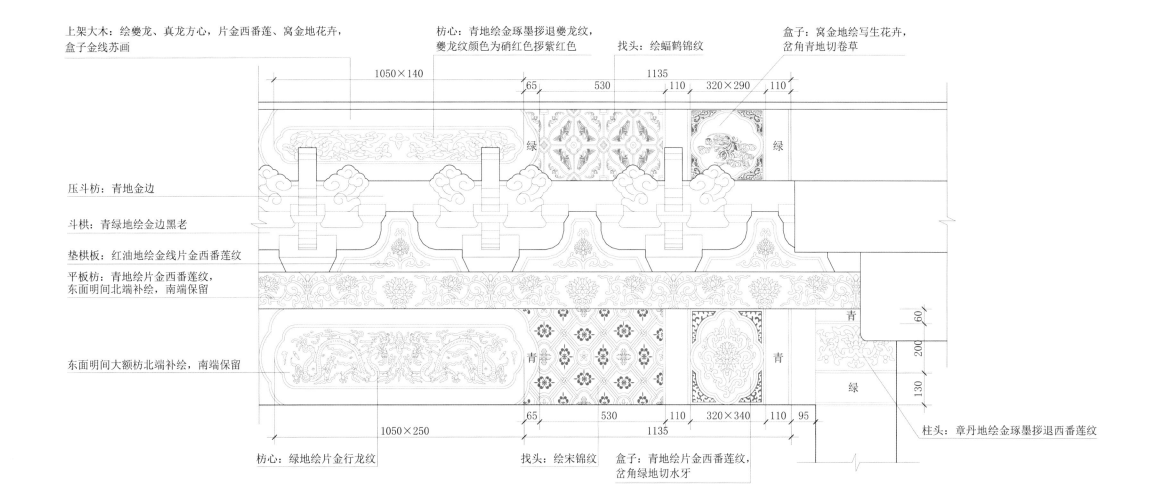

1050×140

1135

65 530 110 320×290 110

绿

绿

青

青

青

绿

60

200

130

1050×250

65 530 110 320×340 110 95

1135

枋心：绿地绘片金行龙纹

找头：绘宋锦纹

盒子：青地绘片金西番莲纹，岔角绿地切水牙

柱头：章丹地绘金琢墨拽退西番莲纹

符望阁三层东面明间内檐彩画设计图
Design Drawing of the Colored Painting of the Central Bay's Interior Side, Eastern Partition Wall of the Third-floor of the Belvedere of Viewing Achievements

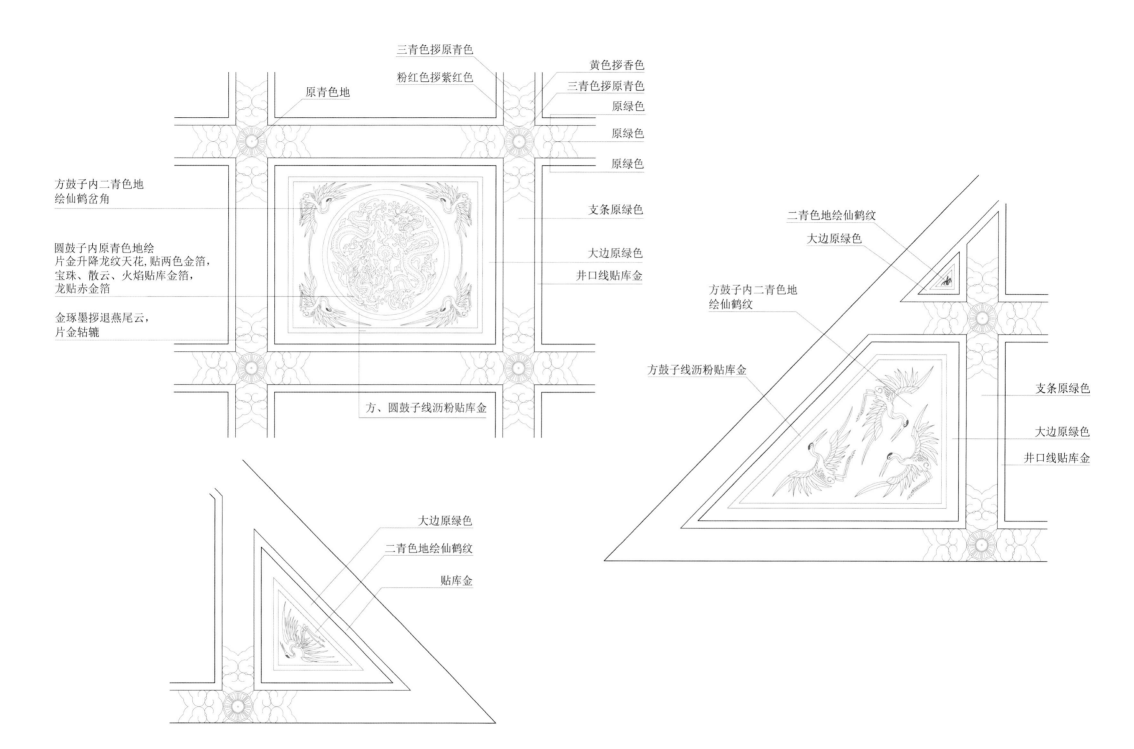

三青色拶原青色

粉红色拶紫红色

原青色地

黄色拶香色

三青色拶原青色

原绿色

原绿色

原绿色

方鼓子内二青色地
绘仙鹤岔角

支条原绿色

二青色地绘仙鹤纹

大边原绿色

圆鼓子内原青色地绘
片金升降龙纹天花，贴两色金箔，
宝珠、散云、火焰贴库金箔，
龙贴赤金箔

大边原绿色

井口线贴库金

方鼓子内二青色地
绘仙鹤纹

金琢墨拶退燕尾云，
片金轱辘

方鼓子线沥粉贴库金

支条原绿色

大边原绿色

井口线贴库金

方、圆鼓子线沥粉贴库金

大边原绿色

二青色地绘仙鹤纹

贴库金

符望阁三层天花彩画设计图
Design Drawing of the Painted Ceiling Panels, Third Floor of the Belvedere of Viewing Achievements

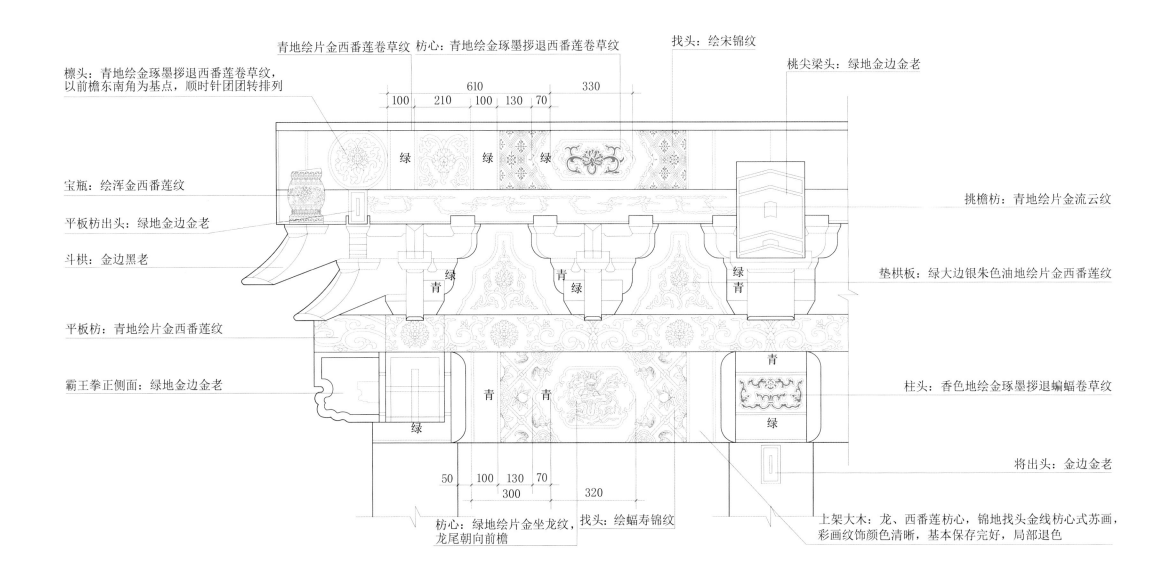

檩头：青地绘金琢墨拨退西番莲卷草纹，以前檐东南角为基点，顺时针团团转排列

青地绘片金西番莲卷草纹

枋心：青地绘金琢墨拨退西番莲卷草纹

找头：绘宋锦纹

桃尖梁头：绿地金边金老

宝瓶：绘浑金西番莲纹

平板枋出头：绿地金边金老

斗栱：金边黑老

挑檐枋：青地绘片金流云纹

垫栱板：绿大边银朱色油地绘片金西番莲纹

平板枋：青地绘片金西番莲纹

霸王拳正侧面：绿地金边金老

柱头：香色地绘金琢墨拨退蝙蝠卷草纹

将出头：金边金老

枋心：绿地绘片金坐龙纹，龙尾朝向前檐

找头：绘蝠寿锦纹

上架大木：龙、西番莲枋心，锦地找头金线枋心式苏画，彩画纹饰颜色清晰，基本保存完好，局部退色

绿   绿   绿

青   绿

绿   青

青   青

绿

青

绿

610   330

100   210   100   130   70

50   100   130   70

300   320

玉粹轩北山面东次间外檐彩画现状图
Present Condition of the Colored Painting of the Northern Elevation's Eastmost Bay, Bower of Purest Jade

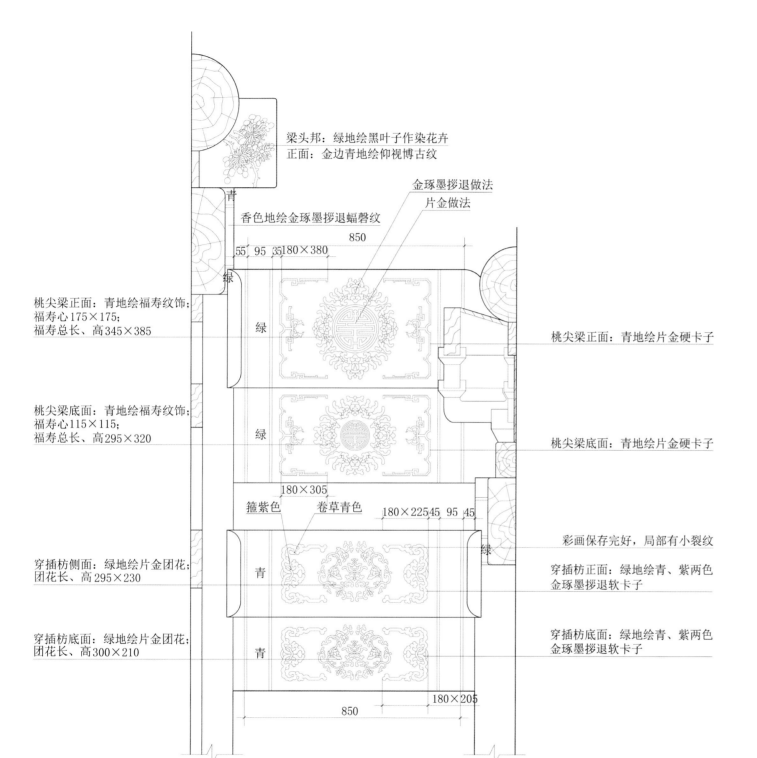

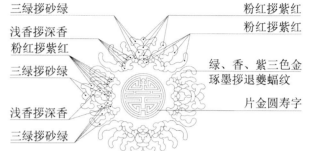

桃尖梁底面福寿纹饰颜色

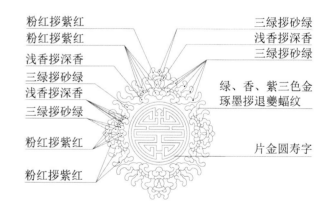

桃尖梁正面福寿纹饰颜色

梁头邦：绿地绘黑叶子作染花卉
正面：金边青地绘仰视博古纹

金琢墨拶退做法
片金做法

香色地绘金琢墨拶退蝠磬纹

主茎：三绿拶砂绿

三绿拶砂绿
浅香拶深香
粉红拶紫红
三绿拶砂绿
浅香拶深香
三绿拶砂绿

粉红拶紫红
粉红拶紫红
绿、香、紫三色金
琢墨拶退夔蝠纹
片金圆寿字

桃尖梁正面：青地绘福寿纹饰；
福寿心175×175；
福寿总长、高345×385

桃尖梁正面：青地绘片金硬卡子

桃尖梁底面：青地绘福寿纹饰；
福寿心115×115；
福寿总长、高295×320

桃尖梁底面：青地绘片金硬卡子

箍紫色
卷草青色

彩画保存完好，局部有小裂纹

穿插枋侧面：绿地绘片金团花；
团花长、高295×230

穿插枋正面：绿地绘青、紫两色
金琢墨拶退软卡子

穿插枋底面：绿地绘片金团花；
团花长、高300×210

穿插枋底面：绿地绘青、紫两色
金琢墨拶退软卡子

粉红拶紫红
粉红拶紫红
浅香拶深香
三绿拶砂绿
浅香拶深香
三绿拶砂绿

三绿拶砂绿
浅香拶深香
三绿拶砂绿
绿、香、紫三色金
琢墨拶退夔蝠纹

粉红拶紫红

片金圆寿字

粉红拶紫红

青

绿

绿

青

青

绿

青

绿

850

55 95 35 180×380

180×305

180×225 45 95 45

850

180×205

玉粹轩廊内桃尖梁、穿插枋彩画现状图
Present Condition of the Colored Paintings on the Head Beams and Penetrating Ties, Bower of Purest Jade

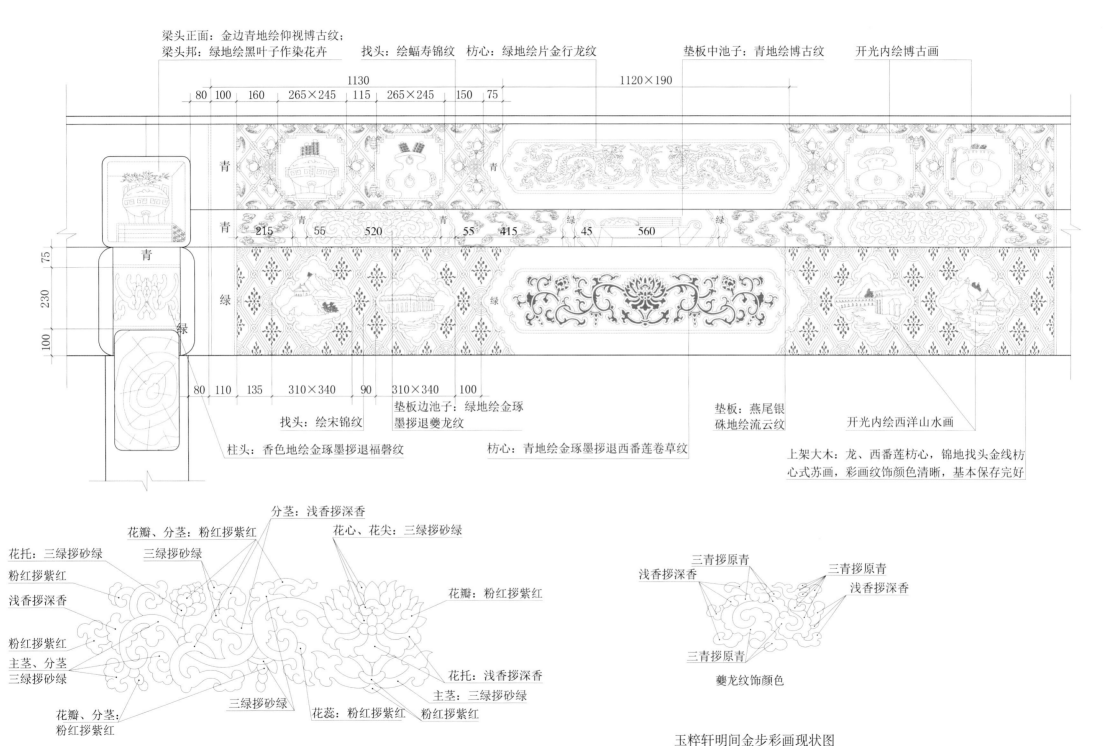

梁头正面：金边青地绘仰视博古纹；
梁头邦：绿地绘黑叶子作染花卉

找头：绘蝠寿锦纹

枋心：绿地绘片金行龙纹

垫板中池子：青地绘博古纹

开光内绘博古画

1130

1120×190

80　100　160　265×245　115　265×245　150　75

青

青

青

青

青

青

青

绿

绿

215　55　520　55　415　45　560

绿

绿

绿

75

230

100

80　110　135　310×340　90　310×340　100

找头：绘宋锦纹

垫板边池子：绿地绘金琢
墨拶退夔龙纹

枋心：青地绘金琢墨拶退西番莲卷草纹

垫板：燕尾银
砾地绘流云纹

开光内绘西洋山水画

柱头：香色地绘金琢墨拶退福磬纹

上架大木：龙、西番莲枋心，锦地找头金线枋
心式苏画，彩画纹饰颜色清晰，基本保存完好

分茎：浅香拶深香

花瓣、分茎：粉红拶紫红

花心、花尖：三绿拶砂绿

花托：三绿拶砂绿

三绿拶砂绿

三青拶原青

三青拶原青

粉红拶紫红

浅香拶深香

浅香拶深香

浅香拶深香

粉红拶紫红

花瓣：粉红拶紫红

主茎、分茎
三绿拶砂绿

三青拶原青

三绿拶砂绿

花瓣、分茎：
粉红拶紫红

花托：浅香拶深香

主茎：三绿拶砂绿

三青拶原青

花蕊：粉红拶紫红

粉红拶紫红

夔龙纹饰颜色

西番莲纹饰颜色

玉粹轩明间金步彩画现状图

Present Condition of the Colored Painting on the Front Partition Wall's Central Bay, Bower of Purest Jade

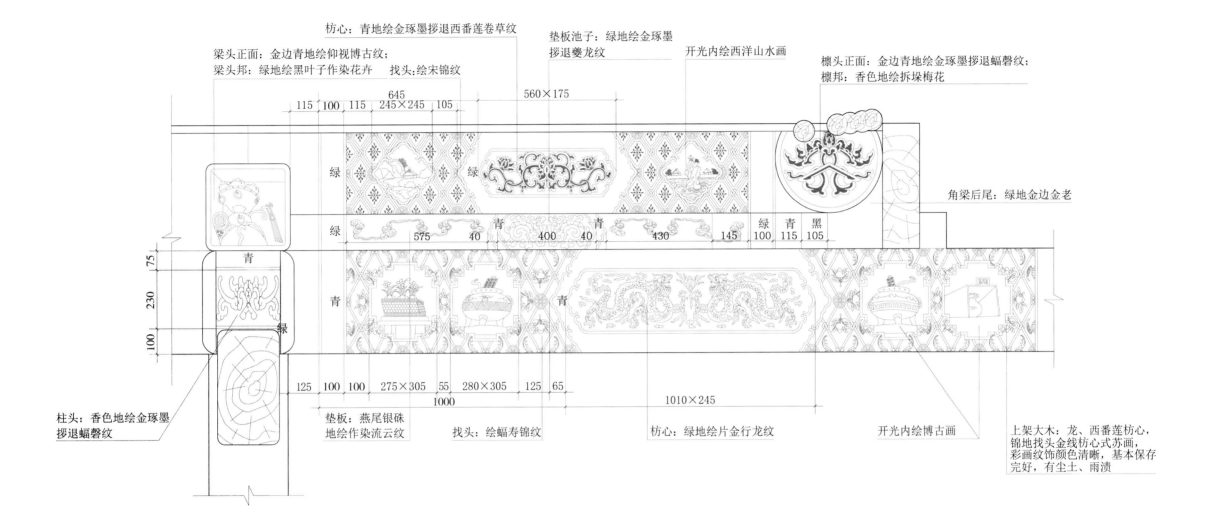

枋心：青地绘金琢墨拽退西番莲卷草纹

梁头正面：金边青地绘仰视博古纹；
梁头邦：绿地绘黑叶子作染花卉   找头：绘宋锦纹

垫板池子：绿地绘金琢墨拽退夔龙纹

开光内绘西洋山水画

檩头正面：金边青地绘金琢墨拽退蝠磬纹；
檩邦：香色地绘拆垛梅花

角梁后尾：绿地金边金老

绿
绿
绿

青
青

青

柱头：香色地绘金琢墨拽退蝠磬纹

垫板：燕尾银硃地绘作染流云纹

找头：绘蝠寿锦纹

枋心：绿地绘片金行龙纹

开光内绘博古画

上架大木：龙、西番莲枋心，锦地找头金线枋心式苏画，彩画纹饰颜色清晰，基本保存完好，有尘土、雨渍

645   560×175

115 100 115 245×245 105

575 40   400 40   430   145 100 115 105
绿 青 黑

125 100 100 275×305 55 280×305 125 65   1010×245
1000

75
230
100

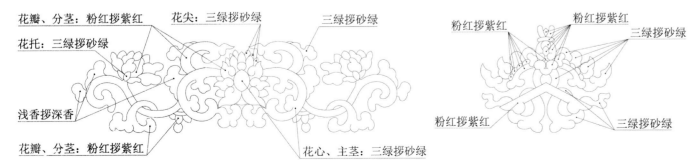

花瓣、分茎：粉红拽紫红   花尖：三绿拽砂绿   三绿拽砂绿
花托：三绿拽砂绿

浅香拽深香

花瓣、分茎：粉红拽紫红   花心、主茎：三绿拽砂绿

金檩枋心西番莲纹饰颜色

粉红拽紫红   粉红拽紫红
三绿拽砂绿

粉红拽紫红   三绿拽砂绿

檩头正面蝠磬纹饰颜色

玉粹轩北次间金步彩画现状图
Present Condition of the Colored Painting on the Front Partition Wall's Northmost Bay, Bower of Purest Jade

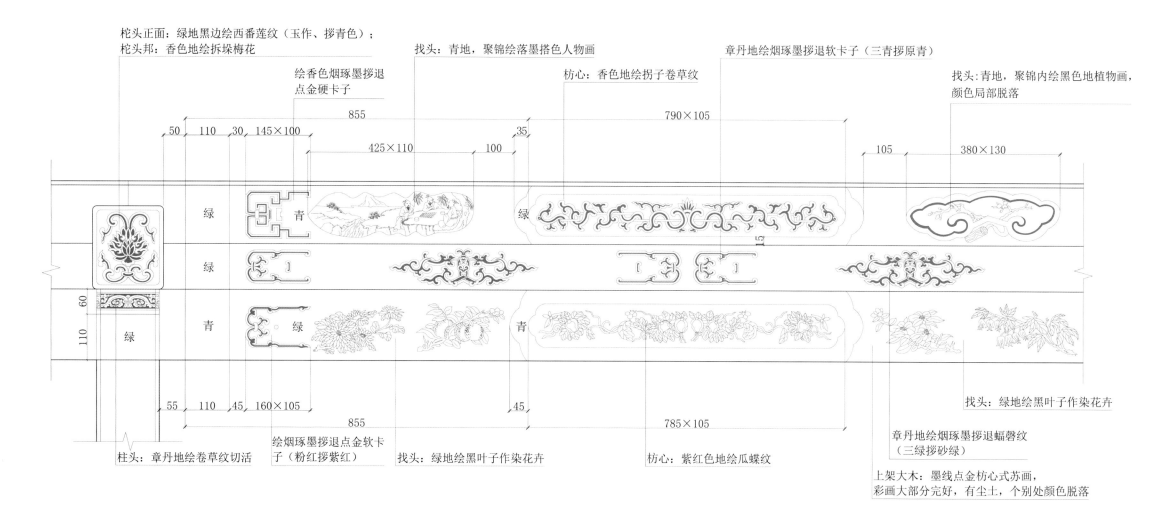

柁头正面：绿地黑边绘西番莲纹（玉作、掭青色）；
柁头邦：香色地绘拆垛梅花

找头：青地，聚锦绘落墨搭色人物画

章丹地绘烟琢墨掭退软卡子（三青掭原青）

绘香色烟琢墨掭退点金硬卡子

枋心：香色地绘拐子卷草纹

找头：青地，聚锦内绘黑色地植物画，颜色局部脱落

855

790×105

50   110   30   145×100

35

105   380×130

425×110   100

绿   青

绿

绿

绿   绿

青

青   绿

55   110   45   160×105

45

785×105

855

柱头：章丹地绘卷草纹切活

绘烟琢墨掭退点金软卡子（粉红掭紫红）

找头：绿地绘黑叶子作染花卉

枋心：紫红色地绘瓜蝶纹

找头：绿地绘黑叶子作染花卉

章丹地绘烟琢墨掭退蝠磬纹（三绿掭砂绿）

上架大木：墨线点金枋心式苏画，彩画大部分完好，有尘土，个别处颜色脱落

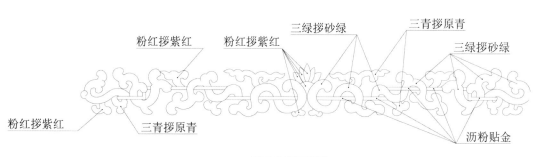

粉红掭紫红   粉红掭紫红   三绿掭砂绿   三青掭原青

三绿掭砂绿

粉红掭紫红   三青掭原青   沥粉贴金

拐子卷草纹颜色

倦勤斋前西游廊北次间前外檐彩画现状图
Present Condition of the Colored Painting of the Bay on the north of the Central Bay, Western Corridor's Western Elevation of the Studio of Exhaustion from Diligent Service

340

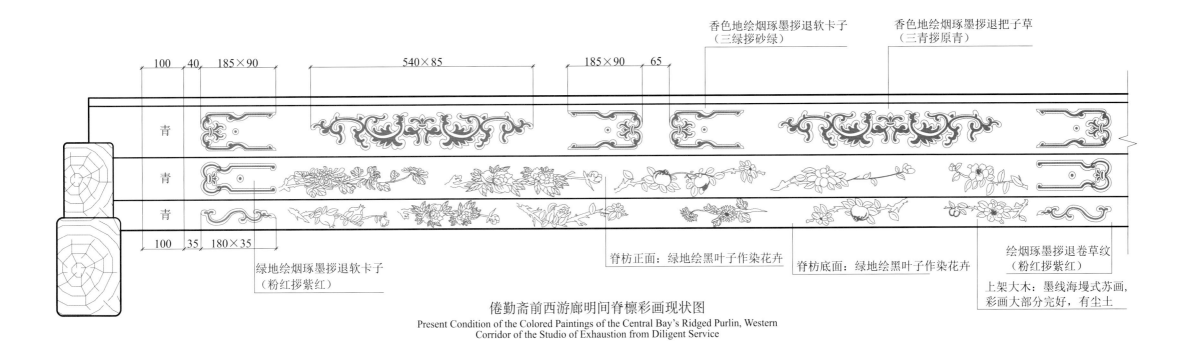

香色地绘烟琢墨拶退软卡子
（三绿拶砂绿）

香色地绘烟琢墨拶退把子草
（三青拶原青）

100　40　185×90　　　540×85　　　185×90　65

青

青

青

100　35　180×35

绿地绘烟琢墨拶退软卡子
（粉红拶紫红）

脊枋正面：绿地绘黑叶子作染花卉

脊枋底面：绿地绘黑叶子作染花卉

绘烟琢墨拶退卷草纹
（粉红拶紫红）

上架大木：墨线海墁式苏画，
彩画大部分完好，有尘土

倦勤斋前西游廊明间脊檩彩画现状图

Present Condition of the Colored Paintings of the Central Bay's Ridged Purlin, Western
Corridor of the Studio of Exhaustion from Diligent Service

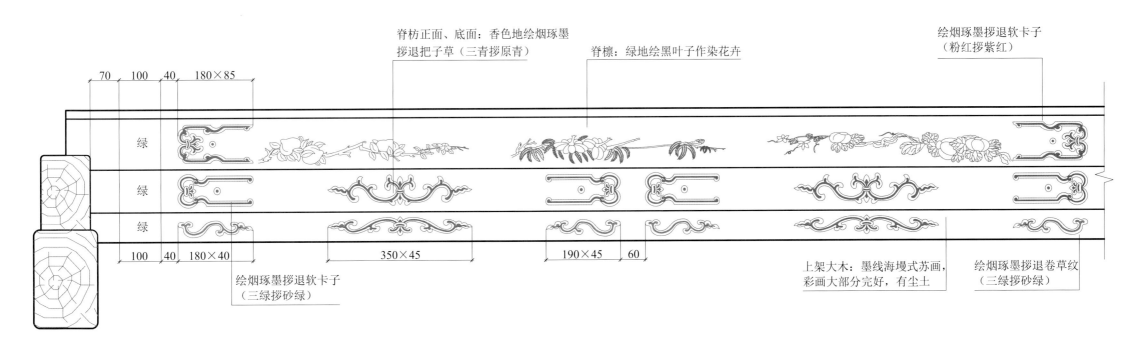

脊枋正面、底面：香色地绘烟琢墨
拶退把子草（三青拶原青）

脊檩：绿地绘黑叶子作染花卉

绘烟琢墨拶退软卡子
（粉红拶紫红）

70　100　40　180×85

绿

绿

绿

100　40　180×40　　　350×45　　　190×45　60

绘烟琢墨拶退软卡子
（三绿拶砂绿）

上架大木：墨线海墁式苏画，
彩画大部分完好，有尘土

绘烟琢墨拶退卷草纹
（三绿拶砂绿）

倦勤斋前西游廊南次间脊檩彩画现状图

Present Condition of the Colored Paintings of the Southern Bay's Ridged Purlin, Western
Corridor of the Studio of Exhaustion from Diligent Service

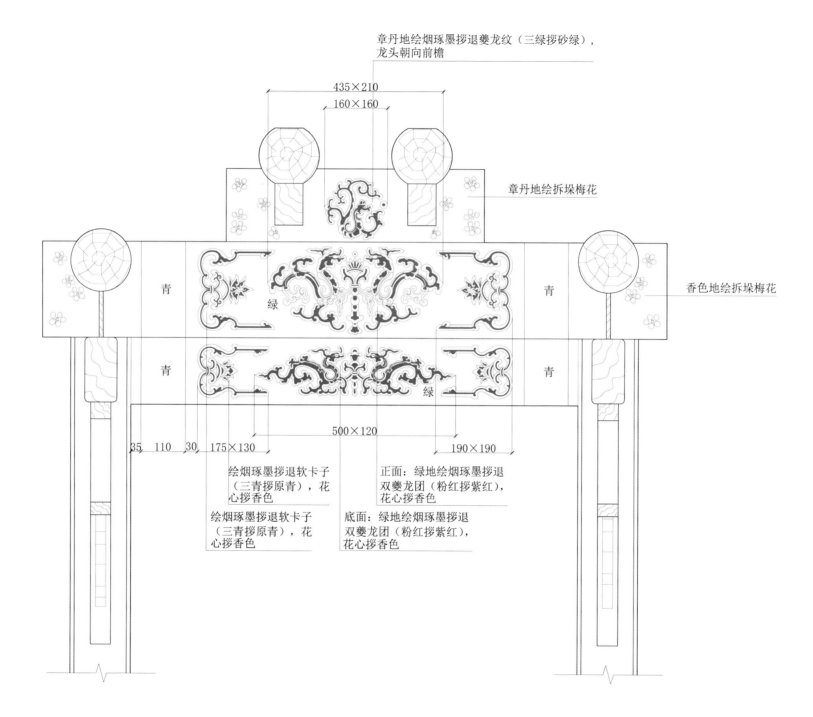

章丹地绘烟琢墨拶退夔龙纹（三绿拶砂绿），龙头朝向前檐

435×210

160×160

章丹地绘拆垛梅花

香色地绘拆垛梅花

青

青

绿

青

青

绿

500×120

35　110　30　175×130

190×190

绘烟琢墨拶退软卡子（三青拶原青），花心拶香色

绘烟琢墨拶退软卡子（三青拶原青），花心拶香色

正面：绿地绘烟琢墨拶退双夔龙团（粉红拶紫红），花心拶香色

底面：绿地绘烟琢墨拶退双夔龙团（粉红拶紫红），花心拶香色

倦勤斋前西游廊月梁彩画现状图
Present Condition of the Colored Paintings on the Crescent Beams, Western Corridors of the Studio of Exhaustion from Diligent Service

Name List of Participants Involved in Surveying and Related Works

1. Survey and drawing of some architecture (drawings achieved with computer-aided software) and its Colored Paintings (in order of surname stroke numbers):

WANG Cong, WANG Wentao, SHI Zhimin, LYU Xiaohong, ZHUANG Lixin, YANG Hong, YANG Xincheng, ZHANG Xiufen, ZHANG Xueqin, ZHANG Yaping, FAN Xuan, JI Xiuyun, ZHUO Yuanyuan, ZHAO Congshan, ZHAO Peng, CAO Zhenwei, CHANG Deshan, CUI Jin, HUANG Zhanjun

2. Participants involved in the compiling of survey drawings for publication

Drawings Arrangement: WANG Mo

Drawings Editor: ZHAO Qi, WANG Biying, WANG Dichen, FAN Qingnan

English Translation: LIU Renhao

参与测绘及相关工作的人员名单

一、部分古建筑（计算机制图）及彩画测绘制图
（以姓氏笔画为序）：

王　丛　王文涛　石志敏　吕小红　庄立新　杨　红

范　暄　季秀云　卓媛媛　赵丛山　赵　鹏　曹振伟　杨新成

常德山　崔　瑾　黄占均　张秀芬　张学芹　张雅平

二、测绘图出版整理

图纸统筹：王　莫

图纸整理：赵　祺　王碧莹　王涤尘　范青楠

英文翻译：刘仁皓

图书在版编目（CIP）数据

故宫 = THE FORBIDDEN CITY / 故宫博物院古建部编
著；赵鹏，王莫主编. —北京：中国建筑工业出版社，
2021.11
（中国古建筑测绘大系. 宫殿建筑）
ISBN 978-7-112-26797-2

I.①故⋯ II.①故⋯ ②赵⋯ ③王⋯ III.①故宫－
宫殿－图集 IV.①K928.74-64

中国版本图书馆CIP数据核字（2021）第211111号

丛书策划 / 王莉慧
责任编辑 / 李 鸽 陈海娇
书籍设计 / 付金红
责任校对 / 王 烨

中国古建筑测绘大系·宫殿建筑

故宫

故宫博物院古建部 编著

赵鹏 王莫 主编

Traditional Chinese Architecture Surveying and Mapping Series: Palace Architecture
THE FORBIDDEN CITY
Compiled by Department of Architectural Heritage, The Palace Museum
Edited by ZHAO Peng, WANG Mo

*

中国建筑工业出版社出版、发行（北京海淀三里河路9号）
各地新华书店、建筑书店经销
北京雅盈中佳图文设计公司制版
北京雅昌艺术印刷有限公司印刷

*

开本：787毫米×1092毫米 横1/8 印张：47$\frac{1}{2}$ 字数：1252千字
2022年6月第一版 2022年6月第一次印刷
定价：**398.00** 元
ISBN 978-7-112-26797-2
（35229）

版权所有 翻印必究
如有印装质量问题，可寄本社图书出版中心退换
（邮政编码100037）